An Alternative Author's Biography

Rick Jolly was *launched in October 1946, coming down the *slipway in *Honkers. His old man had gone in the bag there six years before, but was eventually saved by two *buckets of American sunshine that changed the Japanese Emperor's mind. After *rug rat time in *Singers, Doc J then returned from the *far flung to a college of knowledge for *left footers in Lancashire. From there he did the long *scab-lifter's course in *Smoke, and was going to be a *dagger *fanny mechanic, but joined the *Andrew instead. He got his *green lid in 1972, did the *bubblehead course, and split *watches between the *boot-necks and *wafus, apart from time in the *Madhouse and, later, the *Pompey *Puzzle Palace. He also qualified as an *avquack, and during six years at *Cul-D was the *dope on the rope more than fifty times, even breaking the thing one memorable day.

Throughout the Falklands *shebang he was *Top Quack of the *Green Death, and also ran the Ajax Bay *boneyard. Thanks to the efforts of all the *bootneck, *cherryberry, *matelot and *pongo medics, cutters and gasmen in his teams, the *butcher's bill was much reduced. He *issued an *arduous duty tot on twelve occasions, running up a personal account which Their *Lordships were happy to settle. The *junglie, *pinglie, and *teeny-weeny crews also helped *big style, along with the lone and *mankey (but really *bramah) *shuddering shithouse, in getting all the *WIA to the floating *boneyard UGANDA. From here the *droggies took charge, then the *Crabfat flying *blood wagons did the business as *freedom birds from Uruguay to home. Rick went to *Buck House to meet the *Lord High Admiral when the sweeties were handed out; seventeen years later he received an equivalent recognition from the Argies in Buenos Aires. To be *gonged by both sides in a war is rarer than a *Fleet Jossman's sea draft.

In 1996, Doc J got the *Golden Toecap in a daft series of defence spending cuts, and *swallowed the anchor down in *Oggieland. When not operating a *tripewriter he likes to *goof at the *war canoes playing with their *brown envelopes in the *Thursday War. His *CINC-NAG-HOME since 1970 is Susie; their only son James (who helped with the first edition) *crossed the bar, aged 17, in 1989. As well as JACKSPEAK, Rick has written a couple of novels - and dreams of the day when Hollywood bids for the film rights to his weekly shopping list.

Other titles by Rick Jolly currently available from
Palamanando Publications:

JACKSPEAK - an illustrated anthology of Royal
Navyand Royal Marines slang and usage.

IN CONFIDENCE - a collection of over 600 remarks
made in confidential reports concerning officers
and other ranks of the British Armed Forces.

*The author has directed that his royalties from both
these books are donated to The South Atlantic Medal
Association (1982), and used specifically to maintain
SAMA82's unique electronic Garden of Remembrance.
This is an innovative memorial to the
255 British servicemen and three civilian ladies who
died during the restoration of the Falkland Islanders'
freedom. The Garden can be visited from SAMA82's
home page at www.sama82.org.co.uk*

FOR CAMPAIGN SERVICE - an exciting, detailed
and completely authentic novel about service in the
Belfast of 1972. The godfathers of the Provisional IRA
have undertaken to complete a deadly task.
Who can stop them?

Three other titles (one non-fiction and two fiction)
by the same author are also currently in preparation.
Details of these works in progress, and information
about how to order direct from Palamanando
Publishing may be obtained at the back of this book,
or from the relevant web addresses on the title pages.

Rick Jolly

JACKSPEAK

An illustrated guide to the
slang and usage of
The Royal Navy and Royal Marines
including
The Submarine Service
and Fleet Air Arm

Illustrated by **TUGG**

FoSAMA Books
www.fosama.com
An imprint of Palamanando Publishing

JACKSPEAK

A FoSAMA Book
www.fosama.com

FoSAMA Books is an imprint of
Palamanando Publishing
www.palamanando.com

First edition published in Great Britain 1989 as
*Jackspeak: The Pusser's Rum Guide to the Slanguage
of the Royal Navy and Royal Marines*
by Palamanando Publishing

ISBN   0-9514305-2-1

Typeset in Palatino Light by Palamanando Publishing
on a Macintosh G4 using Quark Xpress DTP software.
Jacket design, imposition, proofing and printing by
Deltor Communications,
Long Acre, Saltash Parkway, Cornwall PL12 6LZ
www.deltorprint.co.uk

Distributed by Maritime Books Ltd, Lodge Hill,
Liskeard, Cornwall PL14 4EL
www.navybooks.com

Dedicated to Jack and Royal,
but not forgetting Jenny.

On their broad and willing shoulders,
the destiny of this island nation
has so often depended.

Who knows what trials of
their devotion to duty
are yet to come..

Author's Preface

This book is the direct result of a hobby which began nearly thirty years ago, on a sunny Mediterranean morning in 1971, and very soon after I had joined the Royal Navy as a rather young and green Surgeon Lieutenant. My memories of that first patient are still embarrassingly clear; a tall and very fit-looking Royal Marines Corporal told me he had *caught the boat up*. As Mintoff was then in the process of kicking us all out of Malta, I presumed that my customer was delighted to have been chosen for a sea voyage back to England - or had he been selected for service in submarines?

Those of you who are familiar with Naval slang will no doubt understand his total confusion at my proferred congratulations! I had to excuse myself rather hurriedly, then pop out to the front office and question the Sick Bay'tiff. This spendid character, the wonderful *Jock Noble*, slid under his desk for laughing, and then dined out on the story for the rest of his career. I returned to the consulting room, sorted my patient out in the conventional manner, and then decided never to be caught out again.

Seventeen years later, during a stint as Principal Medical Officer of the Royal Naval Air Station, Culdrose, I finally had a chance to sit down at the keyboard during the long hours that the airfield remained open for night flying. Of course, if I had known then how much work was going to be required for completion of this little project, I would have abandoned it there and then! It therefore says a lot for the resilient humour of my then Sick Bay manager, the splendid *Sam Parker*, that the Boss was never allowed to flag. We first did a local and self-printed version to raise £2,300 for a Fleet Air Arm Museum project. Then, in 1989, the final result of those highly enjoyable labours appeared, with the computer-collated presentation of hundreds of scribbled prescription pads and bar chits that had been accumulating since Day One in Sliema.

Another eleven years on, and having now become a Naval pensioner, this revision became something of a labour of love. As a former obstetrician, I really should have remembered that labour often lasts much longer than planned! The first edition of JACKSPEAK was a great success, and over twenty thousand copies have sold since we first went to print. The response from those who wrote to us about the book was almost universally positive - apart from the lady who bought it for her Sea Cadet nephew and then thought that some of the definitions and usages were a little inappropriate! She got her money back...

There has been a steady trickle of other letters, which, while thanking me for the industry and effort displayed in collecting all the components of JACKSPEAK, also pointed out its Royal Marines and Fleet Air Arm bias. I apologised proudly, since I was, after all, only the product of my Service experience, but I also agreed readily with their comments. When I asked the same correspondents to help me with this admitted difficulty, they came back without hesitation. The files are bulging with the lovely suggestions, corrections and additions that came pouring in. In addition, I finally got to sea as PMO of HMS BRISTOL, the Dartmouth Training Ship, and that helped too!

I am very grateful to all those who helped with this new edition, and especially thankful to my part-time secretary, assistant and family friend, Mrs. *Rosalie Dunn*. She marshalled all the new potential additions onto the computer, helped me to sort them alphabetically, and then popped them into the text as we revised the book. The first edition was created on an Acorn Archimedes computer, and had to be ported across to a PC, and from there to a G4 Mac. The carry-across was not exactly bloodless, since all the previous text settings were stripped out in the process, and they all had to be replaced and carefully checked. I used my time as ship's surgeon of the unique little inter-island vessel *RMS St.Helena* to good effect in this respect, but it is Rosalie who has borne the brunt of the demanding tasks of textual revision and change.

Something else has changed as well. We had a little sponsorship money (which paid for the cover of the first edition) from *Pusser's Rum Ltd.* The former US Marine who owned the company in Tortola recently sold out to the huge Jim Beam drinks conglomerate in the USA. The new key account executive was of Peruvian extraction, and was also someone who had supported the Argentine cause in 1982. For that reason, he simply hated the image of a White Ensign that used to adorn the original bottle's label! All references to the Royal Navy (plus the White Ensign) were therefore deleted from the new label, an action now reciprocated by cancellation of any endorsement for that product of the kind which was carried on the cover of the first proper edition of JACKSPEAK. However, *Lamb's Navy Rum* has the White Ensign in its rightful place, and the company is generous in its sponsorship of Royal Navy sporting events and facilities. It is a highly recommended fluid, either as *neaters or in a *dark and dirty!

The really key feature of this new edition has been the contribution of *Richard Benham*. After a long and distinguished career as a *salthorse, his final appointment in the *Andrew before *swallowing the anchor was as the *Jimmy of HMS ILLUSTRIOUS. We are *old ships from *Dartmouth and he gave me generously and kindly of his experience and expertise in making some definitions more precise, as well as sorting the wheat from the chaff.

Tugg's wonderful cartoons, of course, need no real introduction from me. They sum up, in just a few deft pen strokes, the very essence of Jack's wry, witty and often self-mocking observations about life in the *Andrew. Some of the drawings are originals, the others are taken from the cartoon strips that have been appearing continuously in *NAVY NEWS* since the very first in February 1973. *Tugg* has retired now from full-time active duty in the cartoon world, but his clever pen remains as sharp as ever. He has drawn a dozen new full page illustrations for this edition of JACKSPEAK, and I am also very grateful to *Jim Allaway*, Editor of *NAVY NEWS*, for permission to include a few more examples of *Tugg's* brilliant *JACK* cartoon strip - which continues to grace his excellent monthly publication.

At least two correspondents have urged me not to be frightened of the 'F word', noting that this barrier was breached long ago by the BBC, and now features regularly in the press, on the radio, and in on-screen dialogue. I have declined to accept their counsel, as the directness of this particular word and others similar to it can still offend. The alternatives will simply have to do while JACKSPEAK remains my editorial responsibility. I suppose that it would also be fair to point out that this product, in modern managerial terms, will never be a source of *complete* staisfaction to all our readers!

What worries me much more is the prospect of our Naval slang and usage falling into oblivion as a direct result of neglect. In the good old days of the *tot, messdeck conversation was witty and vital, stimulated by a daily infusion of *bubbly. Nowadays, that inevitable glass nipple in the corner projects its mind-numbing videos and game shows to an equally-glazed audience, and four hundred years of living, dynamic, unique and constantly-changing spoken exchange is in danger of withering by atrophy.

Despite strenuous efforts on my part, there will also be some errors of both commission and omission. May I ask you now that if you can see some howler of fact, spelling or presentation, will you please let me know? The address is in this fore section, as well as at the stern, along with some blank pages for notes. I promise you that we will do our very best to correct any such errors just as soon as we can.

The charitable aspect also continues. I now raise money for The South Atlantic Medal Association (1982), a group of like-minded veterans of the Falklands Conflict. I was the Founding Chairman of this excellent bunch, but have now been kicked upstairs to become its President! My particular interest, and one which we fund ourselves, is the unique electronic Garden of Remembrance dedicated to the 255 British soldiers, sailors and airmen, plus 3 civilian ladies, who died in the restoration of the Falkland Islanders' freedom. Readers may wish to inspect the website at *www.sama82.org.uk/gor* for themselves. It really is a world first.

Finally, I'd like to thank all the other hard-working people who were involved in the printing of JACKSPEAK. We are still well served by the *Deltor* team, ably led by *Alan Shannon*. The editorial and production gang of *Julie, Dion, Stewart, Lisa* and *Carl* have always been models of kindness and tolerance to this amateur enthusiast! *Andrew Parker*, himself the son of a Naval family, designed and prepared the marvellous cover. Back at the ranch, all the other staff at *Palamanando*, without exception, have been most supportive.

So, please approach and consume this book for what it is. We have attempted to record both the vernacular and the delightful humour of Jack and Royal's verbal shorthand, and have tried to do so in a manner that is both funny and affectionate. We have also gone back to earlier days of the last century, and recorded some of the sharper witticisms of that era, which now (hopefully) out of danger of being forgotten.

As the oldest organised fighting service in the world, the Royal Navy has some significant burdens of expectation. The unpredictable global future that involves British maritime interest is here - *now*. Possession of a good sense of humour will continue to be an important feature of the personal coping strategies that Jack, Jenny and Royal will simply *have* to possess. It is my fond hope that JACKSPEAK, threaded through with the black humour that allows sabbatical relief from reality when danger threatens, will help to keep them - and us - on song.

As our splendid American friends would say - *enjoy*!

Rick Jolly OBE
Surgeon Captain RN (retd)
November 2000   Cornwall   PL11   2YR

ALPHA

1 - 18

A1   The highest level of seaworthiness certificate awarded by Lloyd's Register of Shipping - the letter refers to the hull and the numeral to the ground tackle (anchors, etc.). To *be A1* means to be of the best quality.

A25 (*FAA*)   Aircraft accident / incident reporting form which requires considerable detail for its correct completion. The effort involved in this (plus the actual survival!) is celebrated in the refrain to each of the *A25 song's* verses, which describe some of the hair-raising crashes and escapes of the past:

> *They say in the Air Force that a landing's OK,*
> *If the pilot gets out and can still walk away -*
> *But in the Fleet Air Arm the prospects are grim,*
> *If the landing's piss-poor and the pilot can't swim..*

> (Refrain)   *Cracking show, I'm alive,*
> *But I've still got to *render my A25..*

Some of the other verses celebrate traditional enthusiasms among Fleet Air Arm aircrew, such as:

> *My CO has promised me an old Tiger Moth,*
> *An appalling contraption made of string, wood and cloth,*
> *He says its performance - like mine - is fantastic,*
> *Because we both go like crazy on knicker elastic...*

A's and A's   Abbreviation for *Alterations and Additions*, those adjustments to a ship's machinery, fighting ability and habitability which have been (after a long and tortuous process) approved by the Ministry of Defence and which may - if both money and time allow - be incorporated in a ship's refit; the business of incorporating such corrections into a book like JACKSPEAK is an unending task, but all comments are welcome and all suggestions will be considered! See also Author's Preface.

AB Abbreviation for *Able Bodied,* and denotes the rate (rank) of Able Seaman. Originally, this was someone who was no longer a *landsman,* but someone who could now *hand, reef and steer*; often used in the expression *three-badge AB* denoting a sailor, usually of great experience and character, who has not sought promotion during a naval career that has lasted at least sixteen years.

aback The sails of a square-rigged sailing ship were said to be *aback* when the wind was blowing on the wrong side of the sails. While this could be a deliberate manoeuvre (such as in a close-quarters battle in order to frustrate the enemy's tactics) it was highly dangerous and could cause damage to spars and rigging. The possibility of a sudden change in wind direction has led on to its modern meaning and wider usage, in the phrase *taken aback,* of being completely surprised by a situation. See also *flat aback.

abeam On one or other side of a point of reference (ie not *ahead or *astern of).

ABC (RM) The rather resigned response to any alteration of an official plan: *'Tomorrow is ABC - it's All Been Changed!'* There needs to be some awareness however of the possibility that things will *ABCBA* in the fullness of time - *All Be Changed Back Again!* Also the nickname of Admiral Sir Andrew Browne Cunningham.

accelerated advancement A system of early *advancement awarded to ratings who have done particularly well during training or on a specialist course.

A - 2

a'cockbill   Description of a ship's anchor when it has been eased out of its stowage (hawse pipe) and is hanging vertically in readiness for being let go. Formerly, the yards of a sailing ship were *set a'cockbill* - at an angle to the horizontal - as a sign of mourning.

accommodation ladder   Technically correct name for any stairway or flight of steps leading from one deck to another inside a ship. In the RN it is nowadays used to denote the ladder (formerly known as a *gangway ladder*) rigged against the side of a ship to provide access when in harbour but not alongside a jetty. A temporary rope ladder used for boarding at sea is called a *pilot ladder*. Note that the correct routine when accompanying a senior officer on *Rounds is to allow one's superior up a ladder first and down last, in contrast to the small boat etiquette of *last in and first out.

ace   Two applications:
1. Something or somewhere that impresses Jack as being of really high quality: *'Hey, seen Lofty's new tranny? It's really ace..'* Or else: *'Newcastle's an ace *run-ashore..'*
2. The *Flagship - *the ace* that must be protected.

ackers / ackies   Corruption of the words *piastre* (Egyptian money) or *drachma* (Greek) which then became descriptive in the old Mediterranean Fleet for any form of foreign cash. Overtaken in current usage by its further adaptation to *ickies, but see also *klebbies, *shrapnel and *washers.

acquire   Euphemism for the illegal (or barely legal) process of obtaining a *Naval stores item that is in short supply. See also *proff.

across the Pond   In America, since the *Pond concerned refers to the Atlantic Ocean, as opposed to the *Ditch of the English Channel.

Acting Unpaid   Formerly, a rating who for good reason is granted (*local) permission by his Commanding Officer to wear a badge of rank when he is not strictly qualified to do so, but needs to have some authority over others of the same *rate. The term is nowadays used only in jest; in reality, the captain of a seagoing ship may, subject to strict rules, promote a rating to the local acting rate for which he or she gets paid the salary for the higher rate - but only for the period that the vacancy exists.

Action Messing   The process of feeding the ship's company very quickly whilst at *Action Stations (in a way that McDonalds have never dreamt of). This is a time when *Potmess and *Babies Heads come into their own.

Action Stations   The highest state of readiness in a warship, ordered when action with an enemy is imminent, with all *hands *closed up.

Active Service   An officer or rating of the Regular RN forces, as distinct from those on the Reserve, Retired or Emergency *Lists. A national emergency or specific shortages can lead to *recall to Active Service* from the latter categories.

actual   Three applications:
1. (FAA) Flying in real cloud rather than simulating this experience under a helmet-mounted hood.
2. (FAA) Sleeping in a bunk during an operation or exercise instead of simulating this *kip by lying on the counterpane, exhausted.
3. *Actuals* refer to *actual expenditure*, an accounting process authorized in countries where the cost of living is very high, and where fixed allowances would probably prove inadequate.

Adam and Eve on a raft   Two fried eggs on a piece of toast.

Adam's ale   Drinking water.

addled   Old sailor's term for drinking water that had become stale or putrid; hence the term *addled eggs* for those that have gone off, or *addled brains* for someone a bit *handcarted.

ADDLS (FAA)   Acronym for an Assisted *Dummy Deck Landing Sortie; Naval aviators would do simulated carrier approaches to a specially marked runway with the help of a *Bats, in order to develop or retain the special skills required. When the mirror-landing sight was developed (in Britain!) these flights became MADDLS instead.

Admiral Brown   A turd floating past a ship; on the grounds that it was Royalty (Henry III, Edward III, Richard III, etc.) and therefore it could be saluted.

Admiral of the narrow seas   Jack's historic nickname for someone unkind enough to vomit stale beer all over his *oppo.

Admiralty clown   Physical Training Instructor; see also the terms *club-swinger and *springer (RM).

Admiralty Fleet Order   Precursor of the *DCI and originally abbreviated to AFO; in the Mediterranean and Far Eastern Fleets, *Egyptian AFOs were poorly printed and laughably misspelt pornographic books.

Admiralty ham   Suspicious description of any kind of tinned meat; see also *fanny for further explanation.

Admiralty Rain / Admiralty Weather   Describes the incredible and unfair climate change on a *make-and-mend afternoon, or other time when Jack might be free. Rain and fog seldom seem to occur conveniently to delay *Pusser's work, but often spoil a good *run ashore.

adqual   Hybrid term for *Additional Qualification*; most ratings, and indeed officers, can acquire such a qualification (eg. ship's diver) regardless of their own specialisation. Some *adquals* entitle the holder to extra pay.

adrenalin's brown!   Fundamental discovery about one's personal physiology on being seriously frightened, especially when this happens for the first time. See also *drop a brown for an older version of exactly the same sentiment.

adrift   Late for work or duty: *'Comin' back off *Crimbo leave, Shiner got *legless an' missed 'is train - five hours adrift and *in the rattle..'* The phrase *adrift to hell* (or stronger) implies being very seriously late indeed, as depicted on page A - 10.

advancement   Non-selective promotion for ratings below *Petty Officer. An individual is *advanced* to the next rank, not promoted.

aerobatic teams (FAA)   There are no officially constituted Fleet Air Arm outfits presently on view to the public, although the *Historics continue to delight airshow crowds around the country each summer. The *Sharks (Gazelle) helicopter display team was disbanded in the mid-1990s as a financial savings measure. In the past era of conventional fixed-wing jets there were some really famous teams, including The Ace of Diamonds (Sea Hawks), Fred's Five and Simon's Sircus (Sea Vixens) and the Blue Herons (Hunters). The latter group, comprised of former FAA and RAF aircrew under contract to the MoD, was particularly smooth and proficient; because of its very experienced but rather elderly pilots, it was also known locally as the Phyllosan Four! See also the *Crimson Crabs.

The very first JACK cartoon in Navy News February 1973.

Affirmative!   Jack and Royal's way of saying: '*Yes!*'

aft through the hawse-pipe   Descriptive phrase for a *Special Duties List Officer promoted from the *Lower Deck. The traditional seamen's *messdeck was up in the forecastles, ie. before the mast; the *hawse-pipes* were openings in the forecastle deck through which the anchor cables ran, and the officer's *wardroom and accommodation was generally situated aft. The expression is sometimes heard with *up* substituted for *aft*. See also *Upper Yardie and *Corps Commish.

afternoon watch   The period between midday and 4 pm (1200 and 1600). The RN does not use the word *hours*. See *watches

A - 6

and *bells.

afters Pudding: *'Woss' fer afters?'*

Aggie Weston's The network of Royal Sailor's Rests begun in 1876 by the formidable Dame Agnes Weston. These *Homes from Home* still exist, in Portsmouth, Gosport, Rosyth, Helensburgh and Devonport. Their emphasis remains on home comforts - and temperance. Such was Jack's genuine affection for his *Sailor's Friend* that when the warship HMS WESTON-SUPER-MARE was launched, she was immediately labelled *Aggie-on-horseback.*

agony bags Bagpipes; see also *porridge guns.

ahead In front of a point of reference. *Dead ahead* means directly in front; also used to describe someone who is ambitious or doing well.

Airship The Royal Air Force equivalent of a Sea Lord, because the *Crabfat model of Their Lordships of the Admiralty Board is called The Air Board - hence Their *Airships* of the Air Board! Jack also has his own ideas about the Junior Service - see also *Per Ardua Ad Astra.

Air Tragedy / Air Tragickers (FAA) The professional skill of Air Traffic Control, and thus a group nickname for practitioners of this secret art. *Air Trumpeters* is an occasional alternative.

airy fairy Derogatory term for a person serving in the Fleet Air Arm. Can also be used as an adjective: *'Most airy-fairy *kit ain't nowhere near *bootneck-proof..'* See *Wafu in addition.

Al Jolson Kit (RM) Skin-darkening paste or *cam* (camouflage) cream.

Aladdin's cave Any over-stocked *compartment full of stores.

Alert Three applications here:
1. Bugle call played to mark a specific occasion such as the arrival or departure of an important personage: *'Sound the Alert!'*
2. (FAA) Aircraft's readiness state to *launch - *Alert 5* or *Alert 30* describes the number of minutes that it will take to get into the air and on task.
3. *Be alert* - because the country needs lerts.

all about Someone who is *switched-on: *'You'd have to get up pretty early in the morning to catch him out - he's really all about, just like shit in a fanshaft..'*

all above board   Older description for anything above the deck of a sailing vessel, ie. visible to everyone; this has led to the more general meaning of fair and open business dealing.

all fart and no shit   A noisy but basically ineffective leader. *All piss and wind* means much the same.

all for it   Older term that can still be heard as a piece of lovely cynicism: *'The Job Evaluation team felt that my work here was absolutely vital to the security of the nation, but two of my three assistants had to go. Then they asked me what I thought about that. Of course, as you'd expect, I said I was all for it..'*

all gait and gaiters   Nice description of *Guns and his staff when dressed and prepared for the parade ground. Can also be *all gas and gaiters.*

all nighters   Contraction and mis-application of the term *All Night Shore Leave* to describe an episode of intense overnight (and indoor) activity with a lady friend. Can also be used as *all night in* to describe a watchkeeper whose sleep, for once, has been unbroken.

all of one company   Very important and oft-quoted sentiment applied to the conditions of service in the Royal Navy. Attributed to Sir Francis Drake in 1578 when quelling the discontent that existed in THE GOLDEN HIND between his professional seamen and the attached gentlemen of Court: *'..for I must have the gentleman to haul and draw with the mariner and the mariner with the gentleman. What! Let us show ourselves all to be of a company..'* See also *happy ship.

all parts bearing equal strain   Classic Naval expression describing how everything is under control and giving no cause for any concern or anxiety. This may also mean no strain at all if the person making the statement: *'I'm going to put all parts under equal strain..'* intends to *slope off for a *kip.

all-singing, all-dancing   Sarcastic description of any piece of *kit that is claimed to solve some previously impossible problem.

all teeth, tits and toenails   Deflating description of an individual who is full of his own self-importance.

Ally Slopers   A brand of pungent sauce stocked in naval *canteens in the early 20th century. The sole direction on the label was to *take plenty with everything*. This popular, all-purpose sauce was also reputed to be very effective for polishing *bright-work.

Ambit   Rough, cheap, strong Maltese wine, barely drinkable even when mixed with *7-Up* or lemonade, although some say that gin improved the taste of the white variety; other names included Amtoot, Toot and of course, the Red Infuriator.

amen wallah   A Naval padre or chaplain. See also *Bible bash-er, *Bible puncher, *bish, *Devil dodger, *God botherer, *God walloper, *Holy Joe, *Maker's rep, *sin bosun, *sky pilot.

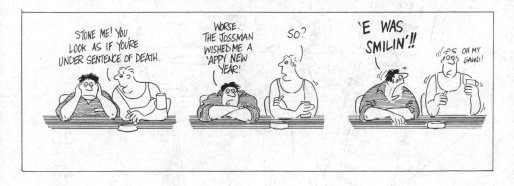

anchor-faced   Someone, usually an officer, who lives and breathes the Royal Navy even when retired, as on page B - 24. See also *Corps-pissed (RM).

anchor watch   A special watch kept while at anchor during a storm, to detect a dragging *pick; also used to describe Jack's anxious and frequent examination of his *toggle and two following success on the previous evening's *run-ashore.

..and like it!   Older expression, usually tacked on the end of an order to perform some unpleasant or dirty job, and which fore-stalls any complaint: *'Right lads - you two, leap away to the top of that mast, clear the jammed halyard..and like it!'*

Andrew (the)   Widespread nickname for the Royal Navy used by all ranks within the Senior Service, especially when referring to length of time in uniform:*'Fifteen years in the Andrew, and most of that spent at sea..'* Nothing to do with HRH Commander The Duke of York (despite his being a serving RN officer) but said to be named after Lieutenant Andrew Miller, a highly successful press-gang officer of the 18th century, and thus also more com-

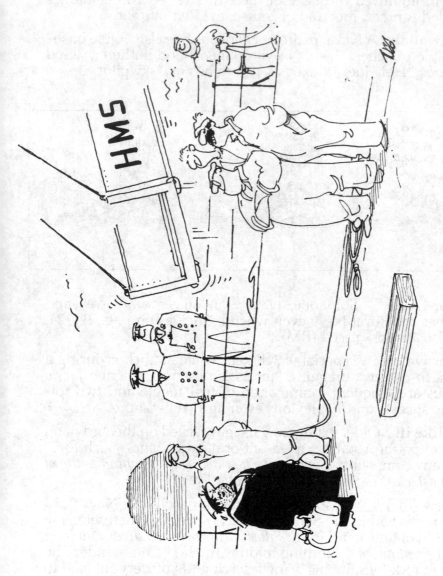

Adrift

pletely referred to by older *hands as the Andrew Miller. See also *Impressment.

Angel's whisper   A *Defaulters parade, nicely depicted in this sense by Tugg on page B - 37.

angles and dangles (SM)   High speed manoeuvres in a submarine, involving large *trim angles of rise and dive.

angry palm tree   A *burning and turning helicopter.

animal   Half-admiring description of an individual whose social and sexual activity would be considered excessive in most quarters: *'Five pints of Old *Doobrey an' then Ginge turns into a right animal, 'e does..'* Can also be used as an adjective (esp. RM) to describe an outstanding or memorable *run-ashore.

ankle biter / ankle snapper   A small child that has just started to crawl. See also *rug rat and *carpet crawler.

ante   A trio here:
1. A *wardroom *ante-room* usually adjoins the dining room itself.
2. *Ante-up* - put one's stake money on the table; also to make one's contribution to the kitty (for a *run ashore).
3. *Up the ante* - increase the stakes in a deal or discussion; hence, to increase the pressure.

any fool can be uncomfortable (RM)   Splendid and sensible advice given by instructors at *Lympstone to recruits learning the business of fieldcraft. All it takes to be warm, dry and happy in the field is a correct attitude - and the determined application of some acquired knowledge.

ape-shit (esp. RM)   Descriptive adjective for someone who is extremely angry or upset: *'The *Boss went totally ape-shit when he heard about that missing weapon..'*

apples   A pair(!):
1. Rough cider or scrumpy.
2. Older term for pay - perhaps derived from the *golden apples* of mythology.

Appointer   Naval officer working in the *Pompey *Puzzle Palace who is responsible for the career development of officers in various specializations, in turn reporting to to the Naval Secretary, who is a Rear Admiral. In the old days, NavSec was Naval Assistant to the Second Sea Lord, and was said to take a keen interest in what the young chaps wanted - in order to be able to disappoint them - hence the alternate title of *Disappointer.

Arch Tiff   The senior Artificer (Engineering Warrant Officer).

Arctic fox (RM)   Someone who is very happy in the Arctic environment, but also a synonym for a frozen turd lying in the snow.

arduous duty tot   A special *tot awarded to men who have completed some particularly difficult or unpleasant operational task, such as the *seaboat crew recovering dead bodies, or First Aid teams exposed to unpleasant or hazardous conditions while tending injured survivors. This issue of spirit is still authorised in *QRRN 4924 para 2; the author utilised this provision in the Ajax Bay field hospital on twelve occasions during the land battles of the Falklands campaign.

Argyll Bowl (RM)   Challenge cup for an annual Rugby Football competition; the trophy was presented to the Corps by the Argyll and Sutherland Highlanders to commemorate the close and happy association between Royal and the Jocks, particularly during the fighting around Singapore during WW2.   See *Tunney Cup for the Association Football equivalent.

ARK   HMS ARK ROYAL, currently the sixth ship to bear her famous name.

Armstrong patent   Nice expression used at the turn of this century which almost boasts of the absence of any mechanical aids on a sailing ship, in that all the hard work is achieved solely through the strong arms of her crew. *Handraulic and *mandraulic are the more modern versions.

arrigones   Tinned Italian tomatoes; one of the major suppliers in the early days of this commodity was a gentleman named *Signor A. Riggoni* who had his name in large letters all over the labels. The eponymous term persists to this day.

arisings   Material left over after the completion of a task; these may be valuable and require accounting for, but they may also be worthless, as in: *'This *civvy *chippy didn't bother to tidy up as he worked. The whole *compartment was knee-deep in arisings..'*

arrival (FAA)   Understatement for the hard touchdown of an aircraft on landing.   Fixed-wing carrier aviation remains a supreme test of piloting skills; conventional jet aircraft like the *Toom and *Bucc had to be placed accurately, at high approach speeds and sink rates, onto a relatively tiny area in order to pick up one of four arrester wires. Each landing was in effect *an arrival* - or a barely-controlled crash. Although the amazing *SHAR is now operated on the *'Why land and stop - when you can now stop and land?'* principle, the older term persists in the FAA. Getting a *Lynx down in severe weather onto a pitching and rolling frigate flight deck requires native ability, a lot of training - and a *navalised undercarriage.

Arrows! Exclamation of admiration and congratulation derived from the game of darts, but can be used in a wider context to mean *Well done!* or *Good shot!*

arse The familiar, although crude slang word for the buttocks or posterior, employed by Jack in a number of phrases:

> *my arse!* - expression of disbelief.
> *arse about* - to waste time ineffectively.
> *arse about face* - back to front.
> *arse bandit* - a homosexual.
> *doesn't know his arse from his elbow* - he's rather
>   unsure of his job.
> *tear the arse out of it* - overuse or exhaust a good thing.
> *arse over teakettle* - head over heels (*Wardroom).
> *arse over tit* - as above (*messdeck).
> *tear him up for arse paper* - give him a really hard time.
> *arse-up duck* - any bottom-feeding bird (eg. a swan).
> *arseholed* Vulgar term, often prefixed by the adverbs
>   *absolutely* or *totally* to imply extreme drunkeness.
> *load of arse* rubbish (verbal or written). See also *feat
>   of arse.

Arthur, Martha or Mabel   Another amusing term for someone unsure of his job, or a little confused: *'He'd had that many *wets he'd forgotten whether he was Arthur, Martha or Mabel..'*   See also *punched, bored or countersunk.

Articles of War   Formidable 17th century document laying down the duties of Royal Navy personnel and the draconian penalties to be suffered by those who fail to carry them out. They have now been ratified by Parliament, and incorporated into the Naval Discipline Act. A copy is secured at some highly visible place in every ship of the *Fleet. The final Article is also known as the *Captain's Cloak because it even authorises pun-

THE WIT and WISDOM of JACK

..... WHOSE SPECIALIST SUBJECT IS BARON STRANGLING.

ishment for any misdemeanour or offence not mentioned in any of the previous Articles.

as long as (your) arse points downwards   Expression used to reinforce some definitive statement: *'As long as his arse points downwards, young Robert won't make it as a *Looker..'* This implies that some rather radical changes will have to take place if this opinion is to be proved wrong.

ashore   Anywhere that is not *on board, or anything on the shore side of the *brow. Jack will also describe the action of passing through the main gate of a Dockyard, Naval establishment or air station as going ashore, whether he does so by car or on foot. See also *run-ashore.

ashtray on a motorbike   Label for some poorly-designed piece of *kit: *'Honestly, it's about as much use as an ashtray on a motorbike..'* See also *chocolate fireguard / teapot.

assault with a friendly weapon   Sexual intercourse; in this context, see also *receiving swollen property.

assy (FAA)   Abbreviation of *assymetric,* and applied to an individual with ears of different sizes or position.

astern   Behind the stern, or if moving astern - going backwards. The advice to an officer that he or she is *going astern* means that his or her shoulder rank straps have been (incorrectly) reversed. The phrase *astern of station* can also be used to describe a programme that is running behind time, as well as something that is to the rear of its correct position.

at the dip   A flag signal is *at the dip* when it is hauled halfway up the *halyard; it usually indicates an action which is about to take place. Hence someone who is ready to do something is *at the dip.*

at the rush   As fast as possible; this expression was memorably abused once when a cavalry regiment was billetted in the Belfast accommodation ship HMS MAIDSTONE, manned in part by Royal. A *pipe was made for a certain Corporal of Horse to go to the *brow *at the gallop!*

auction of kit   The sale, by open bidding as at an auction, of the personal kit of some deceased member of a ship's company or RM Unit. Outrageous sums of money can then be offerred for the most useless items, with the article often returned to the pool for re-auction. The proceeds of such a *kit auction* are then passed by the *Jaunty, via the ship's ledger account, to the deceased's widow or family. The older term for this procedure was a *sale before the mast.

auto   Two meanings:
1. Abbreviation of *automatic,* usually implying loss of temper: *'If you mention the Secretary of State for Defence's name to the Captain he'll simply go off in auto..'*

2. (FAA) *Autorotation* of a helicopter, the process of descent following loss of engine power; the resulting airflow through the rotor disc keeps the blades turning. The aircraft glides down, but limited pitch control is still maintained - and then used to cushion final *arrival on the ground.

Avast! Dated but still used command to cease an action or procedure, and stop immediately.

Avquack (FAA) Aviation medicine specialist.

awash Half-submerged. Sometimes employed graphically with food or drink: *'No thanks, Yorks..I couldn't *hack another mouthful - me back teeth are awash..'*

Away Seaboat / Lifeboat! Verbal order or *pipe for the specified boat to be manned in readiness for being lowered. The urgency is denoted by whether the crew or the boat is called away; eg.*'Away Seaboat's Crew!'* (for a routine transfer of personnel or stores) or *'Away *Lifeboat!'* (the nearest trained personnel man the boat in order to save life).

Awkward Standard name for a ship's defensive operational procedure in harbour when facing attack from underwater.

awning(s) Formerly a canvas, but now terylene (or similar) roofing spread over the main parts of the *upper deck in harbour in warm climates. Their purpose originally was not to provide shade (although they did), but to help keep the inside of the ship as cool as possible in the days before air conditioning. Nowadays only one area (usually the flight deck) is provided with an awning and its use is ceremonial. Also used by Jack to describe a pastry pie crust!

Aye Aye! Technically correct reply from a boat to a challenging ship, on being hailed, when there is an officer on board. If the *captain of a ship is in the boat the reply is the ship's name. See also *No No ! and *Flag !

Aye Aye, sir! The *seamanlike reply given in acknowledgement of an officer's order, sometimes with a slightly sardonic emphasis on the second syllable to indicate Jack's opinion of its worth.

The List

BRAVO

19 - 76

B13   Form of notification from *Drafty that a rating has risen to the top of an *advancement or promotion *roster and that when medical fitness is confirmed, he or she will be advanced on the date specified. Note that advancement is the proper term for a naval ratings' elevation in rank, although in this new TriService era, the word *promotion* is now in increasing use.

B's (pronounced *Bees*) (SM)   Reference to *Mrs. Beeton* and her celebrated cook-book - Mrs. B's and thickers is a rich sponge pudding topped with evaporated or condensed milk.

babies' bag rations   The female breasts. See also *BSH, *lumpy jumper and *double bumps.

babies' bums (SM)   Emergency lighting switches, recognisable by touch alone.

babies' heads   Tinned, individual steak and kidney puddings.

baby clacker   The youngest chef on board.

baby spanner   The male sexual organ; this device dispenses *baby gravy*, or *baby batter*. See also *population paste.

back-afty (SM)   Propulsion machinery *Tiff in a submarine, working *back aft* in the nuclear reactor control area or diesel machinery spaces. The two components of this portmanteau word actually mean the same thing!

back in date (FAA)   Recently successful in sexual terms, because most Fleet Air Arm professional skills require regular inspections and checks, with the need to be *in date* for their currency; another phrase, with an identical meaning, refers to *getting your logbook stamped.

back in the saddle (FAA)   Descriptive phrase for the refamiliarization flying undertaken by aircrew following a leave period.

back teeth awash (RM)   See also *awash, but Royal also uses this expression for someone who is very drunk indeed.

backing and filling   Originally a badly-handled sailing ship whose sails were not catching the wind properly. Nowadays used for someone who constantly shifts his or her ground in a discussion or argument.

backside of the drag curve (FAA)   Expression denoting a fairly hopeless situation in which a wing's increasingly high angle of attack is creating more drag than actual lift. In this state, no matter how much thrust is applied, the wing will eventually stall:*'Running an elderly sports car is like being on the backside of the drag curve as far as my wallet is concerned..'*

backy dips   Extra swimming lessons for backward swimmers.

bad speaking bastard   Someone with a regional accent.

badgeman   Any rating with one or more Good Conduct badges on the left sleeve of his uniform suit. Each gold (or red) chevron indicates four years of completed service. The first one was after three years. Fifteen years of what Jack tends to describe as undetected crime leads on to the *Pea-Doo or *Blue Peter; see also *three badger. Unlike the other services, the chevrons (badges) do not denote rank. Trade badges are worn on the upper arm, and Special badges (divers, parachutists etc.) on the right cuff.

badger (FAA)   Aircraft handlers on a carrier flight deck wear different coloured surcoats for easy identification. In a previous generation of carriers like the *ARK, the stokers (*steamies) responsible for her catapults and jet-blast deflectors had white ones with a broad black stripe, resembling a *badger's coat.* Sad to relate, such skills are no longer relevant in the *SHAR era, and there are no *badgers* to be seen now *topsides alongside the other *roof rats during *flying stations.

baffin's bridge   See *biffin.

Bag   Nickname for the AEW (*Airborne Early Warning*) version of the *Sea King helicopter, whose development was hastened greatly following lessons learned in the 1982 South Atlantic Conflict; this aircraft carries a retractable radar aerial outside the fuselage, housed in an inflatable and pressurised rubber bag.

bag and hammock   Jack's traditional nickname for his wife, but it can also be used to describe the sum total of Jack's personal possessions:'*She kicked him out, bag and hammock..*' The term *up bag and hammock* meant a peremptory move of one kind or another.

bag mealies   Fishery Protection Squadron nickname for the minehunter vessels which *day run from port, whereas the FPS ships may stay out on patrol for two weeks at a time.

bag meals   Snack meals provided for personnel on temporary detached duty, usually rather unpalatable and packed in brown paper bags. The RM version is *bag rats* (rations).

bag of nuts   Signal of congratulations from the C-in-C.

bag off (esp. RM)   Sexual intercourse; note also its application in the phrase *beer, big eats, *bag off* and back on board.

bag shanty   A brothel or red-light district bar (see cartoon on page B - 48); this also used to be the nickname of HMS BACCHANTE.

bagger   Common measure of female beauty - or the lack of it:
1. A *one* (paper) *bagger* implies an unattractive face.
2. A *two bagger / double bagger* indicates some anxiety that one bag might fall off.
3. A *three bagger / triple bagger*? Heaven forbid!
See also *bulldog, *coyote, *stumper, *wildebeeste and *wolverine in this particular context.

Bags of swank!   Exhortation by parade ground *GI to put more effort and pride into a marching drill.

Bagsy   Traditional name for anyone called Baker.

balbo (FAA)   Large formation of aircraft, usually for a fly-past, thus preserving the memory of General *Italo Balbo*. Between the two World Wars this distinguished (and pro-British) aviator was responsible for the development of Mussolini's air power, and is especially remembered for a round-the-world seaplane expedition that he commanded.

bale / bale out   Meaning to remove water, and comes from the old name *boyle* for a bucket. Baling out of an aircraft originates from this term, and it is easy to see why, as the cockpit is emptied - these days by a *Martin-Baker bucket!

ballast   Material used to maintain the trim or stability of a ship but of little other use, hence a description of someone's worth: *'He's reliable, but not very bright - ballast really..'* There is another special usage:*'He can't half carry some ballast..'* in the description of someone who can hold his liquor well.

ball of chalk   Failure, see also can of worms.

ball-bagged (RM)   Alternative version of *chin-strapped; extremely tired as a result of physical endeavour, lack of sleep - or both.

ballerina shit (SM)   Pink blancmange.

ballistic   Similar to *banzai or *ape-shit, but used to indicate some senior officer's especial anger:*'If you dare to comment on the quality of his paperwork, our *schoolie tends to go a bit ballistic...'*

balls-ache (esp. RM)   Something tiresome or very time-consuming, usually emanating from a signal from upon high with regard to previous action taken by the addressee.

balls-out   With maximum despatch, or as fast as possible.

balls-up   An error of quite significant proportions.

banana balancer   RN officer's steward or wardroom waiter.

banana bedstead   Sailor's hammock.

banana boat   Older affectionate term for an escort aircraft carrier, stemming from the *MAC ships of WW2 that had been hastily converted from general freighters. Now used also as an extra name for the *canteen boat in a minesweeper squadron.

banana trim (SM)   A trim which is either light at the ends and heavy in the middle, or vice versa.

bandage head   Indian (Sikh) personnel wearing the turban. *'Hope your head gets better soon..'*

bandstand   Several applications, depending on context:
1. Protective framework around an upperworks gun mounting.
2. A cruet holding salt, pepper and mustard.
3. (SM) Waist-high circular guardrail or support for the Officer of the Watch in a nuclear submarine, allowing him to remain steady behind the seated planesmen if the *boat heels at high speed underwater. See also *angles and dangles in this context.

bandwagon (RM)   Tracked oversnow vehicle - the Bv 202 or 206.

Bandy   Traditional (older) nickname for anyone called Evans.

bandy (RM)   Now any member of the Royal Marines' Band Service, but used to refer to the senior bandsman present, especially at formal mess dinners.

bang   Sexual intercourse, especially when used by Royal in conjunction with the adjective *belt-fed.

bang box   Gun turret.

bang on / banging on   Boring everyone to death about some subject very dear to the speaker's heart. The term used to refer to gunnery accuracy. See also *spot on.

bang out (FAA)   Use an aircraft's ejection seat - its bang seat - or else leave a party that is still going strong. See also *Martin-Baker.

bang stick   A rifle; may also be a corruption of the Arabic word *bundook* for rifle.

banger (SM)   Light which hangs over the forward top part of a diesel submarine's fin, illuminating part of the casing to assist the *trot sentry during the dark hours by improving his night vision particularly during his rounds, thus helping him not to fall overboard that often.

banjo   Three meanings:
1. Hit someone or something very hard.
2. Sandwich, originally created from all (or most of) a French loaf, and then filled with a variety of contents. A common variant is the *egg banjo* involving a fried egg.

Anchor Faced

3. It is also the traditional nickname for anyone called West.

Bank of Israel   The spiritual home of all financial acumen in the world. Someone clever with money or knowledgeable about investments may be described as *drafted to the Bank of Israel - *for instructional duties..*

banyan   Tropical picnic held ashore by a ship's company while deployed at sea. Often the beach chosen is on some deserted island, so clothing becomes bright and colourful - *banyan rig* - and the informal tone of proceedings is both relaxed and refreshing for officers and ratings alike. Its origin lies in the meatless Banyan days of the old Navy which were abolished in 1825 - and not with the pleasant shade that might be afforded by a banyan tree. Jack would try and keep some sort of cooked meat provisions aside to *tide himself over these *barc days.

banzai (RM)   Frenzied, half-crazy: *'When 'e heard about his missus and the milkman, Chalky went banzai..'*

bar   A pound note, when such items of currency existed. Also known as a Bradbury. See also *half a bar.

bar chit   An all-purpose piece of paper supplied in booklet form in *Wardroom bars, exchangable (when signed!) for drinks. It can also be used as an *ad hoc* loose-leaf diary, address book, note-pad or (FAA) an instructional medium for explaining tricky principles of flight, usually after about five pints of beer.

bare buff   Naked from the waist up: *'Do you hear there - Rig of the day is bare buff...'*

bare Navy   Older term for a poorly *victualled ship in which the food conformed to the laid down scales of issue - and no more. Later on it was applied to someone without any additional financial means who had to live bare Navy on his pay alone.

barge   Ceremonial, much-gilded and oared vessel of olden times; the term still applies to more modern methods of transportation. A *Flag Officer's personal motor launch is his barge; any helicopter or aeroplane used to carry a *Flag Officer is also called an Admiral's Barge - when not described by its more usual nickname of *Green Parrot! Apart from Royalty, the only other officers entitled to a barge are Queen's Harbour Masters (QHM). The term may also be used to describe a flat wooden serving dish, such as a biscuit barge or bread barge.

barge pole (to not touch with a)   A barge pole is a long, heavy pole, tipped with iron at one end, and used aboard barges for fending off from other vessels, obstructions, etc. The colloquialism is an extension of the original usage. It means to not go near someone or something, to have nothing to do with it, as in *'she was offered the special class for the remainder of the year, but she said that she wouldn't touch it with a barge pole.'* The expression is one of intensification. The barge pole itself is an indicator that the speaker does not even want first-remove contact, let alone personal contact.

baron   A legendary source of gratuitous issue or generous hospitality. Anything free in the Navy was said to be *on the baron* rather than *on the house*; the process of taking advantage of a well-off *civvy individual or organization is known as *baron strangling*. See also the terms *beer, *rum and *tickler baron for a slightly different application and meaning.

baronial   This meant posh, upper class, and is derived from the word *baron as in: *'I took the wife to this hotel, and it was really baronial.'* Anything baronial was absolutely top notch.

barrack damages   Financial charge levied against the pay account of whoever is responsible for the misuse or breakage of furniture or decorative items, even if these are actually in a Married Quarter!

barrack stanchion   Derogatory description of someone who deliberately avoids sea duty, or who has had a seemingly endless succession of shore jobs in his career.

barracks   That part of a warship's *messdecks occupied by her Royal Marines *Detachment.

Barracuda (FAA)   Important WW2 Fleet Air Arm aircraft of great ugliness which attracted criticism and affection in equal amounts. Designed as a torpedo carrier and dive bomber, early prototypes of this high-wing monoplane had an unpleasant tendency to flick inverted when the dive brakes were extended and flaps lowered. This was cured eventually, but these lethal habits - plus the ether-based hydraulic fluid that could anaesthetize the pilot silently in his enclosed cockpit, and the rivets which had an alarming tendency to spring from over-stressed wings, led to a famous FAA song being composed to the tune of *Any Old Iron*!   Despite all this, carrier-borne Barras did enormous damage to TIRPITZ in Tromso Fjord, before high-level bombing by the Dambusters of 617 Sqn RAF finished off this German battleship. See also *ruptured duck.

barrel fever The hangover caused by a beer *sesh; see also *CSB rash.

barrel See *over a barrel.

barricoe Pronounced *breaker*, with which it is synonymous; a small wooden water cask stored in a lifeboat that could also be partially *broken out or *scuttled in an emergency as a water butt.

base over apex Politer conversational version of *arse over tit.

bash (not to be confused with the Welsh *bach*, meaning little or small) A matey greeting to friend, comrade, shipmate, or fellow Jack.

bash the bishop Masturbate.

basha (RM) Any temporary shelter constructed in the field, usually out of naturally available materials; the origins of this term lie in jungle warfare, a highly specialized art in which RM *Commando *jungle bunnies maintain significant and continuing expertise.

basinful (of that) Sardonic response to a person using some long or learned word; now also employed in admiration of a particularly busty or curvaceous female: '*Wow - I'll have a basinful of that!*' Note the term *BSH as well.

basket of eggs An astronomic fix taken when the sun is almost exactly overhead. The result when plotted looks like a collection of small circles.

Look For The Rules!

bastard   In older usage this was a general purpose substitute word, whether as noun, verb, or adjective. If Jack spotted a mess mate with something that was his, he would say *'Hey, that's my bastard..'* or else, he would grumble: *'I've lost my bastard pencil..'* One could call one's bosom friend a *'miserable, rotten, one lung TB bastard..'* without giving any offence at all, as long as one smiles.

Batch (RM)   Nickname for the annual intake of Young Officers entering *Lympstone for their officer and *Commando training. The members of this grouping will always identify themselves for the rest of their days by that *Batch number*, and usually meet for a celebration dinner at *CTCRM twenty-five years on, what-ever their subsequent destinies turn out to be. The Guest of Honour on these occasions is always their *Batch Nurse*, who is usually delighted to find that the *Batch spirit* still prevails - unless of course they were a bunch of particularly *dank hands! See also *YO.

Bats   Nickname for a small ship's Flight Deck Officer, who guides helicopters onto a frigate using bats made of wire frames and brightly-coloured cloth strips. He is the direct descendant of the aviator who, long before helicopters or mirror-landing sights, was crucial to the process of *recovering aircraft on board. The *Batsman* of that era stood on a raised platform with dive-nets all around in case some *Bloggs got it all wrong!

bats   Naval heavy shoes or (FAA) flightdeck boots with steel toecaps: *'Bill was wearin' this bloody great pair of *pussers' steamin' bats..'* Used also to refer to feet: *'Bungy's got rotten bats..'*

batten down   For foul weather, now also used ashore.

batting on a sticky wicket   *Two's up in the coital sense.

battle bowler   Older name for a tin helmet.

battle ensign   In action a ship wears extra *battle ensigns*, usual-ly much larger than the normal sea ensign, in conspicuous posi-tions to ensure the *colours remain flying whatever damage is received.

battlewagon   Older nickname for a capital ship; see also the term *pusser's battlewagon.

bazzy   Abbreviated use of the word *bastard* when referring to mood or demeanour: *'Watch out for the Chief, Sunshine - he's got a real bazzy on this morning..'*

BDV (RM) *Blue Drinking Voucher* - a £5 note. Interestingly, a *BDV* was also the name of a between-wars cigarette that came with free coupons towards a range of gifts. One correspondent still has his clockwork Basset-Lowke railway from that era.

beached RN retired.

beagle balls Rissoles. At the outbreak of WW2, it was decided that the pack of *beagles* at the Britannia Royal Naval College at Dartmouth should be destroyed. Dinner that night included rissoles on the menu, and understandable conclusions were drawn!

bean stealer Someone who is *RA but slips back on board early for a breakfast that he is not really entitled to. Now used also for the kind of person who never buys torch batteries, but always *acquires them from *Pusser instead.

Beano Jack's nickname for a certain type of Commander or *Jimmy who is always addressing the ship's company in a negative sense: *'There will be no (this) until further notice, and until (such-and-such) improves there will be no (that) either..'* One excellent example was: *'There will be no shore leave until morale improves..'*

beans in a row   Phrase used to indicate a form of general agreement: *'If anyone should raise this point, then we've all got our beans in a row on the subject..'* *Singing from the same hymn sheet is an alternative version.

bear pit   A stokers's *messdeck, or (SM) the lower aft section of a diesel *boat's engine room.

bear up   Sailing expression meaning to *bear the tiller up* to windward in order to keep the vessel pointing as close as possible to the required direction of travel. It is in common use, with the metaphorical meaning of *Keep your spirits up*. The opposite is *bear away* - ie. let the vessel fall away from the wind.

Beastie (FAA)   Nickname for the Supermarine Attacker jet aircraft of the early 50's which was heartily disliked by its pilots for tricks like folding its wingtips in mid-air, or its engine stalling when the guns were fired.

beasting (RM)   Heavy physical training designed to improve muscular strength and general fitness; usually delivered in good humour - see *It's only pain - but recently also associated with bullying behaviour.

Beat Retreat   Traditionally, the formal use of military drummers, either to end an episode of fighting, or to mark the day's completion in the sense that outlying troops and citizens working outside a walled city by day were summoned inside for protection during the night. Later, fifers playing tunes were added and more recently bands, the ceremony being embellished over the years until we come to today's setting which takes the form of a musical pageant. Now combined with the Naval *Sunset ceremony, the RM Band Service's Beat Retreat is a spectacular and moving piece of ceremonial.

beat up (RM)   The process of intensive physical self-preparation prior to an attempt at passing the *Commando course. In the FAA it means a particularly daring (and probably illegal) flying display; the second verse of the *A25 song begins: *'They lent me a Fulmar to beat up the Fleet..'*

becket   Small loop of rope or nylon tape sewn into an item of clothing or safety equipment.

bedroom boatrope   Yet another term for the male sexual organ.

bedstead / double bedstead   Type 965 long-range radar rotating aerial; a huge lattice array fitted in some frigates, destroyers and aircraft carriers - now obsolete.

beef   One of the very few words in general use which can have entirely different meanings depending on context and who is using it:

1. As an adjective - homosexual (*'He's beef'*); hence *beefer* or *beef bandit*.

2. As a verb in the active sense - to complain. In this mode it is synonymous with *drip (*'He's always beefing'* or *'I've got a beef'*).

3. As a verb in the passive sense - to criticise, as in *'He's always beefing at me'*. In this sense, see also 4.

4. In the FAA, a *beefer* is a flying instructor. This label has two possible origins - either *B for bastard* or: *'He's always beefing about my flying.'* Whatever the true explanation is, Royal Marines aircrew trained by the Fleet Air Arm must exercise very great caution when describing this experience to their green-bereted *oppos.

beef screen   A compartment adjacent to the *upper deck where the meat was temporarily stored and cut up in ships. One of the ship's company was trained as a butcher; interestingly, this was usually a *bootneck if a *detachment was carried.

beer baron   Someone who uses tins of beer (illegally) as a form of currency to give and receive favours.

beer, *big eats, *bag off - and back on board   Jack's definition of a superlative *run-ashore.

beer bosun   The messdeck rating responsible for maintaining the *beer locker. Can also be used for someone with an excessive fondness for *CSB.

beer locker   A domestic refrigerator fitted with hasp and padlock, and installed in each messdeck. The keys are collected every evening at *pipe down. Jack's basic entitlement is three tins a day, but many sailors prefer not to drink at sea. The privilege of being able to invite family and friends down to the *messdeck while in port is a jealously-guarded one; it is also one of the few ways in which Jack can repay civilians who have taken him *up homers. The system is self-regulating in that abuse by one individual leads to collective punishment; the padlock is changed and its keys retained by the *Jaunty for a suitable period while the man is *picturised by his messmates. It is also a particular pleasure for Jack and Royal to invite their colleagues from the US Navy and Marine Corps on board for a *wet, since the supposedly bigger and better American ships are also totally dry.

beer tokens (RM)   Pound coins.

beetle bait   Jam or treacle.

beetle crushers   Two versions:
1. Older term for members of the *Reggies Branch.
2. *Jenny's nickname for her flat parade shoes, as worn for *Divisions.

beetle watch   Jack's name for a cheap wristwatch of the era before digital models became commonplace. They were apparently powered by a small insect, which *beetled around* inside the case to work the hands, but then usually went *tits up just as soon as Jack was back at sea.

before the mast   Old sailing ship expression for living in the fo' 'sle as one of the hands.

Beira bucket   A *pusser's galvanised bucket, both artistically and highly decorated, and played for as a trophy by ships mounting the Beira patrol between 1968 and 1974. This was a typically instinctive response to the threat of boredom; the sports involved were specified by the defending ship, and *jungle rules applied. The Beira Bucket has an honoured place in the RN Museum at Portsmouth. The term is now used on occasion to describe any impromptu trophy played for by ships in company and detached from home waters.

belay   Traditionally to make fast or secure a rope or line (using a belaying pin). Also used as a general order to stop, or cease doing something. Can also be an instruction to ignore any previous message as in:*'Belay the last *pipe!'* or:*'Belay my last!'*

bell-bottom trousers   Formerly, Jack's *rig included *bell-bottomed trousers* with reverse creases down the sides and horizontal creases down each leg. This was not a fashion statement! The *bell-bottoms* enabled the trousers to be rolled up easily when scrubbing decks; the creases were necessary so that Jack could *stow his kit, in the limited space available, (a) inside out, to keep it clean and (b) in as small a space as possible. Bell-bottomed trousers have now been phased out.

bell end   The glans penis.

Belle Isle (RM)   *Corps memorable date based on the 7 June 1761 action at the siege and assault of Belle Isle in Quiberon Bay. The laurel wreath of the Corps colours and badges commemorate the spirit and gallantry displayed by the two Marine battalions that fought throughout this fierce action.

bells   Before the introduction of a reliable timepiece, the passage of time was marked by the striking of a *bell* every time the half-hour glass was turned. The sea day was divided into *watches each of 4 hours' duration (but see *dog watches), and the *bell* was struck once after half an hour, twice after an hour, three times after an hour and a half, etc. up to *eight bells* when the watch changed. Thus 1030 was *5 bells* in the *forenoon and 1530 *7 bells* in the *afternoon. The bell was struck with paired clapper blows. Today, the bell is struck at *Colours (8 times if at 0800, *2 bells* if at 0900). Traditionally, at midnight on New Year's Eve, the bell is struck 16 times by the youngest member of the ship's company; hence *ring out the old, ring in the new. See also *seven bells.

Bells, Smells and Yells Jack's wonderful description of the island of *Malta GC which, in the days of the Mediterranean Fleet at least, seemed to consist mainly of churches, open drains, noisy children and goats. See also the *Ghut / Gut.

bells in the head Slightly mad.

belly muster Medical inspection.

below Anywhere inside the ship, ie. not on the *upper deck; thus someone inside the superstructure is *below* even if he or she is above the main external deck. *Below!* is the traditional warning cry when lowering or throwing something down - either between decks or over the side. Can also be *Under below!*

belt-fed (RM) Adjective which increases any descriptive impact by an an order of magnitude, for instance:'*She *bangs like a belt-fed *Wombat..'*

belter Something excellent - or a black-eye!

BEM Officially the *British Empire Medal,* which because of some piece of egalitarian nonsense and political correctness, is no longer awarded. Very unofficially - *Bunk Endurance Medal, Barracks Endurance Medal,* and even *Bathrooms 'Eads & Messdecks!*

bend (noun) A knot which fastens one rope to another, or to a spar, as in a *sheet bend;* (verb) to *bend* a cable or rope is to secure it or make it fast. Similarly, *bending on* a sail is to secure it to a boom or yard; also covered under *bent.

Bends (the) Widely used general nickname for the many manifestations of decompression sickness. If a diver has been breathing compressed air at depth for more than a certain time, and then ascends, some of the extra dissolved nitrogen in his blood may form bubbles within the venous circulation. These return to the heart and are pumped out again; depending on their final destination these bubbles may cause obstruction in the: 　　　Lungs - known as the *chokes.*
　　　Brain and spinal cord - called the *staggers.*
　　　Skin - the *creeps.*
　　　Joints - the *bends,* since the limbs are *bent
　　　　　painfully.

Benny   Current slang name for a kelper (Falkland Islander); the term is reputed to have been banned from use ashore by local military order in 1983. Jack soon got round that problem in his usual inimitable way, as shown by the following selection:

Benny Arcade - Stanley fairground.
Bennydiction - local accent.
Bennydorm - Bunkhouse out in the Camp.
Bennyficial - Sir Rex Hunt!
Bennyficiary - seafood processing plant.
Bennyfit - reaction to any suggestion of parochialism.
Benny Hill - Mount Tumbledown.
Bennylin - locally-mixed cough medicine.
Bennytentiary - the cells in Stanley police station
Bennyton - excessive speed on the Airport road.

See also *Stills and *Whens.

bent   Jack's typical understatement for anything broken, or something that has been severely damaged. A signal flag is also *bent on* to its halyard before being hoisted. Also, because a rope is similarly *bent on* to another one before being spliced to it, the phrase *bent on a splice* refers to a sailor who is about to get married.   Note also the application of *bent* in the diving sense described under *Bends.

bent shot   Homosexual - the term may be Glaswegian in origin.

berseyquack (RM)   Alliteration of the word *berserk*, and hence a very useful alternative to *banzai.

bevvy   Glaswegian and Liverpudlian patter word for a drink, widely adopted: *'Coming *ashore for a few bevvies, *bash?'*

Bible basher / puncher   Vicar; see alternatives under *amen wallah.

Biblical code   Both the Old and the New Testament have a traditional place in the Yeoman of Signal's ready-use library on the bridge of HM Ships. There are times and circumstances when a Biblical reference conveys more understanding and support (and even humour) in a single line than any long and multi-part message could in several paragraphs:

From HM WARSHIP to CinC PLYMOUTH:
ROMAN EMPEROR IN TOW BADLY DAMAGED PLEASE SEND TUGS.
From CinCPLYMOUTH to HM WARSHIP:
*REVELATIONS Chapter 3 Verse 11.1**

Behold I come quickly: hold that fast which thou hast, that no man take thy crown.

Angel's Whisper

Biff Gentleman of non-European and distinctly African origin; derived from the cartoon character of *Biffo the Bear*. Another explanation is a more chauvinistic one, namely that these letters stand for *Bloody Ignorant (Flipping) Foreigner*. Most interestingly, RM usage has this as a general term of abuse for the clumsy.

biff Two applications:
1. Masturbate.
2. (FAA) Break wind: *'Ruddy Norah! 'Oo biffed?'*

Biffin's bridge The female perineum, which Jack might define a bit more succinctly as the shelf between her *playpen and the *gash chute(2). Perhaps the term's origin lies in the fact that it is this structure that he keeps **biffing** against. May also be written as *Baffin's bridge.

Big Dipper A *Sea King helicopter when working as part of a NATO *dip gang with other (smaller) sonar-carrying helicopters.

big eats A large or special meal: *'The hospitality in Miami Beach was unbelievable; big eats every night with a different *grippo..'* See the entry *bag off for an additional applicaton.

big girl's blouse (RM) Wonderful term of abuse, originally employed for bulky and unfit new recruits breathing heavily, but now used more widely for a worrier, or anyone faint-hearted.

big reds (FAA) Large red-handled pliers that are a standard and vital component of a *grubber's toolbox.

big soft Nellie (esp. RM) Enough said!

big style Adjectival enhancement, especially when used in a derogatory sense: *'He's wrecked his car, big style..'*

Biggles Traditional nickname for the Flight Commander embarked in a warship; note that *Pilot is a term reserved for the Navigating Officer.

bight A curl or loop of rope, which may tauten at any time, hence: *'Never stand with one foot in a bight..'*

bilge-free Older term for someone full of booze, but just sober enough to pass scrutiny at the *brow when returning on board. Derived from the description of a correctly stowed and full cask as being *bung-up and bilge-free*.

bilges The lowest part of a ship, where a foul and noxious mixture of sea water, waste water and oil fuel collected. The expression *bilge water* is used to describe something that tastes particularly unpleasant, and an opinion or information that is of little or no value is a *load of bilge*. A *bilge rat* is an unpopular person, usually because of his unpleasant personal habits.

Bill of Health Declaration by a ship's Master that he has no contagious diseases on board and that his vessel has not arrived from a port where an epidemic of some kind is prevalent. This expression has now also come ashore in a non-maritime sense: *'I got the RAC to look at the car before I bought it, and they gave it a reasonably clean bill of health..'*

bill-poster's bucket Jack's description of a busy lady of the night with well-used working parts.

billet Appointment or position within an organization: *'I asked *Drafty for a Married Accompanied billet in *Honkers. Guess what his reply was..'*

bimble (RM**)** Anything slower than a *yomp, whether on skis or on foot (see illustration on page B - 71); the Fleet Air Arm also use this term for a relaxed piece of transit flying.

bin Get rid of, or abandon something. The word can be used in both direct and indirect senses, but is usually employed when referring to the abstract: *'We binned the project, but didn't *ditch the trials *kit - I used that for something else instead..'*

binge The operation of rinsing out a wooden cask to prepare it for new contents. Casks were an essential part of a ship's equipment for they were the only means of carrying food and water over lengthy voyages, hence great care was taken of them (see also *knock down). Modern methods of storage have rendered this word obsolete in the maritime sense, but the idea behind it has come ashore, either to describe the good rinsing out that results from a prolonged drinking session, or else Jack's love of spirits, which he might occasionally have been able to indulge when *bingeing* a rum or spirit of wine (brandy) cask. From a Lincolnshire dialect word *binge*, meaning to soak.

Bingo fuel (FAA)   Minimum landing allowance; if your fuel state is down to *Bingo* levels and *Mother cannot be found, then the *reasons in writing may develop quite quickly into an *A 25.

bint   A girl, or woman, with varying shades of meaning (derived from Arabic). *'Take a shufti at that bint!'* was the same as saying: *'Just look at that lovely creature..'*

bird cage   A *WRNS accomodation block.

birdbath   Two versions:
1. (RM)   Method of maintainng personal hygiene in the field when water is in short supply. The participant stands in a half-filled washing-up bowl, soaps himself all over, and then uses the same water to rinse off.
2. (SM) Canvas receptacle rigged under the conning tower to collect any water shipped inboard during heavy weather while running *opened up, usually used in concert with the'elephant's trunk'.

birdshit and paratroopers (RM)   Non-airborne forces statement as to what is most likely to fall out of the sky.

birmingham screwdriver   A big hammer for fine adjustments.

biscuit   Kneaded cakes of flour that were baked with the least quantity of water possible and then stored, as a bread substitute, on board. It was also known as *hard tack*. The advent of ship's bakeries made this staple feature of Jack's diet obsolete after WW1, but the expression *that really takes the biscuit* - in addition to the technique of biscuit baking itself - now have a wider meaning ashore.

Bish   Padre or chaplain; the FAA has *BISHTAX* as a (taxi) sortie to carry the padre between ships in a group. See *Amen wallah for other descriptive variants.

bite   Spoof or deception played against someone, particularly when he or she has a strongly-held or cherished belief that cannot normally be the subject of humour in their conversation: '*Scribes fancies himself for *Upper Yardie, although he's a right *pickle-jar rating. The boys got him on a cracking bite last week when he volunteered for *splash target coxswain..'* A pleasant way to defuse the situation when the person involved *bites* hard is to ask for your hook back! See also *spoof.

bite (on) **the bullet**   Self-restraint when on the receiving end of what one considers to be an unjustified *bollocking.

BITS   Beans In Tomato Sauce; see also *-ITS.

bitter end   The inboard end of a ship's cable which, in the case of a ship's anchor cable, was secured to special strong points called bitts. If the cable was run out all the way it was *at the bitter end*, ie. there was no more to pay out; hence the popular expression for something at its limits.

bivvy (RM)   Abbreviation of *bivouac shelter*; used as noun or verb: '*Just before dawn, we bivvied-up in a forest near the objective..'*

Black Angus   Near-legendary establishment with a highly dubious reputation, situated in San Juan, Puerto Rico. Reputed to be the biggest brothel in South America.

black as Jack's hat   '*It's dark outside!*'.

Black Book / black books, to be in (the)   To be in disgrace, or out of favour. A *black book* today is one supposedly recording the names of those who are in disgrace or who have merited punishment of some kind. From the *Black Book of Admiralty*, compiled in about 1410 as the English codification of the ancient

Laws of Oleron, a charter for seamen introduced into England by Eleanor of Acquitaine in 1154 when her husband Henry of Anjou succ eeded to the English throne as Henry II. Amongst other things, the Laws of Oleron attempted to protect sick sailors; it also contained an authoritative description of the ancient customs and usages of the sea. The *Black Book* itself took its apparently sinister name from the fact that the colour of the binding of the earliest edition was black. In fact, black books for the recording of offenders' names are regularly mentioned in the literature of the 16th century. The term is still in colloquial use today: *'Ever since he forgot about the dinner party, he has been in her black books'*.

black catter A person who always tries to go one better, whatever your story or achievement. If you had a *big black cat*, then he would have one too, only his would be *bigger and blacker* - see Tugg's brilliant evocation of this concept at page C - 82. (Note however that it is just possible he owns a panther..).

Black Day 31st July 1970, when the last *tot was drawn in the *Fleet around the globe; a rather touchy subject with the old and bold!

black drizzle Diarrhoea.

black gang / black squad Seaman's name for stokers or others who work in engine or boiler rooms.

black ham Collective noun for ladies of the night in Africa, especially in Mombasa; for Jack or Royal to seek their company in the pre-AIDS era was known as going for a *slice of black ham*.

Black Jack   Nickname for the Flag Officer's Deputy whose responsibility for efficiency and discipline in a fleet made him strict and demanding.

black lighting (SM)   State of the control room lighting before returning to periscope depth at night. The illumination is turned right down so that everyone is working in virtual darkness.

black maskers   Sticky masking tape of great durability and adhesive properties: *'If the Russians ever invent a ray that dissolves black maskers, then we might as well *wrap..'*   Also an essential component (along with a large hammer) of the *RM repair kit.

Black Mass   After-hours (and illegal) consumption of *neaters left over as *Queen's and then bottled.

black mat   The medal ribbon of the Order of St. John.

black outs   Black curtain material used in the *evolution of *darken ship.   Also a nickname for the WW2 *black knickers* issued to *Wrens, although whether this was because they totally obscured the target (or because of their actual effect on Jack) is still unclear!   See also *passion killers.

black pig (SM)   A nuclear submarine.

Black Prince   Commissioned Gunner in most training establishments.

black silk   Another item of Jack's *rig, worn under the collar and down the sides of the vee of the jacket, and tied off with tapes at the apex of the vee.   It is not actually black, nor is it worn in memory of Lord Nelson; it is simply the modern-day equivalent of a neckerchief/ sweat rag. These were tied around the forehead in the heat of action, and prevented beads of perspiration from trickling down into the eyes.   Similarly, the three white lines around the light blue collar are not in memory of Nelson's three famous victories, but was the number decided on in the mid-19th century after a surprisingly democratic ballot of Jack's Victorian predecessors.

blackshod (RM)   Military training or operations in mountainous areas that are not actually Arctic in their description.   If they were, and there was lots of ice and snow around, then *whiteshod* techniques would be appropriate.

black strap   RN name for a cheap Mediterranean wine.   By extension, to be *black strapped* meant that you had received an appointment or draft for duty in the Mediterranean.

black stripe navy   Medical branch term for the rest of the RN, ie those who do not wear *distinction cloth between the gold lace stripes of their rank insignia.

Black Stump   Australian expression for somewhere very distant, now adopted by Jack and used in a similar way to *Nagasaki:'*He's the biggest liar this side of the Black Stump..'*

black watch (SM)   The unofficial fifth watch of the normal four-watch system in a submarine, ie. those ratings who have been left *inboard for some official reason, but are still on the *boat's books.

blackie / blacksmith   A rate that was abolished in the '60's. Had special responsibility for anchors and cables.

blank week   When the Navy was paid fortnightly, this was the week just before pay day, since it described the usual content of Jack's pockets. The associated *blank weekend* also forced a penniless Jack to remain on board, unless he got a *casual.

blanket stacker   Dismissive nickname for a *Jack Dusty.

blat   Two possible meanings:
1. A new word for foreign currency where large numbers are involved, like Italian lire. These can then be grouped as required into *kiloblats* (thousands) or *megablats* (millions).
2. Hit someone rather hard, or defeat him / them rather comprehensively (as an alternative to *frapped).

blazer   A smart dress jacket chosen (and supplied) by the Captain of HMS BLAZER for his gig crew in 1845, before the *bluejacket concept became standard as part of a laid-down uniform. It featured a short jacket with multi-coloured vertical stripes, a feature that lives on at Henley each year and is still associated with rowing and oarsmen.

blimp   A senior or rather stuffy *Pongo, from the famous cartoonist Low's expressive 1930's character Colonel *Blimp* - whose dimensions rather resembled those of the small non-rigid airships used by * RN Air Service flyers in WW1. It has been suggested that Naval aviators gave their craft that title because a War Office manual stated that airships were of two kinds - (a)rigid and (b)limp. Probably apocryphal.

blind with science   Waffle or talk around the subject.

blob   Several applications:
1. Floating surface marker used in diving operations.
2. A skin boil. To *blob up* is to acquire a social disease.
3. *On the blob* refers to menstruation.
4. A *blob* is created on an *Uckers board by the process of *blobbing up*, or the creation of a pile of two or more of your own (or your partner's, but separately) counters in order to block the opposition. A *triple blob* requires the throwing of two consecutive *double sixes to overcome, and so on. A *mixy blob* that includes both your and your partner's counters has no obstructive value, and may well be the precursor to a comprehensive *dicking.
5. Older RM usage has *score a blob* in the same sense as *make a boob* or *drop a bollock*.

block sweeps (RM)   A person employed on barrack cleaning duties: *'No use asking me, mate - I'm just the block sweeps..'*

Blockhouse (SM)   Fort Blockhouse, HMS DOLPHIN, Gosport - the spiritual home of British submarines and submariners for over fifty years. The excellent Submarine Museum and HMS ALLIANCE (a preserved A-Class *boat) are both open to the public and situated nearby. See also *Dolphin, and note that the Submarine School has now moved down to HMS *RALEIGH, in Cornwall.

Bloggs (FAA)   Generic name for all student aircrew. This label is borrowed from the Royal Air Force, who even have an excellent cartoon character concerned with the adventures of this mythical chap.

Bloke   Nickname accorded to the *Executive Officer (XO) of a large warship or shore establishment, who is of Commander rank and is officially called *The Commander*. See also *Father, *Jimmy, *Jimmy the One and *Number One.

blood   Several interesting usages here:
1. *blood bucket* - lifeboat; synonym for a *blood wagon* (ambulance).
2. *blood chit* - signed authorisation to fly as a passenger in a Service aircraft.
3. *blood for breakfast* - warning of serious trouble looming.
4. *blood red* - the colour of *distinction cloth inserted into the rank *lace of RN Medical Officers. For this reason the annual RN Medical Club dinner is always known as the *Blood Red Dinner*.
5. *blood-stained* - a meeting or event where serious differences of opinion are anticipated, or have already taken place.
6. *blood money* - older term (esp. RM) for a service gratuity, or a sum of prize money.

bloody good kid in harbour   Description of someone who, when nothing is happening, or when he bears no responsibility, is noisy, loud-mouthed and opinionated. When things get rough or when a decision is required, he becomes quiet and inconspicuous.

blow (SM)   The process of blowing water-displacing air into a *boat's ballast and trim tanks in order to control or adjust her buoyancy. The old method of discharging sewage from a submarine was called *blowing shit* but this has now been replaced by the less noisy and slightly more refined process of *pumping poo.

blow a hooligan   Description of a really strong wind that, in older times, could also *blow the horns off a bull*.

blow the bilges down   Defaecate.

blow through   Euphemism for sexual intercourse.

Blow you, Jack!   Expression characterising official indifference to any real or imagined problem involving the *lower deck. Can also be used to portray a selfish attitude: *'Blow you, Jack - I'm *inboard..'*

blowback   An *Uckers move according to *Wafu rules that is made against an opponent waiting by the *shit chute to *suck back your pieces before they can get home. If this move is carried out around the corner it becomes a *bendy blowback*.

blower   Telephone; this term originated with the early speaking-tube communication system between Bridge and Engine room.

blowing the grampus   The process of waking a sleeping sailor who is supposed to be on watch by chucking bucket of cold water over him. The resulting effect was similar to that of a *grampus* (whale) blowing on the surface.

blubber   Cry; the word originates from whaling days and the globules of fat (mimicking teardrops) that dripped down the carcass during the process of flensing.

blubberguts   A fat person, applied especially to fat officers.

blue   Form of address between sailors and marines unfamiliar with each other's names (still in use in 1950's). This may be the origin of its usage, to this day, in Australia.

blue card man   Blue *station card of a special dutyman who is not required for routine watchkeeping, and therefore available for his special duties at any time. Conversely, a *blue card man* is also able to go ashore at any time providing those duties have been completed.

Blue Circle radar   The first *SHARs were delivered without their *Blue Fox* radar sets; these were temporarily substituted for by a shaped lump of concrete inside the nose cone.

Blue forces   *Light blue* is the colour of NATO , so one side in any NATO exercise always adopts this shade to oppose the *Orange forces of the Warsaw Pact . When friendly forces actually engage their own side in wartime due to some error or terrible misunderstanding, the incident is termed a *blue-on-blue*.

Bag Shanty

Blue liners   Cigarettes of special manufacture which incorporated a thin blue line in the paper, and were supplied as duty-free quota to entitled RN personnel.   Although traditionally regarded as both an important privilege and a vital component of Jack's morale, they were incompatible with the ideals of preventive medicine and are no longer supplied.   See also *DFs and *ticklers.

Blue Peter   Two forms of usage:
1. Blue-and-white flag *P* flown in a ship ready to sail.
2. White-blue-white ribbon of the Long Service and Good Conduct medal.   See also *Pea-do in this application.

blue-and-baggies (FAA)   Proper naval uniform, as opposed to the *green-and-baggies or *green-and-smellies which are both nicknames for flying suits (or *ovies).

blue-and-smellies (FAA)   Aircrew nickname for maintainers.

Bluebell   Metal polish; also the radio callsign of a mechanical or electrical engineer.

bluejacket   Generic and descriptive term for Jack after 1858 when the first blue cloth double-breasted jacket was introduced as uniform.   Before that Jack was simply a *tar, from the *tarpaulin clothing that he wore at sea.

Bluenose   A warship that has operated inside the Arctic circle, and has a small paint job at the *sharp end to show this fact. People serving in such a ship are awarded a *Bluenose Certificate*. The term originated in Newfoundland.

Blues (RM)   No.1 (best) Service uniform, worn with the white Wolseley pattern helmet.

blue unction   Gentian Violet.   An old fashioned remedy for *crabs.   Shave off and apply, but it made your scrotum blue.

blue-veined steak   See *toggle.

blue-water (navy)   Warships designed to sail the oceans of the world, not just in coastal waters like a *brown-water outfit.

bluey   Free airmail letter form used in operational areas such as the Falklands / South Atlantic theatre.

blunt end   The stern of a warship.

blushing and farting   Someone who is severely embarrassed.

boat   There is now really only one kind of boat that goes to sea under the *White Ensign - a submarine, although in the past all Coastal Forces vessels (MTBs, MGBs and FPBs but not minesweepers) were also called *boats*. Misuse of the term where ship is the correct description will *wind Jack up a treat, as well as displaying the speaker's ignorance of matters Naval. Ships can carry boats, but not vice versa. Note also that to *catch the boat up* implies the acquisition of a venereal disease, whereas to push the boat out means that the person described is being generous with hospitality, often in celebration. These two phrases are not usually connected! Note also *liberty boat, from which the more general expression to miss the boat is derived. See also *costly farces.

boatmate   Worth a separate entry. In SM service there were never *shipmates*, and today in the SOCA all the *old soaks refer to each other as *boatmates*.

Boat people (FAA)   Disparaging term adapted from the Vietnamese refugee context to describe submariners.

boatswain   Commonly abbreviated to *Bosun* and so pronounced; may also be written as *bo'sun* or *bo's'n*. Originally a *warrant officer, responsible for all the rigging, *boats and the efficient seamanship functions of the ship. Nowadays, an officer borne for similar duties only in larger warships and some shore establishments. For a while in the mid-20th century, *branch (subsequently *SD) officers of various branches were also called *bosun*; hence *Signal bosun*, *Bosun PR* (for Plot Radar), *Survey bosun* (hydrography) and *Bomb bosun* (specialists in the handling and preparation of air-launched weapons). During this period straightforward *bosuns* were referred to as *Scrubdeck bosuns*, but this expression has now demised. Derived from the words *boat* and *suen* or *swain* - husband. Note also *coxswain (*cog suen*) and see also *buffer in contrast to this role. Also note that *bosun* is a useful catch-all noun to be added to any number of naval activities, from the witty to the nefarious - see various examples throughout this book!

boatswain's mate(s)   Originally assistants to the *bosun, but nowadays the assistant to the *Quartermaster both at sea and in harbour.

Bob's yer Auntie   Occasional and amusing variation of the more common Uncle version, especially when describing the after-effects of a *bricking.

B - 50

Bobby's helmet   The glans penis.

bobstay   The fraenum, a structure which tethers the penile fore-skin, and which is often damaged by Jack as a result of excessive enthusiasm during a spot of *counterpane hurdling.

body snatchers   Older term for *crushers or *Reggies employed on *shore patrol duties.

bog off (FAA)   Phrase used to describe an aircraft disappearing over the horizon: '*Now, before you bog off into the wild blue yonder, make sure you all know *Mother's intentions..*'

bog standard   Description of something that is a basic issue item, unadorned by any frills or subsequent modifications.

bog trotter   A native of Ireland.

bogelscope (FAA)   Radar *gadget carried in a *Bag for detect-ing, tracking and reporting *bogeys with. In the submarine world, a *bogglescope* was a cinema projector.

Bogey   A pair of applications:
1. Traditional nickname for anyone with the surname Knight.
2. (FAA) Descriptive label for an unidentified but possible enemy aircraft; *bandit* is what it becomes when identified as hostile.

bograts (FAA)   Older name for the *Middies and *Subbies serving as aircrew in a front-line squadron.

bollocking (esp. RM)   Very severe verbal rebuke or admoni-tion, usually qualified by the adjectives terrific or almighty.

bollocknaked   Spaghetti (bolognese!).

bollocky buff   Without any clothing; to be *in the bollocky buff* is to be in a naked state.

bolter (FAA)   Name for a carrier-borne aircraft which fails to engage an arrester wire with its tail hook on landing. Two rockets were fired and *'bolter'* called loudly on the radio to ensure the pilot went to *max chat in order to get airborne and go round again - the margin for error and consequent disaster was small. Training sorties where aircraft would conduct approaches to the deck and touch down without actually arresting, were called *rollers*. The term is now used when someone vacates a job or appointment very quickly: *'He's done a bolter..'*

bomb bosun (FAA)   The senior rating Armourer in a squadron; also a term for the Officer in charge of all explosive stores in a carrier.

bomb-burst (FAA)   The result when a formation of aircraft encounters unexpected bad weather: *'Then the boys flew into a rapidly developing warm front. Total chaos - and a massive bomb-burst into practically every airfield in South-West England..'* This can also be used to describe the group action taken when some social pariah turns up in the *Wardroom.

bomb shop (SM)   The torpedo or weapon storage compartment of a submarine.

bomb team   Nickname for a regional Clearance Diving (CD)
unit, as in:'*He's *second dickey of the *Pompey Bomb Team.*'

Bombay   The Indian coastal city that is now called Mumbai.
This new label is unlikely to catch on with Jack, who has three
classic usages:
1. *Bombay away*   Diarrhoea, or Ghandi's revenge; note also the
term *Bombay bum* for those with a chronic affliction.
2. *Bombay runner*   A particularly large and offensive breed of
cockroach. See also *cockie.
3. *Bombay sweat*   Older term for the result when a sailor was
too drunk to leave his hammock, yet needed to *pump ship. The
more modern version refers to the process of *swamping.

bombed out   Depending on context this can mean drunk or, in
a wider sense, weird or bizarre: '*That civvy scientist is completely
bombed out of his box, we reckon!*'   Royal also uses the phrase to
describe mental aberration brought on by extreme tiredness.

Bomber   An interesting pair:
1. A Polaris or Trident submarine; the American equivalent is a
boomer, but see also *boomer for a different SM interpretation.
2. Nickname for anyone with the surnames Harris, Brown or
Mills.

Bomber Command circuit (FAA)   Label applied to a *Bloggs'
efforts when using excessive airspace around an airfield instead
of keeping his circuit line tight and precise. Also used when
prosecuting a submarine in a *Sea King and the *stick monkeys
are not doing *jumps to the total satisfaction of the *dip Boss.

Bomber Queen (SM)   Diesel *boat crew's derisory nickname
for anyone serving in a Trident submarine with air-conditioned
comfort, regular hygiene and generally well-ordered and totally
predictable lives.

bombhead (FAA)   Affectionate term for any member of the old
Naval Air Mechanic (Ordnance) branch, populated by big,
strong *Ugh men who seemed capable of bombing-up an aircraft by hand. See Tugg's illustration on page C - 94 for a perfect summary!   The term is still used for those Weapons
Engineering ratings who specialize in aircraft armament or ordnance (explosive) items, including ejection seats. They wear red
surcoats when acting as *roof rats.

bone   Fourteen different applications!
1. Give someone a hard time about something: *'That's the fourth time I've been boned about this morning's little incident..'*
2. Be selected for some unpopular task or duty: *'Mickey's been boned off for fire sentry in the *middle, poor sod..'*
3. Study a subject with particular interest, eg. for an exam: *'Spent the whole of my *make and mend yesterday boning up on *Sea King hydraulic systems..'*
4. The white feather of water thrown up from the bow of a ship under way - at high speed, a ship is siad to have a bone in her teeth.
5. Older term meaning to scrounge or pilfer, after a legendary 18th century *bosun of that name.
6. Telephone - abbreviation of the rhyming slang *telling bone.*
7. To have intercourse with a female, possibly an abbreviation of the slang word *trombone* or deployment of one's ham bone.
8. Unintelligent, not very smart: *'Tanky's a bit bone, but when he's ashore, he bonks for Britain..'*
9. A *bone orchard* is a cemetery.
10. The Royal Naval Hospitals at Haslar (Portsmouth) and Stonehouse (Plymouth) were known in each area as *The Boneyard.*
11. A *bone dome* is an aircrew helmet.
12. *Close to the bone* is a phrase implying reduced safety margins during an *evolution, or a joke too risky for mixed company.
13. A really lazy individual is a *bone idle* *scrimshanker.
14. Any person wearing a *round* hat (rather than a cap) was a *bone head* compared to superior *tiffs, or more specifically a mechanic under training at HMS COLLINGWOOD. The *tiff apprentices would raid the *bones'* huts, and create havoc.

bongles and dongles (RM & SM)   Special noise-generating devices placed in the water by SBS personnel awaiting pick-up by a submarine.

bonk   Sudden and swerving change of course made by a Seawolf missile at Mach 2 as it acquires directional control and tracks the target; subsequent alterations to track are *mini-bonks!* What the relationship between that and the other definition of *bonk* (ie. sexual intercourse) is unclear.

Bonsai trees   Broccoli spears, often served with *yellow peas.

booby   Tropical seabird that was very easy to catch once it had settled, hence the term *booby-prize* for something that is really no prize (catch) at all.

Boogaloo!   Sardonic dismissal of some claim made, or achievement boasted about; the component syllables can be emphasized heavily:*'So, Rick - you've rewritten a book about Naval slang, eh? Well, matey, all I can say is boo-ga-bloody-loo..'*

book of words   Any manual, including the small ship's surgical directions for medical and surgical treatment, in conjunction with a *wallet of spanners* for operations.

boom   A spar attached to the ship's side, swung out when in harbour for securing boats when they are not in use. Also the spar attached to the foot of some sails, and also swung out from the ship's side when in harbour for securing boats to. When someone got fed up with something and put a stop to it, he was said to have *lowered the boom*. Boats were secured to the *boom lizards* (trailing ropes with a Y spliced in the end, by the boat's *painter (always spelt with a Y in the old days) using a single *sheet *bend. If the weather blew up, duty seamen had to go down the Jacob's Ladder to the boat, and convert the single sheet bend to a *double* sheet bend. Consequently, any rating who was deemed to be a bit *henpecked was said to be *on a double sheet bend*, ie. well secured.

boomer (SM)   Also seen by the USN as *bomber. In the older world of the *diesel dinosaurs, this also refers to the noise that a nuclear-powered *boat makes as it rushes through the water at some phenomenal speed, all its active sonar pinging away, and making enough noise to scare the living daylights out of those in the more conventional diesel/electric boats.

boost / booster (FAA)   Another term for a catapult launch: *'Given a decent wind across the deck and a clear run, the old *Gannet* could *launch herself quite nicely without the booster..' The old cat-apults were operated by cordite charges. It really did give one a kick (as in the *A25 song), but 90% of fly-offs were done by *ranging the aircraft aft, and then flying along the deck at 4 second intervals, with 35 knots of apparent wind generated by the ship's motion from 5 degrees on the port bow.

boot   Basically affectionate term for one's wife or steady girl-friend - *the old boot* - or (indicative of unhappiness):*'You're look-ing a bit boot..'* Also an indicator of handsomeness:*'He must be the ugliest man in the Corps - poor chap's got a face like a busted boot..'*

boot topping   Black line along a ship's waterline.

bootneck / bootie   A Royal Marine; the exact origin of this term is unknown, but the 19th century RM tunic had a leather tongue-fastening to hold its collar closed at the throat. This term only became widespread after WW2 - perhaps as a varia-tion of the US Marine Corps' *leatherneck.

bopper (FAA)   Thunderflash, or *thundie.

born old   Description of a know-it-all youngster.

borne Formal expression, but still used semi-formally, for any-one officially on board a ship at a specific time. The term *borne on ship's books* has gone into disuse, because pay accounts are now computerised and held centrally ashore. Hence, *borne for social duties* only - somebody who is socially smooth but profes-sionally not much use. Naval aviators are sometimes described as being *borne for gin and flying*!

borrow See also *acquire, but in a permanent and dishonest sense.

Boss Familiar, yet respectful form of address for a Squadron CO, Company Commander, Head of Department, etc.

bosun / bo's'n / bo's'un See *boatswain.

bosun's call A high-pitched two-note metal whistle used for making *pipes (passing orders) in sailing ships when it could be heard above the noise of wind and sea, and also shouting; in capable hands it can produce a trill and a gradual ascent/descent from a high to a low note. Its use is now ceremonial, but the term *pipe is still used to describe any instruction or information passed over a ship's main broadcast system. Also known as a *Spithead nightingale.

both oars in the water Someone who has a mental problem or an odd obsession may be described as *not having both oars in the water.*

both watches *Muster of all the *hands at the start of a work-ing day.

bottle Older Navy term for a reprimand or scolding: *'What 'e needs is a big dose from the foretopman's bottle..'* or: *'The Commander was handing out bottles all round..'* The word now describes personal courage and daring: *'Your first night parachute jump is a fairly significant test of bottle..'*

botty sex *Brownhatter's aberration, neatly summarised, and adaptable further as *botty bosun, botty boy, botty bandit* etc.

boulder holder Brassiere; if this item is a 46 inch D-cup extravaganza, it may also enlarge in description to become an *over-the- shoulder boulder holder*. *Tit hammock is an amusing alternative.

bounce (FAA) Attack another aircraft, usually from behind and above.

bow and arrow run   Older term for a dangerous operational task carried out by an inadequately armed ship.

bowline   The *bowline* was originally a special knot used by archers for securing their bowstrings.

bows under   Overwhelmed with work, from the old sailing term for a ship carrying too much sail for the conditions. Also, as a result, another term for being in a drunken condition.

bowse in   When painting ship, to pull your paint stage into the ship's side, under the flare.

box of ____   Collective noun in widespread usage: *'Who are those young chaps? Has someone opened a new box of students?'*

box up   Get something ready for use.

Boy Captain   The youngest Captain on the Navy *List, a feature in the career of many of those whose meteoric ascent will take them to the very highest ranks in the *Andrew.

Boy Seamen   Young men aged 15 years 3 months and upwards who used to be carried as operational members of a capital warship's crew; *almost* equivalent to today's (older) Junior Seamen.

brace of shakes   Measurement of time based on the shivering of a sail that is coming up into wind; the figure of speech has come ashore to describe any very short interval.

braces   In sailing ships, the *braces* were ropes leading from the ends of the yardarms to enable them to be moved horizontally to trim the sails to the wind.

bracket   Get a first salvo of gunfire on one side of the target and a second salvo on the other; note also *straddle which refers to a single salvo with some of the rounds impacting on target.

brag rags   Campaign medal ribbons on a uniform.

brain fart   Any temporary mental aberration.

bramah / brammers (esp. RM)   Something that is either brilliant or highly enjoyable:*'Parachuting into the sea? It's brammers..'* Derives from the great British engineer of Nelson's day, named Joseph *Bramah*. Can also be an adjective, also meaning the very best:*'She's a Bramah..'* or:*'That was a Bramah ship..'*

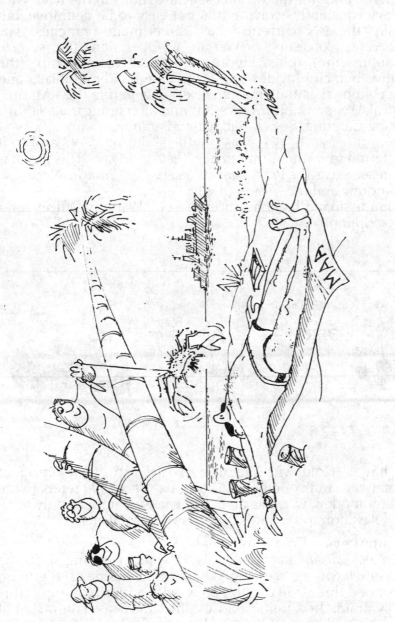

Banyan

Branch   An interesting trio:

1. Generic term for the various specialisations in the RN. With the Navy constantly evolving it is not easy to be definitive, but basically the RN currently has three main branches, viz: *Executive* (X), consisting of Warfare & Operations (air, surface and submarine), plus Hydrography & Seamanship (the Executive branch provides sea-going commanding officers and hence is known as the *master race); *Engineering* (E) - Marine, Electrical, Weapons, Electronics, Air and all training; *Supply* (S) - Logistics, Catering, Secretarial, Administration.

2. The term *Fleet Air Arm* was unofficial during WW2 and so it was referred to by the Admiralty as *The Air Branch*. This name is now preserved as the Royal Naval Reserve *Air Branch*. Note also the *Andrew and the *Trade (SM).

3. Commissioned branch officers - see *Warrant Officer for a full description.

brass hat   Gold wire braiding on the cap of an officer of Commander's rank or higher. *Getting one's brass hat* refers to the actual promotion, whereas an *acting brass hat* implies only temporary elevation to the rank. See also *marmalade.

brass monkeys   Cold. Abbreviation of the phrase *cold enough to freeze the balls off a brass monkey*; in wooden sailing ships the *brass monkey* was a three-ringed brass plate beside each gun on which stood three iron cannon balls, with a fourth on top forming a pyramid. In extreme cold weather the brass contracted at a greater rate than iron, thus making the balls too large for the brass rings, and causing the cannon ball on top to push the lower balls off the plate.

B - 60

brassed off   Quite literally, to be fed up with cleaning brass-work!

Bravo Zulu   The NATO Signal Book's 2-letter signal group meaning *Well Done*. Often abbreviated: *'We got a *BZ from the *Flagship for that attack..'*

break a bit off   A lady of easy virtue would be described as **breaking it off**. Jack would also say that *she collars*. It is quite believable that Jack would tell his *oppo that he had a *Friday while and was going *up the line to the *Smoke to see his *party, and hopefully she would *break a bit off*, but might end *up the spout if he didn't have a *seamshifter.

break out   Order to open up a stores container and prepare some item for its immediate issue or use: *'Break out the *medical comforts and stand by to issue a dozen *survivor's tots..'* See *barrico also.

breaking strain of a warm Mars bar   Description of an individual with little or no willpower when it comes to resisting temptation. The words *chocolate bar* or *Crunchie* are sometimes substituted.

breasts and springs   Traditional way of securing a vessel alongside. *'*Ease springs!'* is another euphemism for a call of nature.

bred in the purple   Jack's term for an officer of noble birth.

brew   The container or urn from which a *wet of tea is dispensed: *'Let's stop and get a brew on..'*

brick / bricking   A number of variants to consider:
1. A naval (gunfire) shell is known as a *brick*. The older term was *projjie.
2. (RM) A half-section of four men mounted in a Land-Rover is also a *brick*.
3. *bricking* is the surgical procedure of vasectomy.

Bridge card   A folding card, published monthly, listing all Royal Navy ships, submarines and Naval Air Command squadrons, together with the names of their Commanding Officers, plus their seniority. The latter aspect is vital when determining the identity of a *canteen boat.

bridle a ship's anchor cable   The process of disconnecting an anchor from the cable, and then using it for securing to a buoy.

brief (FAA)   The process of going over all relevant information prior to a sortie, adapted to more general use: *'What's the brief for that *cocker's P tonight?'*

Brigham   The traditional nickname for anyone called Young, after one *Brigham* Young Esq., founder of the Mormon church.

bright specimen   Sardonic label for an idiot.

brightwork   Brass or copper pipes and fittings that are cleaned during the *middle and morning *watches.

bring to   A seamanship term for applying a rope to a capstan or winch.

bring up with a round turn   Correct someone sharply; another old sailing term from the cabledeck, where a *round turn* was always taken with the inner end of the anchor cable before its cable was *payed out. As the ship dropped astern, the cable gradually tautened until the ship was finally *brought up with a round turn.*

Bristol fashion   Everything neat, tidy and seamanlike in both appearance and function, based on the reputation of ships that used to trade out of Bristol. The full expression, which has come ashore to a wider usage, is *all shipshape and Bristol fashion.*

broach   To break into a cask or bottle; *broaching-to* occurs when a vessel running before a sea is slewed around broadside to the sea - a highly dangerous situation in severe weather.

broad arrow   A mark indicating Government property, first used in the reign of Elizabeth I.

broad pennant   The personal insignia of a Commodore when the senior officer afloat; note that this is not a *Flag in its true sense, which indicates the special authority of an Admiral, and also that this pennant is swallow-tailed rather than square.

broadside messing   The old system of messing in a warship whereby food was prepared in individual messes by the *Cook of the Mess; it was then taken to the *galley to be properly heated though - or cooked. At the *pipe *Cooks to the galley!,* the mess cooks collected the food, and then took it back to their respective messes to be served and eaten. The term was still in use when properly equipped *galleys were installed, and trained cooks employed to both prepare *and* cook the food. Since there were as yet no dining halls, it was still collected by the cooks of the messes and taken to the messdecks for consumption. With the advent of dining halls, the system was then changed to General (Cafeteria) Messing whereby Jack could collect his own meal, choosing from a varied selection at a central servery. The term *Cook of the Mess* is still in use, but now refers to the person or people in each mess who are responsible for cleaning it on a daily basis.

Brock's benefit (esp. RM)   Spectacular battle involving lots of high explosive, tracer and illuminating starshells: *'The attack on Mount Harriet was a real Brock's benefit once the Argies woke up..'*

broke   In addition to the financial meaning, the word also applies to an Officer who is forced to leave the Service, by sentence of *court martial; this stemmed from the older procedure of breaking that Officer's sword if guilt is proven on charges of sedition or treason.

broken brain (RM)   Someone who is not quite all there.

bronzy time   Sunbathing; may also be *bronzy-bronzy* or simply *bronzing*.

brothel creepers   Suede shoes with crepe or rubber soles.

brow   Gangway used to link a ship to shore; on crossing over the **brow** in either direction, all RN and RM personnel pause, whether or not they are in uniform, to salute the *quarterdeck.

brown   Eight usages (so far):
1. A colour traditionally associated with the Army, as in:
    brown clown - Army officer.
    brown job - anyone from the Army and: *'If God had meant the Army to fly, He would have made the sky brown..'*

2. A *brown hatter* can mean a homosexual, or be a general term of denigration implying total uselessness or abject failure: '*Have you seen what the *Crabs did to *Lossie's *wardroom? They've turned the place into a ruddy brown hatter's paradise..*' or: '*Quite frankly, that policy meeting was a complete brown hatter's tea party..*' Note also that a *brown hatter's scrambling net* is a string vest, *brown hatter's overalls* are pyjamas and *brown hatter's teacakes* are haemorrhoids! See page C - 111 for an absolute Tugg classic. *Brown hatters handgrips*, incidentally, are extra long and rather florid sideburns which are not permitted.

3. Someone who spends a lot of time snivelling around his superiors may be described as a *brown noser*, or someone *out for brownie points*.

4. *brown-water navy* - a coastal fleet as opposed to an ocean-going *blue-water one.

5. Lumps of faecal matter floating in a harbour or anchorage are referred to as *brown trout* or *brown admirals*, whereas *Admiralty brown* was *pusser's toilet paper until very recently.

6. *brown envelopes* are special instructions handed out during a Flag Officer's Inspection to test the flexibility and preparedness of the ship in a specific way.

7. *brown neutraliser* - brown sauce twinned with *red lead. Originally *Ally Sloper's (slogan - *Take lots of it with everything*), but later Daddy's.

brown amps (SM)   Diesel *boat term for the poor lighting state in a submarine when the voltage is dropping and the batteries need a good charging.

Brummie   Nickname for anyone originating from Birmingham.

Brylcreem boys   The RAF, due to the advertisments depicting an aviator with *Oh so shiny* (slicked-back) *hair*, modelled by the famous and popular cricketer Dennis Compton.

brush the salt off his shoulders!   Older and wonderfully sardonic remark directed at someone telling exaggerated sea stories; the modern equivalent is: *'He's *swinging the lamp..'*

BS   Acronym for Bullshit, or (if you want to show off your ability to paraphrase English) - Bovine Scatology. See also *flannel, but the two expressions are not entirely synonymous. *Flannel may be designed to, but does not actually baffle brains; *bullshit* is designed to, and frequently does! The wonderful cod-Latin motto for this statement (and the author boasts a Latin O-Level Pass dating from 1960) is *Excreta Tauri Cerebrum Vincit*. *Bullshit* refers not just to words but also deeds. Thus an exaggerated piece of *tiddley work for, say, *Rounds, is also *bullshit*, as is a well-rehearsed and spectacularly-conducted ceremonial *evolution. The US Marine Corps Demonstartion Platoon at ceremonial rifle drill is an example of really serious, but absolutely splendid and wholly admirable bullshit!

BSH   *British Standard Handfuls*, a sizing index for female breasts, otherwise known as *babies *bag rats.

bubble   Once again, a lovely trio:
1. Tell tales or inform on someone: *'Gordon was bubbled about that little scam by his girlfriend..'* To *be bubbled* is to be found out; see also *tumbled.
2. (SM) The *bubble* here refers to the state of a *boat's trim, as displayed by a large spirit level inclinometer in the *Control Room. To *lose the bubble is a term that has now reached General Service, and means that the person so described has lost trim control, thus implying a lack of understanding - or increasing confusion. The phrase *keep your bubble level* means the same as today's *keep your cool..*
3. *bubble in the hoist* - a hiccup or snarl-up. Derived from the delivery of shells to a gun turret. If there had been an error and a shell had not come up on the hoist, there was a bubble in it. Usually based on the effect created by an air bubble in the hydraulic system used to lift ammunition inside a turret.

bubbleheads / bubblies   Ship's divers working with compressed air, which is expired into the water and rises in a cloud of bubbles to the surface. See also *pondlife.

bubbly   *Grog - rum diluted with water, and certainly Jack's champagne in one sense, but not named bubbly for that reason! This is a strict definition, but in general usage the term is employed for almost any form of rum, hence the request in a pub: *'I'll have a bubbly and black please..'* (rum and blackcurrant) or the statement: *'Only * Pussers' bubbly is the real thing..'* When mixed *two and one with water in the rum tub, *neaters took on a foaming appearance. It was in this state that it was issued to the *bubbly bosun* from each *messdeck who came to collect the *Tot in a rum *fanny when *Up Spirits! was *piped.

Bucc   The Buccaneer low-level maritime strike aircraft, operated from carriers by the FAA between 1962 and 1978, and which subsequently rendered yeoman service with the RAF, although it has now been withdrawn from service. May also be modified as *Buccanana* - a particularly lethal form of low-flying fruit.

Buck / buck   Five meanings:
1. Nickname for anyone called Taylor or, inevitably, Rogers.
2. *buck the system* - try to do things in an unorthodox or unofficial way.
3. *Buck House* is a nickname for Buckingham Palace.
4. *pass the buck* - see *slope shoulders.
5. *buck slip*   Slip of paper attached to service correspondence re-routing it onwards, hence the expression *passing the buck*, and President Truman's famous desktop sign *The Buck Stops Here*.

bucket of fog   A situation that is incomprehensible, or illogical.

bucket of shit   Rather surprisingly, this used to be a frequent and affectionate form of greeting between Jack and an old *oppo: *'Me old bucket of shit! Bloody Hell! How's the family?..'*

bucket of sunshine / instant sunshine   Fairly standard euphemism for a nuclear weapon. *CND activists are known as the *Bucket of Sunshine Brigade*; see also *unscheduled sunrise.

buckshee   Free; derived from the Arab word *baksheesh*.

buff stoker   A baby stoker without any length-of-service badges.

buff up   Clean and polish something, usually for *Rounds.

buffalo   Occasional substitute used for *dubs, as in *Oh-five-buffalo* meaning *Oh-five-dubs* (0500).

Buffer   Nickname for the Chief Boatswain's Mate - the Commander or *Jimmy's right-hand man in respect of all work done around the ship to maintain both seamanship equipment (especially lifesaving and survival equipment) and the overall appearance of the ship. Usually a stalwart character of great experience and personality, he directs the *Buffer's party*. Naval Air Stations will have an *airfield buffer* in an identical role. Usually a Chief or PO. There is however another meaning, derived from the term *buff. It refers to a senior rating with a low technical qualification, such as AA3 or QM3. These chaps are / were strong on seamanship and bad language but often rather uncouth NCOs. Known to their peers as *buffs*, this label was not used by officers or junior rates.

Buffs!   Abbreviated exhortation to: *'Buck up, for (flip's) sake!'*

bug blinder   The machine through which all kit had to be put following an infestation by crabs or scabies, ic. a fumigator.

bug out (RM)   Tactical withdrawal, usually conducted in a big hurry.

bug rake   A comb; the parting in a hair style is called a *bug run*.

bugger-about list   The dark-blue equivalent of a hit list on which individuals who have incurred the *Jimmy's displeasure may be placed. Sometimes also called a shit-list for this reason: *'The next man who spills coffee on the chart table goes right to the top of my bugger-about list..'* See also *lurk list.

bugger's grips   Tufts of facial hair specially preserved around the cheekbones as an affectation; these are sometimes also called *muff-diver's depth marks.

buggers' muddle   A complete mess.

Buggins' turn   The process whereby a tri-Service job falls to the next incumbent in strict rotation, rather than being given to the best candidate.

Bugis Street   Eating-house locale in Singapore, sadly now demolished, but famous for its nocturnal population of transvestites. A crucial feature of the atmosphere was Jack and Royal's tolerant and rather civilized attitude to these *kytais. Many a *sea daddy brought his young charges here for educational purposes.

bulkhead   Jack's name for a wall, not formed by the ship's side; if somewhat inebriated he may well be involved in a spot of bulkhead bouncing! A *bulkhead crusher* is a Harvey Wallbanger.

bulldog (esp. RM)   Abrasive description of a female:'*Who was that bulldog I saw you wiv' down the disco?*' Or, used in a different sense: '*That *party's got a *moosh like a bulldog chewin' a wasp..*'

bully beef   *Soup de boulli* - the official term for *corned beef*; also known as *corned dog.

bum   A set of nine applications:
1. *bum bandit* - homosexual.
2. *bum boat* - any vessel holding supplies or goods for sale in large open casks that look like *bombards* (mortars). Alternative derivations include *boomboat* which is either Dutch for a broad-beamed fishing boat, or means a boat which is secured to a *boom in order to trade with the ship's company.
3. *bum fluff* - downy facial hair on a lad yet to start shaving.
4. *bum freezer* - hip-length reefer jacket, still used in Mess Undress.
5. *bum plums* - prolapsed piles.
6. *bum steer* - bad or incorrect advice.
7. *bum, beer & baccy* - one of a landsman's perceptions of the Navy; alternatives include *rum, bum and baccy* or, as Churchill rather unjustifiedly described it, *Rum, Sodomy and the Lash.*
8. *bum burner* - curry.
9. *bum's rush* - A bad deal, foisted on you in a hurry.

bumper   A tool consisting of a heavy block of wood on a pole. This was put on top of a piece of cloth and pushed up and down the floor to polish the Corticene (linoleum). Mostly used in shore bases.

bumph   Time-honoured description of the never-ending stream of printed forms, papers, hand-outs, instructions, orders, cancellations and amendments which arrive in any ship or establishment. The term indicates a wish that it was all printed on much softer - and usefully perforated paper.

bumpy jumper   Female sailor's woolly pully.

bunch of bastards   A length of rope that has become excessively tangled and will require a lot of patience and swearing to unravel and coil properly. Also known as a *bunch of knitting*; and see also *Snakes Honeymoon / Wedding.

bundleman   A married sailor, since he took his *dhobey home in a **bundle** for his wife to cope with; to *drop a bundle* implies an expensive *run-ashore.

bundu   General term for a remote or wild (jungle) area.

bung up and bilge free   A dead body having been in the sea for a while will float face downwards (buttocks upwards) and, like an empty cask, is said to be *bung up and bilge free.*

Bungalow Bill (esp. FAA) Nickname for someone who, just like a bungalow, does not have all that much up top; *Kelvin is an alternative.

Bungey / Bungy Nickname for anyone called Williams or (sometimes) Edwards.

bunghole Old Navy name for cheese.

bunk up *Turn in with a lady friend (Jack), or a chap (*Jenny!).

Bunker Hill (RM) *Corps memorable date of 17 June 1775, and a battle of the American War of Independence in which Marines of the First and Second Battalions displayed conspicuous valour and unshaken steadiness when storming this area of high ground north of Boston.

Bunny Inevitable nickname for someone with the surname Warren.

bunny food / bunny grub Lettuce, or any green salad.

bunting tosser Communications branch rating or (RM) Signals Branch member. *Bunts* was the shortened form. See also *flag wagger.

buoy jumper Seaman detailed to connect the *bridle to the mooring buoy - a hazardous task, especially in bad weather.

burberry / burbs Traditional nickname for a blue Naval raincoat, since Messrs. Burberrys were among the original main suppliers: '*Some big *OD's *razzed me burbs!'* is a complaint that some presumptious colleague has *borrowed Jack's raincoat. The term has also been adapted into other phrases:
> *shiny burbs* - oilskins, or waterproof sailing clothing.
> *Wanchai burberry* - oiled paper umbrella made in Hong Kong, and possessed of a highly pungent smell when put into use for the first time.
> *tin burberry* - sports car.

burble Ramble on in speech, without making anything clear: '*Listen *Bloggs, what on earth are you burbling about?*'

burgoo Porridge; the *burgoo medal* is a RN Long Service and Good Conduct medal, so named for all those years of eating **burgoo**.

BURMA Acronym for *Be Undressed Ready, My Angel.* Anticipatory message on the flap of Jack's final *mailie to his

Bimble

*pash before getting home from sea. See also SWALK and NORWICH.

Burma Road Standard nickname for the main passageway running through the length of a warship. In some ships with city names, the *Burma Road* will have the name (and associated street signs) of the main thoroughfare of that city.

burmadoos Bermuda shorts.

burn Time for a cigarette: *'Right lads, take five for a quick burn..'*

burning and turning A helicopter with its engines running and the rotors engaged.

burnt plum The anal orifice.

bush A lady's pubic hair: *'A hand on the bush is worth more than two birds in the hand!'*

bush baptist Jack's name for any funny church, of the type which appoints you as a pastor in return for $50 forwarded to a PO Box Number in Ohio. The *Church of Turkey is a European alternative.

busking   Old Naval term for pirate vessels cruising along a coast looking for something to attack; now used for itinerant musicians who cruise along a queue of people, still in the hopes of finding some form of treasure.

bust / busted   Jack's typically irreverent way of describing someone who has been disrated (demoted) as a punishment for a serious offence, as in: '*The *Chief got busted down to *killick by the *old man for being *pissed out of his brains..*'

Buster / buster
1. Traditional nickname for anyone called Brown.
2. (FAA) Code word for full speed, or as fast as you can - note also *max chat.

butcher's apron   Nickname for the United Nations medal ribbon awarded for the Korean campaign; it had light blue and white vertical stripes.

butcher's bill   Casualty lists issued after a wartime action.

button / unbutton   Code/decode a signal using a semi-automatic typewriter.

button your flap!   Older exhortation to: '*Shut up* !' derived from the special design of Jack's uniform trousers which had a flap front or *piss flap instead of fly buttons or a zip. The older design is still issued to *Yachties.

button boy   The rating selected for his agility and steadiness to stand on the top *truck or button of the mast at a mast-manning display; he was traditionally given a shilling for his efforts! The origin of mast-manning was that in square-rigged men-of-war entering a foreign port, the more personnel who were visible, the less likely there would be sufficient manpower below decks to serve the guns. Nowadays, of course, we have *Procedure Alpha.

buttons   As worn on the sleeve cuff of a Chief Petty Officer's uniform jacket; promotion to CPO is known as getting your buttons.

buzz   Rumour; a *buzz merchant* is a rumour-monger, or someone who seems to have the latest buzz before anyone else. He will usually claim that his buzzes are *gen as in the drawing at page   Note also the lower grades of *strong buzz* or *good buzz* in this context. '*What's the buzz?*' means: '*What's going on?*' A *duff buzz or *gash buzz is one that turns out to be incorrect. See also *Galley Packet, which predates buzz. The USN version is *scuttlebutt.

Up Homers

buzz box   An intercom system.

by and large   A nautical expression now in common use, meaning *broadly speaking*. Nautically, it means to sail a boat *by the wind* (ie. to weather) but *large* (ie. not very close to the wind).

by the book   According to any laid-down Regulations. A senior member of the Royal family is reputed to have once said: *'If you try to run the Navy by the book, it won't work'* !!

BZ   Well done - see * Bravo Zulu for a more complete explanation.

CHARLIE

77 - 124

C.126 (formerly S.126 but now *Computerised*)   Arguably the least popular of *pusser's various forms - the Report of Stores Lost, Stolen or Damaged.

C.206 (formerly S.206 but now ditto**)**   Confidential Reporting form raised on all officers at regular intervals and thus vital to their promotion prospects. A combination of textual comments and marking points for various personal qualities gives an over-all picture and score which is used to make up ranking lists at the annual Promotion Boards.   Previously, RN officers did not see their S.206s, but were given a *flimsy instead, which should have been an accurate precis of their full report. However, the system was open to abuse, and now Naval officers must physi-cally sight their C.206s. They still get a *flimsy on leaving an appointment, and on change of their CO. A number of classic 206 comments are listed under *two-oh-six, but for a com-pendium of comments from all services, see *IN CONFIDENCE* by the same author, purchase details in the aft section.

C.2641 (formerly C.264 and S.264 before that)   Confidential Reporting form on ratings, and used in a generally similar man-ner to the above.   Ratings, however, do not get *flimsies. Adverse comments which are within their (his or her) power to remedy are underlined in red. See also *Comic Cuts.

CS   Continuous Service as opposed to *HO or NS (National Service).

cab (FAA)   Helicopter or fighter aircraft. A *cab rank* indicates a stack of aircraft waiting to land on, or in olden times, a *trot of RN craft awaiting orders for sea.

cabbage hat   Green beret.

cabin   Sleeping accommodation provided in ships for officers, *warrant officers and nowadays, in most ships, for chief and petty officers. Single cabins are provided for the more important people and *cabins* seldom have more than 6 bunks - above that it becomes a *bunk space* or even a *mess*. By extension, bedrooms in shore establishments, including RM establishments, are also called cabins. In most ships the *Captain will have a *day cabin* (sitting room) plus *sleeping cabin* (bedroom) and always refer to them as such; in larger warships the Captain and other key officers (such as the Navigation Officer and Commander (Air)) will have a *sea cabin* immediately adjacent to, or beneath the bridge.

caboose / caboosh   Combination of store, small office, workshop and hideaway.

cack-handed   Clumsy; probably derived from the Greek word *kakos* for bad. However, *cack* (perhaps for the same reason) can also mean *shit*, and the right-handed majority sneers at the cack-handed (left-handed) arrangements for personal hygiene.

cackle   Excessive and loud talk. One could be told to *cut the cackle*. Note also: *'He's got more cackle on him than a Yankee Gunner's Mate..'*

cackleberries   Hen's eggs.

cackling your grease / fat   Talking out of turn, or failing to listen in a conversation.

CAFO   Usually pronounced *Caffo*, an acronym for the Confidential Admiralty Fleet Order which preceded *pink DCIs.

C - 78

CAG (FAA)   A *Carrier Air Group*, currently of embarked *SHAR and *Sea King squadrons; the EH101 Merlin is in the process of replacing the *Sea King.

cag / *clag (esp. FAA)   Fog, or bad visibility in low cloud.

cake and arse party   Jack's term for any state of total disorganization, often qualified with the adjective *real*. Note that this term is distinct from a *Wardroom *cocker's P which can be called a *cock and arse party.

cakehole   Mouth

call boys   Before the *Tannoy broadcast and loudspeaker system was installed in big warships around mid WW2, the gangway party included boy seamen whose job was to run to all parts of the ship and repeat any pipes using their *bosun's calls.

call for a damp   Break wind silently but very obviously to the olfactory sense: *'Blimey, who's called for a damp?'*

call for Hughie   To vomit.

call round   Invite your *oppo onboard for a few *sherberts, or you go to him for the same.

Call the hands!   Shrill *pipe made at the start of a working day in order to wake everyone up and get them *turned to.

camel   A hollow tank filled with water, paired with another, then placed under the hull of a stricken ship. The water is pumped out and the buoyancy thus generated helps to lift / support the ship.

cam out (RM)   Apply *camouflage cream* to one's face, or *cam nets* and other materials to a vehicle or tent. See also *Al Jolson kit.

camel basher   An Arab.

Camship   WW2 escort ship fitted with a *catapult* capable of *squirting a Sea Hurricane fighter off, in order to deal with the menace of long-range Focke Wulf Condor aircraft. The pilot then had to ditch alongside his ship, the initial letters of which stood for *Catapult Armed Merchantman*. Note the distinction between this and the *Macship; if anyone out there knows of the existence of a Hurricane fighter, whatever its condition, will they please contact the author – or the Curator of the FAA Museum at Yeovilton!

can do   Slightly cynical resignation to the fact that whatever is asked of the RN/RM it will be done, regardless of *overstretch, as the opposite, *no can do, is unthinkable. Jack, Jenny and Royal just wish that someone *up there would acknowledge this in more than words, and provide the resources to fulfil the commitments!

can do paper   Of USN origin, but the term describes a diploma or course certificate.

can man   Civilian embarked in a ship as the *NAAFI canteen manager or *NAAFI damager.

can of worms   Failure:'*We did our best, but then politics turned the whole project into a giant can of worms..*' Also has overtones of something of great complexity.

can spanner   Tin opener. See also *spanner.

Candidate (RM)   A Royal Marine who is working towards promotion as a NCO; the *Roll of Candidates* is a computerized list maintained at *CENTURION.

can't fit that in (esp. RM)   Gentle and rather pleasant way of expressing disapproval of something.

can't make head nor tail of it   Lovely expression used by the Yeoman of Signals when he was unable to make any sense out of a distant *hoist of flag signals; this expression has come ashore into widespread usage.

can't take a joke - shouldn't have joined!   Navy-wide expression of almost amused resignation at some of the crazy things that happen in the *Andrew; (that's) *life in a blue suit is an alternative method of expressing the same sort of sentiment.

canteen   A ship's shop, operated by the *NAAFI.

canteen boat   Title awarded to whichever ship in a task group or squadron has the most junior CO, and therefore performs the most menial and least pleasurable tasks:'*Always first out and last in, then tied up miles from the *run-ashore..*' Derived from the old messdeck system whereby the youngest rating ran errands to the *canteen* for his messmates' tobacco and *nutty.

canteen committee   A body of repesentatives from the ship's company chaired by the Commander or First Lieutenant to consider amenities, now replaced by the *Welfare Committee.

canteen cowboy   A rating who fancies himself with the ladies (see also Tugg on page C - 121).

canteen messing   In the days before central messing each *messdeck's rations were prepared by the detailed cook of the mess, taken to the *galley for cooking, collected from there and then consumed on the *messdeck. If the mess *cates wasn't too smart, the last few days of each month would see *herrings-in for every meal.

canteen socks   Either barefoot, or wearing no socks at all. The canteen connection is a bit obscure, but when ankle boots were compulsory kit, a scruffy rating with an incomplete kit might appear at Divisions without socks. His messmates might then suggest *knee length Cherry Blossom* - black boot polish!

canvas back   Someone who is always asleep. See also *golden gonker, *golden blanket / pillow award, *horizontal champion, *Unknown Warrior and *zeds merchant.

CAP   *Combat Air Patrol.* This acronym, by frequent usage, has become a word in its own right: *'We've got two *SHAR on CAP at a hundred miles, plus another pair at *Alert 5 on deck..'*

Cap Badge (RM)   A prominent feature in the Radfan, on which was positioned an OP manned by men of 45 Cdo RM.

Black Catter

cap tally   Black cap ribbon carrying ship's name in gold lettering. Initially, these were supplied by the *captain at his own expense, but became part of official *rig in 1857. In wartime, *cap tallies* with a ship's name are withdrawn, and ones with the letters *HMS* only are issued. Note also the specific application of *different ships, different cap tallies*, and the term *cap ribbon*, which is Jack's protesting description of the space between the surface of the beer and the rim of a tankard, indicating a short measure.

Cape Horn fever   Older term for an imaginary disease; see also *plumbosis oscillans and *plumus tremens.

Captain   3 definitions:
1. The most senior rank below *flag rank, denoted by 4 gold rings on sleeves or shoulder straps. Formerly described as a *post Captain*, to differentiate from (2).
2. The Commanding Officer of a ship or submarine regardless of the actual rank held.
3. A (usually senior) rating in charge of a *part of ship or station (eg. *Captain of the Fo'c'sle, Captain of the* (gun) *Turret, Captain of the Flightdeck* and, more humourously, *Captain of the *Heads.* There was also a *Captain of the Side* who led the Side party for *manning the side.

Captain-General (RM)   The RM equivalent of an Army Regiment's Colonel-in-Chief. The present incumbent is HRH The Prince Philip, who has held this office since 1953. His insignia of rank are those of a Field Marshal.

Captain's cloak   Nickname for the last of the *Articles of War, because it authorises punishment for any misdemeanour or offence not mentioned in the previous Articles!

Captain's mast   USN version of the RN *Angel's Whisper. Disciplinary procedure at which the Commanding Officer of a US Navy vessel deals with any members of the crew brought before him for investigation and possible punishment.

captain's tiger   A Commanding Officer's personal steward; the term is a legacy from the 19th century and the striped mess jackets worn by some Indian personal stewards of that era.

car smash   Tomato sauce or tinned tomatoes; known as *car smash when bacon is incorporated. The FAA calls a champagne and brandy cocktail *Car Smash* because that's a frequent consequence of consuming too many. See also *train smash, which is car smash with sausages.

card suits   The card suits were as follows: diggers - spades; *sparklers* - diamonds; *tickers* - hearts, and *tealeaves* - clubs.

cardboard fo'c'sle   Jack's description of a *killick's progression to Petty Officer and his consequent moving out of *square rig; this is because the cap suddenly acquires a *cardboard fo'c'sle* as a peak.

cardboard replica   These were what you used to get in breakfast cereal packets, like a cardboard replica of HMS ARK ROYAL. Therefore, anyone who was useless was a *cardboard replica* of something: *'No way he's a ruddy engineering officer! He's just a cardboard replica..'*

Cardiff virgin   Welsh rarebit. The pun lies in the correct spelling of this gastronomic delight.

career-limiting   Delightful understatement of the consequences of an act of gross indiscretion: *'Old Shorty was caught getting his *leg over the Admiral's daughter - a bit of a career-limiting move, I'd say..'*

carpet crawler   A small child. See also *ankle biter / snapper, and *rug rat.

carpet man   RN officer who owes his promotion to influence in high quarters.

carpet tomcat   Officer with a reputation as a womanizer.

carpeted   In trouble; on the carpet in the Captain's office for a spot of *picturising, or else an *interview without coffee.

carrier   Accepted abbreviation of *aircraft carrier*, a class of ship that has had a chequered history recently. In 1965 the RN had 5 fixed-wing and 2 helicopter (*Commando) carriers, with a new class (CVA-01) at an advanced design stage. The 1967 Defence Review (Healey - a name linked forever on the RN's *shit list with *Nott) cancelled CVA-01 and announced the abolition of the FAA's fixed-wing capability. By the mid 70s, there was just one fixed-wing carrier (ARK ROYAL) left. By this time, a new class of *Through-deck Cruiser* had been laid down (the term *carrier* could not be used for political reasons), designed solely for anti-submarine helicopters. However, a spirited rearguard action by naval *Whitehall Warriors successfully secured the procurement of the *SHAR; the through-deck cruiser's flight deck was redesigned with a *ski-jump, the word *carrier crept back into the vocabulary, especially after the Falklands war, and the future of fixed-wing naval aviation was assured.

carry away   Originally, rigging that parted under strain or cannon fire was *carried away* downwind or over the side. The term now has a more general usage, often when someone loses emotional control.

Carry on!   The *pipe or bugle call made, after a period of silence and / or at attention initiated by the *Still (*bosun's call) or *Alert (bugle), to resume normal activities, as in: *'After the two minutes silence, the Carry on! will be *piped at 1102..'* Can also be used as a verbal order, as in: *'Carry on Sergeant Major!'* This is an order given by a young RM officer who doesn't know what to do next.

cash clothing   See *Slops, and very often closed for stocktaking (see also *Jack Dusty and the Tugg cartoon at page @@@@).

casual   Formerly a payment on account made to someone short of cash between fortnightly pay days (see *blank week); the amount of the *casual* was then deducted from the pay due at the next pay day. Its use has gone into decline, since all pay is now credited to individual bank accounts.

cat o'nine tails   Instrument of punishment in the old Navy; if the rope tails were knotted, then it became a *thieves' cat. This device was stored in a red baize bag to conceal the blood drawn by it, hence the expression *the cat's out of the bag* which still means that retribution is imminent. Note also the association with the phrase *hardly room enough to swing a cat*, which implies that the space being described is somewhat cramped, rather than suggesting cruelty to felines.

catch a crab   In a pulling boat, when the oar fails to strike solid water.

catch the boat up   See both the original Preface and the entry for *boat. This is a very old naval expression derived from the fact that Jack was often not allowed ashore, even when sick, in the days of sail - for fear that he might desert. When the Naval hospitals at Portsmouth and Plymouth were built, they were positioned on *creeks and could therefore be reached by water. The sick boat would circulate among the warships anchored off-shore, take off those who were ill or injured, and then transport them up either Haslar or Stonehouse *creeks (which see). *Catching the boat up*, or more simply, *the boat*, now refers exclusively in the RN and RM to diseases of a social nature.

Cates   Nickname for the *Caterer*; although this is now an official branch, the Officers' and the Chiefs' and POs' Messes still elect amateur *caterers* from amongst their members to look after wines, newspapers etc., and they then use that title in an official sense. The *Wardroom Wine Caterer* is traditionally, as the author is proud to relate from his time in HMS BRISTOL, the Medical Officer!

caulk   Old Navy term for a *kip, from the tar marks left on your back from the tar-based *caulking* between deck planks.

caulker   A makeshift head pillow, for instance a rolled-up item of clothing when sleeping other than in one's own hammock.

C-Balls   Acronym for *Carrier-Borne Army Liaison Staff,* subsequently changed to Ground Liaison Officer; a small group of *pongos borne in the older aircraft carriers, to control and co-ordinate Ground Attack mission requirements ashore. An earlier version was *CBALO*, which was short for *Carrier Borne Army Liaison Officer*, irreverently changed to *Carrier Borne Army Looting Official* in one *carrier, following certain smart exchanges starting with a Jeep in exchange for a high speed motor boat, later exchanged for a MFV (motor fishing vessel) in which the person concerned actually sailed back to UK!

C-Troop   A group of not-so-young ladies who used to turn up regularly at the RN Leadership's School's weekly dances.

CD   Clearance Diver - a title now abolished, but still used as a collective noun for those diving on Navy business using gas mixtures, rather than the compressed air of Ship's Divers or *bubbleheads.

CDA Mess   Special *Contagious Diseases Act* Annexe in large warships for men with venereal disease, often described incorrectly as (having) Contracted Disease Ashore.   See *Rose Cottage for a fuller explanation, and note also that these men received the automatic and rather serious penalty of having their *tots stopped.

CDF   Common Dog Factor - the application of pure common sense (a quality not measurable by written examinations) in solving a problem.   See also *pickle jar and *jampot lid.

centrefold   A two-dimensional object of Jack's fantasy and desire; actually to *trap one is classed as an ultimate achievement.

(HMS) CENTURION   The Royal Navy and Royal Marines' computerised Pay, Records and Drafting (see *drafty) establishment at Gosport, near Portsmouth, and referred to as a single word: *'Until CENTURION clear the payment, you can't have any* *money..'* HMS CENTURION is no longer a *stone frigate, but merely a component part of the Second Sea Lord/CinC Naval Home Command's organisation. Note also that the Pay Office of old in ships and establishments has now become the *Unit Personnel Office* - a one-stop office dealing with all aspects of personnel administration. It's all part of the relentless, so-called improvement that is a feature of the modern Royal Navy, and the introduction of what the Civil Service management gurus call modern *human resource allocation*. Ouch!

centurion (RM)   An officer who personally commands more than 100 men in a Unit, ie. the Commanding Officer and his Company commanders.

chacon   Two forms of usage:
1. Wooden shipping container for logistic stores, developed in Chatham Dockyard - hence *Chatham container*.
2. (RM) Personal rucksac packed for Arctic Warfare operations, and usually very heavy: *'The trouble with ski-ing downhill is that the ruddy chacon keeps *taking charge..'*

chain gang (FAA)   *Roof rats dragging aircraft tie-down chains around the flight deck of a carrier, to the general discomfiture and sleeplessness of those *turned in below.

chains   The small platform, with surrounding *chains* to lean against, hinged out from port and starboard bows for a seaman to *heave the lead. It was an unattractive task, especially as the calls usually went completely ignored. Hence any unpleasant duty was sometimes referred to as *the chains*.

chalk bosun   Instructor Officer; see also *schoolie.

chamfer up (pronounced with a soft *ch*)   Tidy up and polish things, especially for *Rounds. From the joinery term. See also *tiddley up and *bougie up.

chammy   See *shammy.

chancre mechanic / chancre bosun   Slang term for a *quack or *Dick Doc.

channel groping   Ships of the Home Fleet patrolling the English Channel (WW2).

Channel night   Traditional, if officially frowned-upon, celebration on the last night of a long *deployment before a warship's return to base port. Derived from the older condition of *Channel* *fever*, or *the Channels* - the excitement which grips a ship's company when approaching home port after a long period at sea. The intensity of this fever still depends directly on the length of time spent away from the United Kingdom; also known as *Up Channel night.

chap   Pleasant conversational substitute for *One* when used in the first person singular; the phrase *One tends to become somewhat tired after cross-country ski-ing* then mutates into: 'A chap needs his *kip in a big way after spending all day on a pair of *pusser's planks..'

char   Tea, from the Hindi word.

charisma bypass   What an unpleasant officer has had during his training.

Charlie buoy   A mooring position at the seaward end of Plymouth Sound; presumably once supported by *Able* and *Baker*!

charlie's coat   RN name for the *Carley Float*. These were wartime flotation devices carried in addition to ship's lifeboats.

Charlie-G (RM)   The man-luggable (as opposed to man-portable) *Carl Gustav* anti-tank weapon which is now obsolescent.

Charlie Noble   An H-shaped galley stove pipe seen in very much older warships, usually bound in brass and kept highly polished. Also used by Jack as a cover name when signing a hotel or night club register ashore.

Charlie time (FAA)   Planned time of arrival.

Chart & Evans   Nickname for a RN church parade, taken from the opening words of the Lord's Prayer: *'Our Father which art in heaven..'*

chase arse   Chaos; life in the *Andrew has been neatly summarised as *chase arse in a blue suit.*

chase the bubble (SM)   The *boat is pitching in a heavy sea. Even at periscope depth, the After Planesman, whose job it is to maintain this depth, is having hell of a time with the indicator bubble in his inclinometer. Planes down, and one would expect the bow to sink, and the bubble to move aft; it won't. Another two degrees of dive / planes down, the bubble shoots even further forwards. Yes, a second later he is smacking his planes to full rise as the boat dips into a particularly deep trough, and the bubble shoots aft - he is *chasing the bubble.*

chase the pisser   Messdeck card game involving the Queen of Spades.

Chats / Chats   The historic Naval port and RM base of Chatham, and also a nickname for anyone called Harris. *Chatham rat* was the name for any lower deck rating from there, because during the war, they all had to sleep in tunnels under the barracks. Note also *Chatham rating* - the one who was first in the queue for *scran, but last in line for ammunition.

chatty   Grubby or unclean.

check away To *pay out / ease out slowly* a rope or wire which is under strain. In the MN it means *hold on.*

Check, check, check! Gunnery order for a temporary cessa-tion of firing (and therefore not the same as *'Cease firing!'*); by extension, it can also used to silence someone in the middle of a verbal tirade.

check the ship for leaks Polite way to indicate your intention to pass water. See also *pump ship and *spring a leak.

cheer ship Pleasant *evolution when Jack lines the rails and gives three cheers in unison. This might occur while steaming past a ship with the *Lord High Admiral or other Royal person-age embarked, or when alongside and saying good-bye to a departing *Father.

cheese down A ceremonial (*tiddley) way of coiling down the stray end of a rope that cannot otherwise be removed or con-cealed; it involves making a flat spiral with the rope's end in the middle. The result is known as a *Flemish coil*; the only other thing that Jack knew as Flemish was cheese - hence the con-nection. It is now also used to describe the process of curling up with uncontrolled laughter. *Cheesing one down* can also be a euphemism for defaecation.

cheese possessed (RM) The tinned processed cheese found in *rat packs.

cheese 'ush (SM) Submarine Service version of a *cheese and onion quiche*; the edge pastry of this creation is called its *guardrails.

cheesy hammy eggy *topsides Standard Naval fare consist-ing of cheese toast with a slice of ham incorporated, and an egg on top. The original version came from the China Station, but even in WW2 it was a gallant attempt to create something inter-esting out of *mousetrap, spam and powdered egg.

chef's delight Unsavoury habit of a chef who spits into his deep fat frier in order to test the oil's temperature.

cherry Virginity (in either sex); hence to *lose one's cherry*, usu-ally during a *spine-shattering run ashore early in one's naval career.

cherryberry (RM) Member of the Parachute Regiment ; their riposte refers to a *cabbage hat.

chew   Three rather different meanings, depending on context:
1. Fellatio; a homosexual indulging in this activity is a *chew bosun*.
2. *chewing someone out* (RM) indicates that someone has erred - and is being seriously *picturised for it.
3. To *chew the fat*, as in discussing general topics at some length, is an expression that has its origins in the steady and extensive mastication required to break down the tough rind of salt beef that had been pickled and stored in brine barrels carried on board, in the era before canned meat or refrigeration.

chicken Chernobyl   Probably the hottest curry now available from your local Indian take-away, and a real *ring-stinger.

chicken shit   American slang term used to indicate something of little real importance: '*I know it's all a bit chicken shit, but the *Boss wants this list complete and handed in by tomorrow..*'

Chief
1. Formal mode of address for a Chief Petty Officer.
2. Less formal address (from a superior or equal) for the Marine Engineering Officer (MEO) of a warship, regardless of rank or rate, or the Chief Engineer of a RFA ship. Derived from Merchant Navy custom and practice. In a big ship his deputy is traditionally known as the Senior Engineer or *Senior*; in other ships he is rather unromantically known as DMEO. Note that the Chief Officer of a MN ship is the First Mate or *Chief O*, and in the RFA a *Choff*.

Chief GI   Chief Gunner's Mate, which evolved into Chief Gunnery Instructor, a semi-legendary figure (especially at *Dartmouth, *Raleigh and other training establishments) responsible for all matters of Ceremonial and parade-ground drill. Regarded with a mixture of awe and affection, but never forgotten once encountered, as on page D - 142. The RM equivalent at *Lympstone is the *First Drill. Note that Gunnery *Instructor has demised as a *rate, but the term *Chief GI* lives on informally. See also *Instructor. Note the SM equivalent of *TI.

chief housemaid   The *Jimmy

Chief Nightingale   The senior medical rating in a larger warship carrying medical staff.

Chief Stoker's method   Hit something hard with a really big hammer! Probably derived from the Chief Stoker's position in the *fo'c'sle capstan party when working cable, and his tendency to strike the chain links with a maul (hammer) in order to get them running smoothly. To laugh like a chief stoker ....To issue a guffaw with sexual innuendoes.

Chief Stokers   Jack's nickname for the sea birds that are always hanging around at the back end, because that's where their souls ended up - picking up the gash and making a lot of noise.

chin-strapped (RM)   To be down on one's chin strap with exhaustion or fatigue: *'After re-running the *thirty miler next day, me and Buck Taylor was totally chin-strapped..'*

chinese fire drill   A panic situation. State of utter confusion lacking order or organisation (US).

chinese landing   Landing an aircraft *Wun Wing Loh*.

chinese national anthem   Very loud throat-clearing, followed by hawking and spitting. (See also *chinky and *chogey)

chinese wedding cake   A *duff made of *pusser's rice pudding with embedded currants and raisins.

Bombhead

chinese whispers   As in civilian life, the law that states: (a) that people hear only what they want to hear, and (b) that superiors sometimes do not hear what their subordinates want them to hear; perhaps best illustrated in this alternative version of *The Creation*:

In the beginning was the Plan, and then came the Assumption;
And the Assumptions were without form, and the Plan without substance.

And the darkness was upon the face of the workers;
And they spake unto their group heads, saying:
'It is a crock of shit and it stinketh..'

And the group heads went unto their section heads;
And they spake unto them:
'It is a pail of dung, and none may abide the odour thereof..'

And the section heads went unto their managers, and sayeth:
*'It is a container of excrement, and it is very strong,
such that none here may abide by it..'*

And the managers went unto their Directors, and sayeth:
'It is a vessel of fertiliser, and none may abide its strength..'

And the Directors went unto their Director General, and sayeth:
'It contains that which aids plant growth, and it is very strong..'

And the Director-General went unto the Deputy Minister,
And sayeth unto him:
'It promoteth growth, and it is very powerful..'

And the Deputy Minister went unto the Minister,
And sayeth unto him:
'This powerful new Plan will actively promote the growth and efficiency of the department, and this area in particular..'

And the minister looked upon the Plan,

And saw that it was good - and so the Plan became Policy.

chinky   Two uses explained:
1. *Chinese*, especially when referring to food - *chinky nosh*
2. Diseased in the tropical sense (without intention of racial slur) as in:*'Worst case of chinky *toe-rot I've ever seen..'*

Chippy   Three applications shown:
1. The Shipwright artificer; now sadly defunct, but selected Marine Engineering Artificers can get an *Adqual (hull) and, when borne for such duties are still referred to as the *chippy*.

2. Inevitably, a nickname for the surname Carpenter.

3. An orthopaedic surgeon

chit / chitty A piece of paper, usually with some form of official permission or instruction written on it. *Bar chits are used for most purchases in the *Wardroom.

chocker see *chokka

chockheads An affectionate term that is best not used directly, unless seeking a serious *bite, for those Fleet Air Arm ratings who are members of the Aircraft Handlers Branch and who are also trained in fire-fighting techniques. A newer term is that of *wedge technician. See also page E - 149.

chocolate fireguard / teapot Another nice version of *He's about as much use as a..* See also *ashtray on a motorbike, *rubber dagger and *third nostril in this context.

chocolate lager Severe diarrhoea.

Choff Acronym of Chief Officer, the Second-in-Command of an *RFA, equivalent to the *mate in a MN vessel.

Chogey Chinese: *'When you get on board, ask the Chogey cobbler to make you a pair of mess boots - half the price and twice the quality of anything you'd get ashore...'* In another special usage, *Chogey knicks* are boxer shorts made in almost any material that you care to provide *Sew-sew with.

Choke his luff! *'Shut him up!'*

chokey Prison; see also *DQs and *slammer.

chokker / chokka Upset, fed up or totally exasperated, always applied in the emotional sense: *'Four months in Crossmaglen my son - and then you'll understand what chokker means..'* Derived from the old warship sailing term of chock-a-block, when two blocks, rigged in a tackle, have come together and no further movement is possible. Can also mean 'full' as in 'the bar was chocker and you could hardly move, let along drink'.

cholera belt Formerly in a rating's kit. Supposed to protect the stomach from tropical or heat induced ailments, particularly for stokers in coal-fired ships.

chop Signature and/or authorisation or approval for a course of action, as in: *'Put your chop on this, please'* From the Chinese for an official seal. Hence also *Chop chop!* - *'Hurry up!'* (literally

'I have approved it, so get on with it!'). Can also be a change of command, or frequency. See also *outchop.

chop one off (RM)   Render a hand salute.

chopped (FAA)   Withdrawn from flying training by formal executive action, after a series of warnings and a *chop ride*: *'Now *Bloggs, your mother's pet name for you is Boo-Boo isn't it? Well, Boo-Boo - you're chopped..'*

chopper   The nickname for anyone aboard who was overfitted with sexual arrangements (*well endowed*). Any Jolly Jack thought to be well equipped acquired this as a nickname. As there was no privacy for the lower deck, such things never escaped notice.

chopper-pukes   *Stovie term of derision for rotary-wing (helicopter) air crew - *Wobbleheads is an alternative.

chrome dome   Abusive term for a slow-witted individual (whose head is as hard as *chrome*).

chuck one up (RM)   Render a salute.

chuck up   Two applications here, both different:

1. Formal congratulations (esp. RM):'*The parade was a *bramah, and *First Drill got a big chuck up from the General.*'
2. Something smelly: '*After seven days and nights in a snowhole one does tend to chuck up just a touche..*'

chuckle gap   The area of bare skin on a ladies' thigh between her stocking top and knickers. So-called because, when you get that far, you know you're laughing! See also **gobbler's gulch*.

chuff   Backside, or even tail-pipe:'*Then this Mirage came screeching past and BROADSWORD put a Sea Wolf right up his chuff..*' See also **jacksie, *six o'clock* and **duck run*.

chuffed   Really pleased:'*When we won the *Argyll Bowl, the CO was mighty chuffed.*' Another expression attempts to quantify this pleasure - *chuffed to ten*. Note that the opposite is **dis-chuffed*. It is interesting to record that this word, forty to fifty years ago, was a synonym for *browned off*! Note also the term *dead chuffed*; either *dead chuffed* or *mighty chuffed* is the complete

opposite of **chokker*.

chufflock   An intimate embrace. (GS) This was any wrestling lock which prevented you doing anything: '*Hooky held his 'oppo in a chufflock, while I smacked him..*' Interestingly, if the same was done to a woman, she was held in a *step over dildo hold*.

Chuffs and Puffs   A pair of applications:
1. Chiefs and Petty Officers.
2. Special **meat pies*, with a sausage embedded in the **clacker*; these items used to be sold by a pie shop just outside the Devonport Dockyard main gate.

chummy ships   Two ships from the same home port between which there are strong bonds of friendship; can also be used to describe an organization which has a benevolent attitude to its employees: *'I really like flying the 747 Classic for Virgin Atlantic. The girls are smashing, certainly, but it's also a real chummy outfit.'*

chunder   An Australian version of the *Technicolour yawn: *'Watch under!'*

chunter (esp. RM)   To mutter, mumble and grumble: *'The men don't seem to be chuntering very much, Sergeant Major - has there been a sudden outbreak of morale?'* See also *draindowns.

church key (RM) A device fitted with every kind of corkscrew, can and bottle opener.

Church of Jock   Church of Scotland and Free Churches; note also the use of the term *Church of Turkey in the same sense as *Bush Baptist, and the entry at *non cangoists.

Church of Turkey   This was also used as a catch-all term for any rating whose religious affiliation did not fall conveniently into the Protestant and Catholic compartments. Even agnostics sometimes heard themselves ordered to get fell in on Sundays with this miscellaneous group! See also *noncangoists.

church pendant   One of the oldest signal flags still in use - a combination of British and Dutch naval colours dating from the Anglo-Dutch wars in the mid-17th century. It signified the temporary (but total) cessation of hostilities, so that both sides could conduct prayers and worship.

chutney ferret   Another of Jack's soubriquets for a homosexual. There is no complete list!

CINC-NAG-HOME   Jack's name for Her Indoors , and a clever play on the more usual acronym of *C-in-C Nav*(al) *Home Command*.

CIP   A *Person* (guest) who is *Commercially Important*. When one of HM Ships pays a visit to some port in the *far flung, the usual pattern for invitations on board is CIPs for drinks and lunch; then VIPs (expatriate Brits especially) for an evening *Cockers P and the *Sunset ceremony.

circuits and bumps (FAA)   Landing practice for pilots.

circular file   Wastepaper basket.

civvy / civvies   Civilian person / civilian clothes - or a group of civilian people; *civvy street* is the same as *outside. RN officers used to use the term plain clothes exclusively, but things have changed...

clacker   Pastry crust on a pie, now used almost exclusively in admiration of the female form: *'Cor - look at the legs on that bit of clacker!'* (See page F - 168 in addition).   A *clacker bosun* or *clacker mechanic* is a chef.

clag   In addition to its bad-weather definition (see *cag), it means to connect two items together, especially fire hoses, either to each other or to a firemain.

clagging on   You clagg on lagging and refractory to replace that which has to be removed. Something like handfuls of mudpies, but it can also be used to invite someone to be generous, as when dishing out the *duff. You would say: *'Go on, clagg it on..'*

clamp / clampers   A peculiar thick fog, often accompanied by high winds, that sometimes affects the Lizard peninsula in Cornwall - and the Royal Naval Air Station at *Culdrose, which then beomes clamped; celebrated in a FAA song/poem *'Harry Clampers never lets you down'* (flying cancelled - back to the crew room to play *Uckers or *RAS a few *zeds). On the rare occasions that fog closed *Lossie, it used to be known as Scotch mist!

clanger   A badly-timed remark that is sufficiently embarrassing to make the ship's bell clang.

Clanky   A *Mechanician specializing in ship or submarine propulsion systems; now there are no more Mechanicians as such, only Artificers or *Tiffs - but the nickname survives.

clappers -   Indicative of speedy or energetic behaviour, as in *hammering away like the clappers,* or *last seen going like the clappers with a couple of crushers after him.*

Classified   Material or information with political or military sensitivity: *'I'm sorry, but I can't tell you that - it's Classified.'* The degree of classification varies from *NAAFI RESTRICTED, via COSMIC TOP SECRET - to EAT BEFORE READING.

clean into   The process of changing from working *rig into clean or fresh clothing; presumably, in the old days Jack used to *clean into* his (filthy) coaling rig! Since all rigs were numbered, you cleaned into a lower number and shifted into a higher one.

clean slate   The helmsman's log slate of old, on which the course to be steered and distance made would be chalked - and then wiped clean at the start of the next *trick. The expression has come ashore to a wider use implying a fresh start, or when *wiping the slate clean* in cancellation or settlement of a debt.

clear   Nautical term with many general applications for tidying up, sorting out, freeing an obstruction, rounding a headland, emptying a space or completing Customs formalities. Note also the phrase *clear your yardarm* for the process of taking precautionary steps to ensure that no blame will attach if something goes wrong: *'As expected, the whole thing went to *rats, but he had managed to clear his yardarm by getting someone else to authorise it.'* (See page F - 177).

Clear lower deck!   A *pipe ordering all personnel (or those specified in the *pipe) to cease work and *muster at a specified location for a particular purpose: *'Clear lower deck - muster in the hangar for an address by the *Captain..'* or: *'Clear lower deck of all junior ratings - muster at the *brow to embark stores.'*

clear stern arcs   Same as an all round look.

cleats   (Big) ears.

clench / climch   A stout fitting securely attached to the ship's structure to which the inboard end of a cable (especialy the anchor cable) or hawser is secured. A rope or cable of which all the free part has run out is thus said to be *out to a clench* (or *clinch*). By extension this has come to mean anyone who is too busy to accept any further work. The expressions to *clinch a deal* and *clench your teeth* both have this maritime and shipbuilding origin. See also **hard up in a clinch*. Traditionally, the ship's navigator is responsible for ensuring, and signing, that the anchor cable is secured to the cable clench after a refit; the first occasion of anchoring after such a refit could be a nerve-racking time for him!

clewed up   *Clews* are the cords from which a hammock is slung or suspended. Derived from the fact that before furling a square sail the clew-lines had to be hauled up to bring the bottom corners of the sail - the clews - up the yard to facilitate the gathering in of the canvas in the process of furling.   So at the end of a voyage you 'clewed up'. To clew up with someone means to serve in the same ship, or join together for some adventure: *'After the reception, most of the boys clewed up in a pub down by the harbour.'*   Note that this has an entirely different meaning to being **clued-up*. Also note that to be *in double clews* implies that you are married, and that your hammock has been strengthened to take the weight of two people!

climb to two feet and level off (FAA)   *Turn in, or go to bed.

clinkers   The results of poor hygiene in the peri-anal region. A clinker maker (from the days of coal) is/was a stoker.

clobbered   Smashed up, or severely punished.

clockwork mouse   Submarine used to train surface ships in anti-submarine warfare techniques; also an older FAA term for an aircraft flown by a very experienced pilot which was used to train new *Batsmen in the art of controlling approaches to the deck.

Cloggie   Any Dutchman, but especially a member of the Royal Netherlands Marine Korps who train, exercise and deploy with Royal to Norway as part of NATO's versatile UK/NL Landing Force. See also *Hertz van Rental and *Tilly van Driver.

close (pronounced as in the verb)   To approach, as in '*The two ships closed to carry out a boat transfer..*'

close quarters   Strong bulwarks erected as a defence against boarders - hence fighting *at close quarters* meaning hand to hand engagement.

close stowed bag meal   Oggie.

close to the wind   Living dangerously, either by word or deed. In sailing terms, to sail close to the wind is risky, as a slight shift in wind direction could result in the ship either being taken *aback or cause her to heel over dangerously.

Close up!   (pronounced as in the verb) The *piped order to proceed immediately to a place of duty: '*Damage control and fire parties close up in the canteen *flat.*'

close-up   (pronounced as in the adjective) A flag signal is **close-up** when it is hauled right up to the signal *yardarm. It also means someone who is fully briefed on a topical subject, as in: '*I'm close up on that new weapon system.*'

clouts   Underpants / knickers; see also *keks and *rompers.

club run   A *run-ashore participated in by most of the *Wardroom, or by all the commanding officers of a Flotilla or a Group deployment.

Clubs / clubswinger   Naval Physical Training Instructor; see also *springer.

clued-up   Intelligent and smart; in possession of all the facts, or *all about. Note that this is not the same as *clewed-up.

CND   Two interesting usages:
1. The *Captain* (formerly Commodore) *Naval Drafting*. Generic name for the organisation responsible for deciding where and when Jack will serve next. See *drafty for a fuller explanation.
2. The *Campaign* (for) *Nuclear Disarmament*; see also *Bucket of Sunshine Brigade. Jack feels that the CND's somewhat unilateral and unconditional stance on removing the present strategic nuclear deterrent rather justifies his alternative explanation of *Criminal Neglect (of) Defence!*

coal-hole (FAA)   The darkened *looker's position in the all-weather Sea Vixen jet fighter (1959-69); his ejection seat was mounted lower in the fuselage than the pilot's, and did not have a clear canopy above it - only an opaque, frangible hatch and tiny window.

coaming rash   The painful result of impacting one's shins on the raised edge of a hatch, hence also known as *hatch rash. Note also the specific application of *Moby rash.

Coastie   Member of Her Majesty's *Coastguard* ; their older nickname was *gobbie.

cobbing   Obsolete *gunroom punishment of being beaten.

cock / cock-up   Mistake: *'He made a complete cock of the first approach, so we had to do a *bolter and go around for a second try.'* Note also the RM usage of *self-adjusting cock-up.

cock and arse party   Cocktail party; see also *cocker's P. Do not confuse this with the specific application of *cake and arse party.

cock one's dish   To break wind loudly while seated.

cocked hat   A navigational *fix on a chart comprising three bearing lines which do not meet at the same point; ideally they should do and so determine precisely the ship's position at the time of the fix. With a cocked hat, *Vasco has to decide where in the triangle so formed the ship is - usually sensibly choosing the point nearest to danger. By extension it has also come to mean a situation which is either confused or where there is room for doubt, or a mistake, as in: *'The plan for tomorow's activity is a bit of a cocked hat..'* or: *'He made a right cocked hat of that *evolution.'*

cocker   Nickname for cockney ratings with a pronounced cockney accent.

cocker's P   Cocktail party; the latter can also be written as CTP.

cockie   *Cockroach*; a particularly unpleasant order of crawling (some species can fly) beetle-like insect, of which the largest is a *Bombay runner. Once they infest a ship (possibly as a result of embarking locally-grown vegetables in warm climates) they are very difficult to eradicate - the cockie is one the few animals expected to survive a nuclear holocaust! Big ones are also referred to as *mahogany mice.

C - 104

Bootneck

cockie die / cock dice   Dice thrown half-on / half-off the playing surface, or otherwise coming to rest against an obstruction in, say, *uckers - and therefore invalid.

cocktail commando (RM)   RM officer equivalent of *canteen cowboy. Implies one whose social graces outweigh his practical soldiering ability. *Hollywood Marine is similar.

cocoa bosun   Someone put in charge of something of which he has little knowledge, ssuch as civilian supply staff who provision aircraft spares without any real knowledge of their function or application.

cocoa rats   Delusions and diarrhoea brought on by excessive intake of *kye. The solid blocks of unsweetened cocoa were brewed all night by the gangway staff to keep the cold out, and a typical victim would be a jetty sentry plied with too much of the stuff.

codes   Each branch of the service has its own unique and discreet code, comprising a word and a group of numbers corresponding to message that can be sent between units. Submariners have the Dolphin code, the Fleet Air Arm the Falcon code, Mine Countermeasure ships the Lion code, and so on. Most messages are humorous, many disparaging and rude, and some downright obscene. Some examples:

dolphin 113   *Oh dear, the Staff are getting active again; which idiot gave the Admiral a shake?*

dolphin 174   *I don't know how we're going to cope without you - but we're certainly going to try!*

falcon 119   *Now that you've successfully screwed things up, I suggest you find a way of unscrewing them!*

There is of course a *Biblical Code* as well, and all good communications *yeomen have their digest of suitable biblical quotes, of which perhaps the most obvious is John Chapter 11, verse 35.

codswallop   Jack's term for a load of nonsense, another word that has come ashore to more general usage. It derives from one Hiram Codd who in 1875 successfully marketed bottled carbonated water, which remained drinkable for longer than the still water kept in casks. *Wallop* was and still is, of course, slang for beer. Hence Mr *Codd's wallop* was useless rubbish to a hardened beer drinker.

coffee boat   Sum of money contributed to by all those in the **coffee** (or tea) **boat** for the purchase of *makings.

coffin dreams (SM)   Occasional unpleasant nightmares expe rienced by nuclear submariners during long submerged patrols.

coil it, flake it, or cheese it   What to do with excess rope. *Coiling* was just that, tidy but not *tiddly. *Flaking* was prepar- ing it in lengths for paying out, but *cheesing* it was coiling it down flat from the centre outwards - all *tiddly.

coil one down   Defaecate, usually other than in the normal receptacle. See also *cheese.

Coke-bottle shoulders   An anatomical feature possessed by those individuals who are unwilling to take responsibility in any matter - after the rounded shape of the classic Coca-Cola bot- tle. See also *sloping shoulders.

cold fish   Efficient and zealous, but apparently unemotional officer.

cold move   Repositioning a warship in a dockyard or harbour without the use of her own engines.

cold shot (FAA)   Steam catapult failure during an aircraft *launch from a carrier; the machine usually failed to get air- borne and fell straight into the sea.

collar   Worn originally to prevent his pig-tail, so popular at one period, from soiling his jumper, and the three rows of white tape which frame his collar, are for pure decoration and have nothing to do with Nelson's three glorious victories.

collision mat   A triplet:
1. Enormous coir and fibre mat used to plug a hole in the hull in the event of a *graunch, secured by ropes fore and aft as well as vertically, and manned by Royal in the larger warships of old.
2. Jack's occasional description of a sanitary towel.
3. A hairy chest.

Colours   Two regular forms of usage:
1. Ceremonial morning hoisting of the ensign (at the ensign staff - aft) and the Union Flag (at the jackstaff - forward). Note that the UK national flag is only properly called a *Union Jack* when flown at the jackstaff of a HM ship. Colours are hauled down at true sunset, when the ceremony is called *Sunset, or at 2100 (if true sunset is later), when the ceremony is called *Evening*

Colours. At RN and RM shore establishments, only the white ensign is hoisted. When underway (ie. not secured to the shore or to the seabed), HM ships wear the white ensign only throughout 24 hours (but see *Dress Ship*). Also note: *nail one's Colours to the mast*, meaning, quite literally, that even if all your spars had been shot away, you were still prepared to fight. Hence today's meaning: even if general opinion is overwhelmingly against you, you are still prepared to stand your ground. Note that there is also a *Queen's Colour* presented by HM The Queen to the various naval commands, which may be paraded on specified occasions in the presence of Royalty.

2. (RM) Abbreviated term of address for a *Colour Sergeant*.

ALL THAT BITCHIN' ABOUT ONE MISERABLE BROKEN ARM.!!

IN NELSONS TIME THEY'D LOSE A LEG AN' STILL FALL IN FOR BOTH WATCHES!

—REPORT TO THE DENTAL SURGERY!

OFF YOU GO! LONG JOHN!

combined operations   An important WW2 branch of the service. Jackspeak for the abbreviation Combined Ops was *brownhatters and comic singers*. Also heard as *confused operations*.

come alongside To reach agreement with someone, especially during a discussion or argument. May also be used, aside from the obvious ship-handler's meaning, as an encouragement to someone having trouble understanding a concept during tuition or instruction: *'You don't think water discipline is necessary in the Arctic? Come alongside, my friend.'*

come ashore, Jack! (RM) Advice to cease telling over-embroidered salty sea stories; see also *swinging the lamp.

come-on (RM) Incident designed to lure Royal into an ambush or booby-trapped area in order to maximize his subsequent casualties.

come the acid Much used by superiors if they suspect that a subordinate is displaying superior knowledge, eg.: *'Don't you come the acid with me..'* Nicholas Monsarrat's classic *The Cruel Sea*, Part Two Chapter 3 describes this brilliantly.

comforts (SM) Not ladies in this case, but extra items such as fruit juice for supplementing Pusser's food rations for submarines proceeding on patrol.

comic Any newspaper or publication that cannot really be given any serious credibility.

comic cuts Jack's *Divisional documents and the written remarks contained therein; also an older nickname for Admiralty Intelligence reports! Note this succinct *red ink comment on one rating's comic cuts: *'a.m. idiot - p.m. gibbering idiot..'* Needless to say, this did not apply after the *Black Day.

Commanche bollocks Tinned tomatoes; see also *arrigones.

commander A quartet:
1. A derogatory name, like *Chopper* or to show a little contempt, as in Killick of the Grot: *'OK Stripey, you dish up while *skerse sweeps out..'* Stripey: *'OK, commander..'*
2. A large wooden mallet used when the topmast had to be struck when passing under a low bridge eg. battleships in the pre-war era had to do this to get under the Forth Bridge.
3. *Commander speaking!* - Followed a loud belch.
4. *Commander's doggie* - Junior seaman detailed to follow the commander around as a messenger.

Commando (RM) A quintet of usage:
1. Battalion-sized unit of Royal Marines. Royal has inherited this specialist forces role created in WW2. Currently there are 3

Units - 40, 42 and 45 *Cdos* - linked into a Brigade (3 *Cdo* Bde RM) along with *Commando* artillery, engineer, logistic and aviation assets; this formation is amphibious and also trained for Arctic operations. Enhanced by two Parachute Regiment battalions, it also did most of the fighting ashore in the Falklands during May and June 1982. See also *Cloggie for a note on NATO roles.

2. *Commando course* A punishing test of speed, agility, endurance and stamina undertaken by all officers and men who wish to serve in, or with the Corps. Success carries the right to wear the *green beret, along with a RN or regimental cap badge in the case of Jack and *Perce. The actual Commando tests and timings have not changed in any way since WW2, but the build-up training period is much shorter.

3. The *Commando Training Centre* - also known as *CTCRM* - is at *Lympstone, Devon.

4. *come and do* this - then go and do that!

5. *commando dagger* - Incorrect term for the WW2 Fairbairn-Sykes fighting knife, a distinctive double-edged stiletto, designed by Capts Fairbairn & Sykes, formerly of the Shanghai Police, manufactured by Wilkinson and issued to WW2 Commandos. One of the finest weapons ever derived for close combat in the hands of a trained man. Used on all *commando* unit badges, ties and flags, but now only used for presentation purposes.

commcen *Communications centre* - the modern version of the Wireless Office of old.

commencing cream A skin lubricant; see also *starters and *stoppers.

commission A pair:
1. Warrant conferred on a Royal Navy or Royal Marines Officer by the *Lord High Admiral.
2. The periods between refits when a warship is in active service, subsequently referred to as her *First Commission, Second Commission* and so on. Nowadays, ships remain in *continuous commission*, even during refits, unless going into reserve or possibly for a major reconstruction, until they are put up for disposal. Note that the opposite of *commission* in this sense is, traditionally, *pay off and not *de-commission*. The usual abbreviation was *commish*.

commissioned ballast (FAA) Pilot's label for an an *Observer.

Brownhatter

commissioned branch officer   Rank now obsolete. Until 1956 Chief POs in a technical branch could be promoted to officers, wearing a thin ring with a trade.

commissioned pie-thatcher   The Catering Officer.

commissioned frogman   A Clearance Diving Officer.

commissioning pennant   A long narrow *pennant with a St George's cross and white tail which is flown at the masthead of a ship day and night continuously until the ship *pays off. See also *paying-off pennant.

commit aviation (FAA)   The sin of enjoying your flying.

commit sideways   commit suicide.

common dog   Common sense, a quality sometimes lacking in university graduates of otherwise high intellect. See also *CDF, *jampot lid and *pickle jar.

companionway   Shipboard ladder; see also *accommodation ladder.

CQMS   Company Quartermaster Sergeant within a RM company. Derived from Troop Quartermaster Sergeant (TQMS) in the old Commando Troop organisation.

compartment   Jack's equivalent of an office *on board, except that the *bulkheads may be curved to fit inside a warship's hull, and there is neither floor nor ceiling, only a *deck and *deck-head!

complain   The block (of a rigging block and tackle) is said to be *complaining* if the centre sheave squeaks when it is in use.

compo (esp. RM)   *Composite* ration pack for troops ashore, of a legendary binding quality with regard to Royal's intestinal functions.

concrete cheeks   A condition produced by laughing so hard that your facial muscles seize up.

concrete parachute   The military equivalent of a nine bob note - a homosexual.

condensing snot   Snoring loudly; *percolating snot* is a similar and possible alternative.

confusion   Four examples:
1. He don't ruddy know if his arsehole's punched or bored.

2. I didn't know if I was on my arse or my elbows.
3. We didn't know what to do, shit, fart or spew, or buy a pair of shoes from slops.
4. I didn't know whether to suck back or blow through.

congenital liar   Either an Officer's Appointer, or a weather forecaster.

conning (the ship)   The business of directing a ship's steering, and nothing to do with confidence tricksters: *'Take the con.'* Or (FAA) : *'Con me back and over that other survivor in the water.'* Her Majesty's submarines have a *conning tower* for this purpose, which called a *sail* on the other side of the *Pond.

cook of the mess   One of two ratings detailed off to prepare the meals for the mess where canteen-messing was in force. Their turn of duty was for one week, during which they 'put up' the food to be cooked (or burned) in the galley; and washed up after meals. They were excused all other work in the forenoon.

copper-bottomed   Protective copper sheathing plates fitted to the wooden hulls of old; they reduced attack by the teredo worm so that the wood lasted longer and - because barnacle and weed growth was less - made the ship go faster. Hence the expression for something guaranteed to be worthwhile as having a **copper-bottomed** guarantee.

cordite jaunty   Chief gunner's mate.

Cordites   Standard nickname for any sporting team emanating from the old Whale Island Gunnery School in Portsmouth.

corkscrewing   The motion of a ship in heavy weather when the sea is on the bow, ie between *ahead and * abeam, which causes the ship both to *pitch and to *roll - very uncomfortable.

corn / corned dog   Tinned corned beef. A corned dog inspector is yet another label for a homosexual.

corporate signal   Someone from MOD HQ at Bath (normally a civilian). Someone paying a once a year visit to the ship, causing chaos* and disappearing. (Not to be seen again for at least another year) *shitting on you from a great height.

Corps Birthday   This *Corps memorable date, 28th October 1664, was when the Duke of York and Albany's Maritime Regiment of Foot was first raised. The Duke was then *Lord High Admiral of Charles II's Navy, and later became James II; his

Admiral's Regiment of fighting troops (who could also act as sailors) was the forerunner of today's Corps.

Corps commish (commission) (RM) Exact equivalent of the RN *Upper Yardman scheme; a bright Marine or Junior NCO can be selected for *Young Officer training and subsequently reach the highest ranks in the Corps. In the recent past, at least one *King's Badgeman has made it to Major General's rank, a unique and proud distinction.

Corps de Ballet (RM) Wonderful *sod's opera routine that is the especial party piece of the *Lympstone *Seniors. The Exeter pantomime performed after *Crimbo by these stalwarts (dressed in ballerina costume and boots) produces tens of thousands of pounds for charity each year.

Corps memorable date (RM) A number of days in the Corps' 380-plus years of history are specially marked in Unit Routine Orders, as well as by various parades and dinners. These are the anniversaries of the *Corps Birthday, *Bunker Hill, *Gibraltar, *Belle Isle, *Trafalgar, *Gallipoli, *Zeebrugge, *Normandy, *Walcheren and the Falkland Islands, and recruits passing through *Lympstone have to learn them by heart. Can also be used in mild sarcasm: *'I don't believe it - Bill's actually buying a round! Is this going down as a Corps memorable date?'*

C - 114

Corps-pissed (RM)   Adjective describing a Royal Marine obsessed with both Corps history and its current activities. The term is applied, almost in admiration, to serving and retired individuals alike. It has no real equivalent in the RN since *anchor-faced, a label which has similar overtones, can also imply inflexibility or lack of warmth. The Army's equivalent, which is exact, is *army-barmy*.

CorrO   Abbreviation of *Corres*pondence **O**fficer, an unpopular job, usually given to the most junior seaman officer in smaller ships which do not have a qualified *Secretary, and involving the opening and handling of official mail.

corticene   A proprietary linoleum that would be nice to get hold of today. Always coloured red.

cossif   The bit between the vagina and the anus, *cossif* it wasn't there, her insides would drop out.

costly farces   Coastal Forces of WW2; all gallant men.

cottage   Older slang term for a *messdeck, now only used in the phrase *Rose Cottage*.

cotton waste   Without which no Engineer Officer, Chief/ERA, Chief/Stoker was properly dressed and without which no ship would have run.

cough in your rompers   Break wind.

cough to coffin   Cheap cigarettes.

counterpane hurdling   Possibly Jack's favourite indoor activity (and Royal's as well!).

country pancake   A cowpat.

court martial   Judicial trial before a court of military officers.

covered wagon   Meat or fruit pie.

coyote   Especial version of a *gronk. See *wolverine for a more complete definition of this term.

cowboy's breakfast   bacon and beans.

coxswain / cox'n   Two usages to remember:
1. A Chief Petty Officer or Petty Officer (depending on the size of ship) from any branch who was trained in disciplinary techniques and borne in ships below cruiser size and submarines as the ship's most senior rating, responsible for discipline, steering

the ship in action and in confined waters, and, in submarines and small warships, *victualling. Nowadays, a member of the *Regulating Branch is borne in all surface ships for disciplinary duties. However, submarines still have *Cox'ns*, and the Regulating Petty Officer in small warships is still called the *Cox'n*. See also *Regulating Branch.

2.   The rating in charge of a ship's boat and responsible for its safety. The word's origins lie in the roots *cog* (a type of vessel) and *suen* or *swain* - husband, and hence also the skills of *ship husbandry*, a descriptive term still in wide usage today. Note also that the word *cox* is not a naval expression, and is only used to denote the person steering a racing rowing boat.

cow juice   Milk.

Cowes rig   Amusing quasi-Victorian *split rig of white trousers, winged collar and blue uniform jacket; used occasionally to enliven and also smarten up a daytime *RPC or *Wardroom function.

crabby   Dirty, filthy - perhaps derived from infestation with the *crab louse*. The term *crabby but happy* could be applied to an older ship.

Crabfats / Crabs / Crab Air   Original nickname for a member of the Royal Air Force following that Service's formation, on April 1st 1918, by an enforced marriage between the Royal Flying Corps and the *Royal Naval Air Service . The colour of RAF uniforms is supposed to have resulted from diversion of a huge but cancelled export order for the Tsar's Imperial Guard following the previous year's Revolution in Russia. This light-blue colour was identical to the greasy mercuric oxide jelly (or *crabfat*) which was widely issued at the time for the treatment of body lice - *crabs*. The descriptive term for the RAF as *Crabfats* is still widely used by senior Naval aviators, although now usually abbreviated in common usage: '*Splot, please ensure that our *tame Crab *puts in to grow a *full set.'   Or: 'What, Crab Air fly at weekends? You must be ruddy joking!' Note also the special application *Crimson Crabs. See Tugg at page G- 199.

crabfat grey   *Pussers' dark grey paint between the wars was so thick and sticky that it virtually had to be trowelled on by Jack when *painting ship. In this case it was the similar consistency of the paint to *crabfat (rather than its colour, as described in the preceding entry concerning the RAF) that remains synonymous with the old Warship grey rather than the light blueish grey now used.

crack A quintet of meanings:
1. Achievement: *'I cracked 3 hours for the marathon last weekend'*
2. To break someone mentally, as in *'You can't crack me, mate - I'm a rubber duck!'*
3. *cracked it* - solved the problem (not necessarily mathematical).
4. *crack on* - continue, usually at an increased speed - from the days of sail when setting more canvas would initially cause the sails to make a *cracking* noise as they filled. Also note the application *get cracking!*
5. *crack up* - 2 sub-definitions:
   - to suffer a mental breakdown
   - used as a past participle as a substitute for 'claimed' or 'made out', as in *'Free-fall parachuting ain't all it's cracked up to be.'*
6. *crack regiment* - Women's Royal Army Corps.

crag rat (RM)   A Mountain Leader - the specialist climbers of the Corps.

crappers   Drunk; *Harry Crappers* is a frequent form of usage.

crash barrier (FAA)   Strong nylon net suspended across the flight deck to catch and stop a fixed-wing aircraft that is unable to engage the arrester wires with its tailhook when *landing on; this evolution was termed a *barrier prang*. Crash barriers can still be *rigged at a number of military air bases to arrest aircraft which for some reason are unable to stop within the runway length.

crash draft   Sudden and totally unexpected appointment to a new ship or job, usually with very little notice to move.

crash / crash out (esp. RM)   Fall asleep, especially when *crashing one's swede* . See also *gonk and *zeds in this context, and note the charming *He's doing a bedding muster* as an alternative. To *crash out your smalls* means the same as to *dhobey your *keks!

crawl through   To have intercourse.

cream in (RM)   To collide with something, fall over while skiing (see also *yeti in this context) - or make a poor parachute landing.

cream-crackered (RM)   Rhyming slang for *knackered* , meaning very tired or exhausted.

creamer (FAA)   A really smooth landing, also a *greaser.

crease up   Double up with laughter at a funny sight or joke. See also *cheese down.

creased   Face showing signs of severe tiredness or great pain: '*Spraining my ankle on landing really creased me..*'

creep the reep   Visit Hamburg.

creek   A narrow inlet, usually within a natural harbour or river estuary which is therefore tidal and often dries out at low water. The Naval Hospitals at Haslar (Portsmouth) and Stonehouse (Plymouth) were built at the head of *creeks* of the same names (see *catch the boat up). Thus, given the poor standard of medical care in olden days, to be *up the creek* (with or without a paddle) was to be in a precarious situation.

crest   Emblem of a ship, submarine, naval air squadron and shore establishment. Together with the motto, it has to be approved by the College of Arms.

Crimbo   Christmas. *Crimbo routine* at sea is very interesting; among many other traditional customs observed at sea, the most junior rating embarked borrows *the Jaunty's uniform and then does formal *Rounds of the ship!

crimp   A variety of applications:
1. Old term for an agent commissioned to find the crew for a ship, often by drugging and kidnapping.
2. Use a special compression tool on a piece of detonator fuze.
3. To *crimp off a length* is to defaecate.
4. (FAA) To *crimp out* is to pass into a deep sleep, whether from booze or fatigue:'*Don't bother talking to him - he's crimped out ..*'

Crimson *Crabs (FAA)   The RAF *Red Arrows* formation aerobatic team.

crippler   An unexpected set-back that must be coped with. (RM) Unexpected task given at short notice, particularly to a student on a command course as a means of assessing his ability to cope with the unexpected - he is *slipped a crippler*. To slip a crippler to a lady implies that she is going to get more than she bargained for during a *bunk up with Jack or Royal.

critical (SM)   Term used to describe a nuclear boat's reactor after it has been started up by the process of pulling the control rods.

crocadillapig   Any fierce-looking animal, of whatever size or type. If the beast is especially large and evil, the description may be enhanced by the adjectives *gynoferous or *gynormous. There some other variants, including the lesser blotched hipporhinoflumboduck, and the rhinosnorarse!

cronnick   Derived from the word *chronic*, and referring to anything unpleasant or objectionable.

cross his bow Annoy or insult someone more senior, usually unintentionally; it is both custom and good manners for a junior to give way to a more senior officer in command (of a ship), or to seek his approval to pass ahead, thereby avoiding the slight possibility of collision (in the nautical sense) which could result from *crossing his bow*.

cross the bar Pass away, as a result of leaving life's harbour.

Crossing the Line Traditional, but completely unofficial ceremony enacted whenever a warship crosses the Equator. His Oceanic Majesty, King Neptune, together with his Court, come on board to initiate novices into the Brotherhood of the Sea. Splendid fun, with no distinction made between officers and men in the normal sense as they are lathered, mock-shaved with a huge cut-throat razor, and then thrown to the Bears by being tipped backwards into a tank full of water.

cross-dressing A Writer in coveralls.

cross-hatched (FAA) Drunk, confused, or incapable. Derived from the magnetic indicators of the *Bucc instrument panel which became *cross-hatched* when the instrument went off-line, or failed.

crossomicle To cross over two lines or to misunderstand or to get things arseway, as in: *'You've got all that crossomicle..'*

crow's nest Senior female rating's accommodation.

crows in working dress seagulls.

crozzy A crossword puzzle.

crumb brush (SM**)** Officer's steward.

crumble *'There's been a bit of a *crumble..'* means that someone has failed to do his or her job properly.

crumpet A particularly delicious-looking bit of *clacker: *'I'd crawl a mile over broken glass just to sniff the exhaust of the van that takes that bit of crumpet's knickers to the laundry..'*

crunchy pasty (RM) Tortoise.

crusher A member of the *Regulating Branch (equivalent to the ship's police); originally he was the ship's corporal, an assistant to the *Master-at-Arms whose job was to seek out miscreants; hence he went around in soft-soled shoes and the only way he could be heard coming was by the *crushing of the *cookies* under his feet. Tugg has visualized this at page H -212.

Canteen Cowboy

crushers cramp   Hand held behind the back of a regulating PO's back, half-open to receive bribes (*Fear God and tip the crusher*).

crutch rot   Used to refer to a skin rash caused by incomplete rinsing of clothes. In these days of washing machines, if not civvy laundries, the newer description of *crutch rot* as a fungal skin infection has now taken over.

crystal cracker   Older nickname for a *Pinky, or a radio technician.

CSB   Abbreviation of **Courage Sparkling Bitter**, a high-gravity and powerful keg beer especially brewed by Messrs. John Courage for Her Majesty's sea-going ships. Anyone suffering from the effects of over- indulgence in this excellent ale is said to have *CSB rash*.

cuddy   A cabin situated aft for use either by the Captain or an important passenger. A *cuddy rat* is an officer who spends too much time *brown-nosing there.

cuds (RM)   General term for the countryside, ie. the place where cows chew their cuds. May also be derived from the Hindi word *khud* for a valley. Can also be used to describe the area in which an operation is to be mounted or an exercise held.

cuff it / cuffmanship   Playing things as they come.

Culdrose   HMS SEAHAWK , the Royal Naval Air Station situated south of Helston in Cornwall. It is the biggest helicopter base in Europe, and parents the squadrons and flights of over 100 aircraft of various types. With over 2000 men and women on strength it is, in effect, the largest ship in the Royal Navy. The airfield's elevated position on the Lizard peninsula can lead to some very peculiar weather conditions varying from a thick and clinging *clamp to a forty mph fog; also known as *Cul-D*.

cummerbund   Wide waist band worn as an alternative to a waistcoat under formal evening wear, and with *Red Sea rig; the *pusser's issue cummerbund is black, but most ships, submarines and naval air squadrons have their own cummerbund which features the individual unit's *crest. Can sometimes also (incorrectly) be seen spelled as *kamarband*.

cumshaw   Pidgin Chinese word for *Thank you!* In effect, it is an unofficial payment for services rendered and made in the expectation that such service will continue, but to call it bribery would, in general, be putting it too strongly.   Adopted by Jack for anything that comes under the category of something acquired for nothing; see also *gizzit.

cumulo-granite (FAA)   When conventional cloud comes down to the level of mountain tops, this feature should be avoided by aviators because it can really *spoil your whole day if flown into. Note also the term *cumulo-nasty* for a thundercloud.

cupid's measles   Pubic lice.

cushion creep (FAA)   The process of using the extra lift that is generated by a helicopter's rotor downwash close to the ground, in order to transition an overweight aircraft (or one at high altitude) into forward flight.

cushy number   Rather envious description of a comfortable appointment or job.

custard bosun   The Chief Cook - see page H - 225.

cut and run   Another old navy expression that has come ashore. It derives from the process of furling the sails on their yards and *stopping them there with light rope yarns; these gaskets could be *cut* with a knife so that the sails fell, drew almost immediately, and the ship would begin to move (*run*). In extreme emergency, the anchor cable could also be cut.

cut his painter   Refers to death, since the painter here is a personal one and describes a sailor's link with life.

cut of his jib   The shape of a person's nose in older times, since an efficient lookout could tell the nationality of another vessel purely by recognising the shape of its jibsail. This has now been adapted to comment on a person's style: *'He's a bit prickly sometimes, but overall I rather like the cut of his jib..'*

cuts very little ice   A wooden ship can make very little progress in pack ice, hence the modern usage to describe something that has made almost no impression at all on the speaker.

cutlass   Short, heavy and curved naval sword used by Jack in hand-to-hand combat when boarding an enemy ship. Supposedly last used in anger when sailors from HMS COSSACK boarded the German prison ship *Altmark* in Jossing Fjord, Norway in 1940. *Cutlass drill* was sometimes presented as a visually attractive item at the Royal Tournament.

cutter   Next size up from a *whaler; it had light oars and a lugsail with a transom (flat) stern. *Cutters* could also be towed by a pinnace if lots of *libertymen had to be ferried ashore. Interestingly, all US Coastguard ships are called cutters, even a big 14,000 ton ice breaker.

CW List   Commissions and Warrants List; older equivalent of what has become the *OAL, or Officers' Appointments List. Was also used for those non-commissioned ratings who have been selected for officer training as Senior *Upper Yardies.

DELTA

125 - 152

D   Formerly, a Direction Officer, responsible for anti-air warfare, aircraft direction (control) and airspace management in aircraft carriers and other suitably-equipped warships. Now replaced by the *PWO(A).

D2 (SM)   A D2 was a comprehensive planned maintenance sheet for the engine room department, and also used ashore to indicate a properly detailed job, as in: *'A quick dickie run on the carpet, fire a couple of air shots and then upstairs for the full D2..'*

dabber / dabtoe   Denigratory term for a seaman rating (see also *AB) used by Royal, or by Jack when in a Specialist branch. Sometimes abbreviated to Dabs and see page J -243 for Tugg's lovely visualization.

Daddy S   Affectionately informal nickname for the Supply Officer of a big ship or shore establishment who is of Commander's rank; this official title is more usually abbreviated to *Commander S*.

Daddy's yacht   An ignorant, slow-witted or otherwise useless sailor might well be addressed: *'Where the 'ell d'yew think yew are - yer bleedin' Daddy's yacht?'*

Dagenham Dave   A rating who is a bit unstable or crazy - in fact, he's just the other side of Barking! For those unfamiliar with what has been termed (Thames) *estuary slang,* Barking is a place in Essex, and the word is also a component of the term *barking mad!*

dagger ()   An officer (or Warrant Officer Gunner) who has specialized in Aeronautical Engineering, Communication, (aircraft) Direction, Gunnery, Marine Engineering, Navigation or Torpedo and Antisubmarine Warfare, and then passed the Advanced course in that subject:'*He's a dagger N..*' The term is derived from the way that these facts are recorded in the *Navy List, with a typeface symbol very like a dagger - but not to be confused with the fighting knife insignia used by the *Commandos. Instructor Officers with Honours degrees were also *Dagger Schoolies.*

Damage Control The professional art of containing fire or water ingress to a ship in order to prevent its loss. Jack also uses the term to describe his *pash in the process of applying her make-up! **Damage** was the affectionate nickname for the DCO.

damager Manager, as in *NAAFI damager.

My Dearest Jessica.
Sorry to hear about your teaching job being put at risk by government cuts...

I know how you must be feeling because it's the same with us ...

...and my Share of the ink is finished.
Love Jack
x

dance of the flaming arseholes A dangerous dockyard canteen entertainment when as a forfeit, Jack - clenching an ignited sheet of paper in his buttocks - would run the gauntlet as pints of beer were thrown at him to put the fire out.

dandy funk Obsolete name for a kind of pudding or cake made of crushed ship's biscuits, mixed with molasses and water, then baked. (RN).

dangle the Dunlops (FAA) Lower an aircraft's undercarriage prior to landing.

dank When used in the description of someone, this adjective pinpoints a rather anti-social and characterless individual. *Dank* *hand is a regular application, or *dank runner* when referring to *runs-ashore.

daps *Pusser's white plimsoles, or more recently - training shoes. Someone in a real hurry on official business is said to be

D - 126

moving just like *diarrhoea with daps on* - a nice alliteration, but rather unlikely.

Darby   Traditional nickname associated with the surname Allen.

dark and dirty   Rum and Coca-Cola; see also *light and dirty.

darken ship
1. The defensive process of ensuring that no light whatsoever emanates from a ship at night.
2. Advice to a seated female officer or rating wearing a skirt, to pull the hem down a bit and preserve her modesty.

Dart   A *Dart* was an officer who started as a 13 year old at the RN College, Dartmouth. They were differentiated from other main method which was *Special Entry* at 17, sometimes called *Direct Entry* or *Public School Entry*.

Dartmouth   Location of the *Britannia Royal Naval College* in Devon, with the College often referred to simply by this name. Jack would probably describe *Dartmouth* to you as the place where young Naval Officers are taught half-a-dozen different ways to say to their men:*'If you want me - I'll be in the *Wardroom..'*

dash across the prairie   A matelot's way of describing the male movements in a vigorous act of sexual intercourse. Taken from the cowboy films that were an important component of cinema shows at sea.

DASO'd (SM)   The term comes from *Demonstration and Shakedown Operations*. Only included as it is a big carrot in the *bomber world, because of travelling to the East Coast of the USA in order to fire a practice missile or two down the Atlantic range. It's also normally the only run-ashore that SSBN crews will get in a commission. The boat and individual members of the crew then become *DASO'd*, which is a big *tick in the box for future drafting and appointing.

DAUNTLESS   The former *WRNS training establishment near Reading. A *draft chit to this particular *stone frigate was Jack's pipedream until it closed in 1980; there is now a *DAUNTLESS* block at HMS *RALEIGH. The name will return with the new *Type 45 warships.

Davy Jones' locker   The *duffy* (ghost) of *Jonah*, corrupted down the ages to mean the grave of the sea; note also *Old Grey Widow Maker.

dawn strike   *Assault with a friendly weapon on waking up early; see also *morning glory.

dayman   Rating employed on duties requiring normal working hours, eg. a Writer, and therefore excused *watches; also used for someone in a ship which is day running from port. See *bag mealie in this respect.

days of famine (SM)   Yet another scourge that the diesel driven submariner had to endure. When playing serious war games, the *old man was always concerned to *keep the box up* (keep the battery at as high a charge as possible). Some days he would declare a *day of famine*, ie. no cooking, as in: *'Do you want the good news? There's no bread left, so it's hard tack and bungo..'* (a corruption of *bunghole* - cheese). Note that the concept of *bad news* was not good for morale, so any news, and it didn't matter how bad it was, was always presented as good news!

DCI   Defence Council Instruction ; these may be single service, or applied to all three services. A DCI(RN) is the successor to *AFOs.

DD   Entry in the ship's *muster book of older times to indicate that a sailor had died on board and been Discharged Dead. Jack might say, with typical grim humour: *'E's gone *outside - DD..'*

Dead End Kids (FAA)   Young wartime RN Volunteer Reserve Sub-Lieutenants not considered for promotion to Lieutenant, ie. juniors without a future, but still employed in (dangerous) operational flying.

dead horse   See entry for *flog a dead horse.

deadlight   Hinged metal flap which can be lowered and clamped over a *scuttle *sidelight in order to *darken ship. See also *spoof.

dead marine (RM)   An empty wine bottle; the Duke of Clarence is supposed to have extricated himself nicely from possible offence to his hosts at a dinner party by suggesting that, just like a Marine: *'..that bottle has done his duty once and is now ready to do it again..'*

dead steam   Water!

death   *'You look like death warmed up..'* might be a statement to someone who has a bad hangover. Another greeting in a sim-

Defaulters

ilar situation might be: *'Oh death, where is thy sting?'* After a long period of action stations and watchkeeping, this word might also be heard in: *'Roll on death, and let's get some bloody sleep..'*

Death Slide (RM)   Laconic nickname for the aerial ropeway at *Lympstone down which all aspirants to a *green beret must descend.

decimal bosun   An Instructor Officer; see *schoolie for the complete list.

Deck Landings (FAA)   A *Wardroom game sometimes played after mess dinners in a carrier. A long table surface is slicked with water or ice to simulate the wet deck, and then many napkins and elastic braces are tied together to make an *arrester cable*. Participants pretend to be aircraft that are landing on, by running at, and then hurling themselves headlong at this table top - and catching the arrester gear with their toes. A higher sea state can be simulated by moving the table legs up and down. Then, when the lights are turned out, night flying begins!

deck / deckhead   The former is the equivalent of a floor, the latter of a ceiling. A *deckhead inspection* or *survey* is carried out in the horizontal position from one's bunk. See also *Egyptian PT, *Mulley and *zeds for some alternatives.

Deeks   The usual pronounciation of the acronym *DQs.

deep down, you know it makes sense (SM)   'Nuff said!.

deep one   Secretive or reserved individual, difficult to predict or divine: *'He's a really deep one, he is..'*

deep sea steak   Kipper.

deep sea tot   Short measure - caused by the excessive rolling of a warship just as a *tot was being drawn.

deep six   This refers to the Lead Line, which was the only way of measuring the depth of water before the advent of echosounders. The hand lead line was 25 fathoms long (1 fathom = 6 feet) and was marked (in a variety of unique ways) at 2, 3, 5, 7, 10, 13, 15, 17 and 20 fathoms. The leadsman was stationed in the *chains and cast the leadline forward so that the lead would hit the bottom as the line became vertical. He reported depth as *by the mark* or *by the deep* if he had to interpolate between marks. Nowadays, to invite someone to give something the *deep six* is like suggesting that it be subjected to a *float test - *six* perhaps being chosen as 6 fathoms (36 feet), which is greater than the draught of most warships.

Deeps   *General Service ready-use nickname for a submariner. Often used for the very first time when a *draft chit for SM training comes in:*'Tell Deeps Smith to come to my office..'* Can also be used for the Diving Officer, as he will have gone to at least 130 feet deep in training.

Defaulters   A formal muster and parade for hearing of charges of indiscipline; also the collective name for a group under punishment (mispronounced as *undernourishment*!). See page D -129.

defence watches   The second degree of readiness in a warship, with 50% of the ship's company *closed up and 50% *turned in although fully-clothed and ready to *close up at *Action Stations at short notice. Although a very tiring routine, it can, with imaginative management, be maintained for long periods, and is essential if the ship is to be kept at a high state of readiness for action.

definite maybe (RM)   Classic piece of non-commitment:*'Yes, I can give you a definite maybe on that one..'*   See also *positive perhaps.

demo (RM)   Abbreviation of *demonstration* as in:*'Just had a demo on that new S10 respirator - great bit of *kit, I reckon..'*

DEMS rating   Wartime sailor sent to a MN vessel to man its defensive armament - *Defensively Equipped Merchant Ship*.

Detachment   The ship's embarked Royal Marines personnel; they live in an area of messdeck that is always called the *barracks.

detailed off (RM)   Told to go and do something; see also *boned off and *jobbed.

Devil and the deep blue sea / Devil to pay   Both expressions have a naval origin, although the locations of the *Devil* appear to be slightly different!   In the first instance it was the seam between deck and hull, meaning that there was only the thickness of the ship's hull planking between the *Devil and the deep blue sea.* The other Devil was the long plank running from stem to stern and immediately adjacent to the keel. The caulkers who had to keep this seam waterproof by *paying it* with oakum (hemp fibres unpicked from condemned rope) and then sealing with hot pitch (tar) found the procedure very difficult, since this was the wettest and most inaccessible hull area of a careened vessel. The full original expression (which has now come ashore in a slightly different sense - to mean serious trouble) is the *Devil to *pay, and no pitch hot.*

devil dodger   A Naval padre; see *amen wallah for a complete listing.

Devil's islands   Scapa Flow.

DFs   *Duty Frees* - cigarettes supplied by the *Pusser. Note also *blue liners.

dhobey   Original Hindi word now adopted for the business of washing clothes; may also be spelt as *dhobi* or *dhoby* in many variants.

dhobey crusher   A rather fiendish *Chogey laundry machine on board HM Ships which is apparently designed to rip the buttons off Jack's shirts and then fire them through his socks!

dhobey dust   Washing powder.

dhobey hitch   Any *Wafu's knot which slips undone when it becomes wet; note also the *stoker's dhobey hitch,* which is any totally unrecognisable knot.

dhobey itch   Skin rash from incomplete rinsing of clothes; see also * crutch rot.

dhobey palace   Laundromat / washeteria.

dhobey wallah   Laundryman.

diamond piece   The central, crucial and strategic component of a lady's knickers.

dibs   Money, from a long-distant Dockyard Incentive Bonus Scheme of the 60's.

Dick Doc   Nickname for the most junior of three Medical Officers appointed to the old aircraft carriers; to a certain extent descriptive of his duties, because there was *Big Doc*, *Little Doc*, and *Dick Doc*.

dicked   To be beaten comprehensively, especially in a sporting encounter. Being **rubber dicked* implies that this *dicking* was achieved by unfair or illegal means; an **eight piece dicking* is the highest level of defeat possible at **Uckers*.

dickey   An interesting, multipurpose word:
1. Weak or damaged: *'His heart's a bit dickey..'*
2. A (false) white shirt, laced at the sides, but open at the back for wear in tropical climates is a *dickey front*.
3. *dickey bow*   A bow tie, usually one that is made-up commercially.
4. *second dickey* - the deputy leader (from *secon di/c*).
5. *dickey seat* - occasional seating arrangement in a vehicle or boat.
6. *dickey run* - a trial run.
7. In a **Chatham ship, a *dickey* was a donkey or horse.

dickhead   Idiot.

diesel deafness (SMD)   An affliction suffered by the engine room branch, especially when ordered to turn to.

diesel dinosaur   Conventional submariner on a nuclear boat, whatever his age!

diesel-electric drainpipe   A conventional (diesel-powered) submarine.

dig out   Work hard or with great enthusiasm to achieve an aim: *'We wuz diggin' out blind to finish the job..'* Can also be used as an invitation to help oneself: *'Need a **wet of coffee? Dig out, mate..'* See also **fill your boots in this latter respect.

digit   The finger, paraphrased as *Extractum digitum!* for: *'Get your bloody finger out!'* as an exhortation to get moving. The FAA in WW2 also had *De-digitate!* with exactly the same meaning.

Dilbert Dunker   An imported term from the US Navy that was sampled by FAA pilots trained to fly there. The *Dilbert*

Dunker   consisted of the cockpit of an aircraft, into which a student was strapped, and then shot down a ramp into the water to simulate a ditching. Now based at *Yeovilton, the rotating helicopter cabin of its modern successor is simply called the *Dunker.

dim   Not very bright, hence:*'He's as dim as a NAAFI candle / Toc H lamp..'*

Ding dong!   *'I don't believe it!'*

Dinger   Nickname for the surname Bell.

dingleberries   Prolapsed haemorrhoids (piles).

dining in / out   The tradition of inviting a new Commanding Officer or *HOD to *dine in* with the *Wardroom (or RM Officer's Mess) for the first time in his or her appointment. Other officers may be *dined out* at the same function, as guests of the Mess; all members of the Mess are supposed to attend a *Dining-In Night*.

Dink / Dinky Dai   Jack's generic nickname for an Australian, presumably to do with the words *dinkum* and *G'day*!

dip   Multipurpose word with several distinct meanings:
1. Fail an examination or test:*'I dipped on the pass-out run..'*
2. Lose a rate or rank: *'She dipped her *killick's..'* Or:*'He's been dipped down to Corporal again..'*

3. To *dip in* is to strike lucky: *'He's always dippin' in, the jammy git..'*
4. Lose out, or not receive a fair share: *'I'm always dipping out..'* See also *plums.
5. Dive. *Monthly dippers* are the regular dives made by qualified personnel in order to remain current for pay; *dip money* is an item paid as a special supplement for dangerous or experimental diving. See also *backy dips.
6. *Dip Boss* (FAA) is a term used by helicopters hunting submarines, and refers to the on-scene tactical commander of the *dip gang* who could be a young *Sea King or *Merlin *looker. Note also that the aircraft involved in this hunt will, at various stages, be *in the dip* - hovering with their sonar equipment lowered into the water.
7. To *dip one's wick* is to engage in sexual intercourse.
8. *Dipping the ensign* is a warship's method of returning a salute.
9. A signal flag which is *at the dip* is just below *close-up, and means that it is ready to be executed. Note that, in contrast, *at the *full* indicates that it is to be executed immediately. Thus, if an order is to be carried out smartly, after giving it one may add: *'..and that's at the full!'*
10. *dip rod* or *dip stick* for measuring a tank's liquid contents, the latter term also an insult when applied to a person.

Dipsu Gapsu (SM)   A Mark 27 torpedo just before it leaves the tube is set to run at depth by DIPSU, the hydroplane setting unit, and its course by the gyro angle / rudder setting unit or GAPSU. When coming off shore and trying to walk a straight line, if one staggered a bit or if something didn't travel along a straight course, it would be: *'Whoops! A little bit of Dipsu Gapsu there..'*

dirk   A short sword (about half the length of the present officer's sword), formerly carried by midshipmen on ceremonial occasions. Nowadays, a *pusser's dirk* is a seaman's clasp knife, comprising knife and *marline spike, and issued to all RN personnel on joining. This is a device of great versatility because, as Jack himself would point out, it has to be capable of doing everything from splitting rock to spreading butter!

dirty dive / dirty dash (FAA)   Flying very low (and possibly illegally) beneath low cloud or bad weather in order to make the objective.

dirty windows (a pair of)   Older RM term for two black eyes.

discharge   There is a variety of ways in which Jack, Jenny or Royal can leave the service, other than *in the normal course* (ie. at the end of his or her *engagement). The most severe of these is *dismissal*, which is a punishment awarded by *Court Martial and usually accompanied by a spell of imprisonment (see *DQs). Then there are the various discharges, viz:

1. *Discharge SNLR* (for *Services No Longer Required*). Not a punishment, but an administrative measure taken usually as a result of a series of disciplinary offences which, while not amounting to grounds for dismissal, are such that the continued retention of that person is not in the interest of the service. Very rarely used, because of the effect it is likely to have on the person's future employability in *civvy street. See also *Queen's bad bargain.

2. *Discharge Shore*   Again, an administrative measure taken as much in the interest of the person as in that of the Service. While this might be for continuous minor indiscipline, it is just as likely to be for medical, temperamental or possibly psychological reasons, such as chronic seasickness, alcoholism, financial irresponsibility or, in the case of very young people in their first 2 years of service, unhappiness. The process is designed to ensure that, as far as possible, it should have no effect on the person's future employment prospects.

3.   *Discharge by purchase* is now called *Premature Voluntary Release* but because Jack, Jenny and Royal can usually nowadays submit 18 months' notice to leave the service anyway, it is seldom used.

See also *DD* as a separate entry above.

dischuffed   The direct opposite of *chuffed. Someone who is *mightily dischuffed* is rather angry and disillusioned; see also the term *gruntled.

dismissed his / her ship   *Court-martial sentence on an officer or a senior rate who is tried and found guilty, but not actually thrown out of the Service. He or she is then put on half-pay while awaiting a new ship or appointment.

dist   A basic abbreviation for the word *distribution* which in turn can be used as a verb as well as a noun: *'Didn't you get the letter I disted on that subject? You were definitely on the Dist (list)..'*

DISTEX   A *Disaster Control Exercise*, as practised for near-real during *Operational Sea Training (formerly *work-up).

distinction cloth   Coloured bands interleaved between the gold lacing of an officer's uniform sleeve. The older colours of white (Supply and Secretariat), green (Electrical) and purple (Marine Engineering) have been retained in the Merchant Navy. The blue of *Schoolies has disappeared totally. In the RN, only *blood red (Medical), dark red (Dental) and salmon-pink (Medical Services) are still in current usage, although the Royal Naval Corps of Constructors, when in uniform, sport a silver-grey colour, and the RN Supply and Transport Service have dark green.

dit   Any written (or spoken) account of an incident or event in a sailor's life. A *dit spinner* is a good story-teller, especially if the **dits** are a bit exaggerated. See also *electric dit.

Ditch   The English Channel, as opposed to the *Pond.

ditch   A trio of applications:
1. (FAA) Land an aircraft in the sea.
2. Discard something (eg. *gash) over the side.
3. Get rid of something (or someone) ashore: '*She ditched him just before *Crimbo..'*

ditty box   A lockable wooden container, often elaborately carved or embellished, in which a sailor kept his most prized or unusual possessions. See Tugg's cartoon on page J - 248. This item was originally issued as a *commodity* box for toilet gear etc., but then replaced around WW2 by a small brown suitcase, which is no longer issued. The modern equivalent is a *mess-deck locker which, thank goodness, may now contain a *ditty box*. HMS *RALEIGH's Daily Orders, referred to in the Preface, has a section called *The Ditty Box* which attempts, right from the start, to introduce a new generation of Jack to the delights of *JACKSPEAK*!

diversion kit (FAA)   Toothbrush, credit card, clean underpants, a small amount of folding money and a *franger - carried at all times in a flying suit pocket.

Diving Stations (SM)   The state adopted prior to leaving surface; see also '*Open up for diving!'*

Divisional system   Personnel management system whereby the sum total of Jack's and Jenny's overall well-being, welfare, education and advancement is supervised and recorded by a *Divisional Officer* or *DO*; they report to *HoDs who, in turn, are responsible to the Captain for these matters. A good DO is very much at ease with his / her people, able to talk with them on a wide variety of subjects, and always accessible to them as a source of personal advice, help - and encouragement. It was devised and introduced in the mid-18th century in an attempt to improve the appalling conditions that then existed. Whilst it has evolved over the past 250 years, the basic principles have remained unchanged. Any serious outbreak of indiscipline over the years has usually been traced back to a breakdown in the *Divisonal System*. Today, in the era of *Human Resource Management* and *Investing in People*, new *wrigglestuff terms for a much older and proven way of doing things, it remains a shining example of good personnel administration. See also *set of papers.

Divisions   A formal parade held on special occasions, ranging from *Church Divisions* (every Sunday) all the way up to *Lord High Admiral's Divisions* held at *Dartmouth in the presence of Her Majesty The Queen (or her representative).

divvy   A *dividend* or share; to *divvy up* means to pay up, or share out the spoils.

dixie   Nickname for any large mess tin (esp. RM) or cooking pot, but note also the *scab-lifter's special usage to describe an inflamed *appendix* prior to its removal in a *Boneyard.

do the honours   Pour out the wine for your neighbour while seated at table.

Doc   Traditional nickname for the Medical Branch *killick carried in frigate-sized warships, as distinct from the *Quack embarked for long deployments - or in wartime.

docket   Naval name for a file cover and its contents, which together make up a *pack.

dockey / docky   Shortened version of *dockyard matey.

dockyard goldfish   An alternative name for a *brown trout.

dockyard jellyfish / oyster   A floating *green grolly that has been *flobbed up by a bronchitic *docky, or someone with a productive cough.

dockyard matey   Traditional nickname for industrial personnel working in the (now privatized) HM Dockyards: '*How many dockyard mateys work in Devonport? I should think about fifty per cent of them..*'

dockyard Olympics The old process of refitting a warship whereby all the tradesmen lined up at the start of the day and then raced off to various places inside the ship. The first one to reach an area fitted his pipe, wire, duct or whatever - thus leading to a totally unco-ordinated jumble and a *snake's honeymoon! At the other extreme was the *dockyard shuffle* describing a *dockyard matey*'s speed of progress when detailed to do a job close to knocking-off time.

dockyard omelette / pizza The results of a *Technicolour yawn lying on the road; *pavement pizza* is a variant of this theme.

dockyard runaround Common practice of being referred from one office to another in an attempt to find the person, authority or information that you really want.

dockyard tortoise A Cornish pasty.

docs Abbreviation of *documents*, referring to a rating's *service documents*, held on board a ship either in the *UPO or with the DO (see *Divisional system).

Doctor Fog (FAA) Met man; see also *Professor Fog, *weather guesser and *congenital liar.

doddle Something really easy.

dodge Pompey A very old and time-honoured expression meaning to avoid duties, a draft or other trouble in the Portsmouth Command. Hence a *dodge* is a crafty scheme to evade a job of work.

Dodger Traditional nickname for someone called Long.

dodger   Two forms of usage:
1. Canvas or fabric weather screen on an exposed part of the ship.
2. A messdeck cleaner or sweeper is the *messdeck dodger*; note that Royal's term for this function ashore is *block sweeps.

dodges and wheezes   Ways of making life a little easier while still carrying out the allotted task; see also *wrinkles.

dodgy deacon   Vicar or cleric with homosexual tendencies; *pulpit poofter and *raving rev are recognised alternative forms.

dog   Diarrhoea and vomiting, especially when associated with a particular place, eg. *Malta Dog; see also *bite!

dog and basket (RM)   Nickname for the lion and crown beret badge of Royal Marines Officers and *Warrant Officers.

dog days   Popular name for the hottest part of the year in June and July - it is the time when Sirius the *dog star* rises and sets with the sun.

dog end   Cigarette butt; see also *doofer.

dog fat   Common sense, as in *CDF.

dog robbers   A RN officer's *shore *rig for casual or relaxed occasions.   Originally described as a really incongruous, loud check sports jacket, worn by the type of person who would prowl around smart neigbourhoods with the intention of stealing pedigree dogs for resale or research! Now used for a casual jacket and slacks, with a tie/cravat or polo-neck sweater, and generally a bit smarter than either *scruff rig or *rat-catcher's rig.

dog-shit day (FAA)   Poor visibility in low scudding cloud and rain.

dog watches   Two (short) two-hour periods, inserted in the ship's routine to equalize the duty *roster.   To say that someone has only been in *half a dog watch* implies that he or she has only been in the Navy for a comparatively short time.   Probably derived from *dodge watches* since they were incomplete in one sense; other sources suggest that these were normal watches that had become *cur-tailed*! *The dogs* refers to *both* dog watches together. *Dogs* can also be the watertight clips on a hatch cover or bulkhead door.

Dogger Bank dragoons   Jack's nickname for RM *Commandos during WW2; now more commonly heard as the *Green Death.

doggie   Junior officer, usually under training, appointed as assistant to a senior Executive Officer or the Captain: *'I was *Wings' doggie for that first month - and a dog's life it was too..'* See also *gofer. Note also (faithful) *doggie* as a destroyer following astern of a carrier in order to pick up any aircraft which fail to aviate on *launching.

doggo (esp. RM)   Ugly, when referring to the opposite sex, and probably abbreviated from *doghouse* or *dog-like*. Can also be used to describe the process of being still and silent: *'We just lay doggo in the stream until the Argies got bored and cold - and stood up. Then Jumper Collins followed them back through their minefield and marked the route..'* In the MCM world, the term *doggo* denotes the embarrassing situation of two MCMVs locked stern-to-stern with a sweep wire stretched between them, when matters go awry during conventional minesweeping. Derived here from the similarity of this position with mating dogs.

doing things around the edges   Older term implying peripheral involvement without any real contribution.

doldrums   An area straddling the Equator of light winds, oppressive heat and high humidity; sailing ships could be stuck in the *doldrums* for days on end, experiencing thoroughly unpleasant conditions. Hence to be *in the doldrums* - to be in low spirits and/or very short-tempered.

dollar bosun   Warrant Writer responsible for pay accounts (RN)

dollar pick-up   Older *Singers term for a cheap taxi or *fast black.

Dolly   Traditional nickname for the surname Gray or Grey.

Dolphin (SM)   A quartet:
1. *HMS DOLPHIN* This used to be the traditional home of the submarine service at Gosport, across the harbour from Portsmouth, and formerly the Headquarters of Flag Officer Submarines (FOSM). Now FOSM has moved to Northwood, and the Defence Medical Services have taken over.
2. *Dolphins* - The gilt uniform brooch awarded to all ranks who have completed submarine training and passed the qualifying Boards; they are worn throughout a man's career in the Navy. No women have this distinction. Those associated with the Submarine Service ashore and awarded *honorary Dolphins* (not worn on uniform) may be required to *drink for their Dolphins* in

THAT MAN THERE! REPORT TO ME!

Chief GI

the Chief's Mess or Wardroom. The brooch is placed in the bottom of a glass and covered with a mixture of spirits that must be *yam-senged until the Dolphins are trapped in the recipient's teeth! Tugg applies his special sense of humour at L- 265.

3. *dolphin(s)* - a large wooden pile or group of piles serving either as mooring points or as navigational beacons in harbour.

4. *the Dolphin code* - see *Codes.

donk (Abbreviation of *donkey) Any petrol or diesel engine. The term has been widely adopted in the aviation world: *'When the gearbox failed and both donks stopped, it suddenly became apparent that we were rather poorly placed..'* Or: *'The Heron aircraft has four piston donks bolted to its wings..'*

donk shop (SM) Engine room.

donkey A prefix to describe any auxiliary or other labour-saving machine; hence *donkey boiler* - a small auxiliary boiler to make steam to heat water (during a rcfit this could be a contrivance looking like a steam traction engine on the jetty); *donkey engine* - a small engine on the *upper deck to power a winch or capstan; *donkey winch* - to assist bringing in ropes (usually only in the Merchant Navy; the RN still relies on people-power!); *sailmaker's donkey* - a sewing machine. Note also the *Nagasaki connection, in which a chap who is rigged *like a Nagaski donkey* is especially well-endowed with regard to his wedding tackle.

donkey walloper (RM) Generic term for any cavalry officer; see also *Ruperts, *wah-wahs and *seagulls.

donkey's dick A short rubber tube inserted in the stern of a *RIB, which acts as a self-baler. The FAA also have this term for a fuel dumping hose fitted below and to the rear of a Sea King fuselage. Also known as a *donkey's plonk*.

don't be afraid of the badges! *'Speak up, lad - I won't bite your head off!'*

don't flush through yet! (CD) Colloquialism for *Calm down!* derived from the drill for divers using mixture gas rigs when in trouble.

doofer A catch-all name that will do for anything Jack can't describe instantly or accurately. *Johnson is a Fleet Air Arm variant. Alternatives are *doobrey, doofrey* and *doodah*. The original doofer was the stump of a home-made *tickler which had been extinguished and carefully stowed inside Jack's hat as something that would *do for later*. The sudden order **Off caps!* at Divine Service would often produce a veritable snowstorm of doofers falling to the deck.

doolally   Crazy, crackers, off his / her trolley.

dope on a rope (FAA)   A **SAR aircrewman on the winch wire.

Doris   Standard nickname for a Naval Nurse. **Boris is the newer, male eqivalent.

dose   When used on its own, this word implies the acquisition of venereal disease, but it can also be qualified in a more general way, eg. *a dose of 'flu* or a *dose of the *dog*. In the latter context, see also **catch the boat up, **nap hand and **Rose Cottage.

doss down   Go to sleep somewhere other than a bedroom or sleeping **cabin; (RM) usually in a **green slug.

double-breasted matelots   Female ratings of the Royal Navy, ie. **Wrens. Sometimes described also as *double bumps*; see page M - 276 for Tugg's lovely interpretation.

double-clews   Twice the number of **nettles **clewed to a hammock meant the ability to support a greater load. This is an example of Jack's humour from older times, in that a fellow sailor who had *embarked* or *entered double-clews* had just got married!

double-dipper   US Navy term, occasionally heard in RN circles, for a retired officer re-employed as a civilian, thereby drawing both a pension and a salary.

double-hatted   An officer with RN and NATO responsibilities (can also be *dual-hatted*); note also the even more responsible term of **triple-hatted.

double-six   Crucial dice throw in **Uckers, also extending into real life: *'How the hell did he get that job? Did he throw a double-six or something?'*

doughbag (RM)   An overweight, slow-witted and generally useless individual.

Down the hatch!   Drinking toast similar to *Bottoms up!*

downbird (FAA)   Helicopter that has made a precautionary or emergency landing somewhere other than its intended destination, and which needs attention from the **grubbers of a *downbird team* before it can fly again.

downstairs (SM)   Anywhere below the casing of a submarine. A *downstairs trot* is the *'tween-decks duty sentry in a submarine that is alongside.

dowse   Older RN term for switching off, or covering a light.

Do you (d'ye) hear there?   Preliminary announcement made over a *Tannoy or broadcast system to alert the ship's company just prior to an important *pipe.

dozy (esp. RM)   Word used for a *doughbag:*'You dozy individual..'*

DQs   Her Majesty's Royal Naval *Detention Quarters* in the Portsmouth Naval Base, now closed and used (of all things!) as the RM School of Music. The term may also refer to any military corrective training centre staffed (or patronized) by Jack and Royal.   Nowadays, if Jack, Jenny or Royal are sentenced to Detention, he or she goes to the Military Corrective Training Centre at Colchester. Note that Detention is not imprisonment but *corrective training*. Imprisonment is a separate punishment, only awarded by *Court Martial, spent in a civilian prison, and invariably followed by dismissal from HM Service. See also *deeks.

draft   Either:
1. Set out an outline plan or letter.
2. Transfer to another ship or station. Note that this has nothing to do with the US of A concept of draft as a process of military call up.

Drafty   Generic nickname for the various Desk Officers who work for *CND (Captain Naval Drafting). Up until after WW2 *drafting* was the responsibility of the various Port Divisions (Portsmouth, Devonport, etc.) and a *Pompey rating would in general only be drafted to a Pompey ship (even if she was in the Far East). This became very uneconomical in manpower terms, and nearly impossible to manage in wartime, so in 1957 the office of Commodore Naval Drafting was set up at a rather elegant country house in Haslemere, Hants and since then Jack, and now Jenny as well, has been drafted centrally. He and she can let *Drafty* know what they want, using a *drafting preference card* (see *dream sheet), although the needs of the Service remain paramount. Drafty now resides at *CENTURION in Gosport.

dragging anchor   Departing from a prior agreement, or not adhering to a previously agreed plan or routine.

dragon Jack's occasional and charming description of his wife; see also *Field Marsha, *Generalissima and *CINC-NAG-HOME! May also be used by Royal on sighting a *gronk during a *run-ashore: *'If I was St. George, I'd finish that dragon off right-away..'*

drain down (SM) To urinate, taken from the operation of draining down the *snort mast. *'Drained down, bore sighted clear!'* was a report given to the control room immediately after finishing snorting. It meant the snort mast was clear and the boat was not taking in water, but could also be used to signify happiness or contentment, as in: *'I banged the arse off it, and by the end of leave I was well and truly drained down and bore sighted clear..'*

drain out all over Torrent of complaints, equivalent to *manking or *dripping all over someone.

drain-sniffer Any medical officer or rating involved in Public Health and Hygiene duties. Also the name given to the executive team on the staff of *FOST, who frequently carry out short-notice, unprogrammed inspections of ships during *Sea Training to ensure that standards of habitability, health and hygiene are being maintained despite the busy training schedule.

draught Depth of the lowest part of a ship below the water line.

draw a drop off This was the engine room stokers' phrase to tell you he was going to the heads for a *jimmy riddle*.

drawing too much water *'You're in the bloody way!'*

dread / dreaded lurgie Jack's term for whichever form of virulent influenza is circulating in the ship or establishment at the time.

dreadnought Contraceptive sheath, issued free on board to Jack en route to his *run-ashore. Also known as a *fearnought, but see also *wellies, *forget-me-nots and *frangers.

dreamsheet The computerised *Drafting Preference Card on which Jack and Royal state where they would like to serve in the future. The Fleet Air Arm also use this term to describe the daily *flypro.

dress ship In harbour, ships *dress overall* with signal flags (bunting) from fo'c'sle up to the mastheads(s) and back down to the quarterdeck on special occasions such as the *Lord High

Admiral's Official Birthday, or for *Navy Days. Also, if a foreign warship is in harbour on one of that nation's major occasions, then HM ships will dress overall and fly the appropriate national flag from the masthead. Ships proceeding under their own power in a harbour on a *dress ship day* do not dress overall, but it is one of the very few occasions when they do fly the Union Flag at the *Jackstaff whilst *underway.

dressed up to the nines   Jack or Royal's lady when overdressed for a function.

drift   Implied meaning: *'You get my general drift, Sunshine?'*

drill   Naval procedure: *'What's the drill for tonight's *Cockers P?'*

drill round (RM)   An inert round of small arms ammunition, used to practise weapon handling drills. Also used in the RM expression: *'He's about as much use as a drill round in an ambush..'*

drink   The sea; note also *oggin and *ogwash.

drip   Multipurpose word to describe a moan or complaint. To present *a drip chit* implies the stating of a complaint in the official sense; *dripping all over* someone means complaining to him or her volubly, and at some length. RM usage also has *drip sesh* for any gathering where problems are discussed. There is a lovely remark: *'Any drips? Then see *Freshwater Tanky!'*

drive   Relaxed slang for a ship command: *'Who's driving IRON DUKE at the moment?'* The plural form *Drives* is both a standard nickname and means of address for any RM vehicle driver.

Droggy Nickname derived from a contraction of Hydrog rapher, a member of the service that is responsible for all the Royal Navy's maritime charts. It used to refer to the Hydrographer of the Navy himself, but that individual is now the *Chief Droggy*.

drongo (esp. RM) Rather nice term of general abuse for a slovenly or ill-disciplined individual. The usual qualifying adjective is *complete*, hence: *'As far as I'm concerned, the man's a born-again *tosser and a complete drongo..'*

drop Another useful *Jackspeak* word with a variety of uses:
1. *drop a bollock* - Make an embarrassing mistake; see also *blob(5).
2. *drop a brown* - WW2 expression concerning the effects of fear; the modern version is *Adrenalin's brown!*
3. *drop of all right* - Expression of admiration for a drink (or an attractive lady).
4. *drop your guts / handbag* - Break wind.
5. *drop ..... in it* - Lay the blame for something at someone else's door.
6. *drop of port / starboard* - Any red / green alcoholic drink.
7. *dropping anchor* - Going no further to seek requirements.

drown the miller An archaic expression for the process of diluting *grog by more than the statutory two parts water to one of rum. This might be done by a corrupt purser who sought to extend the ration further - and then pocket the difference.

drumhead service (RM) Short religious service taken in the field, or on *Corps and Unit memorable dates, when fallen comrades are remembered and mourned. Although a number of *side-drums* may feature as a centrepiece for such a service, the real origin is strictly Naval in that a *drumhead* was the top part of the capstan barrel of old - the section perforated with *pigeon holes* for inserting its capstan bars before *weighing anchor.

drummer A drum roll preceded most bugle calls in action - the nickname has passed on for RM buglers, but see also *Sticks. For some reason a *drummer's hook* is the *deck, so that *to hang something on a drummer's hook* means to drop it on the floor.

Dry List Contains the names of officers from the Executive and Seaman specialisation not earmarked for sea command.

dry as dust Description of a Naval person who has not been to sea for a long time, like certain *Whitehall warriors and other forms of *barrack stanchion.

dry bag   Descriptive term for a diver's black rubber and dry diving suit.

dry idler   Jack's traditional nickname for anyone other than a seaman or stoker.

dry run   A rehearsal without actions; see also *dummy run.

DSM - SMR!   *Don't See Me - See My *Relief!* meaning: *'I can't really be bothered to assist you with your problem, because I'm leaving this ruddy job in the very near future..'*

DTS   Popular abbreviation for a Dinner Time Sesh (lunchtime drinks), but it also used to be the *TLA for the *Dartmouth Training Squadron.*

Dubs-40   *WD-40*, a waterproofing, preservative and generally indispensable spray fluid familiar to most motorists; also known as *pussers fix-all.

dubs   Double-O suffix to a time, meaning exactly *on the hour*: *'The meeting is due to start at oh-eight-dubs..'* (0800).

duck run   A lady's posterior - the bit that waggles as she walks, and is also devoid of vegetation. A chap with duck's disease is rather short, ie. his posterior is very close to the ground. Note also the *duck run derby*, a game played on a relay basis by inserting a coin in between the cheeks of a participant's *duck run*. The player then perambulates to the other end of the course and drops the coin into a bucket. The next player then goes.

duckboards   Latticed wooden floorboards found in showers and at the bottom of boats; presumably the term originates from their help in keeping Jack's feet dry - just like a duck! Certainly, the duck's overall waterproofness is a feature that is much admired and envied: *'The whole thing was as watertight as a duck's arse! 'Ow do I know that a duck's watertight? Well, 'ave you ever seen a duck sinking?'*

ducks   White tropical uniform, in the days before Terylene. If short in crutch space, the trousers might be described: *'Just like a small hotel - only one ballroom..'*

duff   Multipurpose word:
1. A pudding, eg. *figgy duff, plum duff*.
2. Useless: *'The radar's duff..'* or (esp. RM): *'We've been given totally duff *gen again..'*

3. To *come one's duff* is vulgar slang for an orgasm, but see also *vinegar strokes and *Fratton.
4. *ear duffs* are hearing protectors.
5. To be *up the duff* is to be pregnant.
6. *duff up* - fill someone in while fighting.
7. *duffo* - A Westcountryman.

dummy deck   Airfield runway area marked to look like an air-craft carrier's flight deck. Designed for pilot's landing practice, or the training of *chockheads; see also *ADDLS.

dummy run   Complete rehearsal of a military *evolution, but without actually firing any of the weapons involved.

dump   Another word with three completely different applications:
1. Defaecate.
2. (FAA) *Dumping the lever* means reducing a helicopter's collective pitch as quickly as possible.
3. (FAA) Get rid of surplus fuel by *dumping* it.

dung button   Anus; see also *burnt plum, *freckle and *rusty bullet-hole.

dung hampers   Underpants or *keks.

dunk (FAA)   Two meanings:
1. Lower a sonar device into the sea from a helicopter.
2. The *Dunker* is a helicopter underwater escape trainer in which all FAA aircrew undergo regular *dunker drills*. See also *Dilbert Dunker.

dunkers (SM)   This was obviously to *dunk* (dip) your bread in your oppo's soup, or your biscuits in his tea, but was also used to ask for a bit of anything as in: *'Give us a dunk of your nutty..'* or *'Give us dunkers on your nutty..'*

duskers   The penultimate stage of a FAA pilot's *working-up to the ultimate level of proficiency in British military aviation - becoming night qualified in the *SHAR.

Dusty   Also two applications:
1. Traditional nickname for the surname Rhodes and Miller.
2. A *Jack Dusty* is a Supply and Secretariat rating, abbreviated from the historic nickname *Jack o' the Dust* - a seaman of yesteryear who issued the flour provisions. Note also Tugg's absolute classic at T - 465.

Dutch ovens   Breaking wind under a double duvet - origin obscure.

Dutchman's log   Originally a method of measuring a ship's speed by throwing a piece of wood into the water, and noting the time it took to pass between two points along the ship's side. Still used, but nowadays only when a ship is manoeuvering to recover a man overboard, or to pass a tow - as a visual confirmation that she is stopped in the water.

duty beauty   Originally a female duty officer (but see the next entry!) Now, by general extension and usage, it can refer to *any* duty person.

duty dog (SM)   *'Who's the duty dog?'* was/is a question asked to find out who's on duty that day. The *Deputy Dog* is the Officer of the Watch in harbour.

duty hag   Jenny's own term, perhaps based on the *Scottish play*, for the duty female rating in an establishment.

duty skirt   The unfortunate *liver-in WRNS officer who is encouraged to leave the peace of her cabin and join a (male) gathering at the bar in the evenings.

dwang   Trouble: *'You, my son, are in the dwang, *big style..'*

ECHO

153 - 160

ear pounding   Heavy verbal criticism, as at page M - 289.

ease / easy   Six entries:
1. *Stand at ease!*   Static positions whilst on *divisions (parade), progressively more relaxed than being at attention.
2.   The act of doing something carefully, slowly or with less vigour; hence *easy does it*.   This is generally used in a descriptive sense; the actual order to do so is *Handsomely!*
3.   *Stand Easy* was also a 15-20 minute break in the day's work when the *canteen would be open; the bugle call for this could be sung to the words '*If you want a cup of tea go now..*' Nowadays, with a more relaxed and self-disciplined approach to the working day, any informal break is called *a stand-easy*.
4.   *Ease to ten!* (from the wheel order) *Calm down!*
5.   For Jack, *springs* are special mooring lines which come under tension as a ship moves fore and aft with the tide and current. The order to *Ease springs!* can relieve tension in these arrangements, and can also be used to describe a visit to the *heads.
6.   (RM) The same order *Ease springs!* has a different meaning.   It is given following a weapon safety inspection after firing on a range, and involves releasing the compression forces acting on the *spring* which operates the weapon's working parts.

Easter egg (RM)   Royal's nickname for a *Bandie wearing a red sash.

eat a cow between two bread vans / horse between two hammocks   Splendid piece of RM exaggeration indicating great hunger: '*I'm that bloody famished I could eat a cow between two bread vans, *no probs..*'   Another alternative concerns a *scabby donkey between two mattresses*.

eating irons   Cutlery; see also *KFS, *gobbling rods and *port & starboard oars; also known as *scran spanners.

egg on legs   A short, fat person.

eggs-adj   Written it as it is said, and a corruption of the word **exaggerate**, but used like this: *'Three days stoppage for one hour adrift? That's bloody eggs -adj, that is..'*

Egyptian   An amusing trio, retained from Jack's long experience of service at the far end of the Med:
1. *Egyptian 'flu* - a lady who is unwell because she's shortly going to be a mummy!
2. *Egyptian PT* (RM) - sleep; see *gonking or *zeds for some alternatives.
3. *Egyptian *AFOs* - crudely printed pornography that caused as much laughter as sexual excitement: *'Stoq, - Oh pleise STOQ !' she crid in Exeters as his hand crapt slowley up her theigh..'* Also called *half-hard books.
4. *Egyptian medal* - having a fly button undone.

eight piece dicking   The most comprehensive form of defeat possible at *Uckers, in that your opponent has managed to get all eight of his counters home before you've even managed to deliver one.

electric dit   Fax machine.

electric ears   Headphones.

electric hat (FAA)   A *Chockhead's hard hat and *electric ears.

electric lemonade   Strong lager.

electric string   General term for any insulated cable.

elephant's arsehole   A shiny brass hawsepipe installed aft on the stern of towed (sonar) array frigates, and used to stream the long, thick transducer cable through.

elephant's footprints (SM)   Spam fritters immersed in batter and then fried before being served for breakfast.

elephant's trunk (SM)   Canvas water chute rigged beneath a submarine's *conning tower, in conjunction with a *birdbath, to collect any seawater entering while the *boat is running *opened up in rough weather.

elk's nest (RM)   Enormous hole left in the snow by Royal when he *yetties on *planks, especially so when fully-laden with a *chacon.

Elmer   General term for an American tourist, or the wrong kind of US Navy exchange personnel. In its fully expanded version, the reference is to one *Elmer P. Chickenshit Junior - the Third*.

Elvis medal (RM)   The Victoria Cross; this supreme British accolade for courage in the face of the enemy has not been awarded to a living person since the Indonesian Confrontation (to a Gurkha) and the Vietnam War (to an Australian). After the Falklands Conflict, two Victoria Crosses were awarded posthumously, leading to this wry comment that if you win the VC, you will receive it from *The King* rather than HM The Queen!

embuggerance factor   Something random or unforseen that does not exactly prevent the execution of a plan or *evolution, but merely delays and impedes it; may also be spelt *imbuggerance. Jack is convinced that there is an *embuggerance committee* that sits somewhere up above, in permanent session, ready to step in whenever things are going well.

empire builders   Any generously-cut shorts, but especially an older pair of *pusser's white tropical ones.

end for end   Reverse the position of something, or as Jack might put it a little more directly, make it *arse about face.

endex   Abbreviation for *end of exercise*, but applied much more widely, for instance as a euphemism for death: '*Touch those terminals, mate - and it'll be endex for you..*'

Ensign   The US Navy equivalent of a midshipman.

ensign (pronounced *ens'n*).   Dates roughly from the early 17th century, when the Fleet was divided into three squadrons: Red, White and Blue (in that order of seniority), each commanded by a *flag officer - hence Rear Admiral of the Red, etc. At about the same time (and confusingly), the merchant service began to adopt the *Red Ensign* as its distinguishing flag, and this was legally endorsed in 1674. The Fleet continued with its three-squadron division (Nelson was a Vice Admiral of the White at *Trafalgar) until 1864, when the *White Ensign* was authorised to be worn by all HM ships; at the same time the Red Ensign became the exclusive property of the merchant navy, and the *Blue Ensign* that of the newly-formed Royal Naval Reserve.

equaliser   Two different usages:
1. A hammer, used to great effect when employed in the *Chief Stoker's method. There used to be sub-specialisation among stokers called a boilermaker. The tool kit of a boilermaker had twenty four different hammers!
2. (SM) A process usually done alongside, with a charging to full capacity in order to *equalise* all the battery cells. Can also be used to describe a welcome period of uninterrupted sleep - to catch up with the body's needs after some exercise or lengthy *evolution.

essence   A wonderful and easily emphasized word that indicates beauty:'*She's essence!*' Or, perfection in form and function: '*It's an essence piece of *kit..*' It may just be an abbreviation of the word quintessence, but it is especially common in RM usage.

ESSO rating   *Every Saturday and Sunday Off,* as in:'*I'm sure the chief stoker fancies the lad, he's a complete ESSO rating..*'

ETA / ETD   *TLA for *Estimated time of arrival / departure.*

ETBs   *Elastic top and bottoms.*   *Pusser's issue *Wrens' knickers, otherwise known as *passion killers. See also *free-traders.

Every man for himself!   Final order given when a warship is on fire or badly damaged and about to sink; it means that nothing more can be done by way of damage control and firefighting, and that there is no longer any need for Jack to await further orders.

everyone's mess but nobody's watch   Said of someone who is always around when there is fun to be had, but who disappears quickly when hard work is in prospect. See also *bloody good kid in harbour for a similar, but slightly different context.

everything on a split yarn Old naval expression meaning *In every respect ready for instant action.* From the practice of having sails or other gear ready and secured in place by a piece of thin twine, or a *split yarn.* This could be easily and swiftly broken or cut, thus releasing the sails or gear, ready for immediate use.

everything you know about that subject could be written on the outside of a gnat's bollock bag '*You are not quite as clever as you think..*' Note also that a *flea's tit* is the alternative geographical location.

evolution This used to be the exercise process of sending parties of different personnel like marines, stokers, or torpedomen to parts of the ship that they would not normally frequent. As a result, all members of the ship's complement became conversant with every part of the ship. This was often an hilarious practice, with disembodied groups of lost souls rushing around trying to find the location they had been ordered to report to. Nowadays, the term refers to any important seamanship task requiring co-ordinated action for its successful completion, especially in an emergency. The term is also widely used in RN usage for other procedures not directly related to the operation of a ship.

-ex Suffix for *exercise*, tacked on to a number of words, eg.:
   Distex - Disaster Control Exercise.
   Endex - the time that an exercise is declared complete.
   Gloppex - a *run-ashore or party where some serious
       drinking is planned or has taken place.
   Navex (FAA) - navigation training sortie.
   Smashex - an exercise that simulates a submarine's loss.

exag See *eggs -adj (the phonetic spelling).

Excreta taurii cerebrum vincit Pig-latin for *Bullshit baffles brains!* See also *BS.

excused boots Originally a foot ailment resulting in a medical to get off what the Army would call *square bashing*, but has now come to mean any excuse to prevent someone doing an arduous job at all: '*What, me play water polo for the ship tomorrow? On a weekend? Not me, mate. I'm excused boots..*'

Executive Officer (*XO)   The second in command of a warship or shore establishment, and responsible to the *captain for the efficient running of the ship in her entirety. In a big ship, the XO will be of Commander rank, and known as The Commander (see also *Bloke); in smaller ships and submarines, the XO will either be a *two and a half or *lieutenant, known as the First Lieutenant (see *Jimmy, etc.); big ships may also have a First Lieutenant, who in this instance assists the Commander with specific responsibility for seamanship and *ship husbandry. Note that in the Royal Navy the XO is the *de jure* President of the *Wardroom Mess; the *captain is an honorary member, and only enters the *wardroom by invitation.

exhibish   An alcohol-induced display of a lewd nature such as the *Zulu warrior ritual, but more especially the sort of live sex acts seen in clubs along the Reeperbahn during a *reepcreep.

Exocet   Jack's wry and self-mocking humour applied to a cocktail barman's special mix: *'Just one - and you're wrecked..'*   Also used to describe his mother-in-law, because just like an *Exocet missile*, you can see her coming, the timing is always very awkward, there's very little you can do about it - and it tends to ruin your whole weekend.

exped   Adventure training *expedition*.

explosion in a marmite factory   What a toilet looks like, the morning after the night before.

Express or local?   This was a rating's response to a request to *pass the (salt) please*. Anyone foolish enough to reply *express* got the item thrown at him. See also *long call.

extenders   An extended long weekend, ie. Thursday to Monday, or Friday to Tuesday: *'Mitch ain't here Monday - he's on extenders..'* Some would have you believe this is normal *Wafu weekend!

extra   Additional musical item often played by the *Bandies towards the end of a formal dinner. A solo or duo piece featuring musical ability and/or great humour is presented, usually to the enormous approval of those who are dining.

extra lights (RM)   The custom of paying a barman an additional sum of money when the bar is kept open after hours. All present are expected to make a contribution.

extracting the Michael   Politer version of *taking the Mickey / taking the*piss*.

E - 158

Chockhead

eyeball Still the most valued sensor in a ship or aircraft, and hence referred to as the *Mark One eyeball* (although usually found in pairs!), as it can't be improved upon. To *eyeball* something is to inspect it visually or, when manoeuvering, to conduct the manoeuvre using visual judgement (rather than working it out on a plotting sheet).

eyelid inspection Sleeping; see *gonking for a list of other versions.

eyes in two watches Description of an individual whose eyes appear to be moving independently of each other as a result of drunkeness, or tiredness - or both. Also, note *eyes like two poached eggs on boathooks*.

eyes like a dying gazelle A quality possessed by a particularly attractive lady.

(made his) eyes water (RM) Laconic understatement applied to the effects of controlled military violence: '*A *Milan anti-tank missile arriving in an enemy *sangar doesn't half make the occupants' eyes water..*'

FOXTROT

161 - 186

Face aft and salute!   Order given to those on the upper deck during *Colours; also a tacit acknowledgement that whatever Jack's different opinions on some aspect of his ship's operation, he will ultimately obey orders: *"The *Boss tried to alter our *Ripple 3 crew *rosters; *Wings wouldn't wear it - told him to face aft and salute.."*

face like a _____   There are some amusing variations to be heard on this theme when discussing *gronks:

> *She 'ad a face like a bulldog chewin' a wasp, and teeth like a*
> *   row of condemned 'ouses..*
> *Her face was like a walking *Hurt Certificate - with a mouth*
> *   like a torn pocket..*
> *She had the face of a messdeck scrubber, and eyes like*
> *   a Dogger Bank cod..*
> *Her face? Well, her *moosh was like a ruptured custard - an'*
> *   the rest looked like a badly-packed kitbag..*
> *Not only was her face like a bag of smashed crabs, she was as*
> *   rough as a badger's bum into the bargain..*

fag bracket   An ear.

fagged out   Tired, from the *fagging out* of an old rope's end. Hence also the term *fag end* for a frayed and stamped-on cigarette butt, and (presumably) the actual derivation of the word **fag**. Note also the original meaning of the term *doofer as a cigarette that has been half-smoked, extinguished, and then carefully stowed inside Jack's cap as something that will *do fer later..*

fair   Favourable, or unobstructed, hence the applications of a *fair course* to steer, the *fairway* of a channel or harbour - and the similar application in golf. A *fairlead* **is** a small opening on the deck-edge of a ship through which ropes or wires are passed; and a *fair copy* is an error-free version of the original. The expression *Fairy snuff!* meant:*'I agree!'*

fair wind   Especially favourable conditions, which may be direct - as when calculating the helpful effect of a following wind on an aircraft's progress, or oblique as in: *'The Admiral very much approves of this idea, so he's given the proposal a fair wind on its way up to the Minister..'*   Also used to ask for the cruet at table: *'Give the salt and pepper a fair wind in this direction please..'*

faith to plant acorns   Nice expression for someone with strong convictions, ie. he intends to plant acorns now which will grow into the oak trees from which his grandson's ship will be built.

fake (often wrongly pronounced *flake)   To lay out a rope or wire in coils, which then becomes faked down and *tiddly. See

*flake for a more detailed explanation.

fall   A trio:
1. The front flap of square rig trousers.
2. *Fall down in a snotty heap* - unable to stand due to a large intake of booze.
3. *falls* - the blocks and ropes used at each end of a sea boat / motor boat for lowering and hoisting.

familygram (SM)   40 word message that is sent weekly to each member of a *Bomber crew when on Trident patrol; some of the words become a bit garbled in transmission, so Jack tends to call any form of computer-generated rubbish a *familygram*. Can also be called a *grumblegram.

fancy waistcoats   Figure of speech that implies unnecessary embellishment on a story - which is not quite the same as suggesting it is inaccurate. It is also used of things physical: *'We've just spent the whole forenoon rigging the ceremonial awning and tiddlying up the quarter deck with Turk's Heads on the stanchions. All this fancy waistcoats stuff give me the pip - a warship's supposed to be a warship, not a tart's boudoir..'*

fang bosun / farrier   Dentist; see also *gnasher basher, *toothwright and *Top Gum.

fanny   Two distinct applications:
1. Oval or cylindrical mess *trap with a handle, originally used for the collection of a messdeck's rum issue, or for the making of *limers or *kye, etc.   It originates from *pusser's first attempt, in 1867, to provide canned meat (in this case *mutton*) as an alternative to salted meat in a cask. This technique was regarded with great suspicion by Jack, especially as a young girl named (Sweet) *Fanny Adams* had just been murdered and dismembered in particularly grusesome circumstances. The tins, however, once a wire handle had been added to the top, were a welcome addition to a messdeck's utensils, and the coincidence resulted in Fanny's name living on in a completely unintended way. The *messdeck fannies* used for *grog were also called *monkeys, about a half-gallon in size, and highly polished and decorated. Note that the word has nothing to do with the more general British term (see below), or the vaguely similar usage involving the posterior on the other side of the *Pond.
2. An intimate part of the female anatomy. Four examples:
> *fanny mechanic* - gynaecologist; *quim quack is a
> recorded alternative.
> *fanny rat* - chap who chases after ladies, often with
> considerable success; see also *lead on MacDick.
> *fanny scratchers* - fingers.
> *fanny boat* - these are vessels run by civvies showing
> holiday-makers the fleet. The ladies are always
> waving to Jack as they pass.

far flung   Anywhere away from the home waters of the United Kingdom, but especially east of Suez.

farewell jetty   South railway jetty, Portsmouth, usually the last berth of a capital ship before leaving on a foreign commission (WW2).

farm   An old expression, when in rough or cold weather:*'Who'd sell a farm and go to sea?'* There was a classic signal exchange when a destroyer had made three unsuccessful attempts to secure to a buoy, under the eye of the Port Admiral, who signalled:*'What do you intend to do next?'* to which the reply was: *'Buy a farm..'*

fart   Almost onomatopoeic term for the anal emission of intestinal gas. A useful sextet:
1. *fart in a collander* - descriptive of indecisive or effectual behaviour:*'Look at you lad, you're rushing about like a fart in a collander, not sure which hole to come out of..'*
2. *fart in church* - a serious misdeamour. *'E's got ten days' number 11's; serves 'im right for farting in church..'*
3. *fartarse about* - pretend to be working, or sometimes *fanny about*.
4. *fart* - when you're beaten in an argument with a senior. *'It's no use trying to fart against thunder..'*
5. *fart in a spacesuit* - Jack's phrase for something not only unwelcome and unpleasant, but which also has an enduring and persistent quality.
6. *fart in a thunderstorm* (RM) - indication of someone or something's general worth:*'His announcement had just about as much impact on the proceedings as a fart in a thunderstorm..'*
7. *fart in a trance* - description of somebody who is a bit dreamy and unable to make decisions; has also been heard as:*'You look like a lost fart in a haunted milk bottle !'*
8. *fartleberries* - yet another name for *bum plums or haemorrhoids, and also for baked beans.

fast black   Official (black) saloon car, although the older Singapore usage referred to the *dollar pick-up black Mercedes taxis (unlicensed) that would take Jack and Royal from RNAS Simbang to the TERROR Club, or to downtown *Singers and the delights of *Bugis Street. Now an almost universal term in Jackspeak for a taxi, anywhere in the world.

fast cruise (SM)   The process of exercising a submarine's crew in various emergency drills whilst fast alongside with the *lid shut; now also carried out by *skimmers.

Fat Albert   RAF term, now adopted in the *Andrew, for the C-130 Hercules transport operated by *Truckies which performed prodigious feats of workload and endurance during (and after) the 1982 Falklands campaign. Jack grew to love Fat Albert and his *mailie drops at sea.

F - 164

fat, dumb and happy (FAA)   Failing to pay proper attention to the exacting business of flying: *'There I was, sitting fat, dumb and happy in a forty-foot hover - when the Doppler threw a monster *wobbly..'*

fat knacker pie (RM)   Any food rich in calories, but especially puddings and sweets. May sometimes be heard as *naughty pie*, or even more simply as a *fat pill*.

fat soft   A **lazy lob*.

Father   Respectful (and affectionate) nickname for the Captain. See also the *Old Man; properly, he should not be called *Skipper, but in practice he frequently is. Although female officers have now been appointed in command, the author is not aware of *Mother*, or even the *Old Woman* being used as yet!

Father Famine   Traditional nickname for the Supply Officer in charge of catering; note also Tugg's absolutely superb and Rowlandson-like caricature on page N - 301.

fathom   Standard measurement of depth or the length of ropes and cables. Derived from the Old English word for an embrace, it was the distance between the outstretched arms of a man and became standardised as six feet. 100 fathoms = 1 *cable (200 yds) and 10 cables = 1 *sea mile. Measurements and dimensions are now metric, but distances are still measured in yards, cables and sea miles. *Droggy used fathoms in the *exact* sense of six feet. Everything is now metric on charts.

fearnought suit (FAA)   Thick jacket and trousers made of worsted felt, worn by fire-fighting crews: *'Listen lad, I was in a fearnought suit when you was still in a romper suit..'*

feat of arse (RM)   Rather mocking derivation that is the complete opposite of a feat of arms; an older play on words also has this phrase as a *feed of arse* for a *botty bandit.

feathered varieties   Name for FAA flying personnel.

feed 'em rice   See under *rice.

feet under the table   Expression meaning that Jack has made himself at home (while away from home) and is getting on very well. May also be used to describe good progress in the pursuit of some attractive lady.

fell in three deep   Expression applied to some event that has been organized properly: *'When we got there a *tame Crab who'd flown *Tooms off *ARK in '77 fell us in three deep and marched us from one party to the next in what turned out to be a fantastic *landaway weekend..'

fell off his perch   Description of some self-important or pompous individual's sudden come-uppance - and subsequently damaged reputation.

fend off   To push off / fend off, - hence the term *fender*, for stopping boats being damaged by banging against a ship or jetty. Note also *fender belly* for a pregnant lady, and see *pudding club.

Ferchristsake wire (FAA)   The last arrester cable, or the one nearest to the *sharp end of an aircraft carrier.

ferret   An unusual trio:
1. Occasional rhyming slang for a *beret*.
2. Sending a *ferret in* is to try and find out about a situation.
3. *ferreting* is also another word for sexual intercourse.

fetch up   End up somewhere after a *run ashore, or arrive suddenly on deck in an emergency, eg. after striking a submerged object: *'All of a sudden there was this *gynoferous crunching sound, and we all fetched up *topsides..'

(a) **few laughs and a few beers** (RM)   Very unofficial translation of the Corps' motto *Per Mare Per Terram.

fid   A wooden spike, tapered for splicing rope; nowadays a handful or sheaf of papers, eg. *a fid of* signals. Also a cylinder of very hard wood shipped through the heel of a top mast or top gallant mast, to hold it in position.

fiddle   Nautical name for a violin, also the raised wooden edge to a table, designed to hold your food in place during *roughers.

Fiddler's Green   An imaginary sailor's Heaven full of pubs, dance halls and enthusiastic ladies. When he *cut his paynter and shuffled off this mortal coil (of rope which made up that paynter!) Jack was said to have gone *aloft to Fiddler's Green.*

Field Marsha   The military equivalent of Her Indoors; *Generalissima and *CINC-NAG-HOME are splendid alternatives.

Field officer (RM)   Officer with the rank of Lieutenant Colonel - or above. When in *blues they wear tight-fitting overall trousers with boots and spurs.

field gunner   A member of the Devonport, Portsmouth or Fleet Air Arm field gun crews who used to train between *Crimbo and summer for a competition held during the annual Royal Tournament at Earl's Court. The results were signalled world-wide to the *Fleet; the participants were famous for their speed, size and strength, and the way that these qualities were combined into a spectacular display of teamwork. Sadly, the heartless accountants who seem to run naval matters these days have decreed that the Royal Tournament is to be no more, and the field gunners have also taken their permanent place in Naval history. See also page O - 310.

FIFO (RM)   Fit In - or *Foxtrot Oscar :*'Look, mate - in this little outfit you've got to FIFO - see?'* *SUSO has a similar meaning.

Fifteen-two that bastard!   General challenge for anyone to do better, having just made a good play or stroke. Can also be used on non-sporting occasions; derived from the card game of *cribbage* where the sum of fifteen is unbeatable and results in two points scored. Sometimes misquoted as fifteen-love (as in tennis) but the meaning is identical.

fifth five   Older term for Extended Service; the normal full-career commitment for Jack is twenty-two years. A *fifth five* took this to twenty-seven, but has now been replaced by the Second Open Engagement which is written as 2OE. Also called a *fifth pricker.*

fifty up   Masturbation, hence the old tombola call: *'Five-oh, under the blanket - fifty..'* or *'Five-oh, change hands, fifty..'*

figgy duff   Any stodgy or suet-based pudding.

Clacker

fighting gear   Table cutlery; see also *KFS and *gobbling rods.

fighting knife (RM)   Correct name for the *Commando dagger emblem.

fighting order (RM)   Weapon, spare ammunition and magazines, water bottle, field dressing, poncho cape and mess tins, with all but the first item carried in special pouches or rolls attached to a close-fitting upper body harness.

fights, (to be) **in the fights**   *Fights* were the wide strips of canvas that were rigged above the sides (*bulwarks*) of a man-of-war before she went into action. The intention was to conceal the seamen who were working on the deck, from the sharpshooters who were stationed in the masts and rigging of the enemy ships. They were also known as waist-cloths, because the waist of the vessel was where the crew were assembled at their posts. These fights or *waist-cloths* were abandoned by the end of the 16th century because they were a serious fire hazard during battle. To be *in the fights* was to be in the thick of things, since the enemy's guns and marksmen poured their fire into the general deck area anyway. Colloquially, the expression carries the same meaning - to be in the centre of the action, to be closely involved in a quarrel or struggle, or to be at battle (either literally or figuratively). Often also expressed, especially of children, as *to be in the wars*.

figurehead   *Figure heads* (the technically correct form) as decorative art have almost disappeared in the 20th century, and only a few vessels - predominantly one or two Scandinavian lines - carry a figure head of the traditional style. Perhaps the best known in recent English maritime literature is that of the *Cutty Sark*, the famous tea clipper built in 1869. She survives, fully restored, in a dry dock at Greenwich, on the Thames. Her figure head is of a woman (in fact a *witch*) in flowing garments, reaching out with outstretched arms in an effort to grasp the tail of the grey mare belonging to the young farmer who spied on Nannie and her companion. The name *Cutty Sark* refers to the short shift or skirt worn by Nannie.

The carved figures, usually human or animal, were fixed on the stem just beneath the bowsprit. It was intended as a decorative emblem that expressed some aspect of the ship's name or function. The origin of the figure head is probably both religious and personal, and was part of an attitude that treated the ship as a living entity. Eyes were an important part of all figure heads, in the belief that the ship needed to be able to see her way across the waters. The religious element arose from the sailors' need to propitiate the sea deities while the vessel was at sea. The form that figure heads took through the thousands of years of mans' seafaring exploits include lions, birds, horses, boars, warriors, swans, dragons, saints, and so on. Figure heads of females gradually became the most popular form of decoration; a rather interesting outcome, because while women were considered by seamen to be unlucky to have on board ship, the torso of a naked woman was supposed to be able to calm a storm at sea. Metaphorically, a *figurehead* is a person who is nominally the head of a society, community, etc. An apparent leader, but one who in fact plays no real part in leading; without real authority or responsibility, but nevertheless, one whose social or academic position inspires confidence.

file 13   Wastepaper basket; see also *circular file.

filibuster   To *filibuster* is from the Dutch word *vrybuiter,* or free-booter, which came into English from the French form *flibustier;* it is the old name under which buccaneers or pirates were originally known in Britain. Literally it meant one who obtained his plunder or booty free. In the 19th century the term described the bands of raiders who operated out of the United States in their efforts to invade and revolutionise certain Spanish - American territories. At about the same time the phrase came into use in the USA to mean the use of obstructive tactics in the legislature, as a derivation from the original idea of raiding and blockading.

filled in   *'He was a bit stroppy, so the three badger filled him in..'* - thumped him, or gave him a *bunch of fives.*

Fill yer boots!   *'Join in - help yourself!'*

fin (SM)   The structure above the casing containing the conning tower, masts and aerials (called a *sail* in the USN).

Find, *Fix - and Strike   The operating philosophy of the Fleet Air Arm.

finger out   A time-honoured, if vulgar, colloquialism, much used in Australian speech. It means to hurry, to get on with it, to look alive, and don't be so stand-offish. The expression is, more immediately, a warning to be not so stuck up, don't be so absorbed in oneself (less delicately rendered by *pull your finger out*) and take note of what is going on around one. Used as in:

'The boss told him that if he didn't get his finger out he would find himself without a job..' Apparently, the expression dates from the days of muzzle-loading cannon on board ship. When the powder and shot were being wadded home into the breech, one of the gunners would hold his thumb over the vent hole at the base of the gun so that oxygen from the outside air could not enter the chamber and ignite the hot gases from previous firing. When all was ready, he was ordered to *get his finger out*; any slowness here would probably mean a burning from the slow-match that was then applied to the vent hole in order to ignite the powder.

finger trouble   Slang term (and excuse) for selecting a wrong switch, or using some piece of equipment incorrectly: *'Sorry, wrong number - finger trouble!'*

Fire-and-Lights   Older nickname for the *Master at Arms in a warship, because of his nightly responsibilities to arrange patrols 'tween decks and ensure that all fires were *dowsed and all lights extinguished, for obvious reasons, inside the wooden hull.

fire, flood, famine (SM)   Name for the Disaster Control exercises carried out during a *boat's *work-up.

firm   The operator/s of a private service to shipmates, such as a *dhobi firm, barber, shoe-mender; not allowed unless sanctioned by Jimmy.

first ashore - best dressed   From the belief that the first man to finish for the day and get ashore, helped himself to the choice of any female civvies hanging around in or outside the barracks.

First Dog   The first of the two *Dog Watches:
  First Dog   1600 to 1800
  *Last Dog   1800 to 2000

First Drill (RM)   The *Senior NCO at *Lympstone responsible for all ceremonial, drill and parade-related matters. Equivalent to the parade *Chief GI at *Dartmouth.

First Watch   2000 to 2359.

first parade service (RM)   Any action that must be carried out at the start of a working day, eg. checking the engine, electrics, fuel and tyres of your vehicle. This phrase can also be used for anything else that usually begins a day in the office.

first push (FAA)   The initial serials of a *flypro.

first turn of the screw pays all debts   The newer version of *paying all debts with the topsail sheet,* ie. starting afresh in one's social or financial transactions just as soon as the ship leaves harbour.

fish (SM)   A torpedo.

fish-head (RM / SM / FAA)   Three applications,, depending on context:
1. Identifying label for a *skimmer officer or rating in *General Service:'*Unfortunately, I've then got to go and do some fish-heading time in order to get my frigate *ticket..'*
2. Army / RAF slang for anyone in a Royal Navy uniform!
3. Fishhead Hall - The Admiralty in London (pre *MOD).

Fishing Fleet   Originally, the group of unmarried young ladies, daughters or nieces of serving officers and colonial administrators, who gathered (or were gathered by pushy Mamas), most famously in Malta, when the *Fleet was in, in the hopes of finding a husband. The Mediterranean Fleet was always considered to be the crack fleet, and a well-heeled junior officer was considered an eminently suitable catch. Nowadays used to describe the small group of unattached young people invited to leaven the otherwise rather stodgy list of official guests at ships' cocktail parties. The term could also encompass the Staff Officer's daughters and nieces who hung around every Commander-in-Chiefs station abroad.

fish's tit (esp. RM)
1. '*I couldn't give a fish's tit..'* :'*I couldn't care less..'*
2. '*That's like asking someone to suck on a fish's tit..'* - demanding

the impossible.

fist   Effort, or attempt:*'I must say, that project was a real swine, but he's made a damned good fist of it..'*

fitted (RM)   Hit a person:*'Nobby fitted him one..'*   Can also be used in a more passive sense:*'He got fitted up a *bramah while he was home on leave..'*

five-finger salvo   A well-landed punch. Note that a *bunch of fives* is a frequent but similar usage.

five-finger spread   The result of having a hand in front of the mouth when creating a *dockyard omelette.

five lace-holes deep   A measurement of enthusiasm:*'..and if he pulls a little stunt like that again it'll be *reasons in writing, and my boot five lace-holes deep up his backside!'*

five turd crap   An American import indicating a great sense of pleasure and personal satisfaction at some achievment.

fix   Enter an accurate position on a navigational chart; see also *cocked hat and *Find, fix and strike!

fizzog   *Physiognomy* - facial appearance and features as in:*'Get your rotten fizzog outa here!'*

Flag!   Reply to a challenging ship from a launch carrying a *Flag Officer; also a designated sentry's warning shout on sighting a car or launch *wearing an Admiral's Flag.

Flag Eight   Warning signal:*'Women on board!'*. To *flag up* a problem means that someone has drawn attention to it, in writing.

Flag Officer / Flagship   An Admiral in charge of a large organization or group of ships, who flies an Admiral's flag when he is in command. The ship which wears this personal flag then becomes the *Flagship*; *getting one's Flag* means being appointed to the rank of Rear-Admiral. Note also the term *private ship.

Flags   Nickname of an Admiral's Flag Lieutenant (naval equivalent of an Army ADC, or *aide de camp*):*'The real perks of being FONAC's Flags is that you get to fly his *barge everywhere..'* Note that it is also a nickname for an officer of the communications specialisation, even when not a Flag Lieutenant.

flag flapper / wagger   Signalman; see also *bunting tosser.

flake   Two usages:

1. A cradle or stage lowered over a warship's side for re-caulking (older times) or re-painting.
2. A rope can be *flaked down*, but not in a coil, rather laid out tidily in long, non-kinking and overlapping figure of eight bights, for easy and trouble-free running when pulled. To *coil* a rope down is to *fake it, and each turn of the coil is called a *fake (without the *l*.) Coils, especially *tiddly ones, usually end up as a *snake's honeymoon when pulled.

flakers   Dead tired, but especially so in *Harry flakers*.

flame-out (SM)   An obvious FAA use, but also the crash stop of both engines in a *snorting diesel *boat due to poor handling in rough weather, or the collapse of an individual due to sheer fatigue.

flanker (work a)   Achieve your aims by dubious or deceitful means.

flannel   Elaborate story-telling, or a plethora of weak excuses:

'*That man's got more flannel than a *pussers' blanket..*' See *BS. Also the white shirt-like garment that Jack wears under his outer jumper. It has a square, blue-bordered neck.   In pre-war days it really was made of a cream-coloured, *flannel* material.

flannel bosun   Someone who pretends he knows all the answers; it is a politer term than bullshit artist. See also *BS and *black catter!

flap   see *fall.

flaps down, and downwind (FAA)   Aviation term adapted to describe two or more sailors, in the old days when Jack's

F - 174

trousers were equipped with *piss-flaps and bell-bottoms, all *springing a leak in the *heads.

flash   A trio:
1. Smart, all dressed-up: *'He looked as flash as a rat with a gold tooth..'*
2. Pass a message to another ship with an Aldis flash-lamp; now also applied to the process of passing a message in radio silence: *'Flash him that I intend to pass to his starboard side..'*
3. Sudden, unexpected glimpse of a female's knickers, sussies or stocking tops. A *good flash* was regarded as the next best thing to actually getting a bit. *Flashing his parts* is what a dirty old man in a raincoat does.

flash to bang time   Taken literally, the difference between the speed of light and the speed of sound, but used here to measure the specific irascibility of a senior officer (see also *short fuse), or the time elapsing between a decision being taken and the subsequent action being completed.

flash-up   As in boiler, so in temper: *'..and for Heaven's sake don't mention that chap John Nott - unless you want the *Old Man to flash-up a treat..'*

flat   Open space between decks, eg. the *Wardroom, tiller, canteen or Sickbay *flats*; a sectioned-off area becomes a *lobby.

flat aback   Describes a cap being worn on the back of Jack's head rather than being *on square*.

flat top (of US origin)   Aircraft carrier.

flat-cock sailor   An older nickname for a member of the *WRNS.

flat-hatting (FAA)   Flying at high speed and low level (in a non- regulation manner); see also *wazzing.

Fleet / fleet   Four variations of this word:
1. Collective term for all HM Ships: *'This decision will have to be promulgated throughout the Fleet..'* Since the early 1970s, the RN has had only *one* Fleet.
2. To *fleet something* is to move a large / heavy object (or a group of men) in small, careful amounts.
3. The area of a ship's side that can be reached using a painter's stage.
4. A creek or ditch - hence *Fleet Street* in London on the site of the old *Fleet Ditch*.

Fleet Chief   This rank existed between 1972 and 1985 when it was replaced by the more Tri-service title of *Warrant Officer. The only conversational relic of that era is the nickname of the *Warrant Master-At-Arms as in: *'That's about as likely as a Fleet Jossman's sea *draft..'*

flex   Flexibility: *'Stacks of flex, boys but - please, nothing limp..'*

flid lid (FAA)   Occasional version of *bone dome.

flight level nosebleed (FAA)   Helicopter crew description of any altitude in excess of about 5,000 feet.

flimsy   A Naval Officer did not sight his *S206 or sign to say he had read it; this has now changed with the more recent *C206. It was however normal practice for RM officers to be shown their confidential reports, whereas the RN officer received a thin and small piece of paper - aptly named a *flimsy* - which was supposed to summarise the salient features. That flimsy could however leave a lot unsaid, giving a falsely favourable impression of what was in the main report. Flimsies were given when an officer left a ship, or when his Captain changed.

flipper to the front   Formal salute to the Priest, before punishment is awarded in older wardroom games like *The Priest of the Parish.* The *flip* was carried out with a rolled-up towel or newspaper. The phrase is now used to describe a bright spark whose talents and performance single him (or her!) out from contemporaries.

float test   *Ditch something overboard. Also used as a euphemism for getting rid of something: *'Any dirty caps that are impounded by the Commander and which remain unclaimed after three months will be subjected to a float test..'* An alternative is: *'Give it to the splosh-maker!'*

floating gin palace   A luxury cruise liner or motor yacht.

flob   To expectorate (spit) phlegm. The product may well become a *green grolly, or a *dockyard jellyfish / oyster if floating.

flog a dead horse   The process of paying off a month's advance wages at sea was known as *working off a dead horse*; when this month was up, a straw effigy of the horse was hoisted aloft, and then dropped into the sea. To *flog a dead horse* was to expect, in vain, that the crew would be willing to work any harder during that first month - since they had already been paid for it!

Clear your Yardarm

flog the glass   The intervals between *watch changes used to be timed by an hour-glass, in the days before chronometers were carried on board. There was a fond belief among *watch-keepers that the sand would fall through more quickly if the globes of the hour-glass were shaken vigorously, or warmed under a coat as in * warm the bell. These terms are still used for someone who tries to shorten his *watch or *trick.

flog the jockeys (FAA)   Operate a *Sea King's engines using the (overhead) manual throttles.

flog yer log   Masturbate.

flogged round the fleet   An old punishment, but only for the most serious crimes. The man thus sentenced was *lashed down to a grating in a small boat and then rowed to each ship in a port or harbour. That ship's company would then be *mustered on deck, to witness a dozen strokes of the *cat administered by one of their own *Bo'sun's Mates, before the whole unpleasant process was repeated further on.

Flood Q! (SM)   Emergency tank in a diesel *boat which could be filled rapidly, allowing the boat to change depth quickly, and dive away from an impending surface collision. The sea water that rushes in is sometimes described as fifty friendly tons! The expression   can also be used to describe a rapid departure: *'When the Jimmy said that, that was me - flood Q - dive, dive, dive - gone..'*

flot can (FAA)   *Flotation canister* device for use in emergency, and fitted on a helicopter's undercarriage sponsons.

flotsam   Cargo, stores, equipment etc., which has inadvertently been lost overboard, and can legally become the property of the finder - but see also *jetsam.

fluff your pinky   Break wind; see also Tugg's drawing at P - 321.

fluffy suit   WRNS best uniform, made of a more woolly material than the working dress.

flunkey   Officer's steward; note also *crumb brush and *soup jockey.

flutterbug   Older term for a helicopter.

flutter-by   The massed flypast of helicopters which traditionally opens a Naval Air Station's annual Air Day.

FlyCo *Flying Control* position in an aircraft carrier, where *Wings and *Little f reside during *Flying Stations. Also known as *The Balcony.*

Flying Stations The state of operational readiness which a ship must be at for the *launch and *recovery of aircraft. *Piped as:'*Hands to Flying Stations!' and repeated once.

flying fish sailor Jack's derogatory term for the fair weather sailors lucky enough to spend most of their sea time in the balmy waters of the Indian Ocean.

flying plumber (FAA) An Air Engineering Officer who is also qualified as a *Pirate.

flying speed The minimum speed required for an aircraft to get airborne and off the *deck, with a parallel in social life:'*We're going round to Splot's house to get up some flying speed for *Taranto Night..'* Jolly Jack's equivalent is *steerage way.

flying the blue pigeon Taking depth-soundings with a lead line.

flypro (FAA) Standard abbreviation for a squadron's *flying programme,* and also known as the *dream sheet.

FOD-plod (FAA) *Evolution designed to prevent *Foreign Object Damage* to aircraft engines or equipment. A line of personnel is formed to walk slowly across an area and then *skirmish it, in order to pick up any *gash lying on the *deck that might be sucked into a jet intake or drawn up into spinning rotor and propeller blades.

follow through Means to foul yourself as in:'*I went for a piss, thought I'd call for a damp* (fart)*, but then I followed through - and now I've got a big Japanese sunset in my *keks..'*

foo-foo (dust) (may also be spelt *phoo-phoo) Any talcum powder used by Jack, sometimes violently scented. *Pusser's foo-foo* (RM) is a foot and body powder issued in tropical zones to combat perspiration and the skin condition known as prickly heat. See also Tugg's cartoon at page P - 330.

foo-foo junks The Shanghai junks which used to carry human excrement to fertilise the fields up-river, causing much rapid closing of scuttles and hatches on board HM Ships.

fore-and-aft rig A Petty Officer's blue suit, consisting of peaked cap, reefer jacket, and trousers creased fore-and-aft. See also *square rig.

fore-endy (SM)   A submariner who works in the *fore-ends* of a
*boat, as opposed to a *back-afty.

forecastle (fo'c'sle)   The area at the *sharp end of a ship, and
which used to be built up specifically, in a Tudor sailing warship
like the MARY ROSE as a *forward castle*.

foretopman's bottle   In the old days this referred to a bottle of
medicine which was the mainstay of primitive medical treatment, and was dished out indiscriminately. A man could report
sick with a headache, back-ache, a cut, a bruise, the *trots, constipation, cold, stomach ache or just be *under the weather*, but the
treatment was the same in all cases: '*A drop of jollop from the foretopman's bottle and back to duty..*'

forget-me-nots   Contraceptive sheaths; note also *frangers and
*wellies.

forty fathom duff   A really heavy steamed suet pudding likely
to put one *hard-a-zizz.

FOST   *Flag Officer Sea Training* - the Admiral, and the generic
name for his staff, responsible for devising and supervising
operational *sea training (formerly *work-up) of RN ships, and
increasingly of ships of allied navies. They were originally based
at Portland, but are now at Devonport. *FOST *funnies* are no-
notice, impromptu drills during *sea training, designed to keep
ships' companies on their toes.

foul   A *foul anchor* exists when the *pick is caught up in something like a rope or cable. Hence a foul anchor for a *Killick's
Hook, as well as the design on the old Admiralty Flag.

foulies   Foul weather clothing.

four by two   Vies with *maskers and *dubs-40 as the most useful item of pusser's kit.   It is a soft cloth which comes in large rolls four inches wide, and is marked off into two inch strips. Originally provided for use in rifle pull throughs, but used universally *(when obtainable) in Ops rooms to rub out chinagraph markings on *Tote boards. Stokers sometimes refer to a piece of rag as a 4 x 2 irrespective of size: *'Rip us off a piece of 4 by 2..'*

four fingers   Unofficial measure of a gill of spirit when issued in a straight glass. The classic *tot is therefore a double by normal standards - and about *four fingers high* off the bottom of the glass.

Fox One!   R/T call transmitted when a *Toom fired a head-on Sparrow guided missile.

Fox Two!   R/T call transmitted when a *Toom fired a Sidewinder missile from the rear quarter.

Foxtrot Oscar!   The classic, phonetically-expressed invitation to investigate sex and travel.

frame a charge   The process (undertaken before *Defaulters) of setting out the exact description of an offence and that part of the Naval Discipline or (RM) Army Acts so contravened. The phrase has no connection with the *civvy usage which implies a fabrication of evidence.

framework of hospitality   In the days of yesteryear, when rum was still issued to Jack, two *snifters equalled one *wetter; two *wetters (wet lips) were equivalent to one *sippers, two *sippers equated to one *gulpers, and two *gulpers equalled *sandy bottoms or *grounders - the volume of a single *tot.

franger   Contraceptive sheath; see also *wellies, *freds and *forget-me-nots.   For some rather obscure reason, a *franger* *sangar* in the RN is a fried egg sandwich.

frapped   Three applications here:
1. (RM) Hit: *'We frapped the opposition good and hard..'* Note also that the French strategic nuclear deterrent is carried by their *Force de Frappe!*
2. Cut someone down to size.
3. Bound: *'That tarpaulin needs to be well frapped down to prevent it blowing away..'* Ropes and shrouds can also be *frapped together* in order to increase the tension force exerted.

Crack out some Zeds

Fratton *Getting out at Fratton* is Jack's expression for *coitus inter-ruptus* - the withdrawal method of contraception. This term is explained by the fact that on the railway line from London to Portsmouth, Fratton is the penultimate station before *Pompey.

-freak (RM)   A total enthusiast who devotes time, energy and (usually) lots of money to his obsession:
>*kit-freak* - always has the best and latest equipment.
>*nutty-freak* - heavily into chocolate and/or sweets.
>*sports-freak* - forever playing or training.
>*mailie-freak* - cannot wait for the daily post.

freckle   Anus.

Fred Quimby   The original producer of the *Tom and Jerry* cartoons; to the cognoscenti, he made the only ones worth watching. If a T&J cartoon (otherwise called a *Quimby*) was shown on video or at a Cinema Night, Jack would usually be heard shouting for *Good old Fred!*   Later on, *Fred Quimby* became the so-called artistic director of the T & J series. You can tell, in these films, that he was no longer in a postion of influence.

fred / freddie   Condom; see also *franger for some alternative names.

free and easy   Old sailing term, widely adopted elsewhere these days, for a ship whose *sheets (sail control ropes) have been eased off, and is now running free before the wind.

free gangway   This stems from describing the control of access from establishments, or seagoing ships in Harbour Routine, to shore. Before civilian dress became the norm and standards of dress in uniform were rigidly maintained, all libertymen would be fallen in and inspected by the Officer of the Watch / Day before being allowed to proceed ashore. This inspection was usually carried out for the first two *liberty boats. After that, the *Free Gangway is now open* *pipe would be made. No more formal dress inspections took place, and ratings could freely proceed ashore after handing in their *station cards.

Free the *slide!   *Pass the butter!*

free-traders   French (loose, open-legged) knickers, in contrast to *blackouts, or *passion-killers.

freedom bird   Of US and Vietnam origin, but now widely used by Jack for any aeroplane taking him home, but especially from the Falklands.

fresh air connection   A torpedoman / *sparker's way of saying there was a break in a wire or cable causing a malfunction in electrical equipment.

Fresh out!   The equivalent of *No chance!* in reply to a request for some stores item or perk.

fresh out of ideas (FAA)   The consequences of a poorly-judged or badly-executed manoeuvre: *'Lift the collective lever too early at the bottom of an engine-off *auto and you'll end up too high, too slow - and fresh out of ideas..'*

freshen the nip   A rope or wire which passes out through a *fairlead at a very tight angle is said to be *nipped*, and could be chafed; thus to *freshen the nip* is to *pay out or * heave in the line slightly to change the point of strain.

freshen your hawse   Another old sailing term for a swig of rum or whisky taken when working long hours on deck in stormy weather.

Freshwater Tanky   Seaman responsible for the daily sounding of all freshwater storage tanks. In earlier times he was also part of the team that went to the Spirit Room to draw that day's rum allowance for the *Tot's distribution to the ship. See also *Tanky.

Friday whiles   Older expression (esp. RM) for a long weekend leave, or as they still say up North, *Friday While Monday.*

frisp   Acronym for something worse than a *Jockroach - an *eff-ing, revolting, ignorant, Scottish pig.* Sometimes seen or heard as the (only just) politer version of *risp*.

frock coat and sword   Prior to 1939, officers making formal calls on Admirals wore *frock coats and swords*. The expression is therefore often applied metaphorically to an affair which must be handled officially by higher authority.

frog in a bog   The culinary dish of *toad in the hole.*

front up   Take an active role in leading a team, or take the lead when presenting some case or argument.

Frozen Chosen   Royal's laconic description of the *Commando Unit that was specially selected for Arctic Warfare training - before the associated clothing and equipment were up to a reasonable standard.

fruit machine (SM)   A primitive fire control computer still used in submarines until the early 1960s. It was situated in the control room of diesel driven *boats. As the boat moved in for an attack, the target's course and range from the periscope readings were fed into the *fruit machine*. This updated the *DIPSU GAPSU settings on the torpedoes before they were fired. From this, of course, all computers became *fruit machines*.

fruit salad   Campaign and medal ribbons, especially the multi-coloured American displays. See also *brag rags.

FUB   Acronym for the Fat, Useless (offspring of an unmarried mother).

FUBAR   Another version of *SNAFU, in this case *Fouled-Up Beyond All Recognition*.

fudge packer   Yet another of Jack's allegedly homophobic but amusing descriptions of one who practices *the love that dare not speak its name..*

fudging the issue   Faulty aims or reasoning processes in an argument or discussion.

fujiama   *'Eff you Jack, I am alright..'*

full chat (FAA)   Aircraft engine(s) developing full power; in contrast, *max chat usually refers to velocity.

full power trial   Part of a warship's *work-up following a refit; adapted by Jack in a subtle sense: *'The *bricking went fairly well - I was able to run a full power trial just six days later..'*

full set   A beard, ie. the *full set* of moustache, sideburns and neatly-trimmed facial whiskers. Nothing less is permitted for Jack; Royal has the right to grow a *'tash, but not a full set. Note also *skers, and have a laugh at page P - 343.

fungus face   A bearded individual; see above!

funnies   The particular pet subjects (or dislikes) of a senior officer: *'Watch out for officers knowing their blood groups - it's one of the Admiral's particular funnies at the moment..'*

funny fags   Cannabis; see also *wacky baccy.

funny farm   Any psychiatric hospital, but originally that at Netley on the eastern shore of Southampton Water.

furcle / furgle   *Grope and fumble with a female acquaintance.

furious palm tree   A helicopter; the nickname was derived initially from the gently-waving motion of its rotor blades when the aircraft is *shut down and at rest. When *burning and turning, it then becomes either a *furious* or a *rotating palm tree*. See also *paraffin pigeon and *kerosene budgie.

FWMMASFOHSBOTASHTSTTCNATTCUFN   *Finished With Main Motors And Steering, Fall Out Harbour Stations Below, Open The Accommodation Space Hatch, Trot Sentry To The Casing, No Access To The Casing Until Further Notice.* Last entry into the log by the Control Room Log Keeper, abbreviated as such, so he can beat the rush to the Forward Mess and be the first to - the beer / get changed / get a seat!

gadget Two completely different usages:
1. Radar set:'*I hold you on my gadget, *squawk 4543..*'
2. An engineering officer cadet in the MN and RFA.

gaff The spar which secures the upper edge of a four-sided, fore-and-aft sail. To *blow the gaff* was to show the ship's *colours suddenly from this point, and now (colloquially) means to betray or give away a confidence.

galley Any area of food preparation and cooking (never a kitchen).

galley packet rumour In the days of sail, the *galley was the only place below decks where smoking was allowed, and smokers would congregate there to *chew the fat and hence generate rumours. A *packet* was a ship carrying mails (and passengers); the *Falmouth Packet* was (and is) Falmouth's local newspaper and, because of the town's geographical position, was often the first place to get news from overseas. Nowadays, the term *galley packet* has been replaced by *buzz, which dates from the introduction of wireless telegraphy.

galley pepper Jack's nickname in older times for the soot and ashes that would on occasion fall into the *victuals as they were being cooked; still used on a *banyan when sausages or steaks are being grilled over an open fire.

Galliano shoulders A more extreme version of *Coke-bottle shoulders (which see), and nothing to do with the effects of a Harvey Wallbanger.

galligaskins Very old name for the wide breeches or petticoat trousers worn by Jack up until the early 1800s; the canvas material, impregnated with tar, was the only form of waterproofing then available for men lying across the yards aloft and handling wet sails.

Gallipoli (RM) Spring *Corps memorable date from 28 April 1915 when RM Light Infantry units of the Third Royal Marine Brigade and First Royal Navy Brigade took part in two weeks of very heavy fighting.

galvanised donkey Nickname for the Silver Horse saloon, on the *Ghut, in Malta.

game of soldiers (RM) Exasperation with all things military. The phrase: *'Stuff this for a game of soldiers!'* means: *'I have become rather disillusioned, and also I am not entirely happy with your plans for the further conduct of this operation..'*

gammy Adaptation of *game* for an injured limb or digit.

gangs (RM) Lots of (something); *gangs of *redders* implies that the weather, or the object being described, is very hot. The word has a traceable origin in that a *gang* described the full set of standing rigging attached to the mast of a square-rigged sailing ship.

gangway A free path through a barrier or obstruction, but not a word to be confused with the *brow. The cry *Gangway!* on board means that an officer or rating on some important mission needs to get past a group of men blocking a passageway or hatch. A *free gangway* is the usual state pertaining when a ship is alongside, or in a naval establishment operating normally; this can become a *closed gangway* for ceremonial or security reasons. The phrase: *'Gangway before I make a bastard!'* is a rather neat piece of double meaning, inviting someone to get out of the way - or be knocked down fatally.

gannet A quintet of applicatons:
1. A sailor who is so hungry that he eats leftovers, or is always going *round the buoy for more to consume.
2. (RM) Someone who eats quickly, and often.
3. (FAA) HMS GANNET, situated at Prestwick Airport on the west coast of Scotland.
4. (FAA) Former A/S and AEW aircraft, still flying in America for propfan research.
5. *gannet strop* - rather like *green oil for a starboard lamp*. It was a becket on a bucket, for hauling smoke out of a smoke-stack, when raising steam by hand!

gapped Something left vacant for a short period, eg. an appointment within a ship or shore organization. In theory, a crucial job or position cannot be *gapped*; Royal Marines have been referred to (very, *very* discreetly) by Jack as *trained gaps*.

gardening (FAA) The process of aerial mine-laying during WW2; the aircraft involved were sowing *cucumbers* into the sea.

gardening leave Nice slang term for a spell of leave spent at home between appointments, usually when the change-over arrangements do not dovetail perfectly. Can also imply trouble in that an officer has been relieved of his command earlier than expected, perhaps because there has been a problem requiring investigation, or else he has just been *court-martialled.

gas and gaiters A nickname in the Navy for the gunnery branch. The phrase *gas and gaiters* is a quotation from Charles Dickens' *Nicholas Nickleby*.

gash A widely-used word with four distinct meanings:
1. Anything surplus to requirement: *'You can have it - it's gash..'*
2. Anyone useless: *'Don't take him - he's a really gash hand..'*
3. Rubbish or refuse: *'*D'ye hear there - *ditch no gash..'* Note that a *gash bucket* is a waste bin, while a *gash chute* was a ramp for *ditching gash at sea. Jack also adapts the latter term on occasion for the lower end of the large bowel.
4. *'Any gash talent here?'* is a question posed when entering a night club or dance hall, and is an enquiry as to whether there are any nice young ladies present who are not inextricably committed to someone else.

gasoline gig The ship's motor boat.

gassing (SM)   This occurs when the battery charge is high or when charging at a very high rate, and the cells give off hydrogen. The *pipe is then made: *'No smoking throughout the boat, battery gassing..'*

Gatling gob   Someone who talks far too much - and far too often.

gauntlet   A form of punishment in older times involving the whole crew. The man to be punished by *running the gauntlet* ran between the lines of his shipmates, each equipped with a knotted cord or *nettle, and was *lashed up by each of them as he passed. This could be done up to three times; for more serious crimes the perpetrator would be drawn past the lines more slowly, sitting in a sawn-down wooden cask. The more modern version of running the gauntlet describes someone having to face severe criticism.

GBH of the earhole (esp. RM)   Condition suffered by someone being *picturised, or receiving a severe *bollocking.

gear   Possible contraction of the French *de rigeur*, used in Liverpool originally as *gear*, meaning *first class,* or *of high quality*. This became national usage at the time of the Beatles, with expressions such as: *'It's gear - fab!'* The single word, emitted with a loud belch at the dining table, also implies great enjoyment of the meal just consumed.

gen   Two different forms:
1. *Genuine,* or truthful: *'The ship's going to Aussie next year - it's gen!'* Or: *'Gen *buzz - we're off Down Under!'* Note also that incorrect information is *duff gen. See page R - 356.
2. General information: *'What's the gen for tomorrow?'*

General Service   Two variations in usage:
1. Any non-specialist aspect of RN service. For instance, a Fleet Air Arm *Looker commanding a minehunter without aviation assets has returned temporarily to General Service (for his fish-heading time!). Note also *return to Gens,* which was the ultimate penalty for failing specialist training in either air or submarine branches; both outfits still use it as a means of broadening experience.
2. The initials *GS* are often seen in the pattern number or stock description of some piece of *kit that is widely issued, eg. a *Raincoat Man's Blue GS.*

Generalissima   The military equivalent of *Her indoors*; see also the title of *Field Marsha and also of *CINC-NAG-HOME.

Dear Mum,
This is the life....

Commando

gentlemen captains   See also *tarpaulin captains and *all of one company in this reference to officers of a distant era, who took command because of connections and privilege - rather than proven ability at sea.

george   Euphemism for the act of defaecation: *'Now, before we get *yomping, has everyone had a morning george?'* In older times it was also the standard nickname in the FAA for an automatic pilot. Supposed to date from the reign of King George VI. You had to go and say good morning to him twice each day, at *colours and at your morning *dump.

Gestapo   Yet another soubriquet for *Regulating Branch personnel.

germs and gigglegogs   *Germs* are always pronounced with a hard *'G'* as in *girders*. *Gigglegogs* are bacteria and various cocci which Jack never knew the full or proper name of, as in: *'This place wants a good boujie out, it's full of germs and gigglegogs..'* Or: *'Don't drink that - it's full of gigglegogs..'*

get scraped   *'Go away!'* (expressed most forcibly).

get up to speed   Two applications:
1. Absorb all the current or necessary information about a subject: *'I'm up to speed on that one..'* means: *'I've read all about that..'*
2. *Getting up to *flying speed* describes the first few *wets of a drinking session or *run-ashore.

Get your hat!   Said to a rating who has just committed an offence, since he will need his *hat* to take off as an offender when he sees the *Bloke. *Get both hats!* is a jocular way of suggesting that the *dwang that Jack is in is very deep indeed this time.

gets on my tits / gets right up my nose   Jack's usual way of describing something or someone that annoys him; note also *grudge fight.

getting the logbook stamped (FAA)   Recent sexual activity; see *back in date for explanation.

getting yards   Admiring and slightly jealous description of a sexual athlete.   See also *stacks rating and the contrasting *plums.

getting your own back (SM)   This refers to the method of sewage disposal in submarines, even more of a hazard in older boats. A holding tank was enough to contain the excrement of the operator. Conected to this was a high pressure air line that charged the tank and then blew its contents to sea. The problem lay in the fact that it was also possible to open the tank top valve. That meant, instead of the odious content being discharged outboard, it discharged back in the face of the pillock who got the sequences wrong. In newer *boats, with a much larger tank, you received not just yours, but half the ship's company's residues as well. Only God could preserve the man who decided to depress the foot pedal of the crapper when the Outside *Wrecker or the Stoker PO were *shooting shit or *pumping poo at the same time.

GIB (FAA)   Acronym, amongst many others, for an *Observer - usually in a two-crew *stovepipe such as the *Toom. The initials stand for **Guy In Back** as opposed to the GIF who sits in front of him.

gibbering (pronounced with a hard 'g')   Somewhat under the influence; see also *comic cuts.

Gibraltar (RM)   Another *Corps memorable date, celebrated officially on 24 July (the date of its capture in 1704), but the place was under siege subsequently for so long that you could raise your glass to Royal and his *Cloggie comrades-in-arms of *Gibraltar* on almost any day of the year, and not be corrected for it. *Gib* is the standard abbreviation, and *Gib Gut* the local version of *Montezuma's Revenge / Aztec Two Step / Galtieri's Gallop* - all intestinal disorders that appear to be associated with a Spanish-speaking influence.

giggle   Collective noun for a marching squad of WRNS.

giggling pin   The male member.

gimpy (RM)   Two meanings, depending on the pronunciation used:
1. Hard 'g' - Unwell or not functioning correctly: '*He's got a bit of a gimpy leg..*' See also *gammy.
2. Soft 'g' - Slang acronym for GPMG, or *General Purpose Machine Gun*.

gin pennant   Green and white triangular pennant flown to indicate an invitation on board for drinks. Smaller versions may be seen in some *Wardrooms; when an officer wishes his colleagues to join him in celebration of some happy event, he will fly this *gin pennant* on the bar.

gingerbread   Decorative carving and scrollwork on the stern of 15th to 18th century warships; this was often gilded, and has led to the modern expression of *knocking the gilt off the *gingerbread*.

girl's time (RM)   Self-disparaging description of any non-pensionable service completed by Royal before the age of 21; see also the term *man and boy. It used to refer to service before the age of 18, ie. before a *man's* rate of pay was paid.

girt big knockers   Large breasts.

give it a draft chit / float test   Ditch it (common usage).

give the ferret a run   Indulge in sexual intercourse; see also a rather different meaning for *ferret.

give the other end a chance   Comment to a perpetual talker!

gizzet / gizzit   Contraction of *give us it*, ie. something attractive or useful which has been acquired for free: '*Where'd I get these pen and pencil sets? They were gizzits from the brewery rep, and keep yer thievin' mitts off..*' Tugg has this at page W - 498.

gizzmo   Similar to *Doobrey or *Johnson.

GL   An Officer of the *General List* , from which all the future Admirals (except Medical and Dental) are appointed. The majority are Seaman Officers, but there are also a number of specializatons within this full-career list, viz. *Pirate, *Looker, *Pusser, *Grubber, *Steamie, *Droggy, *Schoolie, *dagger N etc. The other major groupings are the *Supplementary List (SL) and *Special Duty List (SD) Officers; a *GL transfer* is someone who has changed over from either of these. Note the usual slang terms associated with these groupings - *GL smoothie* and *SL shag.

glad rags   The bright colours that Jack wears when going ashore.

glimpers (esp. RM)   A quick and stimulating glimpse of thigh, *suzzies or any other items of (occupied) female underwear. The associated activity is *glimping*, but under certain circumstances it may well become *perving.

glim / glims   Dim lights (originally tallow candles in sailing warships) now used to mark the edges of airfield taxyways. *'Dowse the glim'* was an instruction to *darken ship. Also an older Navy word for eyes as in:*'Dowse his glims!' - 'Give him a pair of black eyes!'*

glitter   Marmalade or jam; see also *slide - butter. *Glitter* in WW2 was the shredded and metallized foil (*Window* in *crab parlance) that was dropped to confuse enemy radars.

Globe and Bustard / Buster / Burster (RM)   Two rather confusing usages:
1. The crest of the Royal Marines; the *Burster* is thought to have been the *bursting grenade* insignia of the old RM Artillery cap badge, corrupted by general usage to *Bustard*.
2. The excellent bi-monthly Corps magazine - *The Globe and Laurel.*
3. Note also the admiring nickname for Royal Marines as *The Globe Rangers.*

gloom room   A British warship's Operations Room; US Navy parlance has *Combat Information Centre*. This may have something to do with the fact that Brits talk about a hospital's *operating theatres*, whereas across the *Pond they have *operating rooms.*

glop   Any alcoholic beverage; someone who drinks to excess is a *glophead*. The fine wines of France may, in total ignorance, be dismissed as *Froggy glop*. This word can also be used as a verb: *'Since the *Avquack warned me off, I've not been gloppin' it quite as much..'*

glory hole   Originally, a name for the stokers' quarters. Now used for any cupboard or storage space (often discovered during *Rounds) which has become filled with unofficial items while at the same time remaaining hidden from casual view. See also *Aladdin's Cave. For a perfect illustration of this concept, try Tugg on page R - 372.

glum bunny   Another version of someone who is not a very *happy Hector.

glut box   Just one of Jack's descriptive labels for the vagina.

gnat's piss   Said of anything that is weak ie. beer / tea / coffee.

go by the board   Refers either to the *board* from which a sailor was buried at sea, or to the garboard strake, the position from which burials took place because of its sheltered position.

go faster dust (RM)   An essential ingredient of Royal's cuisine in the field - *curry powder*.

go round the buoy   Have a second helping, or repeat a training course having failed the examination first time.

go through the hoop   Standard test of a correctly *lashed-up hammock; if it didn't go through a standard *iron hoop*, implying that the density of material would offer decent protection when stowed against a warship's bulwarks, the whole thing had to be undone and then re-done.

gob-shite   A loudmouth who is always gobbing-off: *'He's so gobby, he could talk a glass eye to sleep!'* See also *Gatling gob.

gob-smacked   Totally speechless with surprise; *gob-flapped* is an older variant.

gobbler's gulch   The gap between suspender belt and stocking top; see also *chuckle gap.

gobbling rods (RM)   Eating utensils; see also *KFS, *eating irons and *fighting gear.

gobby / gobbie   Older nickname for a member of the Coastguard, now better known as *Coasties. The origin of this term is a little obscure, but until 1923 this Service was run by the Admiralty and manned by Naval pensioners. Whether these men tended to be *gobby* individuals (see *gob-shite above) or whether gobby was a slang term for a naval pensioner remains uncertain. *Gobbies* certainly used to be the descriptive label applied to old men employed in a civilian capacity in naval establishments during the war. They swept huts, worked in the galley, tended boilers and generally kept the place tidy.

God botherer / God walloper   Padre; see *amen wallah for some others.

God box Two meanings:
1. Small portable harmonium used by the Chaplain.
2. A chapel or church.

God frog The Officer Commanding the *SBS.

go faster stripes Description of the steel strengthening plates welded and bolted to the sides of *Type 21 frigates and (less obviously) *Type 42 destroyers; they detracted from the otherwise aesthetically pleasing appearance of the *Type 21s, and of course their weight, together with the compensating additional ballast required to maintain stability, actually caused a slight reduction in speed!

gofer / gopher An assistant, who generally needs little brain power to carry out his task: *'Go fer this, and then go fer that..'* See also the term *doggie.

goffer Three very distinct meanings:
1. (RN & RM) A big sea washing *inboard, which may have the disastrous consequences depicted at S - 380 by Tugg.
2. To be *gofferred* can also mean being punched, hard.
3. Any non-alcoholic cold drink sold ashore, or in a Naafi canteen. A *goffer wallah* is the chap from the Indian subcontinent who sells them to Royal.

going deep Taking a nap, as in: *'Well, Number One, I think I shall be going deep for the afternoon..'*

gold-plated Unnecessarily luxurious, or packed with features of doubtful importance: *'They want 16 megabucks per copy for that new ground-attack helicopter - but the whole thing's a bit gold-plated if you ask me..'*

golden blanket / pillow Legendary prize for those individuals who are seemingly inseparable from their bunks. Sometimes heard as the *golden *gonk* award. See also *Rip van Winkle and the *Unknown Warrior.

golden bollocks Possessed by a lucky man, especially when playing tombola.

golden bowler Premature retirement from uniformed service, but on financially advantageous terms, ie. a special redundancy scheme. If the retirement is also compulsory then the individual may receive the *Order of the *Golden Toecap*.

golden eagle (RM) The source of all pay and allowances. If

Royal refers to a future time when the *golden eagle craps all over him*, he is only really talking about his next pay day!

golden rivet   Non-existent final gift from a warship's builder, supposedly fixed somewhere into the keel in order to mark the formal completion of her construction. Any invitation to enter a darkened *compartment down below, in order to inspect this legendary feature, should be treated with considerable caution.

gollies   Nickname for Electronic Warfare (EW) ratings.

gollock (RM)   A long-bladed, wooden-handled device for hacking at jungle undergrowth.

golly shop   Shop or cafe near a naval base run by Indian or Pakistanis; see also *goffer-wallah.

gongs   Campaign or valour medals; note also *fruit salad and *brag rags.

gonk (FAA)   The Fairey Gannet aircraft.

gonking   Sleeping; see also *golden, *zeds and *Egyptian (2).

goodbye-brains night   Social gathering where some serious drinking is intended - or one at which, in the subsequent descriptions, vast quantities of alcohol were consumed.

Good game!   Cheerful expression used when conditions are absolutely miserable, and the work either unremitting or non-existent.

good kit (RM)   The highest praise possible for an item of military equipment, apart from this recommendation, after a war or battle, for some piece of weaponry or ordnance: *'Everyone should have one..'* See also *Gucci.

goodlybylo (SM)   An odd card game, peculiar to submarines. The main object of the game is to divest oneself of all cards dealt.   The rules are many, and extremely convoluted; may include up to seven individual players and has no predetermined order of play or number of cards dealt. It's nearest equivalent is *Snap*.

good run ashore   A booze up, a nosh up, a knees up and a punch up. See also the entry at *beer etc.

goofer (FAA)   Spectator watching aircraft operations in a *carrier, standing in the *goofing gallery* or *goofers*, a platform located high up on the island's superstructure. This verse from the *A25

Crab Air

song is a classic:

> They gave me a Seafire to beat up the Fleet,
> I duffed up the NELSON and RODNEY a treat,
> But then I forgot the high mast on FORMID -
> And a seat in the goofers was worth fifty quid..

goolie chit (FAA)   Safe conduct pass written in several local languages, and carried by pilots operating over tribal territory, offering a reward for their safe conduct if forced down. White prisoners of tribesmen were reputed to hand over captives to their womenfolk, who cut off their *goolies*. (*Goolir* is the Hindi word for ball).

goon bag (FAA)   Aircrew immersion coverall suit, made of Egyptian cotton ventile material, with a single waterproof diagonal zipper plus rubber neck and wrist seals; also known as a *goon suit.*

gopher   See *gofer.

gorilla snot (FAA)   Bailey's Irish Cream and *sticky greens!

goss   A Tiff's expression for his hat, and nothing to do with Pete Goss, the courageous and innovative sailor - and former *Royal.

got ears on it   See *rabbit for more complete background; anything which has been *half-hitched, *proffed, *rabbited or *acquired as a gift can be described as *having ears on it.*

gotcha   Equivalent to *pooh-trap, ie. a common mistake that is just waiting to be made.

grab hooks   Fingers.

grab-a-granny night   Regular evenings at local dance halls when the more mature ladies attend, and Jack is usually assured of the action that he seeks. See also *C-Troop, *School of Dancing and the (*Wardroom) *Fishing Fleet.

grabby   Archaic nickname for infantrymen used by *donkey-wallopers; Jack adopted this term for Royal in older times, but it is now obsolete.

grable-bodied seawoman   During WW2 and after, nickname for an attractive *Wren, parody of *Betty Grable*, the long-legged and luscious Hollywood film star.

graft (esp. RM)   Hard work; often *sheer graft* or *pure graft*.

grand slam   Losing control of all three sphincters when drunk.

granny   Fussy, indecisive officer; see also *two-oh-six for an example of official usage.

granny knot   Reef knot crossed the wrong way.

granny's footsteps (SM)   An irregular and ziz-zag course when dived, named after the children's playground game.

graunch   Sound made when a ship collides with something, or runs aground into the *putty.

gravel belly   *Royal, when operating as an infantryman ashore; the term used to be reserved exclusively for an Instructor in Small Arms.

gravel grinder   A Gunners' Mate (older) or Gunnery Instructor (current) responsible for marching and parade ground drill. See also *tarmac tiff and *tick-tock tiff.

graveyard watch   Midnight to 0400.

grease   A trio of applications:
1. Butter or margarine.
2. A *grease pit* is a ship's engine room and associated machinery spaces.
3. A *greasy spoon* is the generic name for any roadside cafe where hygiene takes second place to almost everything else, and the *dog is the likely consequence resulting from any food ingested.

greased weasel shit   An item which, according to legend, slides easily off a *shiny shovel. Used now as a form of comparision for something that moves or accelerates quickly, or as a definition of *smoothness* when describing a smart talker and dresser such as a TV chat show host.

greaser   A pair:
1. Exact MN and RFA equivalent to Stoker, although the latter term is occasionally heard in conversation especially if talking with an RFA officer who is ex-RN.
2. (FAA) A very smooth landing, see also *creamer.

Green Death   Jack's generic nickname for the *3rd Commando Brigade RM*, a rather awed opinion enhanced by Royal's various activities ashore in the Falklands during 1982; may also be heard as *The Green Machine*.

Green Endorsement (FAA)   Naval Aviation's version of an official *BZ, written in green ink in the paticipant's logbook, and awarded for some above-average or courageous and skilful management of an in-flight emergency.

Green Guide   A Naval publication listing the scale of punishments awardable for various offences.

green   Naive, innocent - or easily misled through inexperience: *'He must have been a bit green to believe the *Appointer like that..'*

green-and-baggies / smellies (FAA)   Flying overalls!

green beret   Symbol of an individual's having completed *Commando training with the Royal Marines, and also worn, when qualified, with varying cap badges by RN, RAF and Army personnel seconded to the Royal Marines. Sometimes referred to as a *green lid*. There is no such thing as an *honorary green beret*.

green coat   To wear the *green coat* is to play dumb and stupid, or feign ignorance; origin uncertain at the time of writing!

green empire   The Electrical Branch.

green grolly   A lump of phlegm or a nasal candlestick. May also be described as a *green gilbert*, and see also *dockyard jellyfish.

Green Parrot   Long before Admirals had flying barges, the **green parrot** was (and still is) a CinC's floating barge. Green was a CinC's colour, other *Flag officers having *blue* barges. An aeroplane which is being used as a CinC's *barge on a regular basis may also become a *green parrot* in the same way.

green rub   An unfair or raw deal: *'A *nap hand from that blonde he met in Fort Lauderdale? Cor - talk about a green rub, eh?'*

green slug   Military-issue sleeping bag which has a quilted outer surface and head cover: *'A dry green slug in the Arctic is an absolutely vital feature in the maintenance of a man's morale..'*

greenie   Nickname for a member of the Electrical branch, signified in a rating's rank by the letter L, or WL in the Fleet Air Arm; also subdivided into *heavy greenies* who get their hands dirty by working on electric motors and suchlike (but who are not really *grubbers), and the *light greenies* responsible for computer-based electrical control systems. The term originates from the green *distinction cloth of Electrical Engineer officers, a feature now sported only by the Merchant Navy. The distinction between *weapon greenies* and *pinkies in the FAA is sometimes very blurred. See also *Green Empire, and note the lovely *'Greenies get their sea time on the Gosport Ferry..'* See Tugg at S- 388.

gremlin (esp. FAA)   A mischievous, elf-like creature who gets the blame for most defects and malfunctions in aircraft engines and machinery, Note also the term for the distaff version - *Wrenlin.

grenade   Scotch egg.

grey funnel line   Traditional in-house nickname for the seagoing part of the Royal Navy, and therefore a useful alternative to the *Andrew in that respect. Also the title of a super book by Cyril Tawney (published by Routledge, Kegan Paul) containing the words of many matelot ditties.

grid   Face, or mouth: *'Get that down yer grid..'*

grimmy   See *gronk; the *Grimmy Trophy* is a rather chauvinistic item awarded by popular acclaim each time a warship leaves after a port visit - to the chap who *trapped the worst-looking lady and brought her on board for inspection. This also used to be called a *Ropey Trophy. See *Gronk's board as well.

grip   Another potentially confusing quartet:
1. (esp. RM) *'Get a grip!'* - *'Take charge of yourself!'* Or: *'It needed someone like him to grip the problem seriously..'*
2. A *pussers' grip* is a standard issue, light brown canvas travelling bag or holdall.
3. *'He really grips my shit..'* means: *'I dislike him intensely..'*
4. *Grips* was also the old nickname for the Hong Kong Hotel

(now probably encased in concrete a mile high). One used to *come to grips* with one's friends there.

gripped by the lower band   Equivalent to grabbing someone by the nether regions, and thus exercising precise and total control over him:'*Grip them all by the lower band - hearts and minds will follow on very soon after..*' It refers to the position of standing at ease for a body of men armed with the No. 4 Lee Enfield. This rifle had woodwork around its barrel, retained by an *upper band* and a *lower band*. When stood easy, the hand was raised from the lower band to the upper one, to allow the body to relax. The hand was then moved down to the lower band in preparation for the next executive order. So, the expression originally came off the drill square to mean *Get ready!*, but now has the controlling overtones mentioned above.

gripper / gripping   These terma applied when someone tried to impress his hearers with a story, usually tall, in which he was invariably the hero, and, inevitably, always happened when he had *gone foreign*. A trained man could recognise a piece of *gripping* coming from a thousand paces, and the way of dealing with it never varied. No sooner were the first words out of a *gripper's* mouth then all hands would begin to hum, slowly and softly, the signature tune from the British Movietone News Reel. This was a great favourite with Jack. Three week old copies would always be run before the film show in the canteen flat and its slogan - *The Eyes and Ears of the World* seemed to be the perfect description of would-be grippers. If the raconteur did not immediately get the message, the humming would grow louder and faster, with the more energetic cranking imaginary movie camera handles in the air, until the point was finally taken and the gripper retired, defeated.

grippo   An acquaintance made (*gripped*) at a party or on a free treat / *run-ashore who then becomes the subject of further social transaction. No real distinction is made between male or female *grippos* in the simplest context; a *baron who has been well *strangled could also be described as a splendid or brilliant grippo.

Grocer   An officer of the Supply and Secretariat Branch (or the *Grocery Dept):'*He started out at *Dartmouth as a Seaman Officer, but then his eyesight failed - so he *remustered as a Grocer..*' See also *Pusser and *White Mafia.

grog   Rum (*neaters) diluted *two (water) and one that, until the *Black Day in 1970 was issued to ratings of *killick or Corporal and below. It was not issued to those marked in the *Victualling Book as *UA (under age) or T (for Temperance), the latter receiving an allowance of 3 old pence per day instead. When diluted in this way, the *bubbly would not keep for very long and so (in theory) could not be hoarded and consumed later, unlike *neaters which would last if re-bottled as *Queen's or *plushers and which then became the centrepiece of a *Black Mass. These illegal actions led to the occasional case of severe drunkeness in the Chiefs and PO's accommodation, and even death through gross over-indulgence. *Grog was named after Admiral Vernon - nicknamed *Old Grogram* after the grogram (*grog - rum*, geddit?) boat cloak that he wore; he first ordered this dilution process to be carried out on the West Indies station in 1740. Note also:

> *grog blossom* - an alcohol-induced flush to the cheeks.
> *grog tub* - any container in which drinks are mixed or
>   diluted.
> *grog money* - substitution allowance paid to teetotallers.

See also *half and half (SM) and Tugg's brilliance at page S - 401.

Groin Exchange / GX   The Plymouth Sailing Club, which prior to a fire in 1999 was a traditional haunt of young Naval officers visiting or working in *Guzz.

grolly   Something green, sticky, unpleasant - and usually associated with a productive cough or nasal discharge.

gronger   Rhymes with longer. Almost obsolete term for the anus, or any other receptacle for unwanted gear: *'Oh just go and stuff it up your gronger..'*

gronk   A lady of less than perfect countenance or physique. Many messdecks have a rather chauvinistic *gronk's board* on which photographic evidence of past non-talent is displayed. Jack takes a rather practical and humanitarian line: *'Booze was invented so that gronks could have an even chance..'* See also *grimmy, *bagger, *coyote and associated alternatives.

groping   The process of feeling a woman's body in an intimate way, using a Braille-based technique.

grot   A *snotties cabin or a room personalized by its owner: *'I'm just going up to the grot for some *Egyptian PT..'*

ground pounding (FAA) *Crab term adopted to describe the *SHAR when operating in a ground attack role; *mud moving is an alternative.

groundbait Box of chocolates, or some other small *rabbit, given to a lady friend in pursuit of a greater prize.

groups To receive / get *groups*, refers to the *groups of letters* in a coded signal, and means to get a hard time from a superior, wife or girlfriend.

group up (SM) Expression for a conventional submarine's main motor power configuration when aligned for high speed rather than endurance; also used by Jack to describe getting a move on generally.

growler (RM)
1. A large chunk of ice which is just awash and difficult to see.
2. A pork pie; *NAAFI landmine is a variant.
3. In the Merchant Navy a *growler* is a towel.
4. At *Dartmouth, *growler* is also the name given to a long and heavy length of rope that the young officers must carry, as a syndicate, from stance to stance in their leadership exercises. The name comes from the cursing and muttering that this item inspires!

grubber (FAA) Air engineering mechanic (or officer): '*The life of a Fleet Air Arm grubber is an appalling mix of blood, snot and lube oil..*' See also *plumber, *greenie, *pinky etc.

grudge fight Older 'tween decks system of sorting matters out when messmates *got on each other's tits. It was applied for officially and run in a boxing ring, under Queensberry Rules, by the *springer. The event continued until one participant either declined or was unable to continue. Generally, this procedure sorted out problems very nicely all round.

grumblegram Alternative name for the 40 word *familygram.

grumpy (esp. RM) Adjective used in a nursery style to imply that someone is not very happy: '*As a result of that Promotion List signal the Adjutant was a rather grumpy frog for a while..*' He could also, in this context, have been described as a not very *happy Hector.

grunt (RM) American import, much liked by Royal, for an infantry soldier.

Grunter Occasional nickname for the *Bloke as a result of his frequent habit of merely grunting in reply to a question.

gruntled Pleased, similar to *chuffed in the sense that the person is not *dis*gruntled or *dischuffed.

G, T or **UA** The former annotation on Jack's *Pay Book indicating his entitlement to rum; G for Grog, *T for Temperance (entitled to 3d (old pence) per day in lieu), and *UA for Under Age (under 20).

guard and steerage Thirty minute lie-in allowed to non-watchkeepers (eg. duty men working after midnight the night before) instead of a *make-and-mend. Because the rest of the messdeck had *turned out and *turned to, it was sometimes an opportunity for a *nifty fifty, hence Jack's nickname for this concession of *guard and flog*.

guardrail critic Someone who comments while standing and watching others at work, akin to the armchair expert ashore.

guardship RN warship performing some important operational or ceremonial duty; hence, Falkland Islands *Guardship* or Cowes Week *Guardship*. Also used to denote the *duty ship* in a group. By extension, Jack, in his inimitable way, uses it to describe a ship that keeps out of the way when there's trouble; thus during the South Atlantic campaign the *flat tops were contemptuously but unfairly described as the *Cape Town Guardships*, by virtue of their disposition well to the east. More recently, during operations in the Adriatic, the *carrier was referred to as the *Bari Guardship*.

Gucci (esp. RM)   A hallmark of excellence as far as Royal is concerned, and referring as much to sleekness of appearance and build quality as to versatility and usefulness. This term of admiration is used as an adjective rather than a noun:*'Those trial ski-march boots are really Gucci. It looks as if *Pusser may have got it right this time..'*

guesstimate   Beautiful amalgamation of the words *guess* and *estimate* which works well in practice as something spontaneous (like a guess) rather than formal and considered (as in a written estimate): *'When will the job be finished? Well, the current best guesstimate is early next week, but if the new parts don't arrive on time, we could be looking at delaying Easter leave..'*

guff   Two uses:
1. A load of rubbish:*'Don't talk such guff!'*
2. The Journal of Royal Navy Medicine (an excellent publication) is known more widely as *The Guffer's Gazette.*

gulpers   A long single swallow of an *oppo's *tot - either repaying some favour owed, or in clearance of a gambling debt. Note that two *sippers equal one *gulpers* in the *framework of hospitality.

gung ho / gunjy   US Marine Corps WW2 slogan, which is Chinese for working together (*kung-ho*). Later the term *gung-ho* was used in the FAA to indicate a keen type, whereas *gunjy* has evolved into an admiring description, on the other side of the *Pond, for someone who definitely does not eat muesli for breakfast, and who uses three colours of *cam cream when out on exercise.

gunna-merchant   An individual who disappoints because he is always *gunna* do this or *gunna* do that - but somehow never does.

gunner's daughter   The name of the gun to which *Boy sea-men were married (tied) when receiving punishment.

gunner's mate   A PO (or CPO, *Chief Gunner's Mate*) immediately subordinate to the Gunner, who might be of Warrant Officer rank or above.

gunny   US Marine Corps *Gunnery Sergeant*, all key men, and highly respected within that huge Corps.

gunny bunny   *Field gunner's groupie.

gunroom   The *Middies' or *Subbies' Mess at BRNC *Dartmouth, and similarly in the Dartmouth Training Ship. Most large ships of cruiser size upwards had a *gunroom* in which to park their *Snotties. It used to be a compartment on the lowest *gun deck* of a warship in the days of sail, but this has now been brought up to the main deck, although it is still separate from the *Wardroom.

Guns   The *Gunnery* officer; see also *Torps and Tugg at S - 412.

gunwales under (pronounced *gunnels*).   Drunk, as in *bows under.   Derived from the appearance and movement of an over-loaded pulling boat.

Guppy   Two usages:
1. (FAA) Nickname for the old AEW Skyraider aircraft.
2. (SM) Nickname for a really fast submarine.

gusting   Jack's term for nearly, or about: *'How much do I think that will cost? I'd say four thousand, probably - four thousand gusting four-and-a-half..'*

Gut / Ghut   Nickname for Strait Street in Valetta, Malta - a narrow thoroughfare which wound downhill in the old city. Jack would buy *sticky greens for his *pash and cold Cisk or Hop Leaf (beer) for himself at the top on pay day; then, as his pockets grew emptier, he and Royal would descend to the lower levels for some sleazier entertainment fuelled by *Ambit and lemonade. Like *Bugis Street in Singapore, the locale has now been cleaned up. The derivation of the word may also have something to do with the beer. The choice was Blue or Cisk, both of which were foul, being made from Maltese water which itself was salty and brackish. Another rot gut was Marsovin, which called itself wine.

gut bucket   Someone with a large beer belly.

guts   Two completely different meanings:
1. Courage; being *gutless* implies the absence of moral backbone in somebody.
2. To *drop your guts* was to break wind. Note also the old naval saying that *'Midshipmen have guts, officers have stomachs, but Flag Officers have palates..'*. Those same officers might also use the phrase: *'I'll have your guts for garters..'* as an admonition or threat of punishment in order to encourage lesser brethen.

Guzz / Guzzle   The naval base of Devonport, adjoining Plymouth. Three possible explanations for this nickname are:
1. *GUZZ* was the wartime signal letter group for the port's call-sign - probably not true.
2. *guzzling* was what Jack did to excess on return from a long spell at sea in the *far flung, especially Janner Jack or a *Westo.
3. *'Cos it's allus rainin' when yer gets in, an' it's allus rainin'when yer guzz out again..'*

gynagorous   Huge.

gynoferous   Frequent description of great size: *'Honest - it was this high! The thing was a sodding great gynoferous *crocadillapig!'*

gyp   A pair of applications:
1. *Egyptian* tummy or *gyppy* tummy; later on, *gyp* came to be used for any pain or aggravation: *'This business of changing *watches every week is beginning to give me the gyp..'*
2. Can also mean to swindle somebody.

gyppo   Another duo:
1. Gravy - *'Pass the gyppo..'*
2. Also an abbreviation for *Egyptian, as in *gyppo PT* (sleep).

gyro failure (FAA)   Nice way to describe the effect of too many *wets; in addition, if the individual affected is unable to stand up, his *gyros have toppled.*

hack   A varied sextet, mostly FAA :
1. Achieve a standard required:*'You can hack it, *Wingsy baby!'*
2. Close down or shut off a piece of mechanical equipment: *'Hack the speed select levers, quick!'*
3. In the tactical sense, shoot down an enemy aircraft:*'The *CAP Sea Harriers hacked the Argentine Skyhawks as they came out from Falkland Sound..'*
4. An aircraft used for general flying purposes is known as the station *hack* (from the equestrian use of the word).
5. *hacked off* – polite version of *pissed off.
6. Journalist - sometimes (though not always!) a person who would benefit immensely from a swift *hack in the fork.*

hackle   A process in rope-making where natural fibres are combed into straight lines by *hackle-boards*, blocks of wood or metal studded with steel prongs. This may have the same origin as an animal raising its hackles when angry or frightened, and when the hair stands up on the back of its neck.

haircut run   Classic description of a quiet *run ashore (usually on the first day in) which might or might not achieve the stated objective, but usually ends up in a bar-crawl; an alternative is a *post card run. In the RM world, it is an equally classic reason given to visit a local town on market day, when the pubs are open throughout the forenoon and afternoon.

hairs on my wrist   An estimate of time, as in:*'By the hairs on my wrist, I reckon it's *tot time..'*

hairy-arsed   Traditional adjective describing the *matelot occupants of a *bear pit.

hairy hoover   Any short-legged, long-haired dog, usually described with grammatical correctness as: *'It was an hairy*

Crusher

hoover..' The *Jockanese hairy hoover* is Dougal of *The Magic Roundabout*, a children's TV programme that is enjoying something of a renaissance in the new Millennium.

half a *dog watch A very short period of time, figuratively speaking: *'How kin 'e know, of all people? The *sprog's only bin in half a dog watch..'*

half-blues Smart *rig of white front and blue trousers.

half-cut An individual who might be described as *in wine, but not fully *paralytic.

half-hard books Egyptian pornography. See also *AFO.

half-hitched Stolen - from the process of putting a rope (in a **half-hitch**) around something in order to drag it away.

half-masted Colours at *half-mast* down the *jack as a sign of mourning - or trouser legs that are too short!

half-stripe The addition of a half-thickness gold lace stripe to a Lieutenant's uniform sleeve, signifying promotion to Lieutenant Commander: *'I *ship my half-stripe next month..'* See also *two and a half.

hammock Classic sleeping method, and a piece of *kit still to be found in Naval *Stores, because with the insertion of metal rods as a frame, the canvas hammock (or *mick) now becomes a camp bed. A properly slung example can be seen in HMS WARRIOR, the warship museum that is part of the excellent Portsmouth Maritime Heritage, along with HMS VICTORY and the immediately adjacent MARY ROSE. See also *stretcher.

hammy, cheesy, eggy topside Classic Naval recipe of toasted ham and cheese with a fried egg resting on the summit; see *cheesy etc.

hand (SM) See *hands, but in the singular used to describe seaman officers below the *First Lieutenant in seniority order (*second hand, third hand*, etc). Note also the wise advice, whether on the *yards of a sailing ship or when clinging to the side of a mountain: *'One hand for the ship, and one for yourself..'*

hand, reef and steer The traditional abilities of a seaman, and the skill difference between him and a *landsman.

hand-organs Look up *holy stones in Christopher Ll,oyd's book *The British Seaman* and you'll find this quotation referring to the late 18th century: *'The decks are scrubbed with holy stones shaped like bibles, or scrapers called hand-organs..'*

handcarted   Well *shot-away !   See the classic Tugg on page S - 420.

handful of sprats   Refers to Jack's lack of success the night before. See also *plums and *no dopples.

hands   Collective term applied to the whole *ship's company; it dates from sailing days when all on board should be able to *hand, reef and steer and thus *hands* were the prerequisite for any seamanship *evolution.   Hence the *pipe *All hands on deck!*, *Call the hands!, Hands to Action Stations!*, etc. Note also that an individual with pleasant social attributes is described as a *good hand*, or the RN and RM equivalent of a good egg, or *TCBO. *Hands to dance and *skylark!* was an older *pipe that meant a period of light-hearted fun, with no holds barred, although it could have a serious purpose, for example if a wooden ship was lightly aground, the capering about of the ship's company could be enough to shake her free.

handraulic   See also *Armstrong Patent and Mandraulic.

hands-on   To be in actual physical control of something, such as an aircraft: *'How much actual hands-on time have you got?'* Also an expression of criticism: *'He's a hands-on manager..'* as someone who interferes a bit too much.

Handsomely!   Instruction to carry out an *evolution slowly, carefully and evenly - as when lowering the *seaboat. See also *roundly for the opposite meaning of *Speed up!*

Hands to dinner! (pause) *'ERAs to lunch!'*

Hands to dinner! - **Starboard 30!**   Jack's rueful *drip that, just as he has time to relax, the *Old Man puts the ship through a series of violent manoeuvres.

hang fire   Term used to describe ordnance which, although the firing circuit has been made, has not actually been fired or launched. The *drill, for a ship-launched or -fired weapon, was to wait for 30 minutes in case it *cooked off, then unload it carefully and *ditch it. For air-launched weapons, the pilot would attempt to release the weapon, or manoeuvre violently to try and shake it off; if all else failed, the aircraft would *divert or be recovered with the ship at a high state of preparedness.   By extension it has also come to mean *Wait just a moment!*

hang out of _____
1. (When applied to the fairer sex) Cohabiting with someone, in the same sense as *crawl through.
2. (RM) A direct threat of violence to a faint-hearted *heap: '*Get your ruddy arse in gear, or I'll hang out of you, you *big girl's blouse..*'

hangar queen (FAA)   An aircraft with a series of problems that spends more time on the ground (in the hangar) than in the air. The natural temptation to rob it for spare parts in order to keep others flying only prolongs its agony; also known as a *hangar Annie* or a *Christmas tree.

hanging judas   A rope, line or halyard that is not properly secured and therefore unsightly. See also *Irish pendant, but the difference is that an Irish pendant shouldn't be there at all, while something that is *hanging judas* should, but not looking the way that it does.

hanging mood   Description of *Father's demeanour when severe punishments are being meted out at *Defaulters: '*The *Old Man must be in a real hanging mood - fourteen days pay for that? Bloody 'ell!*'

hanging on the slack   Waiting to be given an order. This analogy is derived from waiting to haul on a rope.

hanky panky   Old name for brandy and ginger wine; comforting when one has a cold, and presumably something that loosened normal inhibitions and then gave rise to the modern meaning of these words!

Hannah (RM)   Nickname associated with the surname Snell, after the famous female Marine *Hannah Snell* who enlisted and fought at Pondicherry in the 18th century. She later became the landlady of a pub called *The Widow in Masquerade* at Wapping.

happy Hector   '*Hey, Dusty - the *Fleet Jossman wants to see you, and he's not a very happy Hector this morning..*'

happy ship   Any Naval organization with good relationships between all ranks and rates; the resulting shared sense of purpose and high morale are immediately apparent to a knowledgeable visitor. The Commanding Officer may then be the subject of praise: '*He certainly runs a happy ship..*'

harbour cotters (SM)   Fish steaks in batter, named after the *cotter* that is placed in a *boat's main vent actuator to prevent it opening up and accidentally flooding the ballast tanks while the *boat is alongside in harbour.

harbour hassle   The red tape, *bumph, shore routines, demands for working parties, training, etc. that make Jack's and Jenny's return to *base port in their ship a less than pleasurable experience - after the first 24 hours!

hard   Beach or landing place, also a term for a penile erection. The sign *Admiral's Hard* on a wall opposite the RM Barracks at Stonehouse in Plymouth is not a cause for celebration as much as a statement of location.

hard and blind   In a state of extreme sexual excitement.

hard a 'zizz   Fast asleep.

hard liers   Contraction of *Hard Lying Money* - a special allowance paid to Jack and Royal in certain ships with sub-standard living conditions. Minesweepers and the older submarines were examples of this.

hardover   Describes a dashing commander who habitually orders full helm and high speed as if to bring his ship to action when executing a peacetime manoeuvre!

Hard shit!   *'Tough luck, *oppo..'* Note that *Tough titty! expresses much the same sentiment.

hard tack   Ship's biscuit made of mixed wheat and pea flour, with sometimes an addition of bone dust. See also *soft tack - bread.

hard time   Close questioning or extra difficulty: *'I got a really hard time from the Command about that little incident, even though we probably saved the *civvy's life..'*

hard to fathom   Something that is difficult to understand clearly, an expression that has come ashore from the days of the *sounding line and associated problems of establishing depth in shoaling waters.

hard up in a clinch   Jack's older figure of speech to describe a piece of misfortune that has befallen him, adding *and no knife to cut the stopping* if he cannot see a way out of his difficulties either.

hardly out of the egg   Description of a very inexperienced individual.

harness cask   A large open cask kept on deck in the days of sail, containing the salted *ready-use provisions that had been brought up from store below. Since Jack called all his meat provisions *salt horse, in the conviction that most of it had an equestrian origin, the *harness cask* was where the *horse without its harness* had been stabled!

harpic   Mad: '*He's gone bloody harpic..*' This term was derived from a lavatory disinfectant, whose claim in advertisements was that it would *clean round the bend*. See also *Dagenham.

Harry Freeman's   Jack's dated phrase for something that would now be called a *gizzit. *Harry Tate's* is also an older term, for anything amateur in the RN; the word Harry was a classic emphasis for something, eg. *Harry *flakers, Harry *ratters* or *Harry *crappers* (but not, please note, *Harry Krishna!*). *Harry Lashingtons* was a nice term for lots of something. Note also *Harry *pinkers, Harry *stoppers* and *Harry *thickers*.

harvest festivals   A Wren's knickers; all was *safely gathered in.*

Haslar   A *creek in Portsmouth Harbour where the famous naval hospital was built in 1746, and where Fort *Blockhouse is also situated. When Haslar hospital was first constructed, it was the largest brick building in Europe. Its first Physician was the wholly admirable James Lind, who proved that the consumption of fresh oranges and lemons was capable of curing the distressing maritime problem of scurvy. Later on, this source of vitamin C was changed to lime juice, hence the terms *limey and *lime juicer used across the *Pond. In 1998 the prefix *Naval* was dropped from its *Royal Naval Hospital* title, following a Defence Cost Study review by the *Madhouse, which preserved Haslar but also closed the other five Naval, Army and RAF Service Hospitals. Two years later, the place was due to be shut down almost completely, owing to its geographical unsuitability to be the sole Defence Services hospital! This end result could have been predicted by any operationally-committed senior *quack (like the author) who spent his time in or near the front line. Those responsible for this appalling piece of planning nonsense have never been called to account.

hat *flat-aback   Traditional description of Jack at his ease ashore in uniform, drink taken, and, in order to show off his quiff, with his cap well back on his head.

hat rack   Usually a homosexual, but the term can also be used to describe a very senior officer who is a *figurehead without any serious redeeming physical or intellectual qualities beneath the gilded cap.

hatch coaming   The low watertight wall built on the deck around a hatchway, to prevent water running into and down the hatch. Note the spelling - *combings* are the business of barbers, not shipbuilders!

hatch rash   Forehead or shin bruising that results from banging one's head on a closed (or closing) watertight hatch, or legs against the sill; see also *coaming rash.

haul arse   (or rather *ass*)   American slang import meaning to move quickly.

haul(ed) down   A flag signal which has been flying either *at the dip or *close up is finally *hauled down*, which is either the executive order for the signalled instruction to be carried out, or indicates that action is being completed. *Flag officers *haul down their flags* on being relieved of duty, and may also submit a *haul-down report* to their superiors, covering key events during their time in command.

haze   The process of making life on board as uncomfortable as possible for a ship's crew, by forcing them to work extra watches doing menial tasks. This word still exists in America to describe fraternity initiation rites, but on this side of the *pond it has changed to *faze*: 'Smashing his car up didn't seem to faze him at all..'

he-she   A transvestite; the author has also heard this, in the Southern hemisphere, as *Man Mary!*

head down   Description of sleep: '*I'm going to get my head down..*'

head rope   Used to secure the bow, or a *trot of submarines, and the term may be used by Jack when ashore and confronted with the problems of animal management eg. a camel or donkey.

head sarnie   The Liverpool or Glasgow kiss, as opposed to a *knuckle sarnie: *'Does yer Mammy sew? Yuss? Well, get her to stitch this then!'*

head shed (RM)   Alternative for *puzzle palace when describing a Unit HQ.

head-up display   A brilliant system in every sense (when it works) fitted in single-seat high performance aircraft like the *SHAR, whereby the most important elements of instrument data are electronically reflected onto a glass plate in the lower part of the cockpit windscreen, thus enabling the pilot to keep his head up and looking out in front. See also *magic writing.

heads   The ship's latrines, which in sailing days were located in the area between the *forecastle and the beakhead (the forwardmost point of the ship); they were situated on both sides (hence use of the plural), but Jack's forebears were expected to use the *leeward side for obvious reasons.   The term (in the plural) is still used in the RN, but our special relations across the *Pond have always used the singular.   Often cleaned by the *non cangoists.

heads I win, tails you lose   *No matter what happens, I win!*

heads up   Early warning of a problem which may soon develop and cause difficulty: *'Did anyone give you a heads up on that new system?'*

heap (RM)   A pair:
1. *Shambolic individual of poor personal appearance.
2. The *heap system* of keeping papers on a desk. The *deep litter system* of record keeping is rather similar.

(I) **hear what you say, but** -   A dreadful figure of speech being used more and more; it sounds conciliatory but in fact means: *'Your opinion is different to mine and so I won't take any notice of it!'*

Heart of Oak   The Royal Navy's traditional theme, derived from a patriotic song written by David Garrick to commemorate a number of British victories gained abroad in the year 1759: *Heart of Oak are our ships, Jolly Tars are our men..* The rhythm of this song was used by a warship's drummers when beating to *Quarters.

Heartbreak Lane (RM)   Last leg of the *Endurance course at *Lympstone. Its name results from the fact that before entering this feature, the wet and muddy recruit (or doctor!) has been running downhill for some four miles, with the camp buildings in sight for most of that time; suddenly he can only see hedges on either side, and the (now level) road appears to be climbing, as well as heading away from the finish line.

heave   A sextet of different applications:
1. *heave to* - stop in the water.
2. *heaving line* - rope thrown from ship to ship, or from ship to shore, weighted with a *monkey's fist.
3. *heaving tackle* - heavy ropework for lifting and shifting.
4. *heaving his heart out* - being violently sick.
5. *heaving* (RM) - smelly, filthy.
6. (the old) *heave-ho* - good riddance to someone or something.

heavy for'ard (SM)   *Fanny rat, or a chap with a particularly impressive issue of *wedding tackle.

heavy mob (SM)   Submarine Maintenance Group, also the humping and carrying team at *Dartmouth.

H - 220

hedging and ditching (FAA) The process of taking a lady friend for a walk near a Naval Air Station, with a view to a spot of *groping.

helioproctosis Condition in which someone appears to believe that the sun shines out of his or her backside; *procto-heliosis is a similar affliction.

hen-pecked (RM) A hangover induced by the excessive intake of Royal's favourite duty-free fluid - *Famous Grouse* Scotch whisky.

hermit's box The Captain's day and sleeping *cabins, ie. the mechanism by which he can lead a completely separate existence in a warship if he needs (or wants) to.

herrings in Shortened form of *herrings in* tomato sauce . See also *-ITS, and hence HITS. The hated herrings were wonderful for cleaning the flues. The cooks had awful ranges to cook on which sooted up. They would put a tin of *herrings in* into the fire, and then all retreated outside, waited for the bang, then wnt back to clear up. The result was magical.

Hertz van Rental Mythical Dutch officer, along with his *oppo *Naafi / Tilly van Driver, who can be asked for by Royal when getting a *bite out of his *Cloggie colleagues:'*Oi, Pieter - 'ave you seen Cap'n Hertz van Rental? 'E wants to ask you summat..*'

hexy blocks (RM) Small cubes of solid hexamine fuel used, in the tinplate *hexy cooker* that they are issued in, to heat up the contents of Royal's *compo *rat pack in the field.

High enough! The order to stop hoisting.

high hover State of great anxiety: '*Thank goodness that VVIP visit is over - everyone's been in a really high hover for the past few days..*'

Historics (FAA) The Fleet Air Arm's *Historic Flight* operating from *Yeovilton; a splendid sight as well as a glorious sound.

hitched Married; the old advice to naval officers was Lieutenants musn't, Commanders may, Captains should, but Admirals must. Attributed to *Jackie Fisher.

Hit him with your handbag! '*That was a really weak tackle!*'

Hit the deck! Even more urgent order to get down low immediately before a missile comes *inboard; see also *brace, brace, brace!

hit the pit Expression with similar meaning to *gonking or the process of *racking out.

Hitler's Victuallers (Hitler's Vittlers) *Cates and his staff.

HMS / HMHS Her Majesty's Ship / Her Majesty's Hospital Ship.

HO Abbreviation for *Hostilities Only*, ie. someone who served in the RN or RM for the duration of World War 2: *'I was in the Corps in my younger days - but only as an HO..'* Some wags have this as *Helping Out*!

HoD Head of Department; *HoDs 1100* means that a Heads of Department meeting will be held an hour before noon.

hog snarling Qualifying description for drunk.

hog wash / hoggin The sea - usually heard in conversation as the *ogwash or oggin, or even the *og. Also an expression for a story that is not believable: *'This is the second occasion that you have requested special leave because of your grandmother's funeral - it's a load of hog wash..'*

hogging and sagging Unusual strains and stresses are set up in a ship's structure when part of her hull is unsupported. When waves are supporting the bows and stern of a ship, but not her amidships part (ie. when the hull tends to assume a concave shape), the ship is said to be *sagging*; when the amidships part is supported but not the extremities (ie. when the hull tends to become convex), the ship is said to be *hogging*.

hoist in Understand something: *'Look Einstein, it's dead simple. If you ain't got no *ickies then you ain't gettin any *wets! Can't you hoist that in fer Gawd's sake?'*

holdfast Self-explanatory in the instruction: *'Holdfast to that rope!'* but also used in the sense of *belay: *'Holdfast, you lot, where do you think you're going?'*

holdover (FAA) Delay between courses for students in the flying training pipeline; the young *Bloggses are sent to ships or Service establishments to do something varied or useful while waiting on their *holdovers*.

(The) Hole Nickname for the underground bunker of the Fleet Operations Centre at Northwood.

holidays   Two similar applications:
1. Bare patches on a newly-painted surface that have been missed by the paint brush.
2. Gaps in a line of people *fallen in for *Divisions or standing at *Procedure Alpha; as nature abhors a vacuum, so *buffers (1) and *Chief GIs (2) abhor *holidays!*

holy ground   The *quarterdeck.

Holy Joe   Yet another version of padre! See *amen wallah for the complete list.

holystones   Blocks of sandstone used for scrubbing wooden decks, so named, it seems, because Jack had to get on his knees to use them; small ones were called prayerbooks, while bigger lumps were Bibles. See also *hand-organs.

home   *'Sorry, I thought I was at home!'* Token apology for a notable belch or loud fart.

home porting   The base port system for each class of ship; for more detailed explanations, see *base porting and *port divisions.

homeward bounders   Large or crude stitching used by Jack to sew badges on, or make repairs while *homeward bound*, in anticipation that they would then be sewn on properly by the *dragon. Also *Chief's ability to coax a few extra shaft revolutions out of the main engines towards the end of a deployment. The phrase is now also used in the *Boneyards to describe deep surgical suturing of lacerated skin. See Tugg at T - 444.

Honest, Chief - it just came off in me 'and!   Jack's traditional statement whenever anything breaks off or comes apart!

honey monster (RM)   Two variants:
1. Mechanical equipment for sewage handling or latrine (*honeypot*) emptying.
2. Any large, enthusiastic, but not very pretty lady with a particular weakness for Royal Marines.

Honkers   Hong Kong; also known as *Honky Fid*.

honking   A subtle trio:
1. Glaswegian patter word (like *minging) for *handcarted or very drunk.
2. (RM) Smelling strongly.
3. Physically sick; *honking your ring* up is a severe episode of vomiting.

hook   Another quintet:
1. The leading seaman's badge; see also *killick.
2. Nickname for an anchor; the *pick is an alternative.
3. (FAA) Aircraft *tailhook* for picking up an arrester wire on *recovery to the flight deck.
4. *'Can I have my hook back?'* meaning: *'You were on a big *bite there!'*
5. *hook pot* - a tired old warship.

hooker   Tubby little fishing vessel used for line fishing, but also a name for a ship nearing the end of her working days and looking her age. Both aspects of the name apply to the shore-based connotation of a prostitute working the streets and trying to *hook* her clients. At a RN party or social gathering where a senior guest is circulating, an officer acting as *hooker* will precede that guest, lining up the next people to be introduced to him or her.

Hooky   Nickname for a *Leading Hand, so called because of the fouled anchor (or *hook) badge indicating his or her *rate; also a standard nickname for the surname Walker.

hooley   A gale or strong wind. On a stormy day, it will be blowing a *hooley*, from *blowing a hooligan.*

hoop   To go *through the hoop* is to undergo an ordeal. From the old practice in some ships of passing hammocks through a *hoop gauge* to check that they were of uniform size and appearance, before allowing them to be stowed in the hammock nettings.

horizontal champion   Someone who sleeps a lot; see also *Rip van Winkle and the *Unknown Warrior.

Horlicks   Politer alternative for *cock-up:*'Unfortunately, he then made a complete Horlicks of that as well..'*

hornpipe   Properly, an ancient Celtic wind instrument, played as an accompaniment to dancing; hence it has come to mean the name of the dance itself. It was adopted by Jack's forebears in about the mid 18th century, but it otherwise has no maritime origins; the music was (and still is) provided either by a *squeeze-box or a *fiddle.

horoscope   An immediate future that is looking bleak:*'If you let me down just once more, you miserable little toad - you'll get your horoscope read - and no messing..'*

Custard Bosun

horrorscope   A really bad *set of papers or *comic cuts, also something said or read to a junior rating by a coxswain or other senior rating to give him a clear and graphic view of his misdeedss or shortcomings. More feared than Captain's report.

horse   Two meanings:
1. (FAA) Game played by aviators, using the numbers stamped on their aircrew watches, to discover who is buying the wine with dinner!
2. This was also a frequent term used in the late fifties and early sixties. It was used like *wingsybash or *oppo, but had a specific meaning with regard to the opposite sex. Your *horse* was not your regular girlfriend, but something you rode ashore, as in: '*A few scoops with the lads and then round to see my horse..*'

horse box (RM)   The Sergeants' Mess, ashore or afloat.

horse's neck   Brandy and ginger-ale mix, a traditional *Wardroom drink, often written as 2/3 HN.

hot (FAA)   A *Dip gang is *hot* when in contact with a *tube; note also the expression *In hot regarding live weaponry.

hot / hottie   The *buzz, issue or topic of the moment: '*I've heard various figures quoted for the next pay rise, but six per cent across the board seems to be the real hottie at the moment..*' Note also *Red Hot* - a notice board in briefing rooms, offices, etc., on which is pinned the latest vital information or orders.

hot bunking (SM)   Alternate use of bed / bunk space by sailors going on and coming off *watch, as a result of there not being enough sleeping accommodation for all the ship's company; still very much used in *boats, where space as always is at a premium - seldom encountered in surface ships, except possibly in wartime.

hot fog   Steam (this was used frequently in the Cat and Cathedral class frigates which were diesel driven, and where the word *steam* was forbidden.

hot press   Older term for a situation of such dire national need to *impress men for service in the Royal Navy that the press gangs were instructed to take any men that they could find - whatever protections or excuses they carried. See also the *Andrew.

hot run (SM)   A very dangerous occurrence, namely a torpedo running (prop turning) in a closed tube. One of these sunk the *boat HMS SIDON in the early '50s.

hot wash-up   A debrief and quick analysis held immediately after the completion of some event or exercise.

hour hog (FAA)   The *Pirate or *Looker who is getting more flying hours than anyone else in a Squadron's *stats sheets; he may also discover that he has become labelled *hog of the month*.

housewife (pronounced *huzziff*)   A cloth roll containing thread, needles, buttons and all the sewing kit needed for the traditional task of *make and mend.

hover   To wait near at hand; to linger or waver. Originally a nautical usage, to describe a vessel that stood on and off the coast. Derived from the verb *to hove*, or to appear in sight.

howdah (FAA)   The hydraulically-retractable flightdeck-level control position of the old aircraft carriers, where the duty *badger sat and controlled the steam catapults at *launch.

howling (RM)   Drunk; as with *minging, it can also refer to something that smells very strongly.

HQ1   Damage Control *Headquarters* in a ship, and usually co-located with the *Ship Control Centre. It is permanently manned at sea and in harbour. At *Action Stations or in any emergency, it is where all the necessary actions to ensure the ship's survivability are co-ordinated.

hucked out   Somewhere that has been cleaned out for *Rounds.

huffer (FAA)   Engine-starting generator trolley.

hugger mugger   An old naval term meaning slovenly, confused, or generally muddled.

hulk   Originally a large and unwieldy transport/cargo vessel, especially in the Mediterranean (it comes from the Greek word *holkas*). It subsequently came to mean an old dismasted vessel laid up in a harbour and used for stores, accommodation, training, as a prison or even as a hospital (for dangerous, contagious and incurable diseases).

humming (RM)   Stinking; also the secondary meanings for *minging, *howling and *honking.

humungous   Enormous; see also *gynagorous, *gynoferous and *gynormous.

Hurricats   Expendable Hawker Hurricane aircraft catapulted from *CAM ships for convoy protection (WW2).

Hurt Certificate   An official statement of a sailor's wounds that had been sustained in action on duty. This could be purchased by the *Pusser when that sailor retired from the sea - a crude form of lump sum pension. The modern *MOD Form 298 has no such monetary value, but is still called a *Hurt Certificate*. See Tugg's brilliant evocation of this concept on page T - 452.

hussif   Standard pronounciation of *housewife - the roll issued as standard kit to all seamen and marines, and containing a sewing kit of needles, threads, pins and buttons for repairs during a *make and mend.

INDIA

229 - 236

I   Respectful, but shortened form of reference and address for a *GI* (Gunnery Instructor) or *TI* (Torpedo Instructor).

I am IT, and you are SHIT   Something wrong with this instructor's attitude to his duties?

ice / break the ice   An *ice-breaker* is a specially designed and strengthened vessel, built for the purpose of forcing a path through pack ice in extreme latitudes. Frequently, such a vessel is employed to prepare the way for other vessels that need to reach some distant, ice-bound objective - as when opening up a lane in an ice-bound port. Colloquially, an ice-breaker is also anything that breaks down reserve or reticence, such as in one's first meeting with a stranger, or in preparing the scene so that unpleasant or unwelcome news can be imparted. It is interesting to note that the phrase *It cuts no ice with me* comes from an expression of the Iroquois Indians, a tribe from the Great Lakes area in Canada. Not nautical in origin, but introduced into English by the Americans during the War of Independence, in the 1770s.

ice cream suit   White trousers and tunic which button up to the neck, worn by officers and senior ratings in the tropics; now only worn on the most formal occasions by senior officers, it has been replaced by trousers and an open-necked bush jacket.

icers (RM)   Cold: *'Turn the heating up, will you ? It's bloody icers in here.'*

ickies   Foreign currency of any kind, an all-purpose word that is the current usage of the older term *ackies. Although it has a general meaning as in: *'I'm going to get some ickies from the Cash Office..'* it can also be more specific: *'How many ickies do you get to the pound in this place?'* Under these circumstances the *ickie* (whether it be a franc, dollar or cruzeiro) can be further subdivided into a hundred *klebbies. Note also *ickie store* - a bank, and see also *shrapnel.

idler   Jack's current and slightly contemptuous name for any- one not standing night *watches; see also *dry idlers* for those members of the ship's company who are not stokers or seamen either. An idler was originally a member of the ship's crew who worked during the day but did not stand the usual night watches. The carpenter, cook, sailmaker, bosun, and painter were men in this category which had duties that took up most of their daylight hours. They were off-watch at night-time, except (of course) in an emergency. They were also called *day- men*, and much envied by the rest of the crew. This label originally expressed little or no criticism, since idlers worked just as hard as others during their hours of duty. However, the term is now very much one of denigration; an idler is a person who *idles*, a slacker, and someone who is work-shy or habitually avoids work. See also *waister.

If   *If you asked Marconi* for a cat, they'd send you a dog - with a modificaton kit!

If at first you don't succeed..   Then you should either hit it with a bigger hammer, or revert to (RM) *In wi' the boot, an' then the heid!* (Glaswegian origin)

If you want a duff..   This comes from the days of the old method of catering when you prepared everything on the mess deck and then the *slosher cooked it. It really means that if you want something done, then do it yourself, hence: *'If you want a duff - make the bastard..'*

imbuggerance   Alternate pronunciation for *embuggerance.

I - 230

immaculate (RM)   Adjective reserved by Royal to indicate something of high quality or perfect appearance.

Immortal Memory   Traditional speech given by the guest of honour at *Trafalgar Night dinners throughout the Royal Navy, held on or around the anniversary of the 21st of October 1805. The life and achievements of Lord *Nelson are recounted briefly, then some particular quality of his leadership highlighted as an example to those present; finally, a toast to: *'The Immortal Memory..'* is proposed, drunk standing - and in silence.

Impressment   The practice of taking a national subject, whatever his own feelings on the matter, into the armed services of his country in order to make good shortfalls in normal recruitment.   This was a normal procedure for the army (particularly Cromwell's) as well as the navy, and the whole procedure of sending press gangs out into the country was underwritten by Parliament, which also passed the Quota Acts in 1795 requiring each district and town to provide a certain number of men for sea service - because the earlier Vagrancy Acts and their resulting steady supply of petty criminals and vagabonds could not meet the demand for seamen. See also *one of my Lord Mayor's men and *swimmer in this context, and note that the term *prest money*, a form of bounty or conduct money paid on enlistment still survives in the Royal Marines as the title of *Imprest Holder*, the Officer who is responsible for all Cash and Accounts in a *Commando Unit or base. There are some further comments at *Andrew and *pressed.

IMFU   Acronym for Imperial Military Foul-Up.

Imshi! (Arabic)   *Bugger off!*

IMT   Repeat signal in Morse code (or conversation!), used to let a fellow signaller know that what had been transmitted or said was either not heard - or misunderstood: *'I Missed That!'*

In and Out   Jokey nickname for the Naval and Military Club in London; the title is derived from the embellishments of the gate pillars, which have moved, with the Club, from the original site in Piccadilly to St James's Square.

in / on a ship   Not in itself an expression of nautical origin, but inserted here to instruct the neophyte and to remind the faithful. One enters or serves *in* a vessel, never *on* it. And, furthermore, a man is never *in* a *boat unless he actually belongs to the Submarine Service, known as *The *Trade*. To round off the lesson, a warship is referred to - always - with the prefix HMS or the definitive article *the*; so that one served *in HMS WARSPITE,* or *in the Warspite.* Reference to a warship's name without either of the two prefixes traditionally indicates only her captain; this is a long-standing tradition, and is intended to save time in the transmission of signals.

in dock   In hospital - as when a ship goes in for maintenance or repairs.

In - hot! (FAA)   Radio call made by aircraft carrying live ordnance on entering a weapons range.   Quickly adapted to other pastimes: *'As soon as we got ashore, Bill was in hot on a couple of blondes by the swimming pool..'*

in the rattle   In big trouble and liable to appear before *Father at *Defaulters.

in-lier (RM)   An Officer or NCO who lives *on board rather than *ashore. The RN equivalent is a *liver-in.

in (the) **zone**   The *zone* referred to here is the promotion zone, which in turn depends on an officer's seniority. This might be, for instance, three to nine years as a *two-and-a-half in order to be considered for elevation to a *brass hat. Going *overzone will mean a celebration of the *Passover. The behaviour of those *pregnant (for promotion) is sometimes a little contrived: *'Went to a real in-zone dinner party last night. I was the only guest junior to the host..'*

inboard   Two distinctly different meanings:
1. Home and dry, ie. inside or on board the ship: *'I'm inboard,*

haul up the ladder!' is a gently cynical observation applied to those motivated purely by self-interest.
2. (SM) Ashore or in the base, because a submarine's home is often a depot ship which has the *boat moored *outboard.

India rubber man   Another term for a *springer or PT Bosun. His favourite cry was: *'Up the wall bars - go!'*

Indon (RM)   Indonesian.

ineptitude   A definitive statement of ineptitude: *'You couldn't get rated up to Acting Unpaid *OD in a dry-docked dreamboat..'*

inside wrecker (esp. SM)   A chef! See *outside wrecker for explanation of this term.

Instructor   Two sets of applications here:
1 An officer of the old *Instructor* branch, responsible for training, teaching, or *meteorology* and *oceanography* (METOC). The branch has now demised, with the training and teaching aspects now part of the Engineering branch, and METOC as part of the Executive branch. However, the term *Schoolie lives on.
2. The highest *SQ in the old Seaman branch which folded in the early 1970s. Thus the Gunnery branch had a *GI*, the Radar Plot (RP) branch had a *PRI (Plot Radar Instructor)*, the Torpedo and Anti-Submarine (TAS) branch a *TASI*, and so on. Note that it wasn't necessary to be a Chief Petty Officer in order to be an *Instructor*, as promotion / advancement was dependent on a whole range of personal qualities, and not just those in a man's specialist qualification. See also *I.

internal back splint   A *brownhatter's idea of fun.

interview without coffee   A discussion with one's *boss or *father during which one's *horoscope is likely to be read.

IQ   *'This chap has the IQ of a paper clip..'*

Irish   Another manifestation of Jack's somewhat xenophobic habit of attributing the adjective of a foreign country to something when he wants to be disparaging. Perhaps inevitably (and long before their jokes became popular), the *Irish* are first in the firing line, followed by the *French and other (generally European, but not forgetting *Egyptian) nations. Hence the following:

> *Irish confetti* - stone chippings or gravel.
> *Irish hurricane* - flat calm sea.

Irish ice-cream - mashed potatoes.
Irish light ale - Guinness.
Irish mail - bag of potatoes.
Irish parliament - lots of people talking, but no
   decisions being made.
Irish pendant - poorly secured line or hanging
   fender lanyard.
Irish pennants - loose threads on clothing.
Irish pilot - inshore guide who knows every rock
   and sand bar, but not the actual safe passage.
Irish rise - demotion.
Irish toothache - an erection or *stonker.
Irish turkey - corned beef or tinned spam.

Irish horse   A term that deserves a separate entry because it was Jack's nickname in the days of *salt horse (salted beef) for a lump of meat that was even more tough and stringy than usual. This term stemmed from the belief that the Irish, being so poor, worked their horses harder and longer than anyone else, and *'this one died a natural death..'*

iron chicken (FAA)   The (older) piston-engined Whirlwind 7 helicopter.

iron deck   Upper deck of bare steel either side in the waist or mid-section of a destroyer.

ish   Derived from the word *Issue*:
1. A full scale of equipment: *'It's the complete ish..'*
2. Can also mean: *'That's all you're getting!'*
3. Noun to describe a new piece of equipment or an item of clothing that is the very height of current fashion: *'He was in his new *trapping gear - designer jeans, Lacoste sweater, Porsche sunglasses - the ish..'*
4. Also as a single word for approximating a certain figure or level with - ish as a suffix: *'How much did that cost ? A thousand?'* *'Mmm - ish..'*

is / was (SM)   A primitive early torpedo deflection calculator. The precursor to the *fruit machine. *'There it is, there it was, where the hell is it now?'*

Italian teabags   Ravioli.

It's only pain! (RM)   Traditional and jocular encouragement at *Lympstone for recruits who are suffering while undergoing the rigours of *Commando training. Also painted on a signboard in

*Heartbreak Lane to announce the 500 metres distant finish of the *Endurance course.

- ITS   Suffix indicating *In Tomato Sauce.* The variants are:

        B -*ITS*   Baked Beans..
        H -*ITS*   Herrings..
        P -*ITS*   Pilchards..
        T -*ITS*   Tomatoes..

JULIET

237 - 248

JAAFU - Joint Anglo-American Foul Up.

Jack   Generic name for all Royal Navy sailors, derived from *Jack Tar*, the 18th and early 19th century *matelot with his glossy black hat, carefully dressed pigtail, and canvas breeches that, like the hairs on his head, were impregnated with high grade tar. See *tarpaulin for more detail on this aspect of clothing. The usual name associated with Jack these days is *Jolly Jack*, for the cheerful, willing, robust, randy, sharp and witty individual whose common sense, humour and insight have made a book like this possible! Note also:

> *Jack Adams* - older nickname for a stubborn fool.
> *Jack *Dusty* - a stores rating; formerly called *Jack in the dust*, as he worked in a storeroom or storage compartment, amongst the flour and biscuit that were stowed there.
> *Jack Jones* - rhyming slang for *on your own*.
> *Jack Strop* - an argumentative sailor.
> *Jack the Lad* - someone who plays hard socially.
> *Jack-with-Bumps* - originally a *Wren, but now a female RN rating.

Jack of all trades   A sailor who can turn his hand to anything, and almost always had to, since unlike the Army who have infantry, cavalry and artillery, Jack had to provide all these features of military operations by himself!

Jack-me-hearty   As for *Jolly Jack*, usually seen with his cap flat-aback, cuffs unbuttoned and a packet of ticklers protruding from his jumper. As Cyril Tawney records, in a catchy song that was sung to the tune of *The Girl I Left Behind Me*:

> *Oh I couldn't care less*
> *For the Killick of the Mess*

Or the Buffer of the working party,
'Cos I'm off ashore
At a quarter past four,
I'm Jack me (flipping) hearty..

Jack-me-starboard-dhobey-bucket   A sailor who thinks he knows everyone and everything.

Jack-me-tickler   Someone who really believes he is omniscient: *'Don't come that Jack-me-tickler routine with me, you poxy little *scab-lifter...'*

Jack-me-two-eyed-ringbolt   Another term for a real smart arse.

Jackproof   Nothing has ever really been made *Jackproof.*

jack it in (RM)   Give up.

jack it up   Fix it; arrange for something to happen.

jackanapes coat   The original name for a *monkey* jacket which was made of rough wool, and worn by sailors on watch in cold weather. This has now become a *donkey* jacket. The transition may reflect a willingness to be associated with hard physical work (*donkey*) rather than foolishness (*monkey*).

Jackie-boy (FAA)   Nickname for a pilot who is a bit too flashy: *'He's been something of a *Jackie-boy recently, but the *Trappers had his *number just as soon as they started work this week..'*

Jack's dream   This was always described as *being knocked down by a millionaire's twenty-one year old daughter driving a brewer's dray*!

jacksie   Traditional slang term for someone's posterior; see also *duck-run.

jackstaff   Flagpole at the bow (or in the forward part of some ships) from which the *jack* is flown when in harbour. In RN warships the *jack* is the Union Flag, whereas the (White) ensign staff is positioned aft. Note that it is incorrect, although common in *civvy street, to describe the Union Flag as the *Union Jack*.

jackstay   Any taut horizontal rope or wire which is not part of the standard rigging. In other wods, it is only rigged for a specific purpose; hence:
1. *Light jackstay* - manila (or nowadays a special man-made fibre) rope rigged between two ships under way, along which a traveller block runs; it is used for the transfer of personnel and light stores during a *jackstay transfer*.
2. *Heavy jackstay* - as above, but here a steel cable is used to transfer greater loads such as stores, victuals and ammunition, and to support the weight of fuelling hoses, its tension being maintained by automatic winches.
3. *Sea jackstays* - wire ropes rigged on the *upper deck at sea, for safety.

Jacky   Nickname for anyone with the name of Fisher; dates from the early 1900s when the reforming and innovative Admiral Sir John (*Jacky*) Fisher almost single-handedly dragged the Royal Navy, kicking and screaming, into the 20th century. See also the term *hitched.

Jaffa / JAFO (FAA)   Fairly new acronym for *Just Another F(lipping)* *Observer, derived from an American TV series about an amazing helicopter that does impossible things; the *Lynx world quickly adopted this term, which in general usage then became *Jaffa*, as in orange. In turn, *Orange and *Zero were added to the descriptive library for *Lookers. The man who is responsible for *trapping *Lynx *Observers and then saying yes or no about their performance then became, almost inevitably, the *man from Del Monte, after the television advertisement on that theme!

Jago   Jago was the Warrant Cook who invented the central galley and dining halls (central messing system) at RN Barracks

Devonport. The latter facility (now called HMS DRAKE) became known as *Jago's Mansions*. *Jagos* was also a collective nickname for Devonport-manned ships.

jahooblies The female breasts; see also *jamungas.

jam bosun Another term for the Supply (or *Victualling) Officer.

James the First The First Lieutenant; see *Jimmy and *Bloke. Also referred to as *James the Magnificent*. The entry for *Jimmy the One has a more complete explanation for the origin of this term; see also *executive officer.

jammy Lucky: *'Howja fix that little *number, you jammy git?'*

jampot officer See *pickle jar officer.

jamungas (heavy emphasis on middle syllable) Enormous breasts.

jankers Punishment cells, akin to the *pongo glasshouse. Can also describe punishment, at the double, carrying a rifle Men quickly developed the *janker shuffle*.

Jan / Janner Nickname for any sailor from the West Country, and by extension, anything that originates from Devon or Cornwall; strictly speaking a *Janner* is a Devonian - a Cornishman is a *Jagger*, but the two terms have become interchangable in modern usage. *Jan Docky* is a *dockyard matey at Devonport Royal Dockyard, now under private ownership.

Jaunty The Master-At-Arms, or senior *Regulator. This word is derived from the French *gentilhomme* , or *gentleman-at-arms*, and the name tends to go with a position rather than an individual, as in: *'He's NORFOLK's new Jaunty..'* and not: *'He's a Jaunty..'* See also *Joss and *Jossman.

Jeeps (RM) General Purpose Machine Gun (GPMG). The term *gimpy* tends to be used more by the Army.

Jenny *Jenny Wren*. A member of the former *Women's Royal Naval Service*, which has now been fully assimilated into the Royal Navy and no longer exists as a separate entity. Hence the revised dedication of this book, acknowledging that *Jack* and *Jenny* are now one and the same, although of course they aren't! The name *Wren lives on, as (thank God!) *Jenny* is not in general a feminist, even if she considers herself in most respects Jack's equal - if not superior.

Jenny Scribe WRNS writer.

Jenny's side party RN warships visiting *Honkers used to get spruced up there by a formidably efficient team of Chinese women who are still led, after many years, by a charming lady called Jenny. Hers was not the only side party - there was at least one other (Susie's) and the fights between the two when competing for trade were legendary. Jenny was rightly awarded a *BEM before British interest in *Honkers ceased. No doubt, RN warships programmed to visit the Special Administrative Area of the People's Republic of China will still be looked after by Jenny. Furthermore, she will probably have sent the *old man or the *Jimmy a Christmas card, looking forward to the visit, for them to have this formally confirmed some months later! In general, Jenny looked after ships at anchor or out on the buoys, whereas those alongside in Tamar Basin were looked after by Susie and her team.

Jesse The alternative nickname for a sailor named James.

Jesus factor Something extra allowed for in a design to cover those imponderables which have not been (or cannot be) calculated by computer: *'Thirty thousand pounds all-up weight, including five hundred pounds of fuel as a Jesus factor..'*

Jesus nut The all-important feature which actually secures a helicopter's rotor blade system onto its driving shaft. Disconnection or failure of this item while in flight will result in the crew meeting the Man in person.

jet jock (FAA) Member of the *stovie community.

jetsam Cargo, stores, equipment, etc., which has been deliberately thrown overboard (*jettisoned*) in order to lighten the ship in a survival situation, but which legally remains the property of the owner. See also *flotsam.

Jew's march-past The process of examining one's wallet to ascertain either its contents, or else the damage caused by last night's *run-ashore.

jewing firm Older term for a group of sailors running a small tailoring and repair service on board a warship; now replaced by *Sew-sew.

jewing sack A small bag in which a seaman kept his sewing gear.

Jez (FAA)   The *Jezebel* anti-submarine passive sonobuoy system.

jibber the kibber   Older slang term for luring a ship onto a rocky coast, usually by attaching a light to a horse, with one of its legs hobbled, to give the impression of a sailing vessel inshore of the intended victim.

jibbering   *Cackling your grease, usually like a *three-badge parrot. Also spelt as *gibbering, and see also *lipstall; the commonest usage is: '*You jibbering idiot!*'

Jig-a-jig Johnny?   Traditional prostitute's request, now used almost as a euphemism for a brothel visit.

Jimmy / Jimmy the One   The First Lieutenant of a warship, and usually also the *Executive Officer (which see); also referred to as *number one. In older times the word jeminy referred to neatness and spruceness, and the First Officer (beneath the Captain) who was responsible for this aspect became Jeminy the First, or as he is now, *Jimmy the One*!

Job Number   the number allocated to a ship during building before receiving a name.

jobbed   A useful pair:
1.   Told to go and do something - often an unpopular or unpleasant task.
2.   (RM) Killed: '*We sprung the ambush and Smudge jobbed a couple of *Indons with the *jeeps..*'

jobber   Rather like *doobrey, *doofer (or *Johnson), an all-purpose fill-in word employed when a more exact description fails the speaker.

jock frock   A kilt; note also *Church of Jock.

jockanese   The English language when spoken with a thick Scots accent, and sometimes sounding like a foreign language for that very reason.

jockanese cackleberries   Scotch eggs.

jockey   Sometimes used to describe a seaman on the bridge or conning tower, indicating someone having a ride while others provide the horse-power.

jockroach   A persistent, obnoxious, annoying little Scotsman.

Joe   A conrasting pair of usages:
1.   (esp. FAA) Nickname for a rank-and-file member of a

Dabtoe

squadron: *'I'm just one of the Joes..'* or: *'The real trouble with our *Splot is that he can't forget he was once a squadron Joe..'* This leads onto the term *joed off,* or the process whereby a Junior Officer (JO) is *jobbed, usually at very short notice, to take over a duty: *'Charles went sick, so I got joed off as the *Jimmy's *gofer..'*
2. (RM) Officer Commanding Royal Marines (OCRM) in one of the pre-war RM detachments. *Young Joe* was the Second in Command, if there were two officers.

johnson (FAA) Another all-purpose word in steadily increasing usage, similar to *doobrey and *doofer: *'Gimme that double-ended johnson will you?'* In Baltic or Norwegian waters, this item is then supposed to become a *johannsen.*

joining letter Nice custom in the RN whereby a *DO, on receipt of *Drafty's intimation that a rating is due to join a warship at some time in the near future, writes him a pleasant and friendly letter outlining the duties and responsibilities that he will be expected to assume, together with a rough outline of the ship's planned programme.

joke Life in uniform generally, leading to the famous observation: *'Listen chum, if you can't take a joke, then you shouldn't have joined..'*

Jolly Roger The flag flown by submarines on return from wartime patrol, and recording successes with the appropriate symbology.

jolly Two versions (three if you include the author!):
1. Royal Marine, a term later used by Rudyard Kipling in this fragment of verse from his *Barrackroom Ballads:*
    'Sez'e, I'm a Jolly - 'Er Majesty's Jolly -
    Soldier an' sailor too!'
This nickname applied originally to the Trained Bands of the City of London who provided many recruits for the Regiment of Sea Soldiers that were forerunners of the modern Corps.
2. A nice, pleasant trip or sortie that has no real underlying purpose, and which might be undertaken on water in a *jollyboat,* a vessel used only for recreational purposes.

jonnick Genuine, absolute truth.

josie A Maltese person.

joss Two applications:
1. Luck of any sort (from the Chinese); sheer luck or a total fluke

becomes *pure joss*, whereas *bad joss* is bad luck:'*With my bad joss I'd fall into a bucket full of tits and come out sucking my thumb..*'
2. *The Joss* is short for the **Jossman* or Master-At-Arms; see also **jaunty*, and note **Fleet joss* as well.

Jossman   The most frequently used descriptive name for the **Master-At-Arms in a warship; do not, unless you're rather bored and seeking a little excitement in your life, say to this man:'*Hello Chief!*' If he is a **Warrant Officer, then the older nickname (derived from the now superceded rank of **Fleet Master-At-Arms) still persists as **Fleet Joss(man)* or **Fleet Jaunty.

Jossman gin   This nickname for Plymouth Gin probably originated on the China Station - the *Jossman* being the monk depicted on the label.

Judas (hanging)   Said of a rope when insecurely made fast or belayed, ie. false and unreliable, as was *Judas*.

Julie   A technique for turning a pattern of passive sonobuoys into active sonar by dropping explosive charges. *Julie* was a lady in Norfolk, Virginia USA, who had a wonderful ability to make passive boys active.

Julie Andrews   An order for tea or coffee that implies you would like it with milk, but without sugar. (White, nun - geddit?) See also **NATO standard.

jumbo   Two linked usages:
1. The largest foresail in a square-rigged ship, equivalent to a *genoa* in modern yachts; also (2) a large mobile crane carried in **carriers. It is the percursor of the modern usage to describe something huge and elephantine.
2. Big, mobile crane whose lifting capability had to exceed the weight of the heaviest fully-laden and armed aircraft on board. Much beloved by First Lieutenants or Mates of the Upper Deck when rigging for **RAS or heavy **jackstay transfer. When combined with a good Aircraft Handler driver, the *jumbo* was worth both **Watches of the hands of seamen.

jump   Enjoy conjugal relations with someone; also used by FAA **pingers, when chasing submarines, to describe the process of moving from one **dip position to the next.

Jumper / jumper   Nickname for the surnames Cross, Collins and Short, and a clothing item that offers warmth and a little wind resistance, and has no loose pockets to snag on anything.

jumping by numbers   A GI's trick: *'When I say One, jump in the air. When I say Two, come down again - One! What are you moving for?'*

jumping to a conclusion   What happens with a parachute that fails to open.

jungle bunny   Can be a lady of African origin, but is more usually a Royal Marine Commando who is totally in his element when deployed operationally in the jungle.

jungle drums (esp. FAA)   The grapevine or bush telegraph for rumour and speculation: *'The jungle drums say that he's not doing particularly well in the new appointment..'*

jungle rules   Any team game such as volleyball or football, when played without any real rules at all.

Junglie   Pilot or aircrewman belonging to a *Commando helicopter squadron supporting the Royal Marines, in contrast to someone appointed to a submarine-hunting *Pinger outfit. Note also the *Pinglie hybrid which only exists when *Pingers move ashore for land operations, sometimes with unfortunate confusion resulting from a lack of map-reading experience!

junior   Jack or Royal when under 17 years old; mature enough to fight in the Falklands but not, apparently, to serve Her Majesty in Northern Ireland. See also *Boy seaman.

Juniors (RM)   The *Junior Command Course*, compulsory for those *candidate Marines desirous of advancement to Corporal. Held at *Lympstone: *'I'm off up to CTC for my Juniors next week..'*

junk   Proper name for old, decayed rope. Another word that has come ashore to a wider usage.

junket bosun   *Wardroom Steward.

jury-rigged   A temporary and emergency (*de jour*) arrangement or *lash-up designed to get a vehicle, aircraft or ship back to base for repair, hence a *jury mast* or *jury rudder* that has been *jury-rigged*.

just party   Jack, caught on deck when there is a sudden need to form a working party: *'But Chief, I was just -'* Chief Petty Officer: *'I know, I know - just party - FALL IN OVER THERE..'*

Ditty Box

KILO

249 - 254

K Real name-dropping way of describing a senior officer who has been awarded a Knighthood: *'Old Buggins has finally got his K..'* RN/RM officers get appointed *Knights* in the Order of either the Bath (*KCB*) or of the British Empire (*KBE*); really senior officers can subsequently become Knights *Grand Cross* (*GCB* or *GBE*), which gives rise to the congratulatory chestnut: *'Twice a knight - and at your age, too!'*

kag / kaggage (RM)   Unwanted or useless equipment: *'Don't bother with that lot - leave it behind. It's all just kag..'*

kak / kaki   Short for **kaki-poos**, ie. shit: *'Tried to drop me in the kak did he? Right, just you watch me *stitch him up!'*   There is a possible relationship with the Army word (and colour). Someone who is *kak-handed* is left-handed and clumsy, since he also deploys toilet paper with that hand!

Kate   Just as all soldiers were *pongos, so the Army was the *Kate* - rhyming slang from *Kate Karney* of music hall fame.

kecks (RM)   Underpants; see also *shreddies. In Liverpool the word *kecks* is slang for trousers.

keel hauling / keel dragging   17th Century naval punishment where a weighted-down culprit was hoisted up to a yardarm, with a rope tied around his body that ran down beneath the hull and up to the yardarm opposite. He was then dropped into the water and dragged against the barnacle-covered hull, smacked against the *keel*, and then pulled up to the surface again, half-drowned. For additional effect, a cannon - the *rogue's gun - was also fired just over his head. Hence the modern expression: *'If the *Old Man finds out he'll probably keel haul you!'* It may be that the phrase *undergoing great hardship* originated in this way; if you were keel hauled, you had to *under go a great, hard ship.*

Kelvin (FAA)   An amusing abuse of the scientific means of measuring absolute temperature, to describe a not very bright *Bloggs: *'In fact, we judge this man to be a bit of a Kelvin - pretty close to Absolute Zero..'*

kerosene budgie   Another name for a helicopter; see *paraffin pigeon for a fuller listing.

KFS (RM)   **Knife, Fork and Spoon**; see also *eating irons and *gobbling rods.

kick it into touch   Solve a problem by simply getting rid of it.

killick   Older word for a stone or heavy weight used as a small anchor, now used for any *Leading Hand because of the single fouled anchor sleeve badge of a *Leading *rate.

kin 'ell!   The expletive abbreviated; should be listed under *F*!

King's badge / squad (RM)   Royal cipher awarded by King George V's 1918 Order to the best Marine passing out of training from *The King's Squad*; this device is worn on the upper left sleeve of his uniform throughout a man's career, even if he subsequently becomes commissioned as an officer - as many *King's badgemen* have subsequently done.

King's (or *Queen's*) **shilling**   Traditional bounty paid in older times on enlistment into the Sovereign's service, and a development of the original *prest money* described under *Impressed. An unscrupulous recruiter might buy some unsuspecting chap a mug of ale, place the coin in his beer and wait for it to be consumed; the wretch was then deemed to have struck a bargain

K - 250

having swallowed (ie. accepted) the *King's Shilling*. Some pewter drinking vessels still have a glass bottom to guard against this possibility! The term is still used, in a jocular manner, when referring to a person's date of entry into the Corps or the Navy.

kip A pair of applications here:
1. Sleep.
2. A protective sheet of dark-green, tough and waterproof material from which a *basha or *bivvy can be constructed. Derived from the stores item - *Kit Individual Protection* - and also known as a *kip sheet*.

kipper A serious insult: *'You're like a bloody kipper - you've got two faces and no guts..'*

kipper kites Aircraft on Fishery Protection flights.

kipper / kippered (SM) Synonym for torpedo / torpedoed. This is correct for HM Submarines in WW2; *tinfish* is a US Navy term.

KISS Acronym invented by the late Ray Kroc, founder of the McDonald's hamburger chain, and a piece of sound philosophy not always followed by our military friends across the *Pond: *'Keep It Simple, Stupid!'*

kit Two meanings:
1. Equipment, in the general or specific sense: *'It's good kit..'* means that something works well. *'It's a special piece of kit that works underwater..'* could be applied to almost anything designed to function in that demanding environment.
2. Underwear, especially of the feminine kind, referred to in a low growl: *'Get yer kit off, darlin'..'* See also *lagging in this particular sense.

kit muster Formal inspection of a rating's full issue of clothing and personal equipment, often as a punishment for a persistently slack or untidy individual; also a euphemistic term for vomiting, presumably because the stomach contents have also been laid out for inspection.

kit sale It was customary that the sale of a rating's kit took place at the mainmast, in the presence of an Executive officer and an officer of the Supply branch. When the kit is a dead man's, the proceeds go to his next of kin - and it is usual for the ship's company to make high bids for the various articles which, in most cases, are thrown back for resale. Such a sale, which usually takes place during the dinner hour, may last several days before the kit in question is completely sold.

kitty / Kitty
1. Pooling of cash for some joint purchase: '*Anyone for another beer - there's still a fiver in the kitty..*'
2. Nickname for the surname Wells (from the nursery rhyme: '*Ding-dong-dell, Kitty's in the well..*')

klaxon   A very loud electrical horn, in fact used for diving *stations and warning that a *boat's dive has commenced. Hence: '*She's got a voice like a klaxon..*' or: '*Shut your klaxon off..*'

klebbies   Local (foreign) currency. One *ickie - of whatever description - equals a hundred *klebbies*, a term also used to describe small change in a sailor's pocket, because as the ship leaves port, those *klebbies* are rendered almost useless and become *shrapnel instead.

klicks (RM)   Kilometres.

knack-all (RM)   Nothing; a version of *naff-all*, but stronger.

knacker   A quintet of applications:
1. A useless individual, especially if he is an overweight and grossly unfit *fat knacker*. Note also the special use of this latter phrase when referring to any food with a very high calorie value as *fat knacker pie*.
2. Testicle: '*After the *bricking my starboard knacker didn't half give me some *gyp..*'
3. To *be knackered* means to be very tired or *chin-strapped; an inanimate object may also be *knacked* - either broken or seized up.
4. *knacker crackers* are the thighs of a large *party.
5. *knacker lacquer* is hair spray, because if you were crazy enough to spray it on your *parts, the *knacker lacquer* would add lustre to your cluster.

knee-jerk response   Criticism of some quick-response decision made by a higher authority that has not been thought through properly.

knee stripes   Something obtained after entertaining female guests on the ridged rubber mats on workshop and stores decking; matched with bum stripes for the same reason.

knee trembler (sometimes a *KT*)   The process of *giving the ferret a run while leaning against a wall.

knicker python   The penis; in its complete form the phrase refers to a *one-eyed knicker python* or *trouser snake.

knob jockey / knobber   A *brownhatter, but the terms are also used in an asexual, but abusive and derogatory sense.

knock down   The process of disassembling something, derived from the ship's cooper of yesteryear who could *knock down* a cask, when empty, into its component hoops and staves for more compact storage. Also used in sailing for a yacht that has been *knocked down* onto her beam ends by a violent squall.

knock it on the head   Give up; abandon an attempt to do something.

knock the gilt off the gingerbread   Spoil the telling of a joke with an early punchline. This modern usage is derived from a much older one; *gingerbread* was the decorative carpentry and scrollwork round the stern of a warship, often highly gilded or painted. The firing of a broadside, or the impact of enemy shot, rather spoiled this adornment by *knocking the gilt off the gingerbread*.

Knocker   Common nickname for anyone with the surname White or Whyte.

knocking shop   Brothel; see also *bag shanty.

knot   Measurement of speed: 1 *knot* = 1 *sea mile per hour*. A sea (or nautical) mile is the distance on the earth's surface subtended by 1 minute of latitude; although this varies, the mean is taken as 6080 feet (or a shade over 2000 yards). The original method of measuring speed was a long line with a *log on the end and knotted at pre-determined intervals; using a 30 second sand glass, the number of *knots* *payed out in half a minute was counted, multiplied by two, and the ship's speed thereby determined in a standardized manner.

know the ropes   Jack, when properly trained and experienced, knew both the location and function of every component of a ship's general rigging; the phrase has now come ashore with a wider meaning that can be applied to anyone with special or practical experience.

knuckle   A trio of applications:
1. Hit somebody with a fist, or smack him with a *knuckle sarnie*.

2. *knuckle bosun* is the nickname for an aggressive individual who is always getting into fights; *punchy is a suitable adjective.
3. To *knuckle down* is to get on with the job in hand. To *knuckle under* means to yield submissively, probably after not too much of a fight. This stems from the 19th century custom of touching the left fist to the forehead in salute and acknowledgement of a superior's orders.

kouffed (it)   Died; amalgam of *coughed* it and *croaked*.

kronks (RM)   Basic unit of *Noggie currency , but can also be used for any *Skywegian krone (crowns).

KUA   Acronym for *Kit Upkeep Allowance*; formerly, additional money paid to Jack to enable him to replace worn out clothing from the *Slop Room or, if he preferred, from a naval tailor. It has now been replaced by a one-for-one, new-for-old exchange system.

kye / ky (sometimes **ki**)   Hot cocoa drink made from grated slabs of unsweetened chocolate, sugar and condensed milk; this was mixed in a *fanny and, ideally, taken to the boiler room and placed under a steam drain until it reached the necessary heat. The measure of of good mug of *kye* was that a spoon which was stood vertically in it would pause - before falling to one side. Sadly, *pusser withdrew the chocolate slabs (which was also an excellent laxative!) in the early '70s, and whatever anyone says, you can't make kye with cocoa powder.

kytai / kyte   Male transvestite in Singapore, often of Eurasian origin and stunning appearance. Jack's rule of thumb was that the ugly ones were usually real women! See also *Bugis Street; they are also found now in *Gib.

LIMA

255 - 274

laced   Two meanings:
1. Gold *lacing* braid and curl sewn onto the lower sleeves of an officer's *monkey jacket to indicate rank, eg. *Uniform for sale, 40 in. chest, 34 in. waist and laced to Lieutenant Commander.*
2. Extra alcohol added to an otherwise innocuous *wet in order to get the victim drunk (ie. a Mickey Finn).

Lady in the mess!   A cry which would go up if anyone sat at the mess table with his cap on. This was considered a serious breach of etiquette by ratings, and many a *HO in WW2 was surprised to have his cap knocked off by an indignant *CS rating. They were probably surprised that Jack had etiquette at all, but despite the *skates and *Jack Strops and their various highly dubious shore activities, on board Jack had enormous pride and respect for RN tradition.

lagging   A linked pair here:
1. Insulating material wrapped around boilers and steam pipes.
2. A lady's clothing, particularly her underwear: *'C'mon darlin' - get your lagging off..'* See also *kit in this sense.

laid   *'Did you make it last night, Nobby?'* *'Yuh, I laid a tambourine basher - she was *bramah!'*

laid up   Taken out of service for repair or refitting; in the human sense this means being *laid up* in the *Boneyard.

lammy coat   A lamby or *lammy coat* was a woollen *duffel coat* issued for wear on deck during the first half of the 20th century.

lamp   A nice trio:
1. Hit someone, usually in the face: *'Ginge jumped up and lamped him..'* Derived perhaps from the older expression *trim his lamps* as in (2).

2. *lamps* are eyes; *lamp covers* are sunglasses.

3. *swing the lamp* - behave like an *old hand, by talking about experiences at sea or on active service, with the messdeck lanterns swinging gently in a seaway, or in the swell while at anchor. This action can be imitated by a listener! Note also *gripped.

landaway (FAA)   Navigational training exercise which involves a day (or weekend) trip to some pleasant destination.

landman / landsman   In theory, this was someone who had volunteered for sea service in a British warship, but was without any formal naval training. He was paid on a lower scale than an ordinary seaman, although his actual volunteering might have attracted a large cash bounty of *prest money! In practice, however, the term soon came to be used for any *pressed *lubber.

landmine   A hard, loaded bun - as encountered in a *pusser's *bag rat.

larboard   Original word for *port, or left-hand side of a ship; it probably derives from *laden* (or *lading*) *board*, or the side over which ships were *loaded* in port. Probably because it was easily confused with *starboard (or *steering board*), it was officially changed to *port in 1844, although the latter had been in common use long before that.

larbolins   Older term for sailors in the port (*larboard) watch; the opposite (starboard) watch men were *starbolins.

lash-up   Expression derived originally from the process of running the *gauntlet, but now adapted in at least four different forms of usage:

1. Temporary, improvised or home-made construction (esp. RM): *'Even though it was a *right lash-up, the thing worked fairly well..'* See also *jury-rigged in this context.

2. Provide generous hospitality: *'After we *dicked the Army at Twickenham, the whole team got lashed-up *stinking in the Long Bar..'*

3. Traditional early morning call for Jack to get up and *secure his hammock and bedding: *'Lash up and stow!'* to which could be added: *'Heave ho, heave ho, lash up and stow..!'*

4. Any badly *lashed* hammock was a *slack hammock. Men guilty would have to take their hammocks aft to the Quarterdeck every day during the breakfast break. Properly lashed hammocks were stowed in nettings, which were then

positioned against the ship's sides. The tightly compressed, and properly-stowed hammocks then prevented wood and metal splinters from flying about and causing human injury. If the ship was abandoned, a hammock would also float for 24 hours if well *lashed up*. In every sense, a *well-lashed* hammock was an important safety factor.

Last Dog   The second of the two *Dog Watches:
     *First Dog   1600 to 1800.
     Last Dog   1800 to 2000.
This is Jack's favourite *watch at sea, because in a normal 4-watch system he will not have to *turn to again until the 0800 *forenoon watch of the next day, leading to the expression *Last Dog and all night in*, anticipating an undisturbed night's sleep.

last in first out   Normal etiquette concerning the carriage of senior officers in boats, but note also the procedure detailed in *accommodation ladder.

last shot   Final chance of promotion before passing out of the *zone; if this turns out to be a miss, then ceremonies for the Feast of the *Passover will be appropriate.

laughing gear   Mouth:*'Get your laughing gear round this lot..'*

laughing kitbags (RM)   Something hugely amusing:*'Then this *Pongo Major went and split his trousers right in the middle of the parade - the boys were laughing kitbags..'*

launch   A trio:
1. (FAA) Active, and also passive description for aircraft tak-ing-off from a ship or Naval Air Station : '*801 Squadron launched at 0450, an hour before first light, for the attack on Stanley airfield..*' Or: '*The *Lynx was *ranged and launched imme-diately to investigate this new surface contact..*' Note that the term *take-off* is rarely used in Naval parlance, and neither is *landing* when *recovery is actually the process described. However, just to confuse the issue, aircraft will *land on* (board) during the latter *evolution and their crews might well describe this as *being recovered*!
2. Ceremony when a new ship is first introduced to the water; one of the rare occasions when the *Lord High Admiral's Flag is flown in a *private ship, and one of great celebration, but also fraught with dire consequences if anything goes wrong. History is full of sad stories of what happened to ships and warships whose *launch* did not go according to plan.
3. Apart from shipping meanings, it also means to manhandle an item from one place to another: '*Launch that packing case fur-ther aft..*'

Law of the Navy   The seniority system as laid out in the *Navy List. An officer appearing higher in the List is the more senior; in a group of warships, this single fact will determine which one becomes the *canteen boat.

Laws of the Navy   A poem, written by Admiral Ronald A Hopwood CB and dedicated to his *Comrades in the Service*, which appeared in the Army & Navy Gazette in 1898.

lay-apart store   A place where items of *kit not required for immediate use are dumped; can easily turn into something of a *glory hole unless subjected to regular *Rounds.

layer   An unusual duo:
1.. (pronounced *lay - er*)   Older name for the senior member of a Naval gun's crew, sometimes answering to a *turret captain, but who was also responsible for the difficult task of setting that gun's elevation, in conjunction with the *Trainer - who looked after the azimuth.
2. (pronounced *lair*)   An interfacing volume of seawater between two depths where the temperature change is so marked that above (or below) this thermocline *layer*, a subma-rine can hide, in the acoustical sense, with much-reduced risk of detection by *sonar.

lawful occasions   Ships going about their *lawful occasions* are vessels plying their trade in a legal fashion; if doing so under a British flag, they are entitled to the protection of the Royal Navy. From the Naval prayer: *'..that we may be a security for such as pass on the seas upon their lawful occasions..'*

lazy lane (FAA)   Short cut from the runway into a Squadron's dispersal.

lazy lob   Partial erection; see *lob.

lazy paynter   A rope attached from the ladder to the boat at the boom.

lazy shot   A steel or concrete weight, put over the side of a sea boat on a *shot line to assist diving operations.

lead fart   Comparative description of something that has not been well received; see also *fart in a spacesuit!

lead on McDick   Phrase describing someone lacking discrimination or judgement in his sexual activities, and who appears to be careless of the possible consequences: *'Ever since the Falklands he's been a complete lead on McDick *merchant..'* Such a person may also be described as *using his dick as a compass*.

Leading Hand / Rate   The first rung on the Naval promotion ladder, and the first that also confers any authority to the holder, equivalent to a Corporal in Army or RAF terms. Possession of the Leading *Rate indicates elevation from the *Able Rate, and is denoted by the wearing of a *killick badge, hence the general nickname for the rank. The shortened form *Leader* is acceptable when addressing or referring directly to a Leading Hand: *'Leader - will you open a new file *docket, please..'* or: *'Leader Holgate is the *phot who took that amazing picture..'* Leading Hand (or *killick) *of the Mess* - because Leading Hands mess with other junior rates, they may appointed by the *Captain to be in charge of that mess, and also responsible for its overall conduct.

leaf   Once the common pronunciation for *leave* used by Jack.

leatherneck (RM)   Traditional nickname for US Marine Corps personnel, based on a leather strap used to close the collar of their dress uniforms, and probably the origin in WW2 for the term *bootneck. Relationships between the two Corps are traditionally close, as might be expected between two organizations that fought against each other in the Wars of American Independence! See also *Bunker Hill, and any honest account of why the *White House is actually that colour. The best over-all *Candidate passing out from his *Juniors at *Lympstone each year is awarded the *Leatherneck Trophy*, donated by the US Marine Corps. Note also the USMC connection behind the *Tunney Cup.

lecky   General abbreviation for an e-*lec*-trician.

ledger bosun   Another name for *Scribes - a Writer or Pay Clerk.

lee side   The down wind, or calmer side.

left footer   A Roman Catholic; someone who digs with the wrong (*left*) foot. When a ship had Prayers at Both Watches on a Sunday, non-Christians (including RCs, who were considered heathens) were fallen out and doubled away until Prayers were over. The *Buffer might order: '*Roman Catholics fall - OUT! - As you were! At the command fall OUT all Roman Catholics WILL take a full pace forward with the LEFT foot. Once again - Roman Catholics fall OUT..!'*

left-handed bricklayer   A member of the Freemasonry cabal.

left wing   Unorthodox behaviour that offends sensibility: '*Jock got all his type ratings with one airline, then immediately switched to a rival outfit - all a bit left wing if you ask me..'*

leg / shake a leg   A common expression on board, meaning *Come on! Hurry up!* or *Get going!* The allusion is obvious. This should not be confused with *Show a leg!* (which see). In general, it is a cry of encouragement to urge someone into activity of some kind, derived from the traditional call used to rouse or turn out the crew in a sailing warship.

leg it   Run (away) - can also be used when there are no *wheels available, and the only means of getting somewhere is to *leg it*, ie. walk!   Royal's ideal running shoes would be a pair of *Nike Leggits*.

leg over   To *have your leg over* is to indulge in sexual intercourse, but in a horizontal rather than the vertical *knee trembling mode; the phrase *legover and chips* can describe a really success-ful *run-ashore.   See also *beer, big eats, bag-off and back on board in this particular social context.

legless   Drunk.

legoland / moon city   General name for any new barracks or rebuilt shore facility like HMS *RALEIGH, where modern tech-niques have been employed in both design and construction.

length of service   Gentle exaggeration is a key feature of Jack and Royal's humour, and there are some superb visual images for them to call on in order to describe time in the *mob, as con-firmed by the following selection:

> *He was in the mob when Long John Silver only had an egg on his shoulder..*
> *Listen lad, I was in Baghdad when you was still in yer Dad's bag..*
> *I've wrung more seawater out of my socks than you've ever sailed in!*
> *Jim's had a *survivor's tot from the MARY ROSE..*
> *Shiner *signed on when Nelson was a *middy / Cunningham was still a cadet..*
> *I was on the Main Gate when you were still on Cow & Gate..*
> *George was learning to fly when Pontius was the Senior Pilot..*
> *When God actually said 'Let there be light..' Jan was the duty *greenie..*
> *I've had more sea-miles than you've had *pusser's peas..*
> *Bill took the *King's Shilling when *VICTORY was still part of Epping Forest..*
> *Colours must have been in that ruddy store when the Dead Sea first reported sick..*
> *I was in uniform when you was in liquid form..*
> *Clive and Mike joined the *Fleet Air Arm on the day they were scraping Icarus off the duty runway..*
> *Mick led the Attack Party that dealt with the Burning Bush..*
> *When I joined the *Andrew there were no official numbers - we all knew each other..*

*Reckon' he was a regular in the team when Jesus was playin'
full-back fer Israel..*
*Nelson? Never knew 'im - but I reckon his father was a right
hard case..*

less Nott more Speed!   A common *cri de coeur* following the 1981 Defence Review and White Paper, which proposed the near-emasculation of the Royal Navy's surface fleet, especially in its amphibious warfare capabilities. It was conducted by the Secretary of State for Defence, one *John Nott*, and the Navy's rearguard action to preserve some semblance of a fleet was supported by the Navy Minister, *Keith Speed*. Not surprisingly, the latter lost his job, but the worst effects of the Review were discarded following the *Falklands conflict in 1982, which once again proved the need for an effective *blue water Navy and the ability to put troops ashore across beaches, without a harbour or port access. Mr Nott resigned shortly afterwards, but for some strange reason was knighted later on.

let the end go   Failure to pull on a rope - and then actually releasing it, thereby letting the ship and/or team down. Used nowadays to describe someone who has given up without making any proper effort, or has slackened off to a state of serious inefficiency during the process of *RDP.

liar dice   Poker dice, comparing favourably with Uckers as one of the great submariner's games, but also played by *skimmers.

liberty boat / libertymen   Small vessel used to transfer **libertymen** ashore and return them. The *pipe *Libertymen to clean!* orders those so privileged to cease work and *clean into their *shore rig. *Libertymen fall in!* orders them to muster at the *brow prior to boarding the *liberty boat* which, in a shore facility, might well be a *pusser's bus. The expression to *miss the boat is now popular parlance for failing to grasp an opportunity, but its origins lie in *missing the liberty boat* - which wasn't coming back.

licence to breathe   Jack's rather rueful and older nickname for his *station card.

lid (SM)   *Conning tower hatch: *'Shut the lower lid!'* is an order to close and secure this feature. In General Service, *doffing yer lid* is another expression for attending *defaulters, when one's cap (lid) is removed during the proceedings.

lie like a hairy egg   Tell a blatant untruth.

L - 262

lie to   A duo of interest:
1. To cease from doing something, or to take a break. When a boat had been hoisted by hand and *secured, the watch (or part of watch) who had toiled at the task were given the order *lie to*, and they dropped (probably very thankfully) the *falls to the deck.
2. A manoeuvre at sea to prevent a vessel from making progress through the water. This was done by reducing sail and counter-bracing the fore yards so that the wind struck the forward face of the foresails, thereby retarding the vessel's forward motion (see also to be *taken *aback).

lief   Another version of *leave*, as pronounced by the veterans.

lies like a pusser's menu / flat fish / hairy egg / *Appointer / Met man / cheap watch   *'I don't think that person is telling the truth!'*

Lieutenant   An officer's rank to be found in most of the world's navies, including the Royal Navy which has the lower grade of *Sub-Lieutenant* in addition (also known as *Lieutenant jg.* (for *Junior Grade*) in the US Navy). Its origins lie in the French words *lieu* and *tenant*, or the *place-holder* for the Master or Commanding Officer. Both the Spanish speaking and Italian navies omit the prefix, hence *Tenente* and *Teniente* are their versions of this rank. Note that in pure Anglo-Saxon, the word is pronounced *leftenant* or, even more properly in the RN, *l`tenant*; the pronunciation *lootenant* is definitely the sole preserve of those across the *Pond.

lifebuoy / lifebelt   Lifesaving appliance, usually circular and formerly made of cork wrapped in canvas, but nowadays manu-factured in hollow plastic. These are fitted in various places around the *upper deck; some are attached to smoke markers and can be remotely released from the bridge. A *Ceremonial Lifebuoy* is painted white, with the ship's name or *Flag officer's title picked out in gold, and positioned at the foot of the *brow in harbour. The *Lifebuoy Sentry* is a junior rating stationed in the after part of a ship to watch for a man overboard and to keep *look-out astern (also known as *lifebuoy ghost*); nowadays, with much reduced ship's companies, this precaution is only used during hazardous operations such as a *RAS.

life in a blue suit   Resigned acceptance of the vicissitudes of life in the *Andrew:*'Sold your house - and then had the *draft can-celled? Dear, oh dear - that's life in a blue suit I'm afraid, my friend..'* Submariners often extend this joke with a subtle little alteration to *life in a pink frock!*

lifeline Ropes or wires stretched along the decks of a vessel in rough weather, so that men can hang on to them as a safety measure when they are working on deck. Colloquially, any device or means by which a deteriorating situation or collapsing project can be saved. See also *Jackstay (3).

lift one's lid To be in trouble.

lifting the lid Removing cap at *defaulters.

light and dirty Light rum (Bacardi) and Coca Cola.

lightning conductors Gold stripes running down the outer trouser seams of a *Captain's or *Flag Officer's Mess Dress uniform.

like a small hotel - one ballroom Description of a pair of pusser's tropical shorts occupied by someone well endowed.

like rocking horse shit Something rather rare.

limers A soft drink (traditionally prepared from sachets of powder) and issued in tropical zones, or during very hot weather. Now made from ordinary squash or cordials, but the name has persisted, even if orange or lemon is the flavour concerned.

limey / lime juicer Sir James Lind, the first Physician at *Haslar Hospital, wrote a treatise in 1753 that showed *lemon juice* to be effective in treating the sailor's scourge of scurvy, an affliction caused wholly by a deficiency in dietary vitamin C. It was not until 1795, over forty years and thousands of deaths later, that the formal prescription of lemon juice as an anti-scorbutic was instituted by Their Lordships of the Admiralty, and then only because of the persistence of Sir Gilbert Blane, one of Lind's successors. Lemons had to be bought (expensively) in the Mediterranean; *limes* grew in the British West Indies colonies, and one of Their Lordships had some plantations there. So, the less effective *lime juice* was then substituted as a daily issue, and scurvy gradually ceased to be a serious problem in the Royal Navy. Jack's counterpart in the United States of America nicknamed him *Limey* as a consequence, and his ships as *lime juicers*; this name has persisted on the other side of the *Pond for all things British, and is usually prefixed by the word *Goddamned!*

line book (originally FAA) A frequently scurrilous, libellous, scatalogical and invariably hilarious, written and pictorial account of a squadron's activities, both professional and social; since adopted by ships for a similar purpose.

Dolphins

line shoot (FAA) A tall story, or exaggeration in the recounting of some event that is worthy of recording in a squadron line book.

lined up Charged with an offence under the Naval Discipline Act.

lip lock Prolonged kissing; see also *swapping spit: '..an' then she slaps this bloody great lip lock on me!'*

lipstall (FAA) What happens when your brain moves quicker than your mouth; see also *burble.

liquorice legs Shiny black gaiters worn by the officers in charge of a formal Guard, the officer carrying the *Queen's colour, and by the officer or *warrant officer responsible for parade training (formerly *Guns).

List / list Three meanings here:
1. Short form of the *Navy List, an official document published annually by the *MoD, giving a complete listing of all officers serving in the RN and RM, including their seniority, where they are serving, etc. A second volume contains the *Retired List*; in fact, naval officers don't actually retire - they get *placed* instead on the Retired List, thus remaining eligible (if medically fit) for call-up in an emergency.
2. The term is also used when referring to the latest batch of promotions (or alterations to the *List*) signalled annually by the *MoD: *'No good news for me on this List unfortunately. Just one more *shot, then the Feast of the *Passover..'* See Tugg's beautiful rendition of this event at page A - 17.
3. The condition of a ship which, owing to a shift in her cargo or to flooding below the waterline, is not lying horizontally in the water. This is not necessarily dangerous provided the problem is under control, but see also *loll.

lit up Drunk; derives from the broadcast made by a retired naval officer employed by the BBC to cover the Coronation Fleet Review at *Spithead in 1937. He was generously entertained in the wardroom of the battleship HMS NELSON, and by the time he came to describe the floodlighting of the fleet he was somewhat tired and emotional. *'The whole bloody fleet's lit up,'* he announced in slurred and excited tones to a shocked radio audience, and then later, when the floodlights were switched off: *'Where have they gone?'* This incident, captured for posterity in the BBC sound archives, caused a furore at the time.

Little f (FAA)   Official nickname for *Lieutenant Commander (Flying)* in an aircraft carrier or RN Air Station. He acts as deputy for Commander (Air) who is also known as *Wings (but never *Big f*!).

little nibble   Intercourse:*'I'm popping home to get a little nibble..'*

liver-in   Officer or rating who lives on board during the week, even if he has a home elsewhere; the RM equivalent is an *in-lier.

living high off the hog   This expression appears to originate from the occasional welcome relief of pork substituting for the usual *salt horse (beef) in a sailor's monotonous diet at sea.

LMD   Another *TLA, but this one has a degree of wry humour. When the *County class destroyers (the size of light cruisers) were commissioned, they were initially described as GMDs (Guided Missile Destroyers); the mid-seniority *captains who commanded (*drove) them would usually expect, as their next appointment, a spell in the *MoD where they would have charge of a *LMD - Large Mahogany Desk* instead. More junior officers could expect a *Large Metal Desk*, or even a *Little Metal Desk* if they were very unfortunate. See also *mahogany bomber.

loafing stations   Older term for a shore establishment where Jack did very little apart from *loafing* while awaiting his *draft chit for a ship.

loan clothing   Special uniform items issued only to those required to perform a specialist task or job.

lob in (FAA)   Land an aircraft somewhere, usually en route to somewhere else:*'On the way back from Guernsey we lobbed in to Exeter and picked up the Senior Pilot..'*

lob on   To *have a lob on* means to have an erection; a state of partial arousal is described as a *lazy lob*. This meaning is recorded as being in use in the 18th century.

lobbing about (SM)   This is what a *boat does on the surface if not underway, or only just moving.

lobby   A small compartment opening onto a *flat, eg. the *QM's lobby* which is a portable facility used when alongside.

loblolly boy   Older term for a young lad who assisted the ship's surgeon, as described in the novel *Roderick Random* by Tobias Smollett. Still senior to a *pox doctor's clerk! *Loblolly* was the nickname given to a thin, watery gruel served in the Sick Berth. Tugg depicts this role at page T - 474.

Lobs! An alarm call in older training establishments meaning: *'Look Out, Boys - Seniors!'* It could also refer to someone keeping a lookout for authority when doing an unpermitted act.

lobscouse A dish served in sailing ship days, especially in those vessels working out of Liverpool, consisting properly of mutton (but minced salt beef would do), stewed vegetables and broken ship's *biscuit in layers. The term *Scouse originates from this recipe.

lobsters Jack's archaic nickname for the RM Light Infantry of old, because of their scarlet tunics; the RM Artillery (blue) were called *unboiled lobsters* by the same token!

local Local promotion; see also *acting.

Lofty Traditional nickname for anyone tall, or with the surname Lofthouse.

log An important pair:
1. *Ship's Log* An official record (invariably completed in pencil) of a ship's activities on a minute-by-minute basis. A new *log* is started each month, and completed logs are sent to the Naval Historical Branch in London. There are any number of other logs

- or logbooks, either departmental or personal (eg. an *aircrew logbook*) which have to be maintained and inspected from time to time.
2. Equipment used to measure a ship's speed - see *knot for a full description. Nowadays, speed through the water is measured using an *electro-magnetic log*, and speed over the ground by satellite navigation.

logbook stamped (FAA)   Aircrew method of describing successful social activity:'*Went up to *Smoke for the weekend and got my logbook stamped..*' See also *back in date.

logged   The formal recording of a reprimand issued to an officer by the *captain of his ship, in the sense that the event has nominally been recorded as a matter of significance in the *Ship's Log*:'*I got logged for letting off a *thundie in a *Crab mess, yet the bloody *Wafus do that sort of thing all the time..*' Officers cannot be punished other than by the sentence of a Court Martial - a time-consuming process; a *logging*, which may or may not (at the commanding officer's discretion) be reported outside the ship is at the bottom of the scale of retribution. However, an expression of the Commander-in-Chief's severe displeasure is at the top of this scale, and can definitely be *career-limiting.

loggerheads   Three definitions (2 Naval, 1 agricultural!):
1.. Hollow spheres of iron at each end of a shaft; these were heated in a fire, then plunged into a tar bucket in order to melt the pitch for *paying into the seam of a hull's planking.
2. Wooden bitt (see *bitter end) in the stem of a whaling boat, used to control the harpoon line.
3. A *logger* was also a large piece of wood used to shackle a grazing horse's legs and hence prevent it from straying.

It is probably the first of these expressions which has come ashore to mean two people in dispute - hot (angry) and held apart (opposite views).

Loggies (RM)   Nickname for members of the *Commando Logistic Regiment RM*, an organization that contains at least five different cap badges on its *green berets, and which proved itself most convincingly during the land battles of the Falklands campaign. At one stage, the 650 *Commando *Loggies* ashore were successfully re-stocking combat supplies forward to a division of over 7000 men; this quite astonishing teeth-to-tail ratio of more than 10:1 is unlikely to be equalled in any future difficulty.

loll   Condition of a ship when flooded below or near the water-line, and when the floodwater cannot be contained - and is thus able to slop from one side of the ship to the other. This is a highly dangerous situation which can cause a ship to capsize, as most notoriously and tragically illustrated by the ferry *Herald of Free Enterprise* outside Zeebrugge Harbour in 1987.

long burst (esp. FAA)   A lengthy conversation that is mostly one-way.

long call   Expression heard at the *Wardroom dinner table to indicate that something needs to be passed up from further down: *'Long call for the water, please..'*

long course   Play on words derived from the official titles of the deep specialist courses for seaman officers before the advent of the *PWO: *'He got sent into a local Government establishment for the long course in sewing mailbags..'* It was generally felt that about 85% of the theory taught on the *long courses* was not really necessary for everyday practical application, hence (in part) the introduction of the *PWO category.

Long John   Nickname for a sailor who is always quoting Naval history and traditions.

long ship   Older term for a ship which is noted for her poor rations or victuals; now used to describe a *Wardroom displaying poor hospitality, ie. no-one offers to get you a drink when you visit.

long shot   A cannonball, or a shell fired at extreme range and with little real chance of scoring a hit - but considered worth a try in the circumstances prevailing at the time. The phrase has now come ashore to a wider usage.

long Tom   Originally the name given to the bow chasers (2 small-bore, long-barrelled and hence longer-range guns fitted forward in frigates and ships of the line). The term has two modern meanings nowadays:
1. A paintbrush *lashed to the end of a long pole.
2. (RM) A long wheelbase Landrover vehicle.

Look at her, I could make her arse crack walnuts!   An expression of total admiration for a thong-clad lady that would be instantly understood by someone who lived in Brazil.

Look at that arse, it's just like two babies fighting under a pusser's blanket!   A connoisseur's opinion of a female posterior in motion, under a skirt, and expressing much the same sentiment as the above.

Look at the state of that!   Traditional cry of semi-amazement when confronted by a person in outrageous clothing, or someone very much the worse the wear for drink:'*So this is the famous King's Road, eh? Nothing much to see here after all then..ruddy Norah! Will you look at the state of that!*'

Look for the rules!   Excuse to lift the edge of an *Uckers board, thereby causing the counters to slide, and thus effectively ending the game; the size and degree of inebriation of your opponents should be considered *very* carefully indeed before employing this particular tactic. Tugg has depicted this beautifully at page B - 28.

look out for   Stand in for somone:'*Will you look out for me if I *run ashore?*'

looker (FAA)   Traditional nickname for an *Observer:'*Were you a *Pirate or a Looker?*' See also *zero, *talking Navbag, *Pound for pound, *Orange, *JAFO, *commissioned ballast and *winch weight.

look-out   Anyone *detailed off to keep watch using eyes (with or without binoclulars / night viewing device) and ears, and thus emphasising the continued importance of the famous Mark One *eyeball. Also used to describe someone looking after, or briefly standing in for, someone else ('*Look out for me, will you, oppo?*'), or someone on a well-structured *run ashore who deliberately reduces his or her alcoholic intake in order to keep an eye on the others.

looney / loopy juice   Any form of strong alcohol.

Lord High Admiral   An honorary and singular title, formerly held either by the Sovereign or by the Sovereign's nominee, and one of the nine Great Offices of State. Interestingly, the title did not of itself confer sea command on the holder, who also had to be appointed *Captain General of Our Fleets and Seas*. When the Office was vacant (in commission) for any reason, it was executed by Commissioners, who came to be called the Lords Commissioners of the Admiralty (see *Sea Lords). Since 1660, it has usually been in commission, although James Duke of York (later James II) and William Duke of Clarence (later William IV - the *Sailor King*) both held the office for themselves; the latter rather annoyed everyone by exercising his right and power to

take the Fleet to sea! In 1964, when the Admiralty was subsumed into the unified Ministry of Defence (MoD), the title, but
not the Office of *Lord High Admiral* reverted to the Sovereign -
Her Majesty Queen Elizabeth II. The title of *Captain-General
(now purely relating to the Royal Marines) is currently held by
the Sovereign's Consort, His Royal Highness The Prince Philip,
a distinguished Naval veteran of WW2.

Lord Kelvin's balls   The soft iron spheres on either side of a
magnetic compass, positioned to deal with quadrantal errors.

lose the bubble (esp. SM)   The *bubble concerned is located
in the inclinometer spirit level of a *boat. It is used to adjust
trim; if this bubble disappears from sight then there is a danger
of trim control being lost. Hence, the phrase has come to mean
someone who is losing or has lost control of a situation, or else
an individual who is *in wine* and somewhat the worse for wear.

Lossie (FAA)   The former RN Air Station of HMS FULMAR,
now under *Crab ownership, but until recently also the spiritual home of the *Bucc. Locals still refer to the *Wardroom rather
than the Officer's Mess! Aircraft that are *In hot to the Tain
bombing ranges roll in past the Glenmorangie distillery, which
explains why that particular fluid is still the FAA's favourite
whisky.

lost the number of his mess   Euphemism for someone who
has either died in action, or been killed in an accident ashore
while serving in a ship.

louse ladders   Facial sideboards.

lovats (RM)   The No.2 Service Dress of the Royal Marines; this
is *lovat green* in colour. See also *Blues.

Lover's Leap   Nickname for the first train leaving London for
Portsmouth early on Monday morning. Ironically, some of the
occupants may have already got out at *Fratton the night before!

low hover   An anxiety state; see also *Wall of Death.

low stratus   Clouds of steam put out by an unattended boiling
kettle.

lower deck   Collective term for all non-commissioned members
of the Royal Navy, ie. everyone not actually commissioned as an
Officer.   Note that *upper deck does not refer to officers, but to
external areas. For *lower deck lawyer* see *messdeck lawyer.

lubber   An unimpressive or clumsy person; hence a *landlubber* - a *landsman who had yet to prove his worth in a ship. The *lubber's line* is the linear marking on a compass indicating the ship's head, and which is lined up with the course to be steered (so named because a good seaman doesn't need it).

lubber's hole   The opening or hatchway in the platform of a sailing ships' masts. These were provided as a means of access to the *tops* for those *landsmen and *lubbers who were afraid to climb up via the futtock shrouds. These were secured to the outside of the platform and involved climbing up and out on what was effectively a downward facing ladder.

lulu   A lady of comely appearance and manners.

lumbered   Rather like *lurk, but more in the sense that there was no-one else available or suitable:'*One volunteer was required, with a keen sense of duty - and a University degree. Guess who then got lumbered..'*

lumped   Hit some portion of your anatomy against something hard:'*Watch me elbow, *Doc, fer Gawd's sake - I lumped it against that bleedin' hatch cover when I slipped just now..'* Note the distinction between this and *lamped.

lumpy jumper   Descriptive term for a civilian female, in contrast to a *Jenny Wren; can also used to describe a WRNS *woolly pully. See also *bumpy jumper.

lurgie / lurgy   Always qualified by the adjective *dreaded*. An exaggerated name for any comon or simple illness such as 'flu. Sometimesheard as *the dreaded ab-dabs*.

lurk   Similar to *boning off or *joeing off an officer or rating for a particular duty: *'I got lurked to look after the Captain's maiden aunt at the *Cockers P..'* Most *XOs and *Jimmys will maintain a private *lurk list*; see also *lumbered and *bugger-about list.

Lympstone   The Commando Training Centre, Royal Marines (also known as CTCRM or CTC) situated on the eastern shore of the River Exe estuary.   It is the spiritual home of all *Commandos and those who wear the *green beret, and in addition, the base for all NCO, Command, Weapon and other related Specialist training in the *Corps. See also *Royal, *nod, *Endurance course, *Smartie tube, *Peter's Pool, *Heartbreak Lane, *Tarzan course, *speed march, *nine miler, *thirty miler, *First Drill, *Juniors, *Seniors, *King's Badge / Squad and - *It's only pain!*

Lynx   The main frigate-borne ship's helicopter, now that the *Wasp has been phased out (1988). It is an all-weather, combat-proven, two crew and twin-engined aircraft that is capable of high speeds, great agility, and the carriage of missiles, depth charges or torpedoes. See also *Pony.

MIKE

275 - 292

M&B tablets (SM)   These were the panacea for all ills in the submarine service. As diesel *boats carried no medical rating, the coxswain dished these out for every ailment. On one *boat, someone fell down the conning tower (fin) ladder, hitting every rung on the way down. He got two *M&B tablets* and was told to *turn in for one watch.

Macship   WW2 vessel - the initial three letters stand for *Merchantman Aircraft Carrier* - which were an additional feature to the *Camships in Britain's response to the the threat of German long-range *shitehawks(2) operating against Allied convoys crossing the North Atlantic. They were built with flat decks over a tanker or grain-carrying hull. After fighter-carrying escort carriers appeared on the scene, they then began to operate *Stringbags in the anti-submarine role; for a brilliant evocation of these ships and that era, read Lord Kilbracken's book *BRING BACK MY STRINGBAG* (Pen&Sword Books).

mad dog's vomit   Sandwich spread. See also *MDV.

made up   General term for promotion that can be heard in the *Wardroom (with the subsidiary meaning of selection for this) as well as on the *lower deck in its proper sense:'*Splot got made up in in the *List yesterday, but the CO didn't even get a *mench..' as compared with:'My B13 is in and I see the *Old Man next week to get made up..'

Madhouse   Nickname for the *Ministry of Defence* in London; derived from the more official abbreviation of *MoD, but in addition, an accurate description of some of the frenetic activity to be encountered inside that enormous building.

Mae West   Still the unofficial but frequently-used name, after all these years, for an aircrew inflatable buoyancy aid. The large pectoral curves induced to one's outline on operating this life-jacket are reminiscent of the splendid *jahooblies possessed by the late Ms *Mae West* during her cinematic heyday in the 1930s.

Double Bumps

magic binos   Older term for radar, a device which enabled the user to see in fog or bad weather. Now used for the NVG (Night Vision Goggles) which can be attached to a pilot's flying helmet instead of the visor, allowing safe tactical flying in total darkness.

magic writing (FAA)   Flight information presented in glowing letters on the HUD (*Head-Up Display) of a *SHAR.

mahogany bomber (FAA)   Term borrowed by Navyators from the *Crabfats for a desk in the *Madhouse:*'My last trip in a Hunter is programmed in for this afternoon - then I'm off to *drive a mahogany bomber in Whitehall for a pair of years..'* See also *LMD.

mailies   General term for any post, hence *maily-*freak* for someone who is in a state of turmoil awaiting the *pipe:*'Mail is now ready for collection..'* A *maily* in the singular sense is an envelope, although Jack also uses it to mean a letter (*'I'm writing a maily'*); and note *bluey as well.

main engines (SM)   The main propulsion units, without which a ship would not function. Submarine ERAs in Malta had a party piece of representing each piston by a man, in two lines. Each would stand up and sit down in the correct firing sequence. Another operated the muffler valve and another the throttle, and when the revs got to 420 per minute it could be quite exciting.

major smith   To read a signal/letter and make sure that you can understand exactly what the sender is trying to say, a piece of oft repeated advice to submarine COs: *'Always get your First Lieutenant to major smith your important signals; he will often take them away to allow you to sleep on it, and then you will probably decide not to send that signal the following day - when you have calmed down..'* Good advice!

majority (RM)   The process of being *selected for promotion to Major, which, because of differences in comparative rank, used to be equivalent to acquiring a *brass hat - as for a Lt. Col. in the Army, or a Commander RN / Wing Cdr. RAF: *'He got his majority early because of that, and then went straight back out to Northern Ireland..'* At the end of 1999 this difference was abolished, and RM Majors became similar in seniority and experience to their Army counterparts, so the term will gradually fall by the wayside. However, one usage is likely to remain - the Officer in command of a ship's Royal Marines *Detachment is traditionally nicknamed *The Major*, and the most junior RM officer is *The Soldier*, or *Joe.

make   A quartet of applications:
1. *make a signal* - transmit a message.
2. *make and mend* - period in a ship's daily routine set aside for the repair and maintenance of Jack's personal clothing and kit. Nowadays used mainly to describe an afternoon off.
3. *Make it so!* - formal and rather God-like response from the Officer of the Watch when initiating some piece of ceremonial: '*Sunset, sir.' 'Make it so!'*
4. *make your number* - introduce yourself to the *Captain or *HOD on arrival in a new appointment, in a similar manner to a warship signalling her pendant number when joining the Fleet.

make her have it (esp. SM)   An encouragement to hit or pull harder, as in: *'Go on son, make her have it..'*

makee-learnee   Pidgin Chinese for someone who is a novice, but is learning on the job.

Maker's rep   The Padre.

making one aft   To appear as a *defaulter on the quarterdeck.

makings   Three meanings:
1. The ingredients for a *wet of tea or coffee, ie. powder, sugar and milk.
2. Tobacco and cigarette papers for making *ticklers.
3.   In very old navy, the material with which a man made the *cat o'nine tails for his own punishment.

Malta GC   Former strategic base of the Mediterranean Fleet; the scene of much stoic heroism despite strong Axis bombardment during WW2, for which the island was collectively awarded the George Cross.   Although no longer a NATO asset, and following a period of strained diplomatic relations, RN ships are now visiting with increasing frequency, thereby reinforcing strong historical links and introducing a new generation of Jack and Royal to such features as:

> *Malta *dog* - a severe form of diarrhoea and vomiting.
> *Maltese breaststroke* - reversal of the normal swim
>> stroke into a scooping action:*'Gimme your money..'*
> *Maltese gharry horse* - an animal with particularly
>> muscular hindquarters, hence:*'She had a backside / face like a Maltese gharry horse..'*
> *Maltese lace* - any garment with frayed edges or loose
>> threads.
> *Maltese pound* - containing thirteen ounces.

See also the term *my brother in Gozo, and Tugg at U - 483.

Mama-san   Madame in charge of a Far Eastern *bag shanty.

man and boy   Proud statement that usually accompanies any description of length of service: '*I was in the *Andrew for twenty-nine years, man and boy..*' Note that Royal will refer to his service as a *Junior in a different way when making an identical claim: '*I did twenty-nine years in the Corps, including three years *girl's time..*' See also the interesting comparisons under *length of service.

man fat   Another term for seminal fluid; the others are *population paste and *baby gravy.

man from Del Monte (FAA)   The *Lynx *Observers *Trapper; see *JAFO for a more detailed explanation.

man up (FAA)   The crew process of boarding, strapping-in and then completing all the pre-flight checks of an aircraft before *launch.

Manchester slut (SM)   A culinary delight derived from the recipe for a Manchester tart - this was a *clacker with a thin layer of jam, then a thicker layer of some kind of lemon curd custard, and finally desiccated coconut sprinkled on top.

mandraulic   Mechanical apparatus worked by muscular power alone; it is the modern version of *Armstrong patent. See also *handraulic.

mankey   Something dirty or filthy.

manking   Complaining in a whining or repetitive manner: '*Don't come in here and start manking all over me about transport..*'

Marines   There are constant references to *Royal*, his history and terminology throughout this book, but it is as well to remember that many nations have Marine Corps of soldiers who are especially trained and adapted to the problems of war at sea - including the Argentines! See also *Cloggie. *Royal's* origins lie with the 1664 Order in Council that raised 1200 men for the Lord Admiral's Regiment of Sea Soldiers (see also *Jollies); this number fluctuated until 1755 when the force was re-organized into a permanent feature, serving in warships in order to maintain discipline, provide sentries, and play in the ship's band. Later on, artillery functions were added, so that one gun turret's crew of most large Royal Navy warships were all Royal Marines rather than seamen. The distinction between RM Artillery and RM Infantry was abolished in 1923. Later on, *Commando tasks were added; after WW2 this latter role was adopted specifically by the *Corps, with Army personnel supporting the artillery, engineer and general logistic functions.

The relationships between the United States Marine Corps and The Corps of Royal Marines are extraordinarily close, both in terms of current liason and past development, as well as their expertise in the amphibious warfare role. During the Wars of American Independence they actually fought against each other! Although the USMC is technically junior (formed in 1775) it is numerically over twenty times the size of its British counterpart. On both sides of the Atlantic Ocean, the reputations of both Corps are mutually respected as unsurpassed in an unbroken history of fighting spirit and devotion to duty, in the service of their respective countries.

mark   Originally, in order to be paid or victualled, a sailor had to *sign on in the ship's book. Since most sailors were illiterate, they did this by making a mark (usually an X) by their name, witnessed by an officer or the *captain's clerk; hence the phrase *to make one's mark* - literally to exist, but by extension to have established oneself. It can also be a *mark of depth* on a leadline - see *deep six for a fuller explanation.

marlin spike   The part of a seaman's clasp knife used to open up the lay of a rope for splicing. Old salts used to refer to the ideal sailor as having *every finger a marlin spike*.

marry the *gunner's daughter   An old naval expression meaning to be laid over a gun to receive a thrashing.

marry-up   Work two lines as one, or bring things into line: '*The ship sailed long before we could marry-up all the paperwork for those new stores..*'

Martin-Baker let down   Euphemistic description of the procedure for ejecting from an out-of-control and crashing jet aircraft, named after the ejection seat so employed: '*He came into the hover alongside, but then a nozzle failed and it was time for a Martin-Baker let down..*'

master   Formal, abbreviated mode of address for the *Master-at-Arms; also the correct title for the *captain of a merchant ship, including an *RFA - in this sense it derives from *sailing master*, a *warrant officer who was effectively responsible for navigation.

master race   Wry description of the Executive Branch of the RN, used by the other branches. The Executive (X) branch still provides the *captains and *executive officers of ships, as well as the majority of the more senior appointments in the Navy.

Master-At-Arms (MAA)   Technically, the CPO rate of the Regulating Branch, but woe betide anyone who calls him (or *her* nowadays) '*Chief*'! The Master-at-Arms is *de jure* the most senior rating on board, responsible for the maintenance of discipline, the investigation of offences and, as the Whole-ship Co-ordinator, is a key member of the ship's management team. In a big ship the post is held by a *Warrant Officer (*Fleet Joss), and in a small ship by a Regulating Petty Officer (*Cox'n). *Warrant Officer MAAs* and *MAAs* are the only ratings entitled to carry swords; see also *Reggies, *Jaunty and *Jossman. Usually abbreviated to Master.

'ARRY! - OUR JACK!

HE'S BEEN REMANDED! - BY THE PRINCE OF WALES!!

mate   A complex quartet:
1. In the Merchant Navy, the title for deck officers; hence the *Choff is also the *first mate* - not generally used by the *RFA.
2. Formerly an assistant to any specialist, as in **boatswains mate* (which see for its present meaning).
3. In a big ship, assistants to the *First Lieutenant and responsible for cleanliness and husbandry in specific areas - *Mate of the *'Tweendecks* (internal communal spaces) and *Mate of the *Upper Deck* (another name for the *bosun).
4. The *Mate Scheme*, introduced in 1912, was the first formal method whereby selected ratings were given officer training and then sent to sea as *mates* before subsequently being promoted lieutenant; it was thus the forerunner of the *Special Duties list.

matelots   Royal's collective term for Jack (from the French, and pronounced *mat-lows*); the *matelot's shuffle* can be observed whenever Jack gets on the dance floor with his *pash - one step left, one to the right, a quick wiggle - and then the same all over again, at a pace that is often independent of the beat. A *matelot's gorge* was a big meal of steak, egg and chips on getting home from sea, perhaps leading to the term *Guzz!

matey   Civilian workman employed in HM Dockyards. Reported to jump on any snails following him around.

mattress mamba   Yet another term for a penis, as a herpetological equivalent of a *knicker python, or a *one-eyed trouser snake.

maulers   Hands.

mawren / maren   Wren serving with the Royal Marines. Instead of wearing a naval cap *tally, they wear the *Globe and Laurel cap badge backed with a semi-circular scarlet cloth patch.

max chat (FAA)   Flying at full power and high speed (usually at low level):*'The *Boss called *buster, but I was already at max chat and going like a bloody train..'*

max out (FAA)   Become overloaded mentally:*'Flying low level I can handle the *nav and *poling OK, but give me the radios as well and I just max out..'*

mayfly (FAA)   Number of aircraft available for the tasking and completion of a planned *flypro.

measured his length (esp. RM)   Fell flat on the ground after tripping.

Mech / Mechanician   Up to 1983, a member of the engineering branch who had joined as a mechanic (semi-skilled) and who was selected for training and qualification as a (skilled) artificer. Once qualified, the *Mech*, who had earned his qualification through hard graft and who also had wide sea experience, rather looked down on the *tiff, whose training and some apprenticeship had taken place under relatively easy conditions ashore. In 1983 *Mechanicians* and artificers were combined, although it is pretty obvious which avenue a *tiff has come up, even without looking at his *docs.

medical comforts   Special items of food and drink (eg. soup, chocolate, brandy) held for issue only in cases of medical need.

meet her!   Nothing to do with going ashore to meet Pompey Lill; this was an order to the helmsman to put the opposite amount of wheel on.

mega ma'am   A very senior (or very large) WRNS officer.

meltdown   Physical state of a telephone being used by someone who is extremely angry: *'You should have heard the *bollocking that the *Boss got from *Wings! The phone almost went into meltdown..'*

Mench (RM)   Abbreviation for the operationally-awarded honour of being Mentioned in Despatches.

mental dwarf / mental pygmy   Common terms of abuse.

merchant   Frequent suffix in many descriptions; see **gunna-merchant, *whinge-merchant* and similar labels for an individual rich in those qualities.

Merlin   The **Sea King* replacement; also the engine of the *Seafire* fighter aircraft (FAA derivative of the Spitfire) and the ship's name of the wartime Naval Air Station of Donibristle, near Rosyth.

Mess number   A quartet:
1. **Wardroom account number for signing bar chits etc.
2. Conversational way of pointing out a mistake, so that the chap who has it wrong should buy everyone a drink: *'The *rig of the day is No.4s my friend - what's your Mess number?'*
3. (FAA) By long tradition, an officer's outstanding Mess bill is settled by Mess funds if he is killed whilst flying on duty. This account is not formally closed until midnight, so the rest of the squadron can drink on that number in a wake for their dead colleague.
4. *'He's lost the number of his Mess..'* is an older **lower-deck term to describe a sailor who has **kouffed it.

mess traps   Cutlery and crockery, plus knives, forks, spoons, etc. for ratings' messes. This is the technical storekeeping name. Laid out in patterns for Captain's **Rounds.

messdeck   Six usages here:
1. Jack's home in a warship or shore establishment.
2. *messdeck justice* is the informal dispensation of punishment to someone who persistently trangresses either the written (or unwritten) rules. For instance, on the rare occasions when a sailor or marine is reluctant to comply with the normal standards of daily hygiene, a *messdeck scrubbing* may be visited upon him.
3. A *messdeck lawyer* is a **Jack-me-tickler who is always arguing the toss or quoting regulations and rules.
4. The *messdeck *dodger* is a rating employed on cleaning duties there.

5. When *buzzes travel around a ship they do so via the *messdeck* (bush) *telegraph* system.

6. **messdeck champagne** - Maltese marsovin and 7-Up.

messman   Two applications:

1. In ships, a junior rating employed in a senior ratings' mess on general cleaning duties - could be a *cushy number.

2. In shore establishments, this is a civilian contracted by the Wardroom Committee to undertake all supplies and catering.

met man   See *weather guesser or *Professor / *Doctor Fog.

metal moth   Rust: *'This car has been chewed by the metal moth..'*

Mexican hat dance   Highly excitable state displayed by a senior officer towards someone lower in a chain of command: *'When I got up to *Flyco, the Captain was doing the Mexican hat dance all over *Wings..'* See also *wall of death and *high hover.

Mick / mick   A trio:

1. Any Irishman.

2. *take the mick* - to taunt or make fun of someone.

3. Older slang for a hammock or *hammick - mick the sailor's friend.*

Mickey Duck   A cartoon film; the term is an amalgamation of *Mickey Mouse* and *Donald Duck*. *Two Mickey Ducks and a *shit-kicker* has nothing to do with the drinks list of a cocktail bar, but merely indicates that two cartoons are preceding the Western in that night's cinema programme.   There may also be strident demands for a *Fred Quimby.

Mickey Mouse killick   A young *Leading Hand who has not even got his first (Good Conduct) *badge to go with the *hook. The prefix can also be applied in a similar vein to badgeless POs and inexperienced (technical) Chiefs.

middle   The middle watch, and least favoured of all, since it runs from midnight until 0400.

middle for diddle   Take a chance, from the game of pub darts.

Middy / Middies   Midshipman / a group of Midshipmen. See also *Dartmouth and *Snotty.

midshipman's chest / locker   If something is described as being *'like a midshipman's chest'*, it conveys the image of something in a muddle or badly stowed, with *'everything on top and nothing handy..'*

midships ballast (SM)   A submarine wardroom.

Milan (RM)   Portable anti-tank missile of European manufacture, used with great success by Royal and the Paras in the Falklands to demolish enemy defensive *sangars. In this context see also *eyes water!

milestone   See *slamming.

mince prince   homosexual.

mincer   Yet another term for a *brownhatter.

mind over matter (RM)   *'It's quite simple, really - I don't mind, and you don't matter..'*

mindfart   Alternative to *brain fart as an excuse for having trouble with the operation of a bank of switches.

minesweeping   Two related uses here:
1. The process of going around the half-empty glasses at a party and pouring their contents into your own glass, in order to extend proceedings after the bar has shut.
2. Also, eating with your elbows out and looking like a pair of deployed *paravanes.

mineswiping   Nickname for the crucial business of mine clearance, as performed by Jack in a fleet of glassfibre-reinforced plastic *mineswipers*.

Ming (china) Affectionate description of an older warship:*'He took that lovely old piece of Ming down to the South Atlantic and brought her through the whole Conflict without so much as a scratch..'*

minging (pronounced with a hard *g*):
1. (RM) Adopted Glaswegian slang word meaning drunk: *'Jus' two beers an' the boy was mingin'..'*
2. (RM) Depending on the context, it can also mean smelling strongly:*'After three weeks ashore in the Falklands we wuz all minging pretty bad..'*

mirrors (all done with) Something presented very cleverly.

mismuster Arrangement made for those who missed their noon *tot to draw it later on in the day. Now used for any issue process:*'Lima Company will draw Arctic clothing from Main Stores at 0800 today; mismusters 1600..'* See Tugg at S - 433.

missile mary A person who looks after the missiles on a Trident submarine. The term also applies to others in the TWS department that have the job of looking after the Trident weapon and associated systems.

miss pot sit An obnoxious fluid that you have to drink when in *Rose Cottage. Actually *Mist. Pot. Cit.*, a potassium citrate mixture designed to alkalinize the urine!

miss the (*liberty) **boat** Also applied to missing trains, buses, promotion, etc.

mixy blob Weakened and easily surmountable barrier to forward progress around the board in an *Uckers game; also a label for someone of mixed parentage.

mizzy (SM) A seretive submarine patrol, also known as a *sneaky. Derived from the words *Mystery Trip*.

MOA (RM) A *Marine Officer's Attendant*, the equivalent of an Army batman.

mob (esp. RM) Royal's conversational equivalent of the *Andrew, but this term is occasionally used by Jack as well:*'How long you got to go in the mob then?'* This has absolutely nothing to do with swarthy Italian gentlemen, and neither has the term *heavy mob.

MOBI A rather unflattering description of an unpopular superior - *Most Objectionable Bastard Imaginable*.

mobile Navbag (FAA) Another disparaging term for an *Observer.

Moby rash   The damage inflicted on yourself by crashing or coming off one of the *Mobylette* mopeds that can be hired by Jack when visiting Bermuda.

MoD   The *Ministry of Defence*, positioned in a huge building just off Whitehall, in London. See also *Madhouse. A *MoD Plod* is member of the Ministry of Defence constabulary. See also the term *plastic policeman.

modo   Totally useless person with a hint of physical deformity, derived from the character *Quasimodo* in the film *Hunchback of Notre Dame*. Note the RM equivalent of *spaz.

molar mangler   Dentist; see *fang farrier for a complete list.

Mombers   The Kenyan naval port of Mombasa; see also *black ham.

money for old rope   Expression of maritime origin that has come ashore. *Old rope* was condemned as both dangerous and useless; anyone that could sell this was getting good money for something worthless. It was also called *junk, another word that has gone ashore.

monkey   Another useful nautical word used as a prefix to mean small, as in:
1. *monkey jacket* - the double-breasted uniform jacket worn by officers and senior ratings; so called because it was smaller than the frock coat worn on formal occasions. *Reefer jacket* means the same, and is in common usage, but *monkey jacket* is actually the correct term.
2. *monkey *boom* - a smaller *boom used to secure sailing dinghies in harbour.
3. *monkey's orphan* - sailing warship era term for a young sailor who was too small and inexperienced to send *aloft.
4. *monkey's fist* - Small, elaborate knot at the end of a *heaving line to give it weight to carry to the shore against the wind; it should *never* have an additional metal weight inside it.
5. *monkey's island* - the raised part of a ship's bridge, around the binnacle.
6. *monkey in a ball of wool* - Jack's older figure of speech for a face framed by a *full set of whiskers: *"Eh *Skers - yer *moosh looks like a monkey in a ball of wool..'*
7. *monkey on a stick* (FAA) - the *Lookers are fighting back at last! Nickname for a pilot, with the alternative of *trained monkey.*

Moon City   See also *legoland; the term is applied to any group of buildings with a modern or futuristic appearance, especially the married quarters at Faslane.

moosh   Face, also used as a form of address: '*Oi, Moosh - where-ja think you're slidin' off to?*'

More yet!   Classic drill order given when adjusting the straight-ness of line in a parade formation; many other applications in daily life.

moriarty   Classic Jackspeak for *moratorium* - that extraordinary government finance-inspired mechanism whereby there is a sudden cessation of expenditure in one field or another, in order to balance the books in the short term.

morning glory   An erection on awakening; in the right cir-cumstances this may well lead straight on into a *dawn strike.

Morning Prayers   The Commanding Officer's first meeting of the day, when ship's business and the future programme are discussed.

morse   Telegraphist's code, and one of the biggest steps in com-munications history, without which the Fleet could not have communicated by radio and sound, or visually by light. There is a lovely parody of a song title involving the Yeoman of Signal's daughter: '*She only dit dit 'cos her da da dit dit..*'

Moses   Nickname for the youngest man (*Baby Moses*) of a ship's company.

most dangerous thing in the world (RM)   Prior to 1982, this was defined as Jolly Jack with a rifle; now, post-Falklands, the *most dangerous thing in the world* is - an officer with a map!

mothball fleet   Ships lying alongside or at anchor which are in a deliberate state of preservation. Although inactive, they can be made ready for sea again in times of national emergency.

Mother (FAA)   Radio and conversational description of an air-craft's parent ship or carrier: '*Pigeons to Mother - 270 degrees at 65 miles..*'

Mother Carey's chickens   Very old term for stormy petrels, which, along with the albatross, are about the only sea birds not to be generically known as *shitehawks.

motion lotion (FAA)   Aviation kerosene.

motor mouth   Someone who talks too much; see also *Gatling gob.

mouse (pronounced *mowz*)   To pass turns of twine or small wire around the open end of a secured hook to prevent it unhooking; or to do the same around the end of a bolt or shackle pin in order to prevent it working free.

Ear Pounding

moustache   Banned in the Royal Navy by Queen Victoria on the death of her beloved Albert.

mousetrap   *Pusser's basic cheddar cheese.

mozzie   Any flying and biting insect.

Mrs B's   Refers to the celebrated cook of yesteryear, Mrs Beeton; see entry at *B's for example.

MRU   The acronym for Much Regret Unable - the polite declining of an invitation which has now almost become a word in its own right: '26 *WMPs for drinks before lunch on Sunday, sir - and only four MRUs..'

muck or nettles (RM)   No real choice between two unpleasant possibilities: 'You can go either right or left, but not straight up. Take your pick, it's either muck or nettles..'

muck stick   A rifle, derived from musket.

mud moving (FAA)   *SHAR attacking a weapons range; *ground pounding is an alternative term.

mudguard   A Deputy Head of Department - since it is a DHoD's job to take all the mud and muck thrown up by his *Wheel!

muff diver   Someone partial to a spot of oral contact with a female; in this respect the tufts of facial hair more usually known as bugger's grips can also be described as muff diver's depth marks, and the wearer asked about their calibration.

muffler   The valve that lets out the exhaust gases of a submarine. It is a very large hole to be shut off when *snorting.

mufti   Arab word, initially adopted by the Army, but now heard occasionally in Naval circles for formal civilian clothing: 'Should I wear uniform for this interview, or is it mufti?'

mulct   Older term for stoppage of pay, usually as a fine consequent to formal punishment; see also *Northeaster.

mulley   A quick *kip, so named after the Secretary of State for Defence who, while seated next to his Sovereign, dozed off during the (very noisy) 1977 Silver Jubilee Royal Review of the RAF.

multiplying eye   The condition which exists when blind drunk and seeing more than double.

mundungus   A word used in the Navy to refer to any useless or unwanted material (like gubbins, or wiffin etc). It is, in fact, the correct name for the dust of unprocessed tobacco leaves. Must be cleared up for rounds!

muppet   Acronym applied to someone in the *Andrew who is of poor aptitude or competence: *'You, my son, are a complete muppet - the most useless person Pusser ever trained..'* The term is also used for members of the *mineswiping fraternity.

murder face   A *very* ugly individual.

muscle bosun   Someone who practises the art of body building or who trains hard at weight lifting. Some *springers and most *Field Gunners are *muscle bosuns*.

mushroom troop (RM)   Complaining description used by those who feel that they are not being told enough about what is happening:*'We're the classic ruddy mushroom troop we are - fed on shit and kept in the dark..'*

musical veg   Baked beans and/or peas.

muster   Three entries here:
1. The formal inspection of issued equipment which has been laid out in a neat and regulation manner is a *kit muster*. If the standard is satisfactory, then the lay-out is deemed to have *passed muster*.
2. Can also be used as an order to group together at another location, as in the *pipe:*'All *hands muster on deck..'*
3. To *muster one's kit* also, depending on context, means to vomit, as if the stomach contents are laid out for inspection.

my brother in Gozo!   Traditional Naval disclaimer, a conversational device adapted from Jack's experiences ashore in Malta to shift the blame onto someone else:*'It wasn't me - it was my brother in Gozo..'*

my Navy   *'Smoke in front of the general public while wearing your uniform? Not in my Navy, you don't!'*

mystery trip (SM)   No one knew where they were going and, no one ever discussed it when they got back. These *mizzies were, allegedly, well north of the Denmark Strait, and took the diesel *boats and their crews to the limit of their endurance and, because of the ability of a submarine to take on the same temperature as the surrounding water, were also bloody cold. The term *mystery trip* seems more apt than the more modern *sneaky as the crew never knew where they were going, much the same as a summer coach trip of similar name. Although the destination really was unknown to the crew, there seemed to be a lot of photographs being taken through the periscope when they eventually got there!

NOVEMBER

293 - 306

n   Algebraic expression that can frequently be heard in use to describe a degree or quantity: *'The *Boss was n pissed-off to hear that his suggestion had been rejected by the *Puzzle Palace..'* Another version would have him pissed-off to the *nth degree*.

NAAFI   Acronym for the *Navy, Army and Air Force Institutes.*
1.   The *NAAFI damager* is the civilian canteen manager or *can man who is carried in most HM Ships.
2.   Used to further good effect in describing a low-quality individual: *'He's a bit of a NAAFI rating in fact - No Ambition And Flip-all Interest in what's going on..'*

3.   The security *classification of *NAAFI RESTRICTED* implies little or no security at all!
4.   Note also the mythical *Major Naafi van Driver* along with his colleague *Captain *Hertz van Rental*; either name can be used by

Royal when seeking a *bite from his *Cloggie friends.

5. *NAAFI landmine* - a pork pie or *growler.

6. *NAAFI wad* - older term for a slice of cake.

NAC 89 (FAA)   Formal record of training and progress throughout a Fleet Air Arm pilot's career; the aviation equivalent of a *S.206 which may contain gems such as:*'When this pilot lifts into the hover, he initiates a sequence of events over which he appears to have very little subsequent control..'*

Nagasaki   Japanese city which has assumed a place in Naval legend equivalent to Timbuktu in a wider parlance. A rating who is physically well-endowed with regard to his *wedding tackle may be described as being *rigged like a *Nagasaki donkey;* anything larger or faster than life can also become the largest or fastest (whatever) *this side of Nagasaki,* and someone who was conspicuously thin was a *Nagasaki greyhound* (all bollocks and back teeth!). Extreme thirst can also be indicated by:*'My throat is as dry as a Nagasaki bomb-dodger's starboard flip-flop..'*

nagging machine   Another of Jack's nicknames for the missus. However, he is also wise enough to observe that *nagging* can also be endless repetition of the uncomfortable truth.

names   An addition to the listed *Aggie on 'orseback, there were many others eg. a five funnelled cruiser from WW1 was called a *Packet of Woodbines,* a favourite cheap smoke. The submarine with the pennant number P555 was also called *State Express* after the cigarette firm whose logo it was. The early carrier ARGUS was known as the *Ditty Box* since with no superstructure and straight lines, she was one! HMS/M AUROCHS was known as *The Woolley Bull* and her motto, inevitably but unofficially became *Bullshit baffles Brains.* BIRMINGHAM of course was *Brum.* BELLEROPHON was *Billy Ruffian.* PENELOPE was the *Pepperpot* after the Malta Convoys, and many near misses. Her name was also pronounced sometimes as for *Antelope,* while that ship's name was then pronounced as for *Penelope.* CHARYBISDIS became the *Cherry B.* Note also the lovely *Tiddly Quid* for the ROYAL SOVEREIGN, and *Tiddly Acorn* for the ROYAL OAK!

nap hand   Older term for a *dose of gonz and siff acquired during *all-nighters or a *run-ashore. Syphilis, thankfully, is very rarely seen these days, so the phrase now refers to a mixed infection, such as the *boat along with pubic crab lice.

nark   The *Jossman's nark*. Rating who assists the Master-at-Arms but is not actually a regulating branch member. Reputed to be the most powerful man on board.

native leave   Special leave granted to local boys when a ship visits a port near their home towns.

NATO   No Action, Talk Only - at least until the Kosovo crisis!

NATO standard   The equivalent of: *'One milk, two sugars..'* in reply to the question: *'How do you like your coffee?' 'NATO standard, negative two!'* would be a reply indicating that no sugar was needed at all in your white coffee. See also *Julie Andrews.

nause (esp. RM)   Difficulty with authorities, especially civilian ones, and usually when trying to obtain permission to do something: *'Flightplan into the London Special Rules Zone? Not worth all the nause, my friend..'* Or: *'The boys seem to have been quite well-behaved during their *run-ashore in Trondheim - some nause over a missing traffic sign, but nothing too serious..'*

nautical nausea   Seasickness.

nav queen   One of the Polaris or Trident weapon system (P/T WS) *Greenie watchkeepers. So called because of their special protected status - as the Navigation System must be kept on-line and always *navigating* to maintain the credibility of the deterrent, the *nav queens* would be (almost) immune from fire exercises, wearing Emergency Breathing Apparatus, black lighting and so on, in order that they could/can keep a close eye on this equipment. The Navigation Centre is also off-limits to the rest of the crew. Reported to be the only place to go in a *bomber to borrow hair dryers and curlers.

Naval stores   Almost any *pusser's item: *'They are called Naval stores because they are meant to be stored. If *Pusser wanted them to be given out, then he would have called them issues..'* See also *Slops.

naval airman   Lowest band of humanity in the Air Arm. Comes in two classes and pupates eventually into a Leading Airman. *NA 1st class* is equivalent to Able Seaman. They never *ever* wanted to be known as *Able Airmen*!

naval architect   Jack's opinion of a ship is definitive, but especially with reference to her habitability. *Naval architects* come in for undue criticism, and Jack's ultimate condemnation is that a ship (like a camel) was designed by a committee; hence his opinion that a woman was designed by a naval architect, since no one else would have put the recreation space right between the main drainage systems.

navalised   Something that has been made semi-*Jackproof, usually by the process of taking a civilian item of equipment, doubling its weight, attaching a hook and some navigation lights, painting it grey, then increasing the cost ten-fold - and announcing availability in the New Year, without specifying which one.

Navy (*Thank God we've got a)   Muttered when things are going wrong with the RAF or Army.

Navy cake   Older *brownhatter's term for a sailor with homo-sexual tendencies; the modern version is *seafood*.

Navy Days   Bank Holiday weekends especially selected in the major port areas when Jack, Jenny and Royal, and their ships and submarines are thrown open to the public. Various additional exhibitions and flying / marching / handling displays ensure value for money, with all proceeds going to local and national Naval charities.

(The) **Navy List**   See *List

Navy News   Excellent monthly colour newspaper of the RN which regularly wins prizes for both style and content. Widely (and also nationally) distributed, it is read by Admirals and *ABs alike. This periodical also features Tugg's regular cartoon strips about the life and times of *JACK* - some past gems have been reproduced in this book.

NB / NB'd   A verb meaning to note a fact, or some new and (usually) parallel piece of information, taken from the Latin *nota bene,* as in: *'They've appointed a chap to head up this inquiry, but at the same time as they sacked the whole team that he's supposed to be investigating - did you NB that little fact?'*

neaters   Undiluted rum; this was only issued to POs and CPOs, and lasted longer than *grog. See also *Black Mass and *Up Spirits.

neck oil (RM)   Beer; something that you get down your *neck* for internal *lubrication.*

negatory / negative   An answer confirming a negative state rather than the word *no,* as in: *'Any wine left in that bottle?' 'Sorry, chum - that's a definite negatory..'*

Neil-Robertson   A form of bamboo and canvas restraining stretcher that is winchable up a ship's side, or into a helicopter. Also known as a bamboo * burberry!

Nelson's blood   Rum. This label stems from the incorrect belief that Lord Nelson's body, which had been placed in a cask after *Trafalgar, was preserved in rum; in fact, it was a mixture of brandy and the cruder *spirit of wine.* Ironically, this cask was brought home to England in HMS PICKLE.

Nelson's button   On the left hand side of the fireplace in the Board Room at the Admiralty is a white disc about the size of a shilling, let into the oak panelling about 5ft 4ins above the floor. The legend is that this button denotes the height of Lord Nelson but the more probable story is that it was put there to assist the committee interviewing candidates for commissions in the Royal Marines, for whom the regulations of 1847 laid down 5'4" as the minimum height.

Neptune's dandruff   Table (sea) salt.

Neptune's sheep   Jack's older name for *white horses* (cresting wavelets) at sea. The French Navy use the term *moutons blancs.*

nerve gas See *CSB.

nesting boxes WRNS cabins or quarters.

Netley The former *naval nuthouse* or *funny farm situated in an impressive stately home on the eastern shore of Southampton Water. *Netley Annexe* was the name given to any office or workshop in a ship where the famous adage: '..*you don't have to be certifiably mad to work here, but it certainly helps..*' applied.

nettles The cords that make up a hammock's clews; a single, knotted length was also used by each member of the crew to *lash-up a shipmate who had been sentenced to run the *gauntlet. In one sense therefore, he was being *stung* by their criticism of his behaviour, which gives rise to at least one modern application of the word *nettled*. If the plant's name only came into usage in the last century, then it is also possible that this label stemmed from old Jackspeak as well.

Never cut towards your towards your thumb, always cut towards your chum! Jack would say, as he did just that.

new wine in an old bottle The process of upgrading an older warship by the installation of new weapon systems into her, at a periodic refit. This process has not occurred much lately, because the drawdown in the RN's numbers have also reduced its afloat strength. Ships are instead sold to the highest (South American, *standfast Argentine, bidder) and the Fleet gets steadily smaller.

newted (RM) Drunk; single word summary for someone who is as *pissed as a newt*. See also *handcarted, *legless and *shot away.

nibble Sexual intercourse. *Having a nibble* is similar to *getting a bit*. Those showing signs of frustration before shore leave were said to have *minge mice*!

nibblers Personnel working in a shore establishment who arrive at work late and go home early, muttering about travelling time; this is a creeping habit that occasionally requires some spot checks at the main gate.

nice (quiet) **little number** An easy shore job, or any employment requiring minimal effort to succeed; becomes a *quiet* number as well if there is no supervision into the bargain.

nicknames Most of these standard and traditional pairings appear alphabetically in the text, but they are also listed here for completeness:

Bagsy Baker; Bandy Evans; Baz (for anyone called Barry); Bogey Knight; Bomber Brown; Brigham Young; Brum(my) (anyone from Birmingham); Buck Taylor; Bungy Edwards (or Williams); Bunny Warren; Buster Brown; Chalky White; Chats Harris; Chippy Carpenter; Chirpy Finch; Daisy May (or Adams); Darby Allen; Dicky Bird; Dinger Bell; Dodger Long; Dolly Gray; Doughy Baker; Duke Earle; Dusty Miller (or Rhodes); Dutchy Holland; Edna May; Erroll Flynn; Fanny Adams; Flash Gordon; Geordie (anyone from Newcastle); Ginge(r) Jones; Happy Day; Harry Freeman; Hooky (or Johnny) Walker; Izzy Bent; Jacky Fisher; Jan or Janner (anyone from the West Country); Jesse James; Jimmy Green (or James); Jock (any Scotsman); Jumper Collins (or Cross or Short); Kitty Wells; Knocker White / Whyte; Mick (any Irishman) Nobby Clark(e) or Hewitt /Hewett; Nosey Parker; Nosmo King; Nutty Edwards; Oggie (any Cornishman); Paddy (any Irishman); Pansy Potter; Pedlar Palmer; Pincher Martin; Pony Moore; Pusser Hill; Rattler Morgan; Rusty Steele; Soapy Watson; Scouse(r) (any Liverpudlian); Shady Lane; Sharky Ward; Shiner Light (or Wright); Slinger Woods; Smokey Cole; Smudge(r) Smith; Snowy White or Winter/bottom; Spider Webb; Spike Kelly; Spud Murphy; Swampy Marsh; Sweeney Todd; Tab Hunter; Taff (any Welshman); Tank Sherman; Tansy Lea or Lee; Timber Wood(s); Tug or Tugg Wilson; Whacker Payne; Wiggy Bennett; Windy Gale; Yorky (any Yorkshireman).

Note also the nicknames which are alliterative, as in: Andy Anderson; Harry Harrison; Jacko Jackson; Johnnie or Johnno Johnson; Robby Robinson and Sully Sullivan as well as those which merely imitate, such as: Lester Piggott, Scobie Breasley; Bobby Charlton; Ronnie Biggs; Ginger Rogers; Sherlock Holmes; Chopper Harris; Legs Diamond; Nick Carter; Aggie Weston; Danny Kaye; Connie Francis; Fezz (Fess) Parker; Perry Mason and even Sandy Shaw! Also, there are the labels that describe the complete opposite of a person's physical appearance such as Tiny for anyone enormous in the vertical plane, and Slim for the chap whose circumference needs reduction.

nifty fifty Slang term for masturbation.

Nigerian lager Guinness.

Night of the Long Knives The Medical Services Officers' annual dinner.

night bar *Wardroom facility of a small cupboard stocked with beer, spirits and mixers for those Mess members returning *on board after the main bar has closed, but desiring a *wet before *turning in.

nine miler (RM) One of the *Commando tests that must be passed in order to obtain a *green lid. This involves a squad *speed marching, in fighting order and with rifle, over a nine-mile road distance in under ninety minutes (eighty-one for Royal's officers!).

nine o'clockers Traditional snack taken between the main evening meal and *turning in. It usually consists of a sandwich or bag of crisps, along with a *wet of tea or *kye; the term is falling into disuse, as the traditional tea at 1800 has in general been replaced by supper at 1900.

Nines / number nines Extra work and *musters as a scaled punishment.

nipper Short length of rope used to bind an anchor cable to an endless messenger cable that ran from the capstan and around a series pulleys. As the thick anchor cable came up and inboard through the hawse holes, it was *hove to the messenger with a secure (but quickly-releasable) *nipper*. The boy seaman responsible for this procedure (also called a *nipper*) then walked back with it towards the hatch leading down to the cable locker, cast off the light lashing at just the right moment, and then ran forwards again to repeat the process. There would always be half-a-dozen nippers in place as the anchor was being *weighed, and the boys had to be quick, dexterous and agile - hence the modern usage ashore.

nipples Projections from equipment, for application of a grease gun. *'These tubes 'ave more nipples than the 'ole Luton Girls' choir..'* Nipples *like eight piece *mixy blobs* are nipples that are somewhat larger than the average.

Nisum Abbreviation for *Naval Intelligence Summary*, and used to describe essential background information on any matter affecting Naval men: *'I've just had a quick Nisum on those new rules for Lodging Allowance..'*

no can do! Pidgin English form that is in frequent usage to decline some request.

Father Famine

no Dopples (FAA) *Pinger description of a flat calm sea which does not give a good return for the *Doppler* inputs of a *Sea King's flight control systems; this may be extended into social transactions: *'How did you get on with that bird you *trapped last night?' 'No Dopples sadly - complete waste of effort..'*

no man's land The Captain's daughter.

no names no pack drill *I 'aint telling you!*

No No! Response of a motor launch carrying anyone for whom no specific reply exists when it is challenged by a ship, ie. no marks of respect need to be paid.

no probs / no sweat (esp. RM / FAA) Frequent response to a request for help, or in discussion of some task; either phrase indicates an instinctive willingness to overcome whatever difficulties lie ahead. Even if used somewhat ill-advisedly, it is still a much better attitude to take than the one which leads to: *'Sorry - can't be done..'*

no treating rule A *Wardroom custom whereby junior officers do not buy senior officers their drinks, thereby preventing a well-heeled junior from gaining advantage over his or her less wealthy contemporaries. To your superior you would say: *'May I *write for you, sir?'* If the response is positive, it will also be accompanied by a *Mess number: *'Yes - and thank you. A pint of *CSB on Number 6 please..'*

nod / noddy (RM) Royal's equivalent of a *nozzer at *Lympstone. Said to be derived from the issue woollen cap comforter which the recruits wear so badly as to look like *Noddy's hat*.

Nog / Noggie (RM) A Norwegian, or anything belonging to that splendid country; see also *Skywegian.

noggin Small drink: *'Anyone like a noggin? I'm *writing..'*

non-cangoists RC's, Parsees, Pharisees, and Buckshees!

nonch (esp. RM) Abbreviation of *nonchalant* and often used in a sense of admiration: *'Baz cut away from the main parachute, deployed his reserve canopy, and then landed almost in the circle - dead nonch , like it was all a *demo..'*

non-floaters (SM) A repulsive grey, greasy substance applied to moving parts of a WW2 submarine gun.

nooners   A lovely duo:
1. When the sun passes over the *yardarm at midday, time for the first alcoholic drink of the day.
2. Can also be a euphemism for popping home at lunchtime in order to *give the ferret a run.

north-easter (or nor'easter)   See entry for *Not entitled.

nor-wester   Illegal, but locally-sanctioned strengthening of the *grog mix from two-to-one to one-and-one, in recognition of the cold weather indicated by a north-westerly wind - the more the wind *veered to the north, the stronger the mix.

NORWICH   Another of Jack's romantic epigrams across the sealing flap of his *mailie to his *pash -(K)Nickers (or Nightie) Off Ready When I Come Home.

nose bag   Reference to eating: 'I'm off to get my nose bag on..'

not best pleased   Polite description of a senior officer's annoyance at some event that has occurred.

not entitled!   Official response to Jack when, in older times, he stepped up to the pay table and had so many *mulcts against his name that his pay account was not in credit. The initial letters of NE can also be found on the compass rose, hence the additional term of *northeaster: 'Cor - all I got was ruddy soap coupons - a regular bleedin' *north-easter..'

not me, Chief, I'm_____   'This problem is nothing to do with me!' An attitude strongly discouraged, especially in *small ships.

not something that I'd die in a ditch over (RM)   'This is an argument which I will concede without too much heart-searching..'

not three bad   Frequent figure of speech used as an alternative to the expression not too bad.

notice for steam / sea   Specific feature of a warship's *sailing orders when alongside, which can then be used in other contexts: 'No-one seemed to know when the wretched bus was due to turn up, so we all stayed at pretty short notice for steam..' Notice for steam depended on Notice for sea, as raising steam was a protracted business; nowadays, very few vessels are actually steam-powered, but the term Notice for sea is still used.

Nozz ones   No 1's (uniform).

Nozz twos   No 2's.

nozzer   New entry trainee seaman, said to be named after an instructor at HMS GANGES in Shotley around 1910 who was possessed of a particularly large nose. See *RALEIGH also, and note the RM equivalent of *Noddy.

nub end   A *doofer (in its strictest definition sense) of a cigarette that was on the borderline of being worth saving.

number   A number (!) of distinct definitions:
1. *Service number* - formerly an official number, and given to ratings only - it comprised letters to indicate *Port Division and branch, followed by 6 numbers. When pay accounts became computerised, everyone got a Service number comprising a letter, 6 figures and another terminal letter.
2. *punishment* - in reverse order of severity. *No. 1* (used to be death, but is now imprisonment) down to *No. 14* (admonishment). The first five could only be awarded by Court Martial or by a warrant authorised by a *Flag Officer. The least popular summary punishment is No. 9 (see *Nines).
3. *uniform* - typically, different numbering systems are in force for officers and ratings, and they differ also between ratings depending on whether they are in *square rig or *fore-and-aft rig. *No. 1* is Jack and Jenny's 's best uniform, usually known as *Nozz Ones. The numbering system has been rationalised, but many still hanker after the previous, hopelessly haphazard method of numbering.
4. *nice little number* is a pleasant, low-intensity job.
5. *had his number* applies a targetting sense, as seen in the example for *Jackie-boy.
6. *make your number* should also be mentioned in the sense that a *ship's* (pendant) *number* is the internationally-recognised signal group that identifies her, precisely and uniquely.
7. *number crunching* refers to any paperwork or planning that involves *staff tables* - lists of men, equipment and vehicles: '*Trying to fit a *Commando Group and all its *kag into a North Sea ferry demands number crunching of the very highest order..*' RN usage refers to any kind of data processing task using a computer.
8. (his) *number got hoisted* - older expression similar to *lost the number of his mess, but more appropriate to death in action.

Number One   The First Lieutenant. See also *James the First or the *Jimmy.

Number Nine   A powerful panacea and cure-all used by doctors and *coxswains, and certainly guaranteed for constipation. It was a potent cascara-based laxative pill provided in small ships' medical cabinets, and was used for most ailments short of death.

Number nine shovel   This was the largest size of shovel issued by *pusser. A No. 9 shovel always signified hard work digging out. Several sayings evolved around this in the engine room branch: *'He has hands like No. 9 shovels..'* Anything that moved really fast was said to move *'like shit off a No. 9 shovel..'* If any long hard task was completed, you would say: *'You can take my No. 9 shovel, Chief, I'm flipping knackered..'*

Nummer Wun   The Senior Crown Agent in Hong Kong; by contrast, *nummer wun boy* was / is the most senior Chinese contractor's representative on board (laundry, and possibly tailor (*sew sew) and cobbler (*tap tap)).

nuts and bolts   Lamb stew, with the inevitable small bones still in pieces of meat.

nuts and bolts with an awning   Amusing but older description of a steak-and-kidney pie.

nutter   An individual lacking in wisdom and judgement, the description further embellished by the adjectives *total* or *complete*. There are some charming additional phrases to be heard in this context:

> *The lights are on, but there's nobody home..*
> *He's not dealing with a full deck of cards..*
> *That chap's not got both oars in the water..*
> *She's two frigates short of a battle group..*
> *They've made him OSLO - Outer Space Liaison Officer..*

nutty / Nutty   A funny trio:

1. General term for all forms of chocolate and sweets. Someone excessively fond of either is a *nutty *freak*.

2. *Nutty* is an occasional nickname paired with the surname Edwards.

3. Note that *nutty* in Australia refers to a (*nut-*)*brownhatter!

OSCAR

307 - 318

oakum Unravelled tarred rope used for packing seams and for *caulking. Any prisoner in the ship's cells was required to pick two pounds of tarred hemp (or 6 lb of tarred sisal) into *oakum* daily, Sundays excepted, the material to be weighed in his presence morning and evening.

OAL Abbreviation for the *Officer's Appointment List*, a bi-weekly and numbered publication originating from the Naval Secretary's Department. It shows all the promotions and appointments (*never* the postings of *Pongo or *crabair parlance) for RN (and now) RM officers; an *OAL number* is usually essential for the advance of allowances, tropical clothing etc. See also *PARM.

oars   Tradition had it that in days of old, when a sailor finished with the sea and *swallowed the anchor, he walked inland with an oar on his shoulder. When someone asked him what it was, and why he was carrying it, he would explain that he was going *to dig it in the ground and settle down*. This entry was revised as the GB rower Steve Redgrave returned from the 2000 Sydney Olympics, reluctant to retire even after the incredible tally of *five* successive Gold medals!

OBE   Strictly speaking, the post-nominal letters denoting an *Officer of the Order of the British Empire*, but also heard as *Other B**tards' Efforts* or, - a frequent occurrence when decision making processes are slow - *Overtaken By Events*.

obey the last *pipe   Traditional advice to the effect that if there appears to be any conflict or confusion in orders that are being given, then the most *recent* order should be carried out.

Observer (FAA)   See *Looker.

OD   Abbreviation of *Ordinary Deckhand*, a non-existent rate considered to be one lower than the basic rate on entry for Jack, which is Ordinary Seaman, in turn one lower than the Able Rate or *AB. It is figuratively the very lowest rung on the promotion ladder, but also used in a wider context to describe someone of limited abilities, who is either a bit slow to grasp an opportunity, or just grossly immature: *'Not 'im fer Gawd's sake - the big OD..'* The sort of activities worthy of this label might include the chap who walks straight across a freshly-painted deck, despite the *Wet Paint* signs, or the RO who throws the shredded paper waste to windward and gets it plastered over all the radars and aerials. Can also be used to imply general feebleness: *'So your alarm didn't go off? That's a bit OD-ish isn't it?'*

odds and sods   General expression describing a group that is difficult to categorize exactly, such as an *Odds and Sods Mess* in a ship that might contain *Doc, *Freshwater Tanky, the *Jack Dusty, and *Chippy as well.

Off caps!   This order is only given usually at *Defaulters, which in turn has been wrly described as a *cap-lifting evolution*, but headgear can also be removed as a mark of respect at Divine Service, funerals, Services of Remembrance, or as a prelude to *cheering ship. In older times it often led to a snowstorm of *doofers falling to the deck.

off-sider Another, semi-obsolete way of describing an *oppo: '*He's my off-sider..*'

off watch Not on duty; RM usage also has *off-net* for a person who is not listening, or who is simply just a bit *switched-off.

office boy The Assistant Secretary in a Captain's Office, usually a junior *Pusser, who may even be female in these emancipated times.

officer country Jack's nickname for the *Wardroom *flat.

OGs (RM) *Olive green* clothing issued in the far east. The shirts, made of a cellular cotton fabric, were very cool and comfortable and are still highly prized.

oggie Traditional nickname for a Cornish pasty; the name is supposed to derive from a Mr Edward Hogg, a pie-seller who retailed these items at the toll gate on Stonehouse bridge between Plymouth and Devonport, hence also *Tiddy Oggy* as the occasional nickname describing a matelot hailing from Plymouth.

Oggie, oggie, oggie! Cry of encouragement for a Devonport team. In a list of expressions for a *Guz ship visiting Spain, *Arriba Espana!* was translated as '*Oggie, oggie Spain!*'

'oggin / 'ogwash The sea; also spelt as *hoggin / hogwash.

oh-crack-*sparrow (fart) Common expression for *very* early in the morning.

oil fuel sight setter Dismissive label for the new generation of (post coal) stoker.

oilskins With a sou'wester, and sea boots, these items constituted *foul weather gear before it was re-invented.

old and bold An ex-lower deck officer.

Old Grey Widow Maker Nickname for the sea - *A sailor's grave is already dug..*

old hand Two opposing meanings:
1. An experienced and reliable person.
2. Someone who is dyed-in-the-wool, intransigent and always resisting change.

(The) Old Man Affectionate nickname for the Captain; see also the *Owner. The *old man's ears* was the Chief Yeoman of Signals - especially if he was disliked by Jack.

Field Gunner

old sayings   A quartet of politically incorrect funnies:
1. They ruined the Navy when they let civilians join.
2. Why get married? If you needed a wife, the *Pusser would have issued you with one.
3. For her, I would swim the stoker's bathroom three times.
4. A wife is a luxury, children are extravagances.
Note also the *three lies and the *three golden rules.

Old Soaks   Submarine Service nickname for members of the *Submarine Old Comrades Association*, a thriving group of veterans who display great thirst whenever and wherever they meet. Their golden rule is that it is always the President's round.

old ships   Abbreviation for *old shipmate*, someone you have served with before:'*Charlie, come an' meet my *oppo Timber Woods - we're old ships from the *Ark in '79..*'

on board   To be physically present within the confines of a ship or shore establishment:'*Is *Father on board this evening?*' '*No, he's gone *ashore with the *HODs..*' The radio call *On board!* is also used by FAA aircraft on rejoining a formation or *Balbo. This term has now come ashore to mean someone who is in agreement with a proposed course of action.

on the books   Held on the Ship's *muster book and therefore *victualled in for rations. The Army (and occasional RM) equivalent is *held on ration strength*. While the expression *on the books* is still used, the *book* itself no longer exists. In these days of computerised pay accounts and drafting, *Drafty provides a print-out of who is on board - it affords the *Reggies much amusement and frustration as they attempt to match theory with reality.

on the run   Someone who is absent without leave (AWOL) and who, it is suspected, does not intend to return to carry out his or her duties; after 30 days the *runner's service certificate is marked *R for Run*. Note that such a person is not a *deserter* until actually convicted on a charge of desertion. See also *recover.

on the step (SM)   A nuclear *boat at speed, planing on her own bow wave. This *evolution produces more speed for less propulsive effort.

on the trot   A phrase meaning *one after the other* as in:'*We were closed up for days on end, with nothing going on; then it all happened on the trot..*' Also used to decribe someone *on the run (which see). A *boat is said to be *on the trot* when she is tied up alongside a depot ship or even the jetty at Blockhouse, as in:'*I've seen as many as 12 boats on the trot at MAIDSTONE..*'

on your Jack (Jones)   Rhyming slang for alone.

once-only suit   A brightly coloured immersion suit that is not insulated, but really only designed to prevent a survivor getting wet. Being dry, in itself, prolongs survival in cold water. The suit is made in one piece, with elastic wrist and neck seals, but it has no integral buoyancy.

one all round   Command approval for a quick *burn at a time when smoking would otherwise not be allowed - an especial problem in a dived conventional *boat. Usually, the task of the senior rating in the Control Room was to make the request to, or cajole the Officer of the Watch into approaching the captain for permission to smoke. There were many good reasons to limit this habit strictly, most of them to do with the safety of the submarine such as (inflammable) battery *gassing, preservation of night vision, being near the surface, or in a state of Dark Red or *Black Lighting. The success of such a request meant that each of the watchkeepers could then smoke *one* cigarette, providing that only one initial flame was used, each person igniting his fag from the previous smoker's. The whole of the watch were included - Control Room, Sound Room, Radar Shack and Wireless Office.

one eight sixing (SM)   This term describes the mind deadening process that took place somewhere out in the Atlantic. The conventional diesel *boats, hundreds of feet down, would go round in circles for weeks on end - *186ing*. The hybrid word describes the boat's long range passive sonar with which you could hear ships coming days away. *'Log 'em. Plot 'em. Identify 'em. Tape 'em..'* Week after week, after week; no night, no day, no Saturdays or Sundays; just that awful stench of diesel and unwashed bodies.

one for the brow   A last drink for guests before they leave the *Wardroom, ie. the RN equivalent of *one for the road* in civilian parlance; sometimes heard as *one for the plank*.

one for the *linebook (FAA)   *'That's worth recording!'*

one man band (SM)   Colloquial term for the single-operator control system that operates a *boat's hydroplanes.

one night with Venus   The acquisition of syphilis.

one of my Lord Mayor's men   Old Navy term for a delinquent who had appeared before the Lord Mayor in his role as

Chief Magistrate of the City of London, and then elected to enter naval service rather than go to prison. See also *swimmer, *Queen's hard bargain and the notes on *Impressment

one off the wrist   See *bash the bishop.

one one two!   This was perceived to be a little quicker than *two six heave!* when heaving on a line, and there is a pause between the last *one* and the *two* as in: '*Ready? One one - two and you haul on two..*' Interestingly, to then give another heave and to get the heave together you would then say: '*..and another, two six; heave..*'

one two   Means right away, as in: '*I want this done one two..*'

one up the spout (RM)   Live round moved up from a rifle's magazine into the firing chamber; the weapon is now cocked and ready to discharge as soon as the safety catch - and trigger - are released. This expression is also used by Jack to describe an impending state of motherhood.

one yard rule   Informal regulation that can be enforced when the *Wardroom bar is busy and crowded, mostly by people who already have their drinks and are leaning against the rail. The latter are required to move away at least *one yard*, and thereby let those with an unslaked thirst get in closer and be served. No doubt Brussels will soon ordain that this must be changed to a *one metre rule!*

one-armed paper hanger   Nicely descriptive term for someone who is rather busy; a *one-armed paper hanger with crabs* is either the next stage up, or someone who is completely useless as opposed to highly industrious.

one-eighty   Jack's equivalent of a U-turn, both figuratively and literally halfway around the three hundred and sixty degrees of the compass: '*This guy then did a one-eighty right in the middle of the ruddy motorway..*' or: '*The Admiral's gone one-eighty on official policy for using that new bit of *kit..*'

one-eyed steak   A kipper.

one-two-six   Form used to report *stores losses and then apportion blame, now used as a verb in its own right: '*Any items mislaid or not returned in full working order will be one-two-sixed against your pay account the next day..*'

'oosh (properly *****hoosh** / *****hush**, of possible Eskimo origin)
A dish consisting of diced meat with onions and other vegetables, well-seasoned and then baked in an oven; when covered with a pastry pie crust it becomes *'oosh with an awning*. With Jack's penchant for dry, sardonic wit it can also be called *open air pie*, and is the forerunner of today's *pot mess.

oozelum bird   Term used for any winged creature difficult to identify properly; in addition, see *spadger, *shitehawk and *arse-up duck for the sum total of Jack's concise guide to British ornithology! Note that William Shakespeare described an *ousle bird* in one of his plays (MND), and it can also be spelt as *oozlum* or *woozlum*. Its main identifying feature is a remarkable ability to fly in such ever-decreasing circles that it finally disappears up its own fundamental orifice, from which point of vantage it surveys its enemies, cackling its characteristic cry: *'Up yours, Jack, I'm inboard..'*

open up (SM)   The process of opening the hatch or *lid after surfacing; to *run opened up* usually means that the *conning tower lid is open whilst on surface passage. This is a dramatically different evolution to *Open up for diving!* (also SM) when all the submarine's ballast system valves are aligned in preparation for flooding the tanks and diving the *boat.

oppo   An especial friend or chum in a ship or unit; the term is derived from *opposite number*, the person who is on watch when you are off. The American equivalent is *buddy*, leading on to the *buddy-buddy system of mutual support.

Ops Normal (FAA)   Aircraft exercising or operating out of sight or radar control of their *Mother call up at regular intervals to report *Ops Normal*. This can then be applied in the domestic sense when out on a *run-ashore:*'I just made an Ops normal call home - no problems..'*

Orange   An interesting trio:
1. Traditional colour of forces simulating the former Warsaw Pact during exercises and opposing the *Blue (which see) forces of NATO.
2. (RM) Adjective referring in Ulster to those of a Protestant / Loyalist persuasion.
3. (FAA) *Lynx Observer; a *baby Orange* is a trainee. See also *JAFO and the *man from del Monte.

order of the boot   Dismissed in a peremptory fashion.

order of the golden toecap   Made redundant, but with a terminal bonus and pension.

(the) other half   Figure of speech which assumes that no-one ever has only one drink, and also that saying: '*Would you like another one?*' might be misinterpreted as offensive, in that there is the slight hint that the guest has had too many already. Instead, use of this lovely Wardroom convention of: '*Will you have the other half?*' directly implies that this will only be the second *wet! Therefore, drinks can go on being the *other half* all night - and no-one ever exceeds their personal or legal limits!

Out pipes!   Curiously worded *pipe (that could easily be misinterpreted by Jack) which indicates that smoking must cease, the *stand easy is over, and it is time to get the ship's normal routine going again.   It was often followed in chorus on the lower deck by '*and cigars and cigarettes as well*'. The US Navy version of all this is *The smoking lamp is out!*

out of his tree   Oblique expression doubting someone's sanity:'*If *SOBS thinks I'm volunteering for that job, then he must be out of his tree..*'

out of range of the Service slide-rule   Older (and pre-computer era) term for a problem that cannot be solved using officially-supplied data.

out of station   Not in line within a formation. Someone who is *getting a bit, and out of station as well*, is a married officer involved in a spot of extramarital *bagging-off; Jack's equivalent refers to a *turn of leave out of watch (which see).

out piece and *hack! (FAA)   *Wafu exhortation during an *Uckers game to get out and destroy the opposition, carried over into real life as a form of encouragement to tackle a task head on.

outchop   Signal term for leaving a Command area.

outside   Civilian life: *'Things were pretty tough outside. The streets weren't exactly paved with gold; in fact, most of the streets weren't even paved at all, and guess who was expected to get the bloody slabs down?'*

outside walkee   Chinese / pidgin-english for a paddle steamer; a screw-driven vessel is an *inside walkee* ship.

outside wrecker (SM)   The *clanky responsible, in a submarine, for everything mechanical apart from the propulsion machinery. The *inside wrecker is a derogatory term for a chef!

over the fence   Going off a shore establishment without passing through the proper *liberty boat procedure.

over the wall   The state that pertains when either Jack, Jenny or Royal have had their pay stopped and entered *DQs.

overstretch   Management *wrigglestuff for the increasingly frequent state of affairs that pertains when the RN and RM are given more and more global and local responsibilities to meet - with less and less financial and manpower resources to tackle the tasks. The Service is frequently described as being commitment-rich and resource-poor! See also *No probs and *can do.

overzone   An officer who has just ceased being *in zone, and who has also not been selected for promotion is said to have *gone overzone*. In some instances of selection for transfer between *Lists (rather than actual promotion), the *suck back of an *overzone* officer may occur.

ovies   One-piece *overalls* of any kind; (FAA) *flying ovies* refer to a flame-proof flying suits also known as *green-and-baggies or *green-and-smellies.

owner   An older, rather pleasant nickname for the *captain of a *private ship.

Oxygen Pete   Mythical person who lies in wait for *CDs and SBS attack swimmers who go too deep when breathing pure oxygen. Below 7 metres, you run the risk of oxygen poisoning and a meeting with *Oxygen Pete*.

oyster (*Bombay oyster*)   An old maritime name for a laxative draught consisting of a double dose of castor oil in a glass of milk; a more modern name for such a bowel-stirring concoction might be an *elephant-rouser*.

PAPA

319 - 350

P's (the six) *Prior Planning Prevents Piss-Poor Performance.* 'Nuff said!

P7R Lowered *PULHEEMS grading of someone who is temporarily unfit for sea or front-line duty, now used as a word in its own right: *'I'm P7R for the next three months with this broken arm..'*

PDQ *Pretty Damned Quick*, as in: *'You'd better get up topside PDQ - or as quick as Christ will let you..'*

P-J Abbreviation for *poxy Jock*; not too affectionate.

PV's elbows - from paravanes. Any rating taking up too much room at the mess table by protruding elbows would be told: *'Get yer ruddy PV's in, I want to eat too!'*

palm A leather strap going over a sailmaker's palm, with a lead disc set into the hollow for thrusting heavy duty needles into canvas.

paper Navy The administrative and clerical branches. A *paper exercise* is a war plan or similar exercised by staff and headquarters *on paper*, without involving actual forces.

paraffin pigeon Just one of Jack's nicknames for a helicopter; see also *furious palm tree, *kerosene budgie, *shuddering shit-house and *wokka-wokka.

paraffinos (FAA) Term used to describe the mechanical enineering (as opposed to other trades) ratings in the Fleet Air Arm.

paralytic Incapably drunk; also heard as *parlatic*, which sounds nicely slurred for additional descriptive effect.

paravane A metal kite streamed from either stern quarter of a minesweeper. See also *PVs.

parcel   Hemp ropes had to be waterproofed, otherwise they would rot very easily and become useless in *standing rigging. The grooves in the *lay* of a rope were *wormed* or filled out by thin codline, then covered or *parcelled up* with layers of canvas strips, and the whole *served* with an outer coat of spunyarn applied under tension. This word came ashore as the modern parcel in the postal sense. A rope, or part of a rope, is *wormed, parcelled and served* to protect it from chafe, to make it less liable to chafe other ropes and, with a wire rope, to protect the hands of men handling it. The old rhyme went: *'Worm and parcel with the lay, then turn and serve the other way..'*

Parish Magazine   Jocular nickname for the *Fleet Temporary Memoranda* - a rather serious circulating document containing revised instructions etc. which will later be revised and republished into a more permanent form.

PARM   Abbreviation for *Promotions and Appointments RM*, that used to be Royal's equivalent of an *OAL.

part brass rags   Older term, still heard occasionally, to denote the sudden end of a close friendship; you shared your cleaning *rag bag with your close *oppo, or *raggie, up until this (quite literal) parting of the ways. The term can be used as a verb: *'After that little disagreement and punch-up they parted brass rags..'*

part of ship   Strictly speaking, a sailor's place of work; also used to denote an area of personal responsibility: *'Why's he stickin' his nose in? Thass my part of ship..'* The term *parts* also refers to the male *private parts* or genitalia, leading inevitably to the nickname *Parts* (esp. RM) for an individual who is well equipped with *wedding tackle. *'How's your parts?'* actually means: *'Are you in good health?'*

part of watch   A *Watch Bill specifies a man's place of duty, but also divides his *Watch (*Starboard or *Port) into a First and Second part, thus providing for a 1 in 4 watchkeeping or duty roster; at (relaxed) Cruising Stations in a non-operational area it is usually only necessary for one *part of watch* to *turn to in order to meet the daily tasks.

Part Three (esp. SM)   Label for an inexperienced and half-trained individual, derived from the need (with current financial constraints) to provide on-the-job and qualifying experience at sea for *makee-learnees who have been drafted to a warship as part of her war complement. *Part One trainees* are those at

Fluff Your Pinky

*RALEIGH; note also that the FAA uses the term *to part three something* as an alternative to *snagging it.

party   A *female party* who may later become one's *pash; also used for a working group as in *Buffer's party*, or *RC church party* etc.

pash   Abbreviation for *passion* - the Number One girlfriend.

pass muster   Something that is barely acceptable may be described as having *just about passed muster*; see *muster for other applications.

passengers   Non-ship's company travellers from all three services taking passage. Used to be very much welcomed on small ships with canteen messing, because of the accumulated mess savings left behind on their departure!

passion killers   Name **for** *pussers issue Wrens' knickers of an older design, 1940. See also *harvest festivals and *ETBs.

Passover   To be *passed over* means that your seniority in a rank now exceeds the *zone considered by the Admiralty Board for promotion purposes; the day of your *last shot *in zone, if unsuccessful, then becomes your personal *Feast of the Passover!*

pasting   Give (or take) damage to a warship in battle.

patch   Colloquial term for an area where the *Married Quarters are situated.

paternity leave   Relatively new concept in the *Andrew; the old philosophy was based on: *'You was there when the keel was laid, Sunshine - that don't give you a ticket for the launching..'*

patrol report   naval shore patrol report of a misdemeanour.

pay   A number of historic applications:
1. Cables or ropes are *payed out*, rather than let out.
2. The seams of a wooden hull were *payed* with hot pitch (tar) after they had been caulked with *oakum; see also *loggerheads and the various entries associated with *Devil.
3. Semi-formal mode of address (from a superior or equal) for the Supply Officer of a ship; seldom used now. It dates from the time when Supply & Secretariat officers were known as the *Paymaster* branch - see also *paybob. *Pay* is in the same style as *Wings for Cdr (Air).

Pay no regard! (FAA)   Classic Naval wartime version of the RAF's *Press on Regardless!*, and widely used in responding to almost any adversity - from loss of shipmates to a severe hangover. In this sense, the Royal Marines expression *It's only pain!* is identical.

pay-off   Originally, it literally meant the paying off of a ship's company when the ship returned to her home port for refit wearing her *paying-off pennant*, ie. with all arrears paid up and the men now free to leave. In fact, this custom was more often honoured in the breach rather than the observance. Nowadays, ships remain in continuous *commission, and seldom pay off until put up for disposal or sale. Although *de-commission* is a more appropriate term, *paying-off* is still the proper expression. *Paying off* is also the process whereby a sailing ship's bows, having passed through the wind in the process of tacking, falls off to leeward before her sails begin to draw again.

Paybob   Jack's older term for a Paymaster Branch Officer, a specialization now absorbed into the many skills of the *Pusser.

paying-off pendant (pronounced *pennant*)   A long signal flag flown from the masthead at the completion of a warship's *commission, prior to her refit, sale or other disposal; it used to consist of cleaning rags tied together to show that they were now being dispensed with, but then became a larger and extended version of her *commissioning pennant. Its length should be that of the ship, plus one twelfth of the length for every month served over the originally-stated length of the *commission; however, with the amount of expensive sensor equipment fitted to masts nowadays, it is in practice limited to a maximum of the ship's length. It should be flown on sailing from the last port in a foreign station, on last sailing from a UK port, and on arrival at the base port for the last time.

pea-do   An interesting pair:
1. Nickname for pea soup.
2. The Naval Long Service and Good Conduct medal - the origins of this usage are a little obscure, but may be a mispronunciation of the *billet-doux* grant of £25 cash (sadly, now discontinued) which used to come with the *Blue Peter. See also *undetected crime.

pear-shaped   Useful descriptive term employed in two distinctly different ways:
1. *'Play it pear-shaped..'* - be flexible, see how it goes, don't commit yourself too early on.

2. *'It all went pear-shaped..'* - the scheme collapsed or went wrong; see *rats as an alternative.

pebble monkey   Junior officer in the RAF Regiment. It is the diminutive of *Rock Ape.

pebbledash the porcelain / walls   Suffer from profuse diarrhoea; see also *black drizzle, *scatters and *squitters.

peep-stick (SM)   A periscope, and also, like *look stick*, derived from pidgin English. It may be that *look stick* referred to the search periscope, and *peep stick* to the attack periscope.

Peggy   The *Pegasus* engine of the *Stringbag - and now also of the Sea Harrier (*SHAR); there is even a Fleet Air Arm song about the reliability of this splendid radial construction in comparison with that of its successor:

> *The Stringbag relies on her Peggy,*
> *While the modified Taurus ain't sound -*
> *So the Swordfish flies out on her missions,*
> *And the Albacore stays on the ground..*
> (Refrain)   *Bring back, bring back,*
> *Oh, bring back my Stringbag to me..*

peggy   Older word for a messenger - often a *peg-legged* old veteran. In the MN, a ratings' or PO's steward.

pendant number   The letter and side numbers of a warship, usually painted on the hull in big black letters and pronounced *pennant*.

penguin (FAA)   Any non-flying *Wafu!

P - 324

pension trap An understandable reluctance to do anything remotely dangerous when approaching the end of one's career in the *mob, because an accident would save the Navy the bother of having to provide your duly-entitled pension: *'Wot, get me up in a bleedin' helicopter - with only three months left to do? No thanks, mate - that's the biggest pension trap that *Pusser ever invented..'* Can also be used to describe some feature of Service life that induces a person to stay in the *Andrew: *'Boarding School Allowance is a proper pension trap..'*

pepper-potting (RM) Military *evolution for advancing tactically - the members of a rifle section move forwards under control, but in apparently random motion - as if they were being scattered from a *pepper pot*.

Per Ardua Ad Astra *Crabfat's motto which, strictly translated, means *Through Hardship to the Stars*. Jack's version is based on the observation that as most RAF station cinemas are named *Astras*, the real meaning is: *'After work we all go to the movies!'* Or else: *'You have to queue for the upper stalls..'*

Per Mare Per Terram (RM) *Corps motto of *By Land and By Sea* - but note also a *few laughs and a few beers.

per pusser A term meaning to do something in the official way, or exactly in the manner laid down in the *book of words.

Perce (RM) Shortened form of the generic nickname *Percy Pongo*, used by Royal to describe anyone from the Army in exactly the same manner that the terms *Jack* and *Jolly Jack* refer to members of the Royal Navy. See notes on *Pongo as well.

perch A seat: *'Grab a perch..'* Or, a position in an argument or discussion: *'This new information will knock him right off that ridiculous perch..'*

perique Jack's DIY plug tobacco, made from rolled leaf pickled in various concoctions, including honey and/or rum, and bound tightly in canvas and a thin tarred rope for maturing.

Perisher (SM) Famous nickname for the Submarine CO's Qualifying Course, because if you fail this demanding test, your career in the Submarine Service is over. In short, you either *pass or perish*. Alternatively, as some maintain, it is a corruption of the original term *Periscope Course*. Take your pick! See also *Teacher.

personal admin (RM)   Military-sounding euphemism for time spent attending to your own problems during the working day.

perving   Contraction of the word *perversion*, but usually employed in a gentler sense, eg. as an alternative for *glimping.

Peter's Pool (RM)   Partially-damned stream encountered on the *Endurance course at *Lympstone which must be forded chest-high while keeping one's rifle clean and dry.

Petty Officer   RN equivalent of a Sergeant, or Senior Non Commissioned Officer, and abbreviated as *PO*. The word *Petty* comes from the French *petit*, or small; hence, see also *smalley pigs. There is also an underground (*lower deck!) version of *PO* as *Pathetic Object*.

phonetic alphabet   A method of articulating single letters on a voice radio circuit. The original English (and rather whimsical) alphabet had to be changed when we joined NATO, so as to ensure, as far as possible, that the words sound the same when spoken by a *scouser as when spoken by a Greek! The present alphabet is used as chapter headings in this book. Used in communicating to avoid mis-hearing of letters, particularly when background noise is high.

phoo-phoo dust   Talcum powder; see also *foo-foo.

Phot / Phots   Standard abbreviations for the *Photographic Branch* and its members. See also the older term of *snaps, but retired members of the branch should understand that this earlier label now has a rather different connotation!

Pi - R - squared the bastard then!   *'If you're so clever, then work it out for yourself!'*

pick   The main anchor, hence to *drop the pick* for the process of anchoring, and *swinging round the pick* when actually at anchor; see also *hook and *killick.

pick up   The process of official advancement, already described in the passive sense of getting *made up. The same process might be described, with an identical meaning, as: *'My *B13's in and I see the *Old Man tomorrow to pick up my *hook..'*

pickle-jar officer   Jack's delicate and highly observant description of an individual with great intelligence but poor practical ability: *'Your average university graduate these days is the sort of* *bloke who can tell you the square root of a pickle-jar (or *jampot) lid to three decimal places - but can't get the bloody thing off..'*

picturised (RM)   Put in the picture, usually as the result of some misdemeanour or failing: *'That useless *gob-shite Terry needs picturising - in a big way..'* Note also *Rembrandted.

pidgin (note the spelling)   The word *pidgin* is derived from the Chinese for *business*, thus *pidgin-english* was really derived from everyday commercial transactions. The expression *not my pidgin* certainly means: *'That is no concern of mine..'* See also *pigcon.

pie-eyed   Drunk.

pieces   The main armament were *pieces of ordnance* hence the phrase: *'During the afternoon we fired the pieces..'*

pieces of nonsense   Apropos of absolutely nothing, some *pieces of nonsense* might be used by an old hand to his *winger, or to a bemused civilian in a pub.   One of these, often heard, was: *'Have you ever been chased across the wild, wild wastes of the Gobi Desert by a snarling tombola ticket?'*

pied   A newer word that implies a *custard pie* in the face, or rejection in a dramatic or unexpected manner: *'She then went and pied him after a year of living together..'*

pierhead jump   Draft or appointment that has to be taken up at very short notice; derived from the need to take a running jump from the *end of the pier* because your new ship has actually begun to *slip and proceed!

Pier Cellars   An old Seaward Defence HQ that opens onto Plymouth Sound; expedition weekends are held here by the *nozzers from HMS *RALEIGH.

-pig   A suffix to indicate something troublesome:*'It wasn't my fault that the lights didn't work - it was the ruddy switch-pigs..'* This usually indicates that the operator went and had a *brainfart when making the actual selection.

pig / piggery   Highly derogatory terms for an officer and his or her living quarters. The term goes back at least as far as the great mutinies at *Spithead and the Nore in 1797, when a significant number of officers fully deserved the soubriquet. The term is still used by Jack, Jenny and Royal perjoratively to describe an officer who has lost, or failed to gain, their respect (and their opinion in such matters is definitive), and sometimes as a collective noun, but not necessarily with malice. *Young officers are, inevitably, *piglets*. See also *grunters and *ruperts.

pig's breakfast   A very badly done job, or a badly turned out rating. *'You made a right pig's breakfast of that..'* and:*'You look like a real PB..'* are the respective ommets that would apply. See also *pig's ear.

pig's ear   Upper deck urinal on a warship for Jack's use when he is unable to leave his place of duty while *on watch. Can be used as well to describe some hopeless cock-up:*'He made a real pig's ear of the whole thing..'* See also *pig's breakfast.

pig's orphan   Another description of some thoroughly unpleasant person (or task).

pig's ribs!   An older expression of complete disbelief.

pigeon   Two different applications:
1.   Responsibility: *'That particular problem is very much your pigeon..'* See entry at *pidgin, and also *part of ship.
2.   (FAA) Homing pigeon derivation, where *pigeons* are given as the course in degrees magnetic, and distance to be tracked for home or *Mother in the event of a malfunction or emergency: *'Pigeons for *Culdrose are 270 at thirty-seven miles..'*

pigskin pie   A fatty bacon roll.

pigtail   Also known as a queue, but as cultivated by Jack. The hair was twisted or plaited, commonly prettied up by a binding of spun yarn, and the whole applied with a dose of Stockholm tar which gave its gravity-defying look. Unfortunately, the tar stained the neck of the clothing, which had to be protected by a loose, washable cloth. Hence *Jolly Jack Tar* and his separate uniform collar, which still exists today.

Pill   Jack's nickname for certain individuals who are small, white, round - and totally devoid of any conception.

pillock   A term which used to be fairly commonly employed by GIs with new entries, a *pillock* being something equivalent to a *stupid git* or *pea brain*. Perhaps derived from an undescended bollock (testicle) - which is quite useless.

Pilot   Traditional nickname for the Navigating Officer of a warship; see also *Vasco

ping   Discover something, or find out. The derivation of the word is the same as for *Pinger, but its daily use rather different, as in: *'It took us a bit of time to ping him, but eventually we proved that he was fiddling the books..'* Or: *'During the honeymoon, she suddenly pinged the fact that her new husband was a miserable toad..'*

Pinger (FAA)   An anti-submarine warfare helicopter specialist, derived from the *pinging* sound made by active (dipping) sonar. Note also the hybrid word *Pinglie, and a *Pinger's moon* when the skies are clear, the moon full, and the horizon nicely visible.

Pinglie (FAA)   A *Pinger who flies ashore into what is normally regarded as *Junglie territory, and then has to map-read; see also the *most dangerous thing in the world.

Pink / pink   An interesting colour in the RN!:
1. *pink *DCI* - Confidential *Defence Council Instructions* dealing with sensitive disciplinary matters, and printed on *pink* paper.
2. *Pink List* - projected programme of ship movements issued by Fleet Headquarters at Northwood.
3. *pink chit* - A formal warning issued to Jack whenever he came over the *brow in drink and the worse for wear; a second such episode meant a *green* chit and then *get your hat for a talk with the *Bloke. The expression is now used to denote a wife or girlfriend's prior knowledge of a night out with the boys: *'Coming on the section *run-ashore? I've got a pink chit from my *dragon..'*
4. *pink gin* - Plymouth Gin and Angostura bitters, drunk neat or diluted with plain water, and known also as *pinkers*. Officers did not *draw the *tot, so this was the most important *wardroom drink in the Royal Navy of the 20th Century, and especially so in the era before refrigeration and the wider availiability of ice at sea. *Plymouth Gin* (see also *monk) is the only gin that can be

Foo-Foo

drunk, like whisky or whiskey, with water at room temperature. Angostura bitters add colour and a delightful extra flavour. Try this test with any other brand and you will be horrified! Of course, in the traditional *G&T, made in the (relatively) modern manner with ice and lemon, it has an extra breadth of flavour that makes it a top-notch, highly acceptable *cocker's P or pre-dinner *wet.

5. *pink lint* - spam, or any form of processed luncheon meat.

6. *pink sheet* or *the pink* - Whenever a problem or task is set for students at Staff College, the Directing Staff have the relevant answers, discussion points or the staff solution already set out for them on *pink paper*. Hence the real life expression: '*There's no pink sheet* (solution) *for this one, I'm afraid,*' or when something goes wrong: '*That wasn't in accordance with the pink..*'

pink oboe   A penis.

Pinky / pinky   A quartet of widely different applications:
1. (FAA) An artificer specializing in radar and radio equipment; its origin lies in the layout of the old RN Aircraft Servicing Form which used to contain *pink-coloured* log sheets for the radio and radar gear. The current *MoD Form 700 has no such distinction, but the label for this skilled and sea-going profession lives on. Note also the remarks made in *greenie.
2. (RM) Nickname for the surnames White and Panther!
3. Occasional nickname for the anus - as in *fluff your *pinky*, meaning to break wind (see Tugg's cartoon on page P - 321)
4. The little finger.

PIP   *Previously Important Person.*

pipe   Originally, the series of notes produced on a *bosun's call (which see) and which varied depending on the order being *piped*. With the advent of the main broadcast, *pipes* were then made on this (*Tannoy) system. Nowadays, use of the *bosun's call is generally limited to ceremonial, including the greeting of entitled VIPs (see *pipe the side* below). However, any verbal announcement or instruction made on the main broadcast is still called a pipe. Note that the actual instrument is a (bosun's) *call*; it is the actual arrangement of *notes* which it produces that is described as a pipe.

pipe the side   The ultimate ceremonial greeting, the use of which is jealously guarded and only afforded to the Sovereign (the only person entitled to receive it when wearing plain clothes), entitled members of the Royal family (if of Captain RN rank or above and if in naval uniform), *Flag officers and commanding officers of HM ships, all of whom receive it between *Colours and *Sunset only. *Foreign* naval officers, if in uniform, receive the honour at all times. The *side is piped* once for people arriving or departing via the *brow, and twice for those arriving / departing by boat - this latter feature deriving from the origin of this particular pipe, which was the order to hoist (once) the VIP out of the boat in a *bosun's chair and lower (twice) him onto the deck. The side is *never* piped for a civilian (however important) but, uniquely and unprecedentedly, the coffin of Sir Winston Churchill was *piped on board* the Port of London Authority launch at Tower Pier and again when it was disembarked at Festival Pier en route for Waterloo Station, by a Royal Naval *Piping Party*. This particular pipe, which comprises the low note - rising to the high - and falling to the low again, lasts just over twelve seconds, and good lungs are needed!

Pipe the still! / *Carry on!*   These are only other *pipes still in regular use, and used to call the ship's company (or those who are on the *upper deck) to attention for *Colours and *Sunset, to salute a passing warship, and on the arrival of a VIP, who may or may not subsequently get a *pipe the side - see entry above.

piping hot   Shoreside expression with a Naval origin; if food was collected from the *galley as soon as the appropriate *pipe was made, then it could be served on the *messdecks *piping hot*.

Pirate (FAA)   *Looker's nickname for his pilot.

pirate rig   Wear what you like; usually authorised on occasions such as *Crossing the Line. In small ships in the *far-flung this was usually a sarong, T-shirt and flip flops.

piso   A miserable individual who is tight with money; derived from the unusual feature of Indian currency that one rupee consists of sixteen annas - and each of these in turn is made up of four *pais* or *pice*! Apparently, it may also be a Maltese word.

piss   Another word with many other meanings besides the obvious one:
1. *piece of piss* (esp. RM) - something easy, or no problem to achieve; hence also:'*You'll piss it..*'
2. *streak of piss* - a tall, gangling and thin person.
3. *on the piss* or *pissing up* - drinking session, sometimes abbreviated as a *PU*. Note also the terms *piss-head* or *piss-artist* as alternatives for *glop-head, the latter defined (almost admiring-

ly) as someone who can sign his name in the snow in this way. *Pissed* is another term for someone who is tired and emotional through drink, but note that across the *Pond this means something rather different - someone who is angry and upset.

4. *take the piss* - tease or mock somebody in a bout of *piss-taking*. See also *extract the Michael.

5. *pissed-off* - a similar meaning to *chokka or *hacked off.

6. *piss flap* - a feature of Jack's uniform trousers prior to the redesign of the trouser fly to allow the incorporation of a zip; this flap had to be unbuttoned prior to *pumping ship; it was still utilised in the special uniform issued to *Yachties until the *Yacht was *paid off.

7. *piss flaps* - Jack's nickname for the labial lips so often displayed these days in the raunchier men's magazines, and which he may describe as being the size of a *Buccaneer's air brakes, John Wayne's saddlebags, or a blacksmith's apron..

8. *piss poor* is a traditional description of something very poor indeed, probably derived from (9).

9. *gnat's piss* - label for weak beer or poorly-brewed tea.

10. Couldn't *run a piss-up* in a brewery - useless person.

11. *piss strainers* - kidneys.

12. *piss-head* - someone who drinks too much, and too often.

13. *pissed as a handcart* - very much the worse for wear.

14. *pissing contest* - pointless dispute between two individuals in which each tries to pee higher up the wall, rather that settling a point of difference sensibly by discussion and logic.

15. *pisshole Parliament* - a group of men hanging around the *heads, expressing their opinions on something.

16. *pissing fish-hooks* - suffering from a social disease having *caught the boat up.

17. *pisspot porter* - a medical assistant, carrying a urine sample for testing in this context!

18. *pissy cacky all fall down* - description of a group that has been on a run ashore are have had too much ale.

19. *piston broke* - almost invetitable consequence of a run ashore - to be in wine but out of pocket (*pissed and broke!*).

pisser pilot Older FAA and RAF term for an Army Air Corps pilot, or any officer sporting Army wings; needless to say, this implied inferiority puts all the *Teeny-weenies into an immediate *high hover!

pit Bed or bunk space; occupied around the clock by a *pit rat*: '*Sorry I'm adrift, sir - my duvet wouldn't let me go..*'

pitch up   Arrive; *pole up is a frequent alternative.

placcy-bagging (RM)   The sport of sliding down a snow-covered slope while sitting or lying on a plastic bag.

Plan B   Any alternative when things go to *rats, even when contingency plans do not actually exist: *'Aircraft cancelled? That's *no problem. We'll just switch to Plan B..'*

plank   Amusing quartet of varied usages:
1. A dull individual: *'Socially, he's a complete plank..'*
2. (FAA) Helicopter aircrew's description of a normal aircraft wing, and thus *Planky* as a nickname for the pilot of any such aircraft.
3. *pusser's planks* - wooden or fibreglass Norwegian military skis.
4. Alternative word for the *brow; *plankers* (SM) is a declared last drink before leaving, or the *Boat people's equivalent of *one for the plank.*

planter's   Hot weather *rig of slacks, long-sleeved shirt, tie and chukka boots.

planting (FAA)   Burial: *'They're planting him on Friday - it's a *swords and medals job, of course..'*

plastic (RM)   Sardonic appellation for an officer temporarily elevated to *local rank, ie. dressed for that rank, but not *substantively promoted to it, nor paid for it.

plastic policeman   See *Modplod.

play the white man   Do the decent and fair thing even when a more attractive but less honest option presents itself.

player   Label for someone who is good company socially: *'You know, old *Scratch is a bit of a player on the quiet..'*

playpen   Another of Jack's nicknames for the vagina; you'll have to find the others for yourself!

plew   Old lower deck word for tea.

PLM   Plastic Luncheon Meat - spam.

plucky (FAA)   Gentle understatement for a highly demanding or dangerous job: *'Low-level troop insertions at night, high in the Lyngen Alps? Yersst - plucky little number, that..'*

Plug   Label for anyone with projecting ears and/or protruding teeth; the nickname has been borrowed from a character in the *Beano* comic's *Bash Street Kids*.

plug   An old way of rolling up leaf tobacco.

pluke / plook   Any skin infection, but especially when localised into a facial boil or *zit.

plumber   A contrasting pair:
1. Mechanical Engineering Officer in a warship.
2. Gynaecologist.

plumbosis oscillans / plumbus tremens   A pseudo-medical and cod Latin diagnosis of an imagined illness, characterised by a *lead-swinging and trembling fear which will result in a one-way ticket out of an unpleasant theatre of operations - unless the individual involved is firmly *gripped.

plums   The plum-shaped figure 0, or a line of zeros: '*Howja get on with them birds, Taff?*' '*Plums, mate, nothing but bleedin' plums..*' Someone like this, who never seems to have much luck with the opposite sex while *trapping, then becomes a *plums rating*, in

P - 335

contrast to a *stacks rating who always seems to be *getting yards.

plushers / plussers   Residual rum remaining in the tub after the *tot had been distributed; usually an important perk for those involved, if (somehow) this surplus was not ditched down the scuppers. Down in the spirit store, where the rum was initially pumped out of the storage barrel, as soon as the pump sucked dry this barrel was immediately filled with water. After the smaller (transfer) barricoe was taken up to the rum tub, this device was inverted above the rum tub, drained down, and then shown to be empty. In this way, the daily issue of rum was supposed to be continuously accounted for, down to the last drop as well. However, that is not to say that there weren't some dodges and wheezes around, some worthy of the Magic Circle, to ensure that *plushers* were still available to those in need, or as in Tugg's lovely depiction of plushers as currency at page V - 488, used to secure a few favours.

Plymouth Argylls   Name given to he composite force formed by the Royal Marines survivors from HMS Prince of Wales and HMS Repulse, sunk off Malaya in 1940, and the remnants of a battalion of the Argyll and Sutherland Highlanders. They fought against the Japanese in Malaya, and in the defence of Singapore in 1941 / 1942.

Poet's Day   Jack's alternative name for Friday, derived from the first letters of *Piss Off Early - Tomorrow's Saturday*!

polar bear's arseholes   Jack's nickname for those white and gummed paper punch-hole reinforcing rings that come on a peel-off strip.

pole up   Turn up, or arrive; see also *pitch up - the words are interchangable.

poling (FAA)   The actual physical skills of handling an aircraft: *'You know, that boy's brilliant on poling but rubbish at captaincy..'*

Polto (SM)   Nickname for the old rate of *Petty Officer (Leading Torpedoman). The Leading Rate was LTO, the Senior Rate POLTO, and you then went on to TGM (Torpedo Gunner's Mate) and Chief TGM. Officially, the rank went out of use in 1946, but was still in unofficial use over twenty years later.

Pom   *Father Famine's favourite - powdered mashed potato, usually sharing a mess tin with *salt dog (corned beef). Also an unaffectionate Australian nickname for a Brit.

pom-pom   Wartime multi-barrelled, short range anti-aircraft gun, available in 2-, 4-, or 8-barrelled versions and mounted on a *bandstand to form a Chicago piano. Made by Vickers and very noisy - but also rather ineffective - although, as a morale-booster, better than nothing. Unlike the later Bofors gun systems which had a much higher muzzle velocity and a better fuze to deal with the Kamikaze threat in the Pacific theatre, the *pom-pom* was laid visually to the target, using a ring and bead sight or (later) a gyro sight similar to a fighter pilot's.

Pompey   Portsmouth; there are a number of explanations for the origins of this term, and the least likely appears to be Jack's observation, while walking his family / wife / lady on Southsea Common, of the 18th century volunteer firemen (*pompiers*) exercising there. I very much like the suggestion that *Portsmouth Point* was the traditional landing and embarkation point for *libertymen; try slurring this geographical name as if *handcarted and listen to the sound! In some parts of Yorkshire, a *pompey* is a prison or house of correction, so it may just have somehing also to do with the Portsmouth Naval Prison. The true answer seems to involve the captured French prize vessel HMS *POMPEE* which was moored in Portsmouth Harbour along with the FOUDROYANT, and used as an accommodation and *receiving ship before the present Barracks were built. Either way, the Portsmouth Maritime Heritage, with HMS *VICTORY and the Royal Naval Museum; the MARY ROSE; HMS WARRIOR; the Royal Marines Museum and the OVERLORD Tapestry are all splendid and important features of the city.

Pond   The Atlantic Ocean; *across the Pond* refers to the United States of America.

pond life   Clearance diver's nickname for *scoobies and *bubbleheads. Also a perjorative label for someone achieving the lowest possible score on the Naval mathematics and English test.

Pongo   Any member of the British Army - more completely known as *Percy Pongo* or (also) as *Perce. A *pongo* is a hairy African sand-ape native to the deserts south of the Med; Royal will have you believe (incorrectly) that the word is derived from *Perce's occasional failure to wash on a daily basis, so where the Army goes, the pong goes as well. This opinion is strongly endorsed by those with troopship experience to the Far East! Tugg has a lovely vision at page W - 490.

Ponti   Nothing to do with famous Italian film directors, but a new import from the Army, particularly after the Gulf War experience - *Person Of No Tactical Importance*.

pony   The Naval *Lynx helicopter.

poodle-faking   Older term for service in a warship on a cruise designed almost entirely for some VIP's entertainment; still heard on those occasions when commerce rears its unstrategic head. The term is derived from the underlying (and rather base) desires of military men, when cultivating the society of ladies, to emulate their lap-dogs by *poodle-faking*! Can also be applied to any social activity ashore, such as calling on married messmates at home, instead of playing sport or participating in some other all-male activity.

pooh trap   Some common pitfall or easily-made mistake that one should be aware of, as in the *heffalump trap* of AA Milne's classic *Winnie The Pooh*.

poop from group   The official word from on high.

pooped   Seamanship term for the dangerous event of a big sea breaking over the stern (*poop deck*) of a ship. Now also used as a word to describe great tiredness, but see also *chin-strapped and *flakers. There was also a SM version which did not require a following sea. If the boat was running opened up (with both conning tower hatches open) a big wave surge could cause water to arrive in the Control Room and the decks below.

poor as piss   Jack's standard description for low-quality beer in a pub ashore: *'The ale in there is as poor as piss - and twice as nasty..'* An associated abbreviation was *porous*.

pop   Euphemism for booze; a heavy drinker might be described as *on the pop* again or else as having trouble with the *old pop*.

population paste   One of Jack's euphemisms for seminal fluid; see also *baby gravy and *duff(3).

pork / porker / porky   The word **pork** is a useful basis for a number of other terms. Some imply gluttony, such as: *'I really porked out on Sunday lunch - it was excellent..'* or: *'You porker!'* as an insult. Someone who is looking a *little porky* is putting on weight, but just to confuse any reader who is not a native, the term *porky pies* is rhyming slang for *lies!* Inevitably, a *pork sword* is a penis, and in older times this term was used mockingly by Jack in this way: *'I say - well done that man! I shall be putting your name forward for the Most Noble Order of the Pork Sword..'*

porridge guns   Bagpipes; see also *agony bags.

Port Divisions   Formerly, Jack joined up through one of three port divisions, Portsmouth, Devonport or Chatham (regrettably, the *Scottish Navy had to do this as well), and the initial letter P, D or C then formed the first part of his official *number.

Port Said bible   Older term for a pornographic book.

port   The left-hand side of a ship when facing forward. Before the rudder was introduced into ship design, vessels were steered by a large oar or *sweep* mounted on the right hand side of the stern. That side then took its name from the *steer board*, later evolving into *starboard, whereas the cargo and passengers were loaded through the left-hand or *load board* side. Load board then became *larboard, but since this was easily confused with steer board / starboard this was officially changed to **port** in 1844, although the word had been in use for many years before that. Traditionally, **port** is somehow deemed inferior to *starboard.

port & starboard oars   Knife and fork.

porthole   More a Merchant Navy than RN term, although a square window is known in the RN as a *port* or *square port*. The small, round (and sometimes openable) version is a *scuttle, which is also fitted with a *deadlight. Interestingly, the bridge windows of a warship are called just that!

porthole gazer Yet another term for a homosexual.

Portland Formerly a busy Dorset Naval base, dockyard, Admiralty Research Establishment, air station and sea training facility. Warships of the RN and many friendly navies underwent *work-up here, under the auspices of *FOST (Flag Officer Sea Training) to a state of operational readiness. One highlight of this period was the *Thursday (or *Weekly) War. The Naval Base, Dockyard and Air Station have now closed, and *FOST has moved, with his staff and *sea-riders, to *Guzz.

positive perhaps (esp. RM) Inability to make a decision: *'I think that I may just about be able to give you a positive perhaps on that one..'* See also *definite maybe.

Post Captain Older term for a Captain who was eligible for a sea command appointment, and whose name was on the Post List. This has now become the *Wet list.

post card run See *hair cut run.

Postie Nickname for the Ship's Postman, in big ships and in past times usually a RM Corporal.

Postman's Walk (RM) An interesting aerial ropeway that comprises part of the *Tarzan course at *Lympstone.

pot Diving compression chamber; a training dive in this will be entered into a diver's log book as a *pot dip* after the *pot run* is completed.

pot mess Any stew to which ingredients are being added constantly, but which also remains hot and ready (eg. for survivors) at all times. The Biblical expression *mess of pottage* means much the same thing. When qualified with the additional word *proper*, the term can also used to describe muddle or confusion.

POTS   Petty Officer Telegraphist - who later became a RS, or Radio Supervisor, in the modern RN.

pouch (RM)   Belt-order item of a Marine's personal equipment which, for some unfathomable reason, is always pronounced as if it was spelt *pooch*!

poultice-walloper   Member of the Royal Naval Medical Branch - see also *scab-lifter.

pound for pound, I'd rather have the fuel.. (FAA)   Another put-down for the poor old *Observers, who seem to have fewer barbs to direct at their *Pirates in retaliation for this suggestion that the absence of the *Looker would mean a welcome increase in fuel load.

pox doctor's clerk   The figurative lowest of the low in the Medical Branch:*How do they expect me to run a Follow-up Clinic with the help of just two *sprog *scab lifters and a pox doctor's clerk?'* In older times there was an expression referring to someone as having *all the luck of a pox doctor's clerk* since he had immmediate access to all the cures for venereal disease.

poxy   Useful adjective of disapproval, especially (SM) in the alliterative term *poxy Jock* for certain citizens of the far North.

praise in public, rebuke in private   Eminently sensible piece of Naval man-management advice.

pregnant   Officers who are nearing the end of their time *In zone, and still hoping for promotion.

premature   Round or shell which detonates prematurely on leaving the barrel of a gun or mortar, with devastating effect on those nearby.

presento   A small gift given in return for hospitality.

press gang   A group of naval men, acting by the sanction of both custom and law, to carry out the process of *impressment. Men liable for this enforced sea service were described as eligible men of seafaring habit between the ages of 18 and 55 years. There were a few exceptions, but these were often ignored - with disastrous results. The last law on this matter was passed as late as 1835. See also the *Andrew and note the more general expression:*One volunteer is always worth a dozen pressed men..'*

pressure-head   *Skimmer's nickname for a submariner; see also *boat people (FAA).

previous   Alternative word for early: *'We're due to run in on top at zero nine *dubs exactly, but no harm in being upwind and out of sight behind that hill some five minutes previous..'* Or (esp. RM): *'Them as wot's keen gets fell in previous..'* meaning that you will always do well for yourself in life by arriving early.

prick   Two or three interesting, and possibly related, meanings:
1.   Leaf tobacco, formerly issued (on repayment) to Jack's forebears which was rolled up tightly (having previously been soaked or steeped in honey and/or molasses and/or rum), wrapped in canvas and then tightly bound with tarred twine. After maturing, the resulting *prick* was cut as required into *quids* (from cud) for chewing - it was less often smoked, as this involved going to the *galley (see also *galley packet). The derivation of the word prick appears to be from the French *perique* or *peruque* which themselves may be derived from the French word *queue* (tail). This was also used in upper-class English to mean long hair tied back at the nape of the neck (eg. a pigtail) which in some ways resembled a *prick of tobacco*; alternatively it might just refer to its resemblance to (2). Just to confuse the issue, there was a dark tobacco from Louisiana called *Perique*. Apparently, you could even buy a traditional *prick* in certain Pompey tobacconists until the late 1950's.
2. Vulgar slang for a penis, which is not just *Jackspeak*, but has been around at least since Chaucer's time. The word certainly pre-dated the introduction of tobacco. A *prick farrier* is another term for a doctor, and note also this description of a sexually profligate individual: *'He uses his prick as a tiller..'*
3.   Derisory term for an unpleasant person (though what this really has to do with (2) is a good question!

(all) **prick and padded shoulders**   Jack's dismissive phrase for a *canteen cowboy, or some other social boaster without justification for his many claims.

primo   The male equivalent of a *prima donna*, a fussy and demanding individual who is quite good at his job on the few occasions that everything is right for him. Between the wars this word referred to any enormous person such as *Primo Carnera*, the Italian heavyweight boxer - who was eventually canvassed by Joe Louis.

Procedure Alpha   Ceremonial lining of a warship's side and

Full Set

upperworks by the ship's company when entering or leaving harbour.

proctoheliosis The prefix *procto-* concerns the lower bowel, while *helios* is the classical Greek word for the sun; someone afflicted with this condition (or, identically, *helioproctosis) is vain enough to believe that the sun shines from his or her backside.

Professor Fog (FAA) Weather forecaster, or *Met man.

proff Steal or *acquire an item, or benefit from a situation.

projjy Jack's wartime name for any projectile fired from a gun, whatever its calibre.

pronger See * third pronger (FAA) for explanation.

proviso The name of a light messenger rope (or warp) carried ashore by a vessel that is mooring stern on, with a single anchor out in the stream of water. This is used to haul over the bigger sternfast or stern rope. The name has also come ashore in a semi-legal sense.

psc *Practically Senior to Christ* - pun on the post-nominal *TLA that indicates a person as having *Passed Staff College*.

PU Acronym for **piss-up*, ie. a drinking session.

puck A cringle of rope used for the violent sport of deck hockey.

pucker factor Fear as a motivating force! Describes one of the subjective effects of uncontrolled adrenalin flow on the anal sphincter.

pud Two applications:
1. (RM) Royal's term for any officer involved in Logistic supply or administration; the Senior *Loggie in any formation then becomes its *Chief Pud*.
2. Wartime nickname for a Lowestoft fisherman, over 10,000 of whom saw service as *HOs. Derived from their fondness for suet puddings.

pudding club To be *in the pudding club* meant that the lady involved is pregnant. The term is derived from the large and similarly bulbous *pudding fender*.

puddle jumper (FAA) Any civilian light aeroplane.

puffer jets (FAA)   Unjustified term of disparagement directed at the *SHAR (and its pilots) by *chopper pukes and others who recall real fixed-wing carrier-borne aircraft, such as *Buccs, *Tooms and even *Sea Vixens.

PULHHEEMS   Medical assessment acronym which grades from 1 to 7 the individual qualities associated with *Physique, Upper* limbs, *Lower* limbs, *Hearing* (R+L), *Eyes* (R+L), *Mental* capacity and *Stability*. These are usually a string of 1's and 2's, leading to the statement: *'The marks on his *C.206 looked a bit like a PULHHEEMS grading..'* (ie. not very good!)   See also *P7R.

pull / pulling   Jack's term for rowing, when applied to service boats such as the old Montagu whaler, cutter, etc; the oars are not feathered with each stroke, as in rowing, but merely *pulled* through the water as hard as possible in a *pulling race*. The fact that effort is co-ordinated in this way can also be used as a method of encouragement: *'Pull together lads, and we'll piss this bastard..'*

pull pole (RM)   The action of dismantling a *bivvy or tentsheet shelter under Arctic conditions, only undertaken when everyone is packed and in all other respects ready to move. The expression can now be heard in use for any group activity where the exact timing of a final action is critical for success.

pull-through   Device for cleaning a naval weapon or (RM) rifle's barrel.   Can also be used in a personal sense, especially when a messmate had released a particularly noxious odour from his *chuff: *'Cor - you could do with a good pull-through with a Christmas tree - smells like a rat crawled up there and died..'* As usual, there is a sexual connotation too, in that *having a pull-through* describes the effeects of giving the *ferret a run.

pull up a bollard   Quaint invitation to have a seat.

pulpit   Guard-rail around a raised platform.

pulpit poofter   Homosexual vicar; see also *raving rev and *dodgy deacon.

pump up   Another euphemism for sexual intercourse.

pumping poo (SM)   The modern process of discharging raw sewage by diffusion into the wake, as opposed to merely *blowing shit.

pumping (the) **ship** Polite euphemism for urination; see also *ease springs and *check the ship for leaks.

punched, bored or countersunk Mentally confused: *'By the fourth round he didn't know whether he'd been punched, bored or countersunk..'* See also *Arthur, Martha or Mabel.

punchy Interesting adjective that can be used to indicate a tough, aggressive military person: *'He's one of those typically punchy little Paras..'* or, when referring to a letter or position paper, it describes written text in which a logical series of hard-hitting points are developed very well.

punkah-louvre A *cabin or *compartment fitting attached to the ventilation *fan trunking and adjustable for both angle and flow.

PUNS / puns Medical category meaning *Physically Unsuitable* (for) *Naval Service.* In the lower case, men *under puns* have had certain privileges withdrawn while they are *under punishment.*

push out Alternative for *dist, as in: *'Push out this memo, please..'*

push the boat out Throw a party, or buy a round of drinks.

pusher Jack's older term for his girl-friend, or the person that he *pushed around* the dance floor.

Pusser An all-purpose word to do with the Navy that is one of the most interesting used in Jackspeak;
1. The paymaster and supplies officer of the old Navy was the

purser (an appointment still made in the Merchant Navy) which then became slurred in daily usage to *pusser*. This word was noun, verb or adjective depending on the shade of meaning required. *The Pusser* is still a ship or establishment's Supply Officer, whereas *a Pusser* is any officer of the Supply and Secretariat specialization.

2. Anything of official origin was (and still is!) *a pusser's item,* or *pusser's issue,* and in the sense that *Pusser* refers to the whole Royal Navy as an organization, the word crops up in a large number of amusing daily descriptions:

    pusser built - someone who sticks to the regulations
    pusser's bull - naval history
    pusser's camel - a *Wren
    pusser's chicken - possessed of sixteen legs
    *pusser's *crabfat* - thick warship-grey paint
    pusser's crabs - Naval boots
    pusser's daps - white plimsole shoes
    pusser's dip - candle
    pusser's dirk - seaman's clasp knife
    pusser's duck - Walrus aircraft (*Shagbat) or a seagull
    pusser's dust - cheap instant coffee
    pusser's finest - not necessarily complimentary!
    pusser's fix-all - WD-40 fluid
    pusser's grey - warship colour
    pusser's grip - brown canvas holdall
    pusser's hard - coarse cleaning soap
    pusser's item - anything bought in *Slops
    pusser's leaf - rolled tobacco
    pusser's logic - any false economy
    pusser's loaf - biscuit
    pusser's medal - food stain on clothing
    pusser's phoo-phoo - tropical foot powder
    pusser's planks - (RM) military cross-country skis
    pusser's prefect - Regulator
    pusser's red devil - red-painted Naval bicycle
    pusser's shift - see *split rig
    pusser's shirt - any badly-tailored garment fits like this
    pusser's tally - fictitious name given in *Aggies
    pusser's wagon - battleship
    pusser's wipes - Bronco (shiny) toilet paper

3. A *really pusser* officer should also be noted as a singular use of the word to describe someone who is *absolutely* formal and *totally* correct in both deportment and dress. An individual who

is steeped in Naval tradition might also be described as having been *born on a pusser's blanket*.

4. *Pusser's vinolia* was a special soap with amazing properties in that it removed facial stubble whn the face was being washed, thereby obviating the need for shaving. Of course, this was just another of the many *bites that young, *green ratings might be exposed to. Usually, *slops would have just run out of this item, and the hapless victims of this spoof would be encouraged to try Boots the Chemists instead.

5. *A drop of pusser's* is a general phrase for rum. There are some important distinctions to be made here with regard to *Nelson's blood which may at first seem a little pedantic. When speaking of proper Naval rum, Jack will refer to *a drop of pusser's*, without necessarily referring to the trade-marked commercial fluid (with a capital P). *Pusser's Rum* is made in Tortola, but Charles Tobias, the former US Marine who owned the company, recently sold out to the huge Jim Beam drinks conglomerate. One of their key new account executives was a Peruvian who supported the Argentine cause in 1982, and therefore simply hated the image of a White Ensign that used to adorn the original bottle label! The White Ensign was therefore withdrawn, an action now reciprocated, by cancellation of any endorsement for that product, of the kind which was carried on the cover of the first edition of JACKSPEAK. However, *Lamb's Navy Rum* has the White Ensign in its proper place, and the company is generous in its sponsorship of Royal Navy sporting events and facilities. A recommended fluid, either as *neaters or in a *dark and dirty!

put me down for some of that!   *'I fancy her!'*

putting the Queen to bed   Nickname for evening *Colours and/or the *Sunset ceremonial.

putty   Sticky or muddy shallows - as opposed to damaging rocks. However, the process of placing a warship *on* or *in the putty* is still an embarassing *graunch in that the vessel actually goes aground. Also a nickname for the ship's painter of old, an artisan whose rate was abolished after WW2.

PV   *Positive Vetting*, a system of establishing someone's suitability to handle, or have access to, sensitive *classified information; also used by a prospective fiance when meeting his intended's parents for the first time.

PVR   *Premature Voluntary Release* - see *discharge.

PWO (pronounced *Pee-woe*)   *TLA for the *Principal Warfare Officer*, who replaced the old deep-specialist seaman officers (eg Gunnery, TAS, D, etc.) in the early 1970s. The concept provided for officers to be trained sufficiently in all warfare disciplines and tactics, although they could subsequently become more specialised in one discipline such as Air Warfare, Underwater, or Communications. Despite initial headshaking amongst the *old hands, the concept very much came into its own during the Falklands campaign of 1982.

QUEBEC

351 -354

Q   The *Quick-acting* ballast tank in the forward section of a submarine which is used to assist diving in an emergency, as when taking urgent action to avoid collision. Hence **flood Q!* - allowing sea water in to facilitate a fast sink rate without even touching the planes; the **oggin* that comes rushing in is sometimes described as fifty friendly tons.

QRs / QRRN   *Queens' Regulations* (for the *Royal Navy*); these used to be called *QRs and AIs* (Admiralty Instructions). In so far as there is a book that the RN is run by, then this thick, blue-covered and loose-leaf tome is it - but see also *by the book.

QT   *On the QT means on the quiet, or unofficial:'On the QT, old chum - could you slip me a *towpath copy of the minutes of that meeting?'*

quack   Medical officer - as distinct from the *Doc who is traditionally the ship's Medical Assistant. *Avquack* is a FAA variant, but see also *chippy, *gasman, *plumber, *Dick Doc, *fanny mechanic and *quim quack.

Quarterbill   The document produced by a ship's design authority which lays down the number of people required to man the *quarters, ie. to operate the ship when at *Action Stations. As such, it makes no allowance for ancillary tasks such as cleaning, training or other *communal duties. These are shown on the *Scheme of Complement.

quarterdeck   The spiritual heart of a warship, situated in the after part, and where a religious shrine was positioned in the sailing vessels of yesteryear. It was the place from which the ship was controlled by the *captain and the officer of the watch, and thus became the exclusive preserve of the captain and his officers. The custom of removing one's hat, or *saluting the quarterdeck* in passing (which stems from its religious, not its hierarchical, significance), is a tradition that is maintained to this day by all RN and RM personnel crossing the *brow to enter or leave one of Her Majesty's Ships.

quarterly report   Special three-monthly reports *rendered on an officer who is not apparently performing to the required standard.

quartermaster / QM   The senior helmsman - or master of whichever course that a vessel is sailing on, the latter dictated by the wind's direction or *quarter*. The wheel or steering mechanism was also located on the *quarterdeck*. When a warship is alongside, the *QM* runs the *brow and is responsible for the *station card routines, *piping the side, and all other relevant ceremonial. A Royal Marine employed in this role is called the Corporal of the Gangway; this is because Royal thinks of a *Quartermaster* as the officer responsible for all *Unit stores and transport, an appointment similar in function to that of the *Pusser. In big ships, with two *brows, the after brow is manned by the QM, and the forward brow by the Corporal of the Gangway (regardless of whether he or she is sailor, or he is a marine).

quarters   Two definitions:
1. The positions (**quarters**) to be manned at *Action Stations, from which is derived the *quarterbill. In older times the ship's drummer(s) would *beat to Quarters* when action was imminent, using the rhythms of *Hearts of Oak. Nowadays the *pipe *Action Stations! accompanied by an urgent klaxon or bell sound is used for this purpose, although the US Navy still sounds General Quarters.
2. Accommodation (usually ashore), including that provided for married personnel (*Married Quarters*).

Queen Mary (FAA)   Large articulated lorry and trailer used to move an aircraft by road.

Queen Street   The road that bounds the southern wall of *Pompey Dockyard and which in the mid to late 19th century was the scene of such uncontrolled debauchery that *Aggie Weston determined to improve Jack's lot and raised funds to build and open the Royal Sailors' Rests.

Queen to bed   See *put the Queen to bed.

Queen's   Any residue of rum left in the *fanny after everyone in the *messdeck had drawn his *tot, similar to *plusher's and *plusser's in this respect. This was usually the *rum bosun's perks, even though his judicious use of a large thumb had caused short measure to be given. When referring to *neaters, any **Queen's** was on occasion (illegally) stored in a *ready-use bottle, supposedly for visitors and guests to the Chief and Petty Officer's Messes, but very occasionally for a *Black Mass.

Queen's Colour   A special White Ensign, made of heavy silk and adorned with tassels, and secured to a staff topped with the naval crown; one is presented by the Sovereign to the various RN and RM commands and it is also paraded, with much cere-monial, on Royal occasions.

Queen's Harbour Master   Officer responsible for the safety, navigation and general management of water-borne traffic in a Royal Dockyard port. The *QHM* is the only officer below flag rank entitled to a *barge and a distinguishing flag, which is a Union flag with a white border, *defaced with a crown and the letters QHM in the centre.

Queen's (from King's) **hard bargain**   Jack's (much older) description of a fellow sailor who has elected to join the Navy rather than go into prison. Now used for a sailor who serves his time to pension without doing anything really very spectacular or useful during his twenty-two years - and then goes on to draw his pension for twice that length of time. In contrast, a *Queen's bad bargain* is a hardened *defaulter, for whom any amount of corrective training is unlikely to do any good, and is a candidate for *discharge SNLR.

Queen's Hotel   A place where one is a guest of Her Majesty (ie. *DQs).

queen bee   A *Flag Officer's wife or, formerly, the Commandant of the *WRNS; the post no longer exists *per se*, but there is still a senior female officer to whom the term can apply. The senior female officer in a ship or shore estalishment will not now necessarily have any direct responsibility for other female personnel borne.   The term was also used for a pre-WW2 radio-controlled aircraft.

quick burn   Rapidly (and silently) smoked cigarette.

quick coat of paint   A lovely euphemism for the physical activity associated with a rapid *legover.

quick on the uptake   Someone intelligent and smart, or just a little lightfingered.

quickfix (esp. FAA)   An urgent solution to a problem that, in the long run, may not be the best one.

quiet number   Another version of *cushy number, but especially so when there is little or no supervision involved.

quiet *run   Never happens!

quim quack   Alternate for *fanny mechanic or gynaecologist.

ROMEO

355 - 374

RA Abbreviation of *Ration Allowance*. Formerly, a married officer or rating who lived ashore in *base port was paid the value
of his daily victualling rate in order to bolster the family food
budget; hence he became ineligible to eat *on board for free,
and had to pay for any meals taken (see *bean stealer). *RA* is no
longer paid, but the term is still used to mean someone who
lives out. Note also the term *RA's clock* to describe a timepiece
that is running slow - in order to allow late arrival at the place
of work. The RM equivalent of someone RA is an *outlier.
Those who did not bring sandwiches or similar on board when
*day running, and who ogled Jack's meals were detested:
'Little Miss Muffet sat on her tuffet
Eating her curds and whey,
Along came a spider and
Sat down beside her,
And she said: 'Bugger off, you RA bastard..'

rabbit(s) Frequent descriptive term for a gift - or something
that has been *acquired. The word originates from Chatham
Dockyard, where the small island of St Mary's inside the Royal
Dockyard area was overrun with *bunny rabbits*. Although strictly speaking Admiralty property, they were frequently poached
and taken home as a welcome (and free) source of fresh meat.
A *rabbit run* describes an excursion ashore in order to buy presents. To say that something has *got *ears on it* means that the
article being described is really a rabbit, or is something that has
been *rabbited* or *acquired. *Rabbitwork* is material made in a
workshop on an unofficial basis. Note also, as piece of quaint
folklore, that on the island of *Portland it was extremely unlucky
to refer to the animal version of this paragraph by this name -
bunnies, long-ears, white-tails or even *they varmints* were the
terms used instead.

racing snake A person who is extremely thin: *'During the*

Gen Buzz

*yomp across East Falkland, both the *Cherryberries and the *Booties found that their racing snakes and marathon runners were unable to hack the distance under load..'

racing trim (SM)   Everything shaking, a howling gale blowing down the conning tower as the *donks eat up the air; flat out at 12 knots. Twelve and a bit if you got the surface trim right, the wind behind you, everyone smoking and it's downhill. Four days back to Faslane, and every half a knot counts. The *Jimmy and the Chief Stoker go into a huddle in the wardroom. They know exactly where every pound or pint of movable or disposable weight is. Move all beer and tobacco aft. Open stern tubes. Blow all tanks. Pump out all bilges, slop drain and sewage. Transfer 50 gallons of diesel from for'd to aft. The stern goes down a tiny bit, up creeps the bow and the boat increases speed to 12.6 knots. That was *racing trim*!

rack out   Go to sleep; see also *hit the pit and *turn in. The SM world also describe the interesting phenomenon of *rack reversal* - to be half-asleep on watch, yet half-awake in one's bunk. Also note *rack rejection* - being satiated with sleep and unable to lie down any longer.

racking and tracking (FAA)   Fighter-pilot term for the process of turning hard under G forces (*racking*) while trying to get a gun or missile-firing solution on the target (*tracking*).

radhaz   Abbreviation for *radio-frequency emission hazard*, painted as a warning sign near radar aerials and at microwave transmitter sites.

(The) **Rag**   The Army and Navy Club in Pall Mall, London.

rag-bag   Untidy and messy individual: *'You look like a *teased-out rag-bag..'* See also *scran-bag as an alternative insult.

rag-head   An Arab.

rags / raggie   Older term for *oppo, in the sense that the person you shared your brasswork *cleaning rags* with tended to be a particular chum, hence the expression *parting brass rags used to describe the sudden break-up of such a friendship. Also an occasional nickname for someone with the surname Richards.

RALEIGH   HMS *RALEIGH* is the shore establishment near *Torpoint, Cornwall, where all basic new-entry training in the Royal Navy is now carried out. It is an amalgam of the former HMS GANGES (Juniors' training, at Shotley, near Ipswich), HMS St VINCENT (New Entry training, Portsmouth), HMS *DAUNTLESS (WRNS training, near Reading), and HMS FIS-

GARD (Artificer training, Torpoint). All of these are remembered in training blocks within *legoland. The *nozzers spend six weeks here before moving on to their Part Two courses. *RALEIGH* is also the home of the Supply and Secretariat School (formerly at HMS PEMBROKE, Chatham), and now of the Submarine School (transferred from HMS *DOLPHIN, in Gosport), as well as number of smaller specialist schools. See also *Royal Navy School of Dancing.

ram it! Jack's way of saying *Stuff it!* The phrase is used to perfection in the *RDP song.

rampstrike (FAA) Older *stovie term for a misjudged carrier approach in which the landing aircraft's wheels hit the lip of the flight deck's edge. The violent deceleration was disconcerting, and the impact occasionally severe enough to destroy the undercarriage. See *round-down; the much older carriers didn't have one.

ranged (FAA) The process whereby an aircraft is brought up from (or out of) a hangar, and made ready for *launching; the opposite procedure (following *recovery) is *striking down.

rare as rocking-horse shit Not something one comes across very often!

rank & rating In the RN, Commissioned Officers hold *rank*; Chief and Petty Officers are *senior ratings*. Leading Hands and below are *junior ratings* (not just the juniors). Officers are promoted; ratings are *rated up*, or even *disrated*. In the RM army conventions apply ie. Officers and Other Ranks are all promoted.

Rank Inflation Frigates sometimes had Lieutenants in command. That was in the days before *Rank Inflation*, referring to the present tendency almost to have more Admirals than ABs!

RAS (pronounced *raz*) *TLA for *Replenishment At Sea*, the procedure whereby ships can refuel, and transfer stores, ammunition and people whilst underway using *jackstays or helicopters (see *vertrep). It is a term which can also be used as an alternative for *acquire as in: *'Where did he get those bindings from ?'* *'Dunno, sir - reckon 'e must have razzed 'em from the *Noggies..'*

rat-arsed (esp. RM) Also heard as *ratted*, or *ratters*, but in all cases meaning drunk.

rate Naval equivalent of rank, gained on being advanced by the Commanding Officer: *'I got rated up to *killick during my time in BOXER..'* In ascending order, the *rates* are: Ordinary Rate,

Able Rate, Leading Rate, Petty Officer and Chief Petty Officer. In slang it referred specifically to the rating of Petty Officer:'*He's picked up his rate..*' or:'*He's passed for the rate..*'

rating   A member of the *lower deck, ie. anyone below officer rank.

ratpack (RM)   Compaction of the words ration and pack to describe either tinned rations (*compo), or the dehydrated and foil-packeted *Arctic ratpack*.

rats / ratshit (esp. RM)   Term used to describe the collapse or failure of some scheme: '*Then it *clamped and began to rain, so the plan went to rats..*'

rattle   To be *in the rattle* is to be in big trouble, ie. receiving professional attention from the *Reggies. Jack might also ask, in older times, about a lady's sexual proclivities:'*Does she rattle?*'

Raving Rev   A homosexual cleric; see also *pulpit poofter and *dodgy deacon.

RBG   *TLA for *Rich Brown Gravy*.

RDP   *Run Down Period*, usually prior to a ship's paying off, but also used for an officer or sailor who is about to leave a job (or the Navy) and hence is not interested in what's going on. Cleverly used by the singer Shep Woolley in his song - *Ram it - I'm RDP!*

ready-use   A small stock of stores held near to their point of use, eg. an ammunition *ready-use locker* near a gun, with the rest of the ammunition down in the ship's magazine.

rear party (RM)   Those left behind to maintain security or keep things ticking over during a *Unit's deployment or seasonal leave. The RN equivalent refers to *retard leave

reasons in writing   An officer's formal written explanation for a moderate, or more serious lapse in behaviour, which has come to the attention of the authorities. The expression has now become a phrase in its own right: '*When the boys got the Commander's Mini up the steps and into the *Wardroom foyer, it was - as you can imagine - a reasons in writing job all round..*'

re-bore   Surgery for piles.

rec space   A compartment or *flat *rigged for recreational purposes.

receiving ship   Originally, an old and decaying *hulk, permanently moored in a harbour as temporary accommodation for newly-entered or *impressed men, before they were sent off to sea. Nowadays used during *RAS planning to differentiate from the *delivering* or *supplying* ship.

receiving swollen property   Sexual intercourse; the phrase may also be used in conjunction with *assault with a friendly weapon.

Recommend (esp. RM)   Semi-formal expression of praise: '*I think he deserves a Recommend for that..*' or: '*You all did well, so take an official Recommend!*' Note also the subtle put-down implied in: '*A miserable old boot? Saying that about her would be a recommend..*'

recovery   The process of landing an aircraft back onto a carrier or the runways of a Naval Air Station; a *runner is also *recovered* when he or she is back in custody.

Red Dragon (FAA)   Rear Admiral The Prince of Wales KG KT Royal Navy, a fully qualified and operationally-experienced *Junglie.

Red Duster   The Merchant Navy ensign.

Red Endorsement (FAA)   This older system of official comment in a pilot's logbook following the perpetration of some serious error does not seem to be practised nowadays in the FAA , but the *Green Endorsement certainly is. A *red ink* entry in an aircraft's log book refers to an acceptable problem which will be dealt with as soon as practicable.

red ink   A trio:
1. Colour traditionally used by the Captain when writing on minutes or memoranda; see *spilled blood as well.
2. The underlining of any adverse comments, which are within his or her power to remedy, written in a rating's Divisional documents, done to signify that attention has been officially drawn to these.
3. When an officer incurred their Lordship's displeasure, he could be told this by a typewritten letter. If the displeasure was deeply felt, he would be notified in the handwriting of the Secretary of the Admiralty in green ink. If, however, he has thrown the morale of the whole establishment into chaos, it would be in red ink.

red lead   Tomato sauce; *worms in red lead* refers to tinned spaghetti.

Red Plum   Affectionate nickname for HMS ENDURANCE, the Royal Navy's Antarctic ice patrol ship.

red recommend   Older term for an especially good report on a senior *rate which, in a system no longer extant, had the top 10% of candidates' names on an alphabetical list typed out in red.

Red Sea rig   A relaxed evening *rig worn in RN *wardrooms and comprising uniform trousers, tropical shirt with rank shoulder-straps and a *cummerbund (kamarband). Previously it was only permitted in extremely hot weather (hence the name), and up until the early 1970s, officers were generally expected to don mess *undress in the evening. Nowadays it is the accepted evening *rig for all but duty officers, and is inceasingly being worn by senior rates.

red tape   Official Government or Service forms and paperwork. Recently, valiant efforts have been made to reduce it, especially in an attempt to ease *harbour hassle, but they usually come to nought.

redders (esp. RM)   Really hot, abbreviation of *red-hot*, but also used to describe sunny weather. The phrase *gangs of redders* is often used when talking about a plentiful source of heat such as an oven or a sauna.

redemption by *pusser's hard   Old system whereby items from the *scran bag could be recovered on payment of one inch of an individual's personal supply of Naval-issue soap, which was then used for communal purposes.

reeve   This is a proper *sandscratcher's word. To *reeve a rope* is to attach it to another, usually by a splice. You also *reeve a rope* when you take turns around something. The turns are called *reeves*. When required to haul on a rope, you are told to *reeve on*. However, stokers only used the term in the sense of appreciating a nice bit of *clacker: *'Cor, I could reeve a length of that..'* To *reeve a shackle* is a euphemism for defaecation.

regain (RM)   An exercise undertaken over the static water tank at *Lympstone; the special technique of recovery after falling off and hanging from a rope must be demonstrated. Also used in a wider sense: *'After a mistake like that he'll have to do an enormous regain if he wants to get back in the CO's good books..'*

Reggy / Reggies   Polite abbreviation for a member of the Regulating Branch, the Navy's policemen.   Unlike the Army (*Redcaps*) and the RAF (*Snowdrops*), the RN does not recruit directly into a police branch; selected (volunteer) ratings are *sideways-transferred, usually at *Leading Rate, into the Regulating Branch. Thus the Navy, uniquely, is policed by its own and, perhaps for this reason, while no one admits to liking *Reggies*, they are not held in the same disdain as their other service counterparts; apart from anything else, in ships they have to *mess with their peers.   The *rates are Leading Regulator, Regulating Petty Officer (who may be *Cox'n of a small ship), and Master at Arms (MAA).   A Warrant Officer MAA is still known as a Fleet Joss (see *Fleet Chief).   When the WRNS was fully absorbed into the RN, the female variant of MAA was (perhaps sadly) not termed a Mistress at Arms!   See also *crushers, *Gestapo, *Jaunty, *Jossman and *Master-at-Arms.

reindeer juice   Any really strong alcohol: *'A couple of these and you'll be on the roof..'*

relaxed rig   Informal (recreational) clothing.

relief   The person who takes over your duty, watch or job.

religious experience (esp. FAA)   Something that you would like your enemy to have in war, so that he suddenly changes his outlook on life - and then either surrenders or *bangs out!

remuster   In an official sense, to *remuster* something is to check it for a second time; in practice, the word is often used to describe someone who has changed trades or vocations: *'After the attack on Two Sisters, one of the Rifle Company officers asked to remuster as a padre..'*

render   Submit a report or *return; note also that a rope *renders* *to* a block rather than passing through it.

Rentaset   The Royal Navy School of Education and Training Technology.

Report your position and depth at midnight.   Jocular and traditional telegram sent to a Naval Officer on his wedding day

- to be read out at the wedding breakfast by his best man. The Royal Marines equivalent might be this piece of fieldcraft advice which states: *'Don't fire the first time up..'* Either way, the maiden aunts are usually horrified. An optional extra is based on a real-life hydrographic detail: *'..and also nature of bottom'*!

request chit Written request seeking formal permission to do something: *'You want a slot on that *exped up to the Hardanger Vidda? OK, can't promise anything, but put your request chit in..'* In the RN, this idea has more to do with reminding a senior officer of a discussion, after he has had time to think about the problem. In the RN it also used to be necessary for *requestmen (which see).

Requestmen Captain's *table for the hearing of requests by his men for advancement, promotion, redress or recognition following success in academic or sporting matters. Usually a happy occasion, in contrast to *Defaulters.

required on board Informal sanction awarded by the *Captain or *Executive Officer to an officer who has drawn unwelcome attention to himself, eg. by drinking too much. An officer who is *required on board* will be unable to participate in a *run ashore, or accept any invitations to go *up homers, and might also have a *stoppage of wine-bill to suffer into the bargain. Extra duties (or extras) is another sanction, but more often used by the RM. Note that all this only applied to officers.

re-scrub Repeat something, especially an inspection after failing it the first time around.

rest of your natural The *rest of your natural-born* days, ie. for the rest of your life

retard leave Staying back for security or administrative duties during main leave, thus retarding your own leave (or even taking it earlier!) and forming the retard party; the RM equivalent uses the term *rear party.

retinue A *Flag Officer's household staff.

re-tread Someone who is doing a job for the second time, usually after a long absence from it; can also be used as a descriptive adjective for a person who has *remustered from another skill: *'Joe's a re-tread *Looker - he bust his back ejecting from a Vixen and is now an *Air Tragicker..'* A *re-tread bachelor* is someone who is divorced.

returns Routine written or signalled reports on a plethora of subjects required, it always seems to busy sea-goers, merely to satisfy the needs of *red tape. *Nil returns* are also required - even if you've got nothing to say, you've still got to say it!

RFA The *Royal Fleet Auxiliary*, a splendid organisation that supplies stores, fuel and ammunition to HM warships at sea.

RHIP *Rank Hath Its Privilege* - a nice way of deferring to a senior officer in some matter. Note also *boat routine.

RIB *Rigid Inflatable Boat*; it has a fibre-glass vee hull with rubber-composition inflatable sides, is fitted with a powerful inboard or outboard engine, and has superior sea-keeping qualities. Used as the *sea boat in all HM ships

riding on her own milk tins *'She's been there that long she's riding on her own milk tins..'* This was the phrase Jack used to describe a clapped-out merchant ship, usually French, Greek, or Chinese, which was always lying alongside the jetty wall in the same place whenever their ship entered harbour.

rice Two applications:
1. (RM) *Give it rice!* is like saying: *'Let's have more effort!'*
2. *Feed 'em rice, Jimmy!* is similar to: *'Give them a piece of your mind, James!'*

R - 364

ridge ropes   Jack's description of the *VPL.

riff-raff   Alliterative term derived from the rather unsavoury *Riff* and Berber pirates of the Barbary Coast of North Africa.

rig   Originally a general term referring to the masts and sails, which together defined the type of a sailing vessel. Nowadays it is more generally used to describe uniform and other clothing as follows:
1. *rig of the day* - the uniform laid down in Ship's Daily Orders as appropriate for wearing that day; daily orders can also specify if this is to change during the day, or it can be changed at short notice by a *pipe.
2. *square rig* (which see) - smart uniform worn by ratings below the rate of *Petty officer, and comprising jumper and trousers (no longer bell-bottomed) over a *white front and with a light-blue jean collar, and with a round cap (hat) with *cap-tally; derives from the original *bell-bottomed trousers which had horizontal creases and hence gave the impression of a square rigged vessel under full sail.
3. *fore and aft rig* (which see) - smart uniform worn by *Petty officers and above, comprising double-breasted *monkey jacket and trousers worn over a white shirt and tie, and peaked cap. A Petty Officer's rate is shown by crossed anchors on the left arm; a Chief Petty Officers by three *buttons on each cuff; and Warrant Officers by the Royal Cypher on the left cuff.
4. *working rig* - (traditionally called No 8s, but this is changing) - light blue shirt and dark blue trousers, *woolly pully if required, and usually a *ferret (beret!). Note that *rigs* are numbered (the numbering system has recently been overhauled and rationalised). *No 1 rig* is the smartest, and the greater the number the more functional the rig. Traditionally, people *clean into a smarter rig*, and *shift into working rig*.
5. A *split rig*, in which items of uniform issue are mixed with *civvy kit must always be avoided; another name for this is a *pusser's shift!
6. *shore rig* - civilian attire, which may be *planter's or *dog robber's, but will undoubtedly be a *clean rig* - and a *smart rig* as well.
7. *jury rig* - old sailing term for a temporary get-you-home form of mechanical repair, perhaps derived from *de jour*.
8. *rigged like a* _____   See *Nagasaki.
9. *'Excuse my rig, please?'*   Traditional and polite request to the senior uniformed officer present in a *Wardroom for permission to use the facilities despite not being in uniform yourself. This permission is almost always granted - providing that your rig is not too weird!

10. *scruff rig* is not particularly smart, and inappropriate to the formal surroundings of a *Wardroom, so there is often a *scruff's bar* to cater for those dressed in this manner after sport or study. See also *pirate rig.

rigged for action   In possession of a French letter.

riggers   *Dockyard mateys who work on ropes and cables, and handle mooring lines of ships in dockyard. To *run like a rigger* presumably derives from the need to move quickly if something looks like breaking.

right   An adjective which emphasizes the meaning of the noun which it is applied to: *'He's a right *knacker, he is..'*

rigol   A curved, convex gutter attached to the ship's side, like an eyebrow over each *scuttle.

ring eight bells   Older term meaning to die, hence the underlying significance of the Alistair Maclean novel's title - *When Eight Bells Toll.*

ring on / off   Derived from the engine telegraph system that connected the wheelhouse or bridge to the engine room. Movement of the selector lever caused attention-getting bells to ring at both ends, alerting everyone that a change had been made. You would *ring on* a speed, or *ring off* to finish with main engines, hence this latter usage to imply that a task has been completed and it's now time to do something else. Even though everything is now done with computers and power levers, the traditional terms persist.

ring out the old, ring in the new   Pleasant and traditional custom in RN ships whereby the youngest person on board - officer or rating - rings sixteen bells at midnight on New Year's Eve. Eight are for the old year and eight for the new; see *bells.

ring piece   The anus, hence *ring stinger* as a very hot curry; see also *chicken Chernobyl in this sense. Jack may also use the phrase *I puked my ring piece* to describe an episode of persistent vomiting. The phrase can also be used, almost inevitably, for a *Looker.

ring the bell   Two very different usages:
1. (RM) Small brass bell hanging in the *Senior's bar, usually with embroidered and fancy ropework attached to the clapper. Sounding this bell, whether by design or curiosity, will bring a host of new friends to your side - because you have just indicated your willingness to buy a drink for everyone present.
2. Make your girlfriend *squarey pregnant on the first occasion of a little *nibble.

ringbolt   A zero, as in 820 Squadron becoming *Eight-Two-Ringbolt*, and *oh-crack-double ringbolt* (0-00) as midnight!   There is another occasional use to describe the anus, hence a *ringbolt kicker* is a homosexual; note also note the term *ringbolted* for someone who is hopelessly drunk.

Rip van Winkle   Legendary *kip *merchant whose legacy is celebrated in the accusation: *'You've had more time off than Rip van Winkle's bunk light..'*

ripple (FAA)   The maintenance of a squadron's aircraft in the air around the clock; a *ripple three* means that three aircraft are continuously airborne, day and night - a punishing requirement that taxes aircrew and maintainers alike.

ripshit   A wild colonial boy.

rise and dive bollocking box (SM)   The control room area consisting of the planesmen, ship control and panel positions plus *bandstand.

Rise and shine!   Traditional verbal call when making the pipe *Call the hands!* It is repeated once and usually followed by the words:*'You've had yours - now I'll have mine..'* Other versions are:
> *'Rise and shine - the morning's fine!'*
> *'Rise and scowl - the morning's foul!'*
> *'Rise and sweat - the morning's wet!'*
> *'The sun is shining fit to burn yer eyes out'*
> (whatever the actual weather is..)

Note that technically, in a historical sense, the correct usage should be *Rouse and shine!*

RM repair kit   *Black maskers and a big hammer.

robbing chit (FAA)   Written authority to *acquire some spare part off a *Hangar Annie or *Xmas tree.

Robin Hood   Sarcastic name for a do-gooder:*'Proper bleedin' little Robin 'ood..'* Also:*'Some people call him Robin Hood; I call him robbin' bastard..'*

Rock   The Rock is Gibraltar. A *rock scorpion* is Jack's name for a resident of Gibraltar - originally it referred to a Gibraltar policeman, but the meaning has widened. The patriotic, but financially astute Gibraltarians dislike this nickname intensely.

rock ape   A trio:
1. Member of the Royal Air Force Regiment. See also *pebble-monkey.
2. (RM) Occasional nickname for a ML (Mountain Leader) or a member of the M and AW (Mountain and Arctic Warfare) Cadre.

3. The phrase a *real *three-badge rock ape* describes someone of low intellect who can lift heavy weights.

rock up   General expression similar to turn up or *pole up; note that getting one's *rocks off* has a completely different meaning - to do with giving *the ferret a run.

rocket fuel   Any really strong drink, but especially brandy mixed with Benedictine.

rocket shop (SM)   The missile compartment of a *bomber, as opposed to the *bomb shop up for'ard; see also *Sherwood Forest.

OF COURSE I THINK YOU'RE BEAUTIFUL — BUT I'M NOT VERY GOOD WITH WORDS..

OH GO ON! TRY!!

YOU GOT SKIN LIKE THE LEE SIDE OF A TOM BOLA TICKET

rockets   Nickname for the Weapons Electrical Officer of a SSBN.

rocking horse droppings / manure   Form of comparison for something rare or unusual; one politer alternative might concern the even rarer event of a *Fleet Jossman's sea draft!

rocks (esp. RM)   Censure or criticism as when *bollocking someone: *'That approach was OK but I got absolute rocks for the landing..'*

rocky   Nickname for a wartme RNVR officer.

rodneys *RFA collective nickname for Royal Navy officers. The RFA always has a sneaking feeling that the RN are trying to dilute or change completely their rather unique Service way of doing things. It is therefore considered a rather poor show if a RFA officer adopts too many RN habits and attitudes. Any officer found guilty of this is normally labelled a *closet Rodney*.

Roger D! Informal alternative to OK when agreeing to do something; a shortened form of the alliteration *Roger Dodger*.

Roger Ballast Pump (SM) Expression used by the control Officer of the Watch, in acknowledging reports from the ballast pump operator; also found in hotel registers, or offered as one's identity when confronted by naval patrol - a *pusser's tally. Also used in acknowledgment of trivial or inconsequential information - more from habit than anything else.

rogue's yarn Coloured jute thread laid up in the strands of a rope to identify its source and thereby stop thieving; Naval rope commanded a particularly high price ashore if it could be smuggled out of the dockyards and sold. Nowadays *rogue's yarns* are used to identify the different types of man-made fibre ropes, all of which are designed for a specific purpose.

roll on death, let's have a go at the angels Often said during a period of hard slogging of some kind Also heard as: *'roll on death, let's have a long stand easy..'*

rollicking Polite version of bollocking.

rolls on wet grass Description of a ship with poor *sea-kindliness. Another version is *rolls on wet blotting paper*.

ROMFT! *Roll On My (Flipping) Twelve!* Expression used by someone who is on *RDP and impatient to get *outside after the twelve year engagement of old; for *Twelve* in the modern era, now read *Time!*

rompers Underpants, or *keks.

roof (SM) The surface of the sea.

roof rats Those personnel working up on an aircraft carrier's flight deck, and especially the *chain gang.

root'n'toot! Expression of disbelief; see also *Boogaloo! Could also be dscribed as: *'Well I never..'*

Rose Cottage Euphemism for a venereal diseases clinic, possibly because of the rose-pink lesions of syphilis - now very rarely seen. Another explanation may lie in the special messdeck set aside for CDA men in the old Navy - those who were subject to the Contagious Diseases Act, and had their own *heads and tableware which were over-painted with roses. And as if that wasn't bad enough, the inhabitants of *Rose Cottage* also had their *tots stopped.

roster   Duty list; also the waiting list for advancement that kept by *Drafty; a *dry roster* is one with no names on it, so promotion or advancement is automatic when the necessary qualifications have been obtained, in contrast to a *wet roster* which may be very wet indeed.

Rosy Dawn   Potent hangover cure served up in a number of variations, depending on the skill and experience of a warship's *Doc. The ingredients can vary, but are usually based on a red-coloured proprietary tonic, which is mixed with aspirin and Alka-Seltzer, and then served freshly fizzing. Note also the *prairie oyster* - the raw yolk of an egg dropped in a small glass of brandy and covered with Worcester sauce. See Tugg at W - 506.

Rotate! (FAA)   Expression of exasperation: *'So now the Admiral wants us to *scrub round that new procedure and carry on doing it the old way ? Well, bloody ro-tate!'*

rotten   Infected with venereal disease: *'Book me into Rose Cottage, 'swain, I'm rotten again..'*

rough as old boots   *'I'm not feeling very well..'*

roughers   Rough seas: *'I enjoy a spot of roughers - no queues in the *galley for a fried breakfast..'*

roughy-toughy   Frequent descriptive term for Royal, or anything to do with the Corps, derived from Winston Churchill's famous observation: *'The Royal Marines have a rough, tough and glorious history..'*

round the buoy   A second time or second helping.

roundly   Naval word for *quickly*; the opposite to *handsomely*. Often applied when hoisting and lowering boats.

round-down   The rounded after end of a fixed-wing carrier's flightdeck, installed to try and minimise the effect of a *ramp-strike. Since the three present RN carriers only operate the *SHAR, then like the carriers of old, they do not have *round-downs.*

round turn   A hawser being paid out was always held with a *round turn* around a bollard, which could be brought up *all standing by leaning back on the inboard end. So: *'The Argie Navy was brought up with a round turn when we sank the BELGRANO..'*

Rounds Formal tour of inspection through some designated area of a warship or establishment. These may be *Captain's Rounds* or *XO's Rounds,* or simply called *Evening Rounds.*

Royal / royal *Royal* is the traditional shortened form of address for a Royal Marine, and also the generic term for the Corps. There is no specific linkage to the second usage which is as an adjective used occasionally as an order of magnitude: *'He's a royal pain in the arse..'*

Royal Naval Air Service This organization, the forerunner of today's Fleet Air Arm, was founded in 1912 as an unofficial naval air branch of the Royal Flying Corps . Although it developed independently, the RNAS was often in conflict with the RFC, and to resolve these problems the Smuts Committee recommended their amalgamation to form the Royal Air Force, which came into being on April 1st 1918. On the last day of its existence the RNAS had 103 airships, 2,949 aircraft and over 67,000 officers and men!

Royal Navy School of Dancing The Harbour Lights discotheque in *Torpoint, where the young *nozzers from *RALEIGH stand and watch the girls dancing together, around a pile of handbags in the middle of the floor. Also a nightclub in Union Street, Plymouth in the 60's where the seating was all second hand cinema seats and the Ladies came there more for business than pleasure. Another post-war locale with this name was the Paramount, Devonport - obviously the School of Dancing can vary from the popularity of the watering hole at the time.

RPC Abbreviation that has now become a word in its own right - *Request the Pleasure of your Company.* Using the shorthand of signalese, you might hear this instructionreferring to port visit: *'We'll RPC the heavies and CTP the locals..'*

RT *Radio-telephony* - voice transmission, as opposed to the * WT of wireless telegraphy and Morse.

rub / rubber Three usages:
1. A loan of money: *'Anyone give me the rub of a tenner?'*
2. *rub up* - refresher course.
3. *rub of the green* Naval slang expression for an unfortunate mishap. See also *green rub.

Rubber Older nickname for a Physical Training Instructor - or an *India-rubber* man

rubber dicked (esp. RM) Unfairly beaten; see also *dicked.

Glory Hole

rubber Henry   Another version of the above. When you are heavily defeated in some contest, someone will probably have hit you with a *big rubber Henry*.

rubber hubby   Jack's nickname for a vibrator.

rug rat   A small child; see also *ankle biter and *carpet crawler.

rule of the road   A parody rhyme goes: *'In danger with no room to turn, to hell with the ship and have a burn..'*

rum and sand   The legendary cure for *crabs, or pubic lice. The theory was that if you applied such a mixture to your affected *parts, they got drunk on the rum and then threw rocks at each other!

rum baron   Similar meaning to *beer baron, ie. someone who stored the stuff illegally, and wielded power and influence on the *lower deck as a result, particularly among the *rum rats who would do almost anything for an extra *tot.

rum bosun   The man who draws the spirit ration for his own *mess in a rum *fanny at the tub, takes the *two and one *grog, tries not to get it *gofferred, and then dishes it out to his mess-mates, usually ensuring that something extra is left as *plushers.

rum bum and 'baccy   Summary of Jack's supposed social interests in the old Navy.

rumbled   Found out.

Rumour Control   Legendary source of good *buzzes: *'I'm not sure what my next appointment's going to be, but Rumour Control says it's something to do with *number-crunching up in the *Madhouse..'*

run / run in   To *run someone* or *run him in* is the same as putting him in the *rattle, ie. placing that person on a formal charge of disobeying or breaking some section of the Naval Discipline Act. Can also be used in the sense of trying something out, as in: *'Run this up the flagpole and see who salutes it..'* Or: *'Run this past the Boss and see if he's happy with it..'*

run-ashore   A social visit, with various shipmates, to a series of pubs or clubs; those who are your regular companions in these endeavours become your *run-ashore oppos*.

runner   To *do a runner* is to desert or go AWOL (Absent Without Leave). After 30 days absence, the Service Certificate is marked R for *Run*. Note also that a *runner* was also a WW2 term for an exercise torpedo that had no warhead, and in sailing warship days it was part of a ship's rigging. Also used now to signify an assistant, in the sense of *doggie.

rupert   Generic term for an Army officer, but especially one who is from a Cavalry outfit.

rush of shit to the head   This is a sudden brainwave, usually suffered by officers.

Rusty   Occasional nickname for the surname Steele, or someone with red hair.

rusty bullet-hole   The anus.

SIERRA

375 - 440

S.206   See *C.206.

sack rat   Another pithy label applicable to an individual who is addicted to his *pit. See *canvas back for a complete listing.

sad case   A label that was applied to a sailor with a physique so weak, and a countenance so pallid and pimply, and hair so lank and filthy, that it was obvious his only leisure or recreational activity, was *bashing his bishop - in the sure knowledge that if blindness ensued, he could go and sell matches.

sad on   A bad mood, usually caused by a subordinate's failure in some task: *'The first time that happened, the *Boss got a *right sad on that lasted for the rest of the week..'*

Safeguard   Code word used to prefix a message about casualties during an exercise, to indicate that they are genuine and not simulated.

sailing orders   An enhanced state of preparation for sea; when a ship is *under sailing orders*, shore leave becomes somewhat restricted and the penalties for breaking that leave then become much more serious.

sailmaker's suit   A made-to-measure set of *number threes, tailored by a sailmaker using a length of *Pussers's blue serge from *slops, and paid for with a couple of tins of *ticklers.

sailor's sarnie   Jack in horizontal mode with *two* lady friends.

Sails   Nickname for *sailmakers* who were members of a specialisation carried in bigger ships until after WW2. They worked on all canvas gear and usually ran a *jewing firm.

salad gear   Traditional collective description of the *bunny grub, celery and tomatoes etc. that go to make up a salad.

salami slicing   The terrible process in defence budgeting when politicians cannot quite make their minds up about what to cut out of the future acquisitions and procurement programme, so they take a (*salami*) *slice* off nearly *everything* instead.

sale before the mast   Older term for a *kit auction.

salt dog   Corned beef.

Saltash luck   Old maritime expression meaning no success at all. It is said to be derived from the many anglers who sat by the ferry at Saltash for hours, and caught nothing but colds.

salthorse   A naval officer who, formerly, remained a seaman throughout his career and did not sub-specialize in aviation, submarines, mine warfare, navigation, aircraft direction or any of the other black arts denoted by a special symbol in the *Navy List. A *salthorse* frequently took his command exams early, then got command of small ships (up to destroyer size in those days), but was unlikely to reach the highest echelons. Nowadays the term is still used (just) to refer to a Seaman (X) officer who has decided to relinquish his sub-specialisation and is available for more general appointments. The term is derived from *salt horse*, the old brine-pickling method of preserving meat at sea.

sammich (SM)   What a submariner calls his lunch.

sandpaper the anchor   Do something useless.

sandscratchers   The name given, rather unkindly, by communications branch people and stokers to the seaman branch. It was derived from the practice of cleaning wooden decks with sand or *holy stones. *Fishhead, and upper deck ape were alternatives.

Sandy bottoms! Rare privilege, (or the settlement of a *very* considerable debt) involving the *tot; this is a specific invitation to *see off the contents of a glass or mug, ie. to drink until the *sandy bottom* is showing.

sangar (RM) Defensive position constructed with stones, rocks and sandbags: *'I was only away three days, but by the time I got back to my desk, the In-tray had become a ruddy sangar..'*

santan man (RM) A marine trained in field hygiene duties, or a *civvy tasked with emptying chemical toilets. The latter may also be responsible for operating the *honey monster.

SAR Well-established acronym for *Search and Rescue*; this can be part of the national service to which the Fleet Air Arm contributes at a number of locations around Britain's coastline (along with the RAF and certain civilian contractors) - or out at sea. While *SAR Flight* helicopters are specifically dedicated for this job, *SAR* itself remains an occasional (and welcome) challenge for all rotary-wing aircrew.

sardine's revenge A submarine, so called because its occupants are also crushed together in a tin can and covered in oil.

sarnie A sandwich, probably Liverpool in origin. A *knuckle sarnie* is a punch to the face, and note also *sailor's sarnie. You also *salt and pepper sarnies*, but jam was always a jam *wedge as in that well known Chinese chef Wun Jam Wedge (and his brother, the famous gymnast Wun Jim Shoo).

sash for a gash A sanitary napkin.

Saturday night at sea Traditionally relaxed mood and routine in RN *Wardrooms afloat; the junior officer present proposes the *Toast to *Sweethearts and Wives*.

Sawbones The process of limb amputation in the old Navy, now preserved as a nickname for the Principal Medical Officer.

scab-lifter Perjorative label for any member of the RN Medical Branch, but also a description especially reserved for the warship's *Doc: *'Our scab-lifter is an excellent *hand - spent the first six years of his career with the *Booties, and knows more about fieldcraft than most of the ship's *Detachment..'*

Scale See *mulct. When awarding this punishment, *Scale!* was the only word that the *Captain needed to utter.

scandalised The opposite of squared off, originally referring to the yards of a mast, hanging askew.

Scapathy State of complete apathy induced by being stuck at anchor up in Scapa Flow, the Orkney Islands.

scatters A dose of diarrhoea; see *squitters for the main listing.

scend A pair here:
1. Quick vertical rise of a ship's bow out of a trough between two waves, as opposed to its *pitching down. Seldom used in this sense nowadays - the longitudinal rise and fall of a ship in a seaway is just called *pitching (as opposed to the latitudinal movement which called *rolling). See also *slamming and *corkscrewing.
2. The effect of the sea (affected by tide, current, wind and particularly swell) on a vessel in a confined space and especially when berthed alongside. In some harbours the *scend* can be sufficient to part berthing lines unless precautions are taken; also known as *surge. This can occur without there being any noticeable movement of water, yet all the ships are surging at their berths.

scheme of complement The document produced by the MoD manning departments which lays down the number of people by rank, rate, and specialisation required to man a ship in a variety of roles. It is derived from the *Quarterbill, but includes margins for training and *communal duties, etc., and is used by ships' staffs to produce the *Watch & Station Bill.

School of Dancing   See *grab-a-granny night or *widow's hop, as well as the * Royal Navy School of Dancing.

schoolie   Abbreviation for *schoolmaster* and thus the commonest nickname for an *Instructor Officer (now demised); also known as a *chalk bosun or *decimal bosun.

schooner on the rocks   See *straight rush.

scooby-dooby / scooby-doo   Jack's name for a civilian sport (SCUBA) diver.

scope   The length of chain *paid out to allow a ship to swing safely to her single anchor. This has given rise to the shoreside expression *plenty of scope*.

scotchman   Older term for any piece of wood, metal, leather or canvas used as local protection against chafe or wear, such as the metal plate found at the head and foot of a *companionway to protect the decking.

Scottish Navy   Generic name for ships and people based in Rosyth (formerly) and Faslane. (SM - currently).

Scouse / Scouser   Another interesting pair:
1. Any Liverpudlian (native of Liverpool) - derived from the word *lobscouse.
2. Frequent nickname for the Chinese *dhobeyman employed in HM Ships - because, like his Merseyside counterpart, it's often quite difficult to understand exactly what he's saying.

scram (SM)   Emergency shut-down of a nuclear reactor.

scrambled egg   The gold wire braid on the peak of a senior officer's cap.

scran   Food: *'I'm off down the *galley for scran - you coming?'*

scran bag   Any personal possession found *sculling around the ship is placed in a *scran bag*, to be redeemed only on payment of a small fine, with overall proceeds to the ship's Welfare Fund. In older times the fee for *redemption was a square inch of *pusser's hard (soap) per item. The term can also be used to describe an untidy or scruffy person.

Scratch   Traditional nickname for the Captain's *Secretary, and also an Admiral's (more senior) secretary as well.

scratcher   Two variants, depending whether you are above or below the surface:

Goffered

1. A bed; see also *pit, *rack, *sack and *green slug for variants. 2. (SM) The *Coxn's mate. Submarine equivalent to a *skimmers *buffer, and the second Coxswain in a submarine. Always a man from the Seaman persuasion, and not to be confused with the TI - the PO in charge of the torpedoes (Torpedo Instructor). The *scratcher* is the senior rate found on the casing of submarines entering and leaving harbour; he is the man who deals with the seamanship side of life. In turn, his assistant is the *scratcher's dicky*, or *second scratch*.

screamers / screaming abdabs Great irritation. eg: '*He really gives me the screamers / screaming abdabs..*'

screaming skull Label applied to a senior officer who is thin, gaunt and generally rather humourless.

screech An alcoholic concoction, which in Malta was a mix of Coca-cola and an indigenous wine. The wine was not worth drinking alone, but the mixture itself should also have been left alone as well! See also *messdeck champagne.

screen The external *bulkheads of the superstructure of a warship; hence *screen doors*, which give access to the inside of the ship.

screwdriver (RM or stoker's) A hammer.

Scribbles Slang name for a Writer rating.

Scribes More of a standard nickname (see entry above) for a rating of the Writer specialization. Note also *cross-dressing.

scrimshanker Older term for a workshy individual.

scrimshaw Carving or other craft hobby carried out by sailors.

scronk / scronky Untidy and generally grubby individual whose appearance may be described by the adjective *scronky*.

scrote Marvellous term of abuse which rolls well off the tongue, particularly when it is combined with a descriptive qualification such as *born-again*.

scrotum pole An erect penis.

scrub aft An expletive used as in: '*Cor, scrub aft!*', when amazed at something. From an order given when the pre-breakfast scrubbing of all decks was to be carried out: '*Scrub aft, then turn about and scrub for'ard..*'

scrubber   A useful word with a number of meanings depending on the context of its employment:
1. A slightly rough lady - *'A nice little scrubber you was with last night..'* or: *'She's a bit of an old scrubber, but she likes me..'*
2. Do something useful. *'Right, drop that and grab a scrubber..'* is an order to stop loafing around and start working.
3. *'Scrub out for rounds!'* is an order to get things ready for a formal inspection.
4. *wet as a scrubber* is a disparaging remark about a person, with *wet* meaning soft or weak here, or lacking in robustness.
5. *scrubbing a hammock* - sarcasstic response to the query: *'What are you doing?'* when the answer to that question is perfectly obvious.

scrub round   Cancellation of some previous arrangement due to sudden change in needs or circumstances: *'*Culdrose is *clamped, so we'll have to scrub round the planning for that trip..'*

scruff rig / scruffers   Clothing suitable for the garden or building site, or any so-called fashionable style that, at great expense, achieves the same untidy effect. See also further comments under *rig.

scrumpy royal   Triple vintage cider, only drunk on paydays. Incidentally, *bootnecks were never thought to be man enough to drink rough cider, probably they had more sense in the late fifties. They drank *Tutti-frutti* instead (half of rough, half of sweet, top off with blackcurrant). Those who drank *Tutti-frutti* were referred to as *Tutti-frutti soldiers*. A good night on the *apples, and it was said you could *dump through the eye of a needle without touching the sides.

scull   A single oar, or to propel a rowing boat by means of a scull in a notch in the transom. See also *yuloh.

sculling about / around   Something that is lying or rolling about on the *deck: *'Get your kit stowed as soon as you can, lads - and don't leave anything sculling about, or it'll end up in the *scran bag..'* A very old term as used in original context ie. a man ashore alone, but not far away: *'Has Pincher gone up to the *Smoke?'* *'No, he was sculling about the boozers along the High Street when I last saw him..'* Derived from travelling singly in a rowing boat, moving from ship to ship by means of *sculling*, in the days when it was a skill commonly practised by all seafarers in small boats.

scum bag A more general term of abuse, but the phrase also implies a particular dislike of the person concerned.

scuttle A trio:
1. The RN equivalent of a circular window. A *scuttle run* is a dangerous expedition that passes along the outside of a ship using a *scuttle* for both exit and re-entry.
2. Sink a ship by opening her hull to the sea, letting water in and *scuttling her*.   3
Break open a barrel by *scuttling it*, as in a **scuttle(d) butt*.

scuttlebutt Gossip; the original *scuttlebutt* was an open (*scuttled*) fresh-water cask (or *butt*) located 'tween decks, from which issues were made to the messdecks. It served as a focal point for the exchange of rumours, *buzzes or other daily information. The term is particularly used across the *Pond.

SD List Abbreviation for *Special Duties List*, officers commissioned from the *lower deck somewhat later in their careers than the *Upper Yardsmen. This group has now transmuted into the *SUY (*Special Upper Yardsmen*).

sea boat Two distinct usages:
1. Term used when referring to a vessel's handling qualities: '*She may not be very pretty, but she's an excellent deep sea boat..*'
2. Small ship's boat kept at readiness for any emergency and which can be lowered quickly while its parent ship is still under way, eg. to rescue a survivor. A crew for the *sea boat* is *detailed off at all times when at sea, from the watch on deck, but in an emergency the nearest trained personnel will *man it. See also *away. In such a life-saving crisis, the sea boat becomes a *lifeboat* in the pipe: '*Away lifeboat!*'

sea daddy A well-respected older rating or officer, sometimes self-appointed to educate younger men in the ways of the world - and the Navy. Up until recent times this term had no other connotation, but it has now become confused with *sugar daddy*. See *Bugis Street for an example of its correct application. A *Sea Daddy* scheme has also now been started to improve officer recruitment, whereby boys still at school can write to, and then visit RN officers who were at that school themselves. The idea is still in its infancy but appears to be working well. By contrast, a *Sea Dads* programme makes arrangements for the sons and daughters of personnel serving in a warship to take their offspring to sea for the day, or even for the night, during a transit between ports.

sea food!   Expression of anticipation that went up when a uniformed sailor entered a gay bar.

sea dust   Salt.

Sea Jet (FAA)   Nickname for the *SHAR.

sea kindly   A ship which moves and handles well in a seaway.

Sea King   Long-serving and versatile twin-engined helicopter built by Westlands to an original (American) Sikorsky design. This all-weather aircraft serves the Fleet Air Arm in Anti-Submarine (HAS), Commando (HC), Airborne Early Warning (AEW) and *SAR (HAR) variants, all subject to occasional upgrading and changes of Mark number. It is being replaced in service by the EH.101 *Merlin.

sea lawyer   Jack's (older) nickname for a shark. All lawyers are sharks; sharks live in the sea, therefore all sharks are *sea lawyers*! Also an alternative term for a *messdeck lawyer.

sea legs   Ability to walk in a straight line on a leaning deck.

Sea Lords   Before 1964, the Admiralty was a separate Ministry, presided over by civil lords and sea lords; the *First Lord* was a cabinet minister (HMS Pinafore provides a wry description of Sir Joseph Porter's attributes for the job) whereas the *First Sea Lord* was the professional head of the Navy. Collectively, the civil and sea lords were known as the *Lords Commissioners of the Admiralty* and responsible for executing the office of the *Lord High Admiral. The *Sea Lords* were: First, Second (personnel), Third (Controller of the Navy), Fourth (Supply and Logistics) and Fifth (Aviation). In 1964, the Admiralty was subsumed into the Ministry of Defence, the title of First Lord was abolished and that of *Lord High Admiral reverted to the Sovereign. The only Sea Lords to survive in name were First and Second (*1SL* and *2SL*). More recently, *2SL* has combined his functions with those required of Commander-in-Chief Naval Home Command (CinCNavHome).

sea mile (more commonly called a *nautical mile*)   A standard measurement of distance at sea; it is the distance on the earth's surface subtended by one minute of latitiude. Because the earth is not a perfect sphere, this distance varies depending on latitude, but is generally taken to be a shade over 2000 yards. See also *knot.

Sea Queen (FAA)   Nickname for the Royal Air Force's *SAR version of the *Sea King - a machine of really enviable performance and function, except that it has no weapon systems.

sea rider   Member of a sea-going *Flag Officer's staff, and most notoriously those belonging to *FOST (Flag Officer Sea Training) when on temporary detachment to ships undergoing sea training for instruction and assessment purposes. To distinguish themselves from the *ship's company, they wear olive drab *foulies (instead of blue) and are hence also known as *green slime. See also *wreckers.

sea room   Manoeuvering space when handling a ship in a seaway. Note also Friday's *Wardroom *Toast to: '..a willing foe - and sea room..'

sea sick   'He used to start spewing as they flooded the dry dock..'

sea squire   A Warrant Officer of the Royal Navy.

sea story   An exaggerated tale containing variable amounts of the truth.

sea time   Some amusing statements averring to experience in the *Andrew: *'I've spent more time on one wave than you've spent at sea..'* or: *'I've steamed more sea miles than you've had pusser's peas..'*

sea training   Refer to *Work-up.

Sea Vixen   The third and last of a distinguished line of twin-boom jet fighters built for the FAA by deHaviland, the first being the *Sea Vampire* and the second the *Sea Venom*.   The *Sea Vixen* was a twin-engined all-weather fighter which was trans-sonic in a shallow dive, and served the Fleet Air Arm well during the 60's, before being replaced by the *Toom. A *Sea Vixen* *looker sat in the darkened *coal hole inside the fuselage, offset below and to the right of his *pirate.

seagulls (RM)   A group of (Army) Guards / Cavalry officers' wives talking amongst themselves - so named because of the rather high-pitched and screeching collective sound that emerges, in marked contrast to the lower-pitched *wah-wah noise made by their spouses.

seaman (warship)   Generic term to describe a person responsible for the skiled operation of equipment on the *upper deck, the external appearance of a ship, the handling of ropes, wires, hawsers, etc. and, formerly, the operation of a ship's weapon systems. Originally, seamen formed the overwhelming majority of people on board, but nowadays expertise in seamanship is vested in a very small sub-branch, represented in ships by the *buffer and one or two assistants.

seamanlike   Any action or procedure carried out in a neat, yet functional and practical manner. The phrase *seamanlike precaution* is in particular use for any aspect of sensible planning that takes account of possible delay, disaster or damage, such as visiting the *heads before going into a formal dinner.

seaman's eye   Quality of judgement and perception possessed by an experienced *hand when gauging the effects of wind and tide on a ship's movement relative to something else.

seamshifter   A *pussers issue condom. No-one seems to know why!

Second   The *Second* was the *Second in Charge* of a ship's engineering department. The title is still used in the RFA to denote the Chief Officer (E) who fills the post. Just because everybody refers to him as *Second* that does not mean that he is a *Second Officer*! Similar confusion was caused by the fact that Second Officers (E) are known as *Third* due to their previous rank of Third Engineer and that Third Officers (E) are known as *Fourth* for a similar reason.

second dickey The assistant/standby diver during diving training. An important and feared position, as all *bubbleheads can verify.

second thing I'll do when I get home (RM) Lovely phrase, much-heard at the end of an exercise or deployment, indicating a certain base enthusiasm to see one's missus or *pash:'..*and the second thing that I'll do when I get home is - take my pack off!'*

secret squirrel (RM) Anyone employed in an Intelligence role; see also *sneaky beaky.

secretary An officer of the Supply & Secretariat branch, borne in ships commanded by a *captain, and also allocated to all senior appointments ashore, and occasionally afloat - the keeper of his or her master's secrets and therefore someone well worth knowing. Note also the nickname *Scratch.

secure A quartet here:
1. Finish work, or more properly tidy everything away before finishing work:'*Secure is at 1645, and not a minute earlier..*'
2. Cease an *evolution, or change from one work state to another, as in the *pipe:'*Secure from *flying stations!'*
3. '*Secure for sea / action!*' The order given to make sure that all equipment, etc. is either stowed securely, or otherwise *made secure* in readiness.
4. The process of *making fast to something; any potentially floating objects are *secured* when not in the water, whereas shoelaces are tied up! Aircraft however are *tied down.

see Also a quartet:
1. *see over the brow* - welcome arriving guests, or take leave of those who are departing.
2. *seen off* - complaint made when someone has got the better of you, or some injustice has befallen you.
3. *see it off!* - invitation to finish a drink, especially one that has been bought by someone else; of particular relevance to the old *tot, when to be invited to *see off someone else's tot* was the ultimate act of generosity, or else the settlement of a really huge debt.

Greenie

4. *seeing-to* - vigorous sexual activity: *'What that woman needs is an occasional good seeing-to..'*

seggies   Tinned *grapefruit segments*, the standard submarine Sunday breakfast starter.

selected   For promotion: *'Bill was selected for his *brass hat in the June *List..'*

self-adjusting cock-up (RM)   The best-laid plans of mice and men are always going wrong, but especially so when the military become involved. Good plans should always allow for an element of luck in their execution; sometimes the development of a new problem suddenly provides the solution for another pre-existing difficulty. In this way the original error or divergence from the plan becomes a *self-adjusting cock-up*.

send a sausage to the seaside   Officers' version of a *dump.

Senior / senior   Yet another interesting quartet:
1. *Senior engineer* - official title of the *deputy* marine engineering officer in a big ship, and usually abbreviated to *Senior*; it derives from the days when the *first lieutenant was also referred to as *The Senior* (ie. the senior lieutenant). The term *Senior engineer* is only used when he or she has subordinate officers in the department. In smaller ships the rather unromantic term DMEO is used instead.
2. (RM) A *Senior NCO*. The Command course at *Lympstone which all Sergeants must pass before being promoted to that rank is also known throughout the Corps as *The Seniors*.
3. Degree of severity or size: *'Quite honestly, what we're dealing with here is an error of fairly senior proportions..'*
4. *Senior Coward* (RM) Unfair, but still-awarded label for the most senior member of the Corps who is without any campaign medal ribbons on his uniform.

Sergeant-Major (RM)   The senior NCO of a ship's *detachment, irrespective of his actual rank.

Sergeants   Nickname in a ship for those of Commander's rank, because they also have three stripes on their sleeves: *'How many Sergeants are coming to the Wardroom party tonight?'*

sesh (esp. RM)   Heavy beer drinking *session*.

set   A *full set of facial whiskers, ie. beard and moustache. Permission must be sought to cease shaving in order to *grow a set*, and if this looks uneven or stunted after two weeks, the rating may be ordered to *shave off. See also Tugg at @@@@.

set of papers   Jack's *Divisional documents or *comic cuts; a really good rating who is doing well will have an *immaculate set of papers.

set up the backstays   Conceal or make good an *oppo's mistake in order to prevent disciplinary action being taken against him. In contrast, a fair-weather friend is an unreliable, *shifting backstay.

set watch   Listen out on a particular frequency.

seven bells   A total of eight bells are struck to end a *watch; to knock seven bells out of someone implies some pretty severe handling - without actually finishing him off. A seven beller can also be also a really welcome cup of tea taken just before the end of a *watch. Can also describe shore leave that ends at seven bells of the forenoon watch on the following day, ie. from Saturday afternoon, all duties completed, to 11.30 am. Sunday, allowing a run ashore and a lie in.

seven bells of shit   To use excessive force. When something is stuck, Jack will hit seven bells of shit out of it in order to free it up!

seven navies   Figure of speech used as a means of comparison: 'That man is the biggest *skate in seven navies..'

seven seas creases   Creases ironed into the bellbottom trousers of a set of *number ones (turned inside-out and folded concertina-wise seven times). The original rationale was reputed to be that one crease was added for each one of the seven seas that the wearer had sailed upon, so that someone with seven was unusually old and wise. Needless to say, those who affected these adornments were neither old nor wise, and since the effect was distinctly unsmart unless the wearer was particularly tall, the practice was not widespread.

sew-sew   A Hong Kong Chinese tailor carried on board; see also *jewing firm.

shack (SM)   This was your cabin ashore, say in *Dolphin or Faslane.

shacked up with   Living with someone who is a shackeroo or shackerelle depending on their gender.

Shady   Traditional nickname for someone with the surname Lane.

shafted   Slightly more polite version of *screwed* when describing someone who has been *royally *seen off.

Shagbat (FAA)   Lovely nickname for the old and much-loved Walrus aircraft, which was amphibian and also known as a *pusser's duck.

shagged-out   Very tired indeed, derived from the transitive word *shag* - which has connotations of vigorous sexual activity. Note that American usage, up until the recent release of the Austin Powers film *The Spy Who Shagged Me* (!) uses the same word to describe the pile of a carpet, or a high handicap perambulation around a golf course.

shag-nasty   A descriptive term of abuse that contains an element of affection.

shake and pigmy   Steak and kidney pie.

shake a wicked hoof   An older term - to dance.

shake down   Traditionally, a short cruise undertaken immediately after refit, to ensure everything is bedded down and working correctly. Note also *DASO.

shake / Shakes   To *shake someone* is to wake him or her up; *Shakes* is the polite nickname for the person in charge of the *shakes list*, a book containing the name, mess number, bunk-space and time requested. This book has to be signed by whoever is being shaken, to forestall any arguments later on.

shake hands with my best friend   Urinate.

shake out   Wake up from sleep.

shambolic   Nice term that combines the words *shambles* and *diabolical* rather cleverly to describe either a scene of organized chaos, or some event that has gone badly wrong. Can also be described as a *shambollocks* if a noun is needed.

shamfered   Older term for a ship damaged in action, now used to describe the process of tidying up a messdeck for *Rounds, or getting ready to go ashore. The expression *shamfer up!* is an exhortation to do better. The term is derived from shipwright's jargon. When lengths of wood have to be scarf-jointed, or scarfed, they have a *shamfer cut* to fit perfectly. It is exact work usually done with an adze, hence the present-day use to mean something neat and precise. Comes from old French word *chamfraine* hence the soft pronunciation of the *ch*, unlike the word *chamber*.

shammy leather!   Spoken with a heavy French accent, and accompanied by a pronounced Gallic shrug, means: *'That's life..'*

SHAR (FAA)   Standard acronym for the versatile and highly effective *Sea Harrier* (jump-jet) fighter currently serving at sea with the Fleet Air Arm: *'For air combat in the Falklands, the final scoreline was SHARs 27, Mirages and Skyhawks nil..'* Also referred to as a *Sea Jet, and note *ski-jump and *Yeovilton.

Shareholders (FAA)   Briefing and planning meeting held in a squadron which all *shareholders* - squadron personnel - are supposed to attend.

sharp end   The bow of a warship (as opposed to the *blunt end!) but also used to describe the *front line, ie. the place where all the action is.

sharpener   An alcoholic drink taken on a cold morning in order to **sharpen** one's wits.

shave off   A trio:
1. The process of removing a *full set.
2. *Shave off!* is a frequent cry of disgust, disbelief or frustration expressed in response to some unexpected event or a setback.
3. Rant and rave: *'Fer Gawd's sake don't tell him that - 'ave you ever 'eard him shavin' off about them pop singers?'*

shebang (FAA)   An incident that involves explosive activity or wartime action: *'Then the whole shebang mushroomed into a ball of flame..'*

shed a tear for Nelson   Yet another delicate euphemism for *syphoning the python. - a *wardroom version of *going for a pee.*

sheds / shedloads   *'There are lots of these..'*

shellback   A sailor who has been at sea so long that limpet shells and barnacles are encrusting his back, like a ship's hull. The term appears to have been derogatory at first, but later took on an admiring tone similar to that of *Sea Daddy.

sherbert   Alcohol or beer: *'We *called round on Nobby for a few sherberts..'*

Sherwood Forest (SM)   The missile compartment of a *bomber; see also *rocket shop.

shift into   The process of changing clothes.

shifting backstay A supposed *oppo who, instead of supporting you through a crisis by *setting up the backstays, wavers weakly instead and therefore cannot be relied on in future.

shifting tack Alter one's thinking or opinion on some matter by adjusting the line of argument; see also *suck back ten.

shifting timber (SM) This was not necessarily cheating, as in *timbershifting, but just scoring or doing well. It was adapted for other uses, as when trying to move anything by pushing or pulling. After a few attempts - and you got it moving - you would say: *'That's it - now we're shifting timber..'*

Shiner Traditional nickname for someone called Wright or Light.

shiny burbs Oilskins; see also *burbs for a fuller explanation.

ship husbandry The business of maintaining, provisioning and generally looking after a warship in order to maintain her at a peak of efficiency; this process is still performed by the *ship's husband* or *boat swain* - hence *bo'sun.

Shipmate Honorary rank of all members of the splendid Royal Naval Association, which has branches all over the UK and Commonwealth.

shipped his *killicks Promoted to *Leading Hand, ie. a naval term for putting up the fouled anchor (*killick) badges on a uniform.

shipping hazard A floating turd so large that it should be rigged with navigation lights as a hazard to shipping.

shipping it green   Bad weather at sea, with mountainous waves passing unbroken along the ship's length.

ship's cat   Figurative lowest rank onboard, hence the expression: *'Even the ship's cat gets shore leave, but I don't..'* In the days when warships really did have cats to deal with rodents on board (perhaps the most famous being Simon of the AMETHYST) they would often have rank, and appear at the Captain's *Table for rating up from Able Mouser - to Leading Seacat!

ship's corporal (esp. RM)   Title now applied when the duties of *quartermaster are being carried out by a junior (Royal Marine) NCO of the ship's *Detachment.

ship's name   Is commonly used to refer to the Commanding Officer personally: *'I'll tell NONSUCH personally when I see him..'*

ships that pass in the night   A rather nice way to take your leave of someone without using the ordinary platitude of *see you again sometime*; Jack's alternative is: *'Ships that pass in the night will no doubt pass again..'* This is a more modern usage than the older meaning of ships passing in the night, their names not known - and more than likely *never* to meet again. So it is with certain ladies! Taken from Longfellow's Tales of a Wayside Inn:
> *Ships that pass in the night,*
> *and speak to each other in passing.*
> *Only a sign shown*
> *and a distant voice in the darkness..*

shipshape   Neat, tidy and generally seamanlike in functional appearance; the term has passed into general usage, occasionally in the more complete form based on the days when Bristol was the country's premier western coast port, and all the vessels operating from there were described as *all shipshape and Bristol fashion.*

shipside, gangplank, bag off   This was a polite way of saying a man was less than truthful when boasting of rapid sexual success having gone ashore.

shipwreck   Someone suffering the next morning from *CSB rash, or feeling rather *hen-pecked, may well be greeted by his *oppo with a hearty slap on the back and a loud cry of: *'Hello me old shipwreck - how's yer head?'*

shirtlifter   Yet another term for a *brownhatter (which see).

shit   Vulgar but common expletive employed by Jack in a number of specific ways:

> *the shits* - diarrhoea; also:'*He gives me the shits..*' as'*I don't like him very much..*'
> *shit bits* - haemorrhoids.
> *shit chute* - geographical feature of an *Uckers board.
> *shiters* - drunk.
> *shitting bricks / conkers* - externally visible, combined effects of adrenalin and fear.
> *Shitty Death!* - '*Gosh, how unpleasant!*'
> *shitfaced* - totally drunk.
> *shit-fer-brains* - a person who is not very bright.
> *shit hot* - brilliant.
> *shitkicker* - cowboy film.
> *Shitloads!* - '*There is a plentiful supply!*'
> *shit locker* - the rectum.
> *shit off a shovel* - to move quickly or easily.
> *shit or bust* - messdeck card game; or an expression of great determination in trying to do something.
> *shit on a raft* - devilled kidneys on toast.
> *shit on your *oppo* - really anti-social behaviour.

Note also the synonym of *shite* as a variant for most of the above.

shit deflectors   A verbal defence: '*After a cock up like that you'd better have your shit deflectors at the ready..*'

shit fish   All fish swimming in the *oggin, especially those near a warship, were rumoured to be *shitfish*.

shit hawks   Anyone who ate a lot, and also consumed leftovers from everyone else's plate or dish.

shit house flap valves (SM)   Hamburgers.

shit shot, hull valve shut (SM)   Report made to control room when the evolution of *pumping poo was complete.

shit-shower-shampoo-shave   Almost slurred into a single word, these four *S*'s are a neat summary of Jack's usual pre-*run ashore activities; to which could be added, *slide* ashore, for a *slurp* then a *shag*, and *slope* back on board again, thus describing the *eight S*'s of a really complete *run ashore, as an alternative to *beer, big eats, bag-off, - and back on board!

shit together / shit in one sock (get your)   Import of US origin describing the process of getting organised, getting your act together, or generally marshalling all your facts succinctly.

shitehawk   Even a quartet of applications for this:
1. A seagull, and (unless he is an ornithologist) Jack's name for any sea bird, but see *Mother Carey's chickens.
2. An enemy reconnaissance aircraft operating just out of gun or missile range.
3. General term of abuse.
4. The Senior *Rates' bar at *Culdrose is the *The Shy Talk Inn*.

shock   Older term for the process of cooking something; in the days of general *messing, a prepared dish of raw ingredients would be taken down to the *galley with the request to *give it a shock*.

shonk / Shonkey   Nose; someone with a significant nasal adornment to his *fizzog may well be nicknamed *Shonkey* - whatever his surname. It can also a label for someone who keeps poking his nose into your personal affairs.

shoot a line (esp. FAA)   Exaggerate or boast when recounting an incident involving yourself. To *shoot the breeze* with someone is to engage them in general conversation.

shoot through   Fail to keep an appointment or rendezvous. The phrase can also be used as an abusive noun: '*We were there at least ten minutes *previous, but Shiner didn't turn up - the useless ruddy shoot through..*' The original phrase was *to shoot through like a Bondi Tram*, derived from the FAA in WW2. R&R in Sydney involved going to Bondi Beach for the girls (and occasionally, surfing). The Bondi trams had a habit of not stopping - especially if they were full. So the expression came to be used as: *'I tried to trap the Jimmy when he came into the *Wardroom, but he shot through like a Bondi tram and I never had the chance to ask for that weekend off..'*

shop   Service or technical naval matters: *'Please don't talk shop in the *Wardroom..'*

Shore Patrol   A Special Duty *Watch policing the conduct of Jack while on *shore leave - and in some cases protecting him from assault or injury.

shore leave   Permission granted to leave the ship when alongside in harbour; Jack will then change or *clean into his *shore rig*.

short arm inspection (RM)   Medical Officer's examination of the *wedding tackle, usually undertaken in *Rose Cottage, but sometimes (unbelievably) on the quarterdeck as well. A small canvas screen was rigged, the MO and sundry other officers (probably along for the laugh) attended and the whole ship's company was summoned at *Clear Lower Deck! They mustered in the waist, forming a single file to approach the screen; as one pulled up his trousers, so the next stepped forward, dropped his own trousers, feet apart and arms raised. The annoying thing about it all were the *dockyard mateys on the jetty making cat-calls to Jack, who (of course) could not answer!

short arms, long pockets   Tight-fisted individual who is ungenerous with his hospitality, ie. unable to reach down far enough to find the money for a round of *wets.

short arse   Any person of slight stature, or suffering from *duck's disease.

short back and sides   A good telling off: *'The *Joss gave him a good short back and sides - but didn't put him in the *rattle..'*

short chacon (RM)   Nickname for Special Short Service Limited Commission (SSSLC) officer. These are young men of high calibre, likely to do well in civilian business, and specially selected at the Admiralty Interview Board. After a brief period of training, which includes getting a *green lid, they spend a year with the Corps, with the aim of giving them an insight into service life, and hopefully giving the Corps some significant friends in the public sector or industry in years to come.

short course   Any brief introduction to some complex subject, often used in a mocking sense: *'I don't know how he has the nerve to call himself a doctor - it's quite obvious that he's only done the *scab-lifter's short course..'* By contrast, see also *long course.

short fuse   A measure of someone's (usually a senior officer's) *short temper*. A person with a *short fuse* will also have a very much reduced *flash to bang time!

short haircut and over the wall   Alternative term for the process of being sent to *DQs: *'Stealing from the ship's Welfare Fund ? That's a short haircut and over the wall job, I reckon..'*

short rations   Reduced issues of any *stores item.

short think of home   Sleeping, see also *gonking.

short / long basket weaving course   An amusing way of implying that you are about to, or have just *cracked up, and you will be feeling better having attended this facility.

shot away   Drunk: *'By the time he'd had *sippers from about twenty people, the poor chap was completely shot away..'*

shot line   Rope or cable to which a bottom *sinker or *lazy shot is attached during diving operations.

Shotley orphan   A somewhat disparaging term used to indicate that a person entered the navy via HMS GANGES. The *Shotley shuffle* was an older term for *doubling, with the minimum of effort, while under punishment. *Shotley* was the famous Boys Training Establishment of HMS GANGES, near Ipswich, which closed down in June 1976.

Show a leg!   Traditional exhortation to wake up, derived from the old days of sail when women were allowed on board and to stay overnight while in harbour. The females could also linger an extra hour in their hammocks, providing they could prove their gender by showing a (hairless) leg to the *Bosun's Mates as the latter did their rounds of the gundecks.

show the flag   The diplomatic aspect of Jack's visits to foreign ports; by entertaining local VIPs and *CIPs and also allowing others to visit the ship, the image of Great Britain is enhanced.

shrapnel   An interesting, and related pair of usages:
1. Metallic fragments from a bursting bomb or shell, after General *Shrapnel* who invented this munition in 1806.
2. Any otherwise useless foreign coins (see *klebbies and *ick-

ies) that still remain in Jack's pockets as the ship sails from some foreign port. This original definition has now expanded in general usage and applies to almost any loose change; see also *washers. A *shrapnel bucket* is a receptacle placed at the *brow for Jack to empty his pockets into before sailing, with all the proceeds going to a local charity.

shreds / shreddies (esp. RM)   Underpants.

shtum   Keeping quiet; saying nothing.

shuddering shithouse (RM)   Generic nickname for any RAF Chinook heavy-lift helicopter, but especially the fantastic *Bravo November* of 1982 Falklands War fame.

shuff duff (SM)   Older term for an intelligence-gathering mast which was direction-finding at super-high frequencies, or SHF/DF. *Huff duff* similarly applied to high frequency (HF) electronic emissions.

shufti   Arab word used in the sense of taking a look; the fibre-optic and highly flexible endoscopes originally designed for medical use that are now used for looking inside jet engines are known as *shuftiscopes*.

shut   Term for shutting a valve as used in all submarines. The word *closed* is NEVER used as it can be confused with *blows*.

shut-down (FAA)   Stop the engine(s); this could be a *single engine shutdown* in a twin-engined aircraft, in order to save fuel while awaiting another task.

Sick Bay   The *compartment occupied by a warship's *Doc, or the generic name for a collection of medical buildings in a shore establishment. Note also the following specialist applications:
>*sickbay ranger* - hypochondriac, or malingerer.
>*sickbay shackle* - safety pin.
>*sickbay *Tiff* - Medical Assistant, or *Doc.

side (manning the)   It is customary for the Officer of the Watch to order *man the side* when receiving other very senior, or foreign officers on board. At this order, the *quartermaster, *corporal of the watch sideboys and *quarterdeck messengers fall in on the quarterdeck athwartships, at the top of the gangway, to receive the visiting officer. This custom originated in the days when ships were fitted with *sea gangways* which were used by junior officers and all ratings for entering and leaving the ship in harbour, and by everyone at sea. This gangway consisted of narrow wooden steps or rungs, permanently secured to the ship's side. Each alternate step was longer than the ones next to it. The members of the *side party* stood on these longer wooden slats and helped the visitor on his way inboard.

sidelight   The circular glass fitting of a *scuttle, for admitting natural light to a *compartment. This is usually a fixed structure in modern warships with efficient air-conditioning, but it may also be hinged when part of a *scuttle in older vessels. Always coverable with a *deadlight in order to *darken ship.

sidestepper   See *shirtlifter.

sideways transfer   A number of smaller *branches (such as *Reggies, *Clubswingers and more recently seamanship specialists) do not recruit at new entry level; selected volunteers are *sideways transferred*, usually at *leading rate.

siff on his donk (FAA)   Tactic employed in an *Uckers game played according to *Wafu rules; this particular move is designed to prevent the final home run of an opponent's counter.

sighter / sighting shot   First attempt to do something, so that corrections can then be made and the action repeated with a greater chance of success.

sign on   Extend one's service for a longer period: *'I've just signed on for pension..'*

Silent Service   Traditional nickname for the Royal Navy, resulting from the quiet and self-effacing modesty of the *Andrew - and the fact that they don't stamp around the parade ground when doing drill.

silent copy   Extra carbon- or photo-copy of some letter or document whose existence and destination are *not* recorded in the *Dist(ribution) Annex.

silent hours   The (night) period between *pipe down and *call the hands; during this time watch bells are not struck, and only emergency *pipes can be made.

silent routine (SM)   Submarine operating in a manner intended to create a minimum of noise; see also *sock-footed.

silk   The sailor's black silk 'kerchief worn round the throat, is *not* a sign of mourning for Lord Nelson. Originally, it was worn in action - either round the brow to prevent sweat running into the

Grog Rat

eyes, or as a general purpose sweat rag. Nowadays it is a traditional piece of uniform clothing. The *silk* was, until 1935, a piece of black silk 36" square, worn with the two diagonal opposite corners knotted together (the knot being worn at the back of the neck beneath the collar, and bight (known as a *duff bag*) being secured in the tape of the jumper, so that a drowning man's rescuer might have an efficient handgrip. This new pattern *silk* introduced in 1935 measures 50" x 12"; since 1942 it has been made of rayon. Uniform regulations require the ends of this scarf to be stitched together, thus forming a hoop, for the same reason as the old *square silk* was knotted into a loop.

simulated (FAA)   Sleeping on *top* of your bunk rather than being (actually) in it; see also *actual.

sin bosun   A vicar; see *amen wallah for the main listing.

Singapore ear   A fungal infection that gets into your ear when swimming in the sea around *Singers. *Singapore ear* is still the name for almost any kind of ear infection.

Singers   Singapore; until the late 1960s (and except for the 3 years of Japanese occupation), Singapore was a huge British Garrison, the RN/RM element of which was the naval base, dockyard, naval air station and RM camp occupying a vast area at Sembawang in the north of the island, a good 30 minutes' *fast black journey from *Bugis Street and other delights. British military withdrawal was complete by the early 1970s, but the RN retains a couple of berths in the old dockyard. *Singers rules* state that the last man out of the taxi pays for it.

singing from the same hymn sheet   Everyone in agreement about the line to take in a discussion at a meeting or presentation.

single digit salute   The equivalent of '*Up yours!*', expressed with a short upward movement of the closed fist and a fully extended middle finger. A frequent cause of road rage.

sinker   A nice trio:
1. Lead or iron weight on the end of a marker buoy or diving marker line.
2. Suet dumpling!
3. A target submarine's *snort mast or periscope disappearing off radar.

siphon the python   See *pump ship

sippers   Small mouthful of an *oppo's *tot taken in repayment of some favour or debt. Note also the *framework of hospitality, where two sippers equal one *gulpers.

sitrep   Abbreviation of *situation report*: '*Can anyone give me a sitrep on those casualties that we heard about at midday?*'

situate the appreciation   The opposite of what is taught at Staff College - the much easier, but less precise art of making the facts fit a desired conclusion.

six (FAA)   Shortened form of *six o'clock* in the clock code, or right behind you. Hence, the traditional fighter pilot's dictum: '*Watch your six!*' ie. remain alert at all times for someone coming up to attack you from *astern, and by extension, for someone ready to (figuratively) stab you in the back.

six-throwing sod   Difficult opponent to beat in an *Uckers game. Note also the *double six application.

sixteen bells   See *bells for this unique New Year's Eve usage, and *ring out the old, ring in the new.

sizes   Jack will have you believe that everything in the Royal Navy comes in just two sizes, too large and too small!

skate   Ne'er-do-well, workshy individual who appears unable to accept the normal self-disciplines of Jack's life; *scrote is a useful alternative. Interestingly, *skate* (as in fish) was the common nickname in old *Pompey or other towns for the non-commissioned ranks in bell bottoms, used by those *civvies who had no love for the navy.

'Skers / 'Skurrs   Abbreviation of *whiskers*; Jack's *ready-use nickname for any bearded rating or officer whose real name is not known at that exact moment.

ski-jump   Upwardly angled, forward deck ramp of the three RN carriers; this brilliant British innovation devised by Lt Cdr Doug Taylor RN (rtd) markedly improves the safety margins as well as the weapon and fuel loads of a *launching *SHAR.

skidmark   Something to be found in a pair of *keks that are need of *dhobeying.

skimmer (SM)   The *Trade's disparaging nickname for any surface vessel: '*All skimmers are just targets as far as I'm concerned..*'

skimming dish   Was a small high-speed planing motor boat carried by destroyers as a personal run-about for the Captain D or E. Sadly, the high-revving, low-geared engine was no match for jolly Jack coxswains, and they spent most of the time under repair by exasperated Engineering Officers.

skin   Young and unmarked, ie. in a virginal sense. Can be used either as adjective or noun: *'Leave him alone - the poor kid's just a bit of skin! Someone get him back to the ship..'* Also used with the word *essence for someone young and really lovely: *'She's all skin and essence, she is..'*

skinful   Of drink: *'Look after Nobby - he's had a real skinful..'*

skipper   Strictly speaking, only a yacht or a fishing boat has a *skipper*; in practice, the term is often used to describe the *captain of an HM ship, even though *father or *old man is more correct.

skirmishing   Two different, but in a way similar usages:
1. (RM) Controlled fire and movement of ground troops.
2. (RN) Cleaning up an area by picking up all litter and rubbish while *skirmishing through*. A *FOD-plod (FAA) is the ultimate and vitally important example of formal *skirmishing*.

skive   Avoidance of work or duty, hence *skiving, skiver, skive off* etc. Can also be used as a noun; hence *on the skive*, meaning to malinger, or to loaf.

skrinser (FAA)   All-purpose substitute word like *doobrey, *doofer or *johnson.

skulking   Hiding, or making oneself scarce in order to avoid work. Hence also *skulker*.

sky artist   Psychiatrist!

skylark   Light-hearted fun during off-duty time; see *hands to *dance and skylark*. The term is now also used to denote a prank. The word *lark* is a corruption of an Anglo-saxon word *lac*, meaning to play - in fact, in certain parts of Northern England a man who is out of work is still described as *laking* or *playing*. In the early days of the RN, the word *skylark* was used to describe races between young sailors who clambered up to the mast tops and then descended by sliding down the stays (the supports for the masts).

sky pilot   Another word for a vicar or padre: see *amen wallah for the full list.

skyscraper   Originally a small triangular sail, set seventh in ascending order from the deck, but used only in fine and steady light weather. The name has come ashore now, especially in America, to describe tall multi-storey buildings.

skywegian   Older term for anything of Scandinavian origin; see also *Noggie.

slab / slabstone   A particularly boring / unsociable person who somehow always made it to the bar when there was free beer.

slack   Not taut - lazy and indisciplined. Some special applications:
> *slack arse* - anatomical feature possessed by a *sleaze.
> *slack hammocks* - punishment for oversleeping.
> *slack in the programme* - adjustment for delay.
> *slack water* - period between high and low tide.

slag off   Say something unpleasant about somebody behind his or her back.

slammer   Prison, or *chokey, also an alternative name for *DQs.

slamming   The result of proceeding at speed head-on into a heavy sea. The fore part of the ship rises to one wave and either *pitches down into the trough, or onto the next wavetop with a disconcerting shudder. A particularly *heavy slam* is also called *hitting a *milestone*, possibly when meeting a mythical seventh wave.

slap a tingel on it   Strictly speaking, a *tingel* is a wooden tile. The *chippy would repair holes in wooden motor boats with a *tingel*, so any hole that was required to be blocked up had *a tingel slapped on it*. This became adapted in other usages, as when someone was bleeding badly: *'Hang on son, we'll soon fix that, I'll slap a tingel on it..'*

slap in   Make a written *Request by filling in a request chit: *'I'm going to slap in to see some bastard..'* is the classic usage, and the same as saying: *'I intend to make a full and formal complaint about this matter..'*

slap it abaht   During the evolution of *paint ship*, officious types could be heard telling the painting party to *slap it abaht*. Not very good advice for the literal minded!

slaphead   Someone who is follicularly challenged - ie. bald.

Sleaford Tech   Nickname for the RAF College, Cranwell.

sleaze   A *party who offers little or no resistance to *receiving swollen property on being *trapped. See also *sleaze.

sleeping on watch   Always a reprehensible habit; in the time of King Henry VIII there was an instruction: *'If a man within a ship had slept upon his watch four times and so proved, this shall be his punishment; the first time he shall be headed at the main mast with a bucket of water poured upon his head. The second time he shall be armed, with his hands held up by a rope and two buckets of water poured into his sleeves. The third time he shall be bound to the main mast with gun chambers tied to his arms and with as much pain to his body as the Captain will. The fourth time being taken asleep he shall be hanged to the bowsprit end of the ship in a basket with a can of beer, a loaf of bread and a sharp knife, and choose to hang there until he starve, or cut himself into the sea..'*

sleepy juice   Any strong drink or *vino collapso.

slide   Butter and/or margarine. See J.P.W. Mallalieu's book *Very Ordinary Seaman*.

sling yer hook!   A slightly less than polite invitation to go away and *sling* your hammock *clew *hooks* somewhere else. To *sling*, as in the sense of to *turn in, is the process of retiring for the night.

Slinger   Usual nickname for the surname Wood or Woods

slinger   A particular *yardie's skill and trade of moving a heavy item or load with *slinging* wires and a crane.

slingers and gyppo   Sausages and gravy.

slip   Five entries under this heading:
1. *slip right* - when the target time or completion date for a project is getting later and later; this process is called *slippage*.
2. *slip left* (FAA) - is what happens to the *flypro when a sortie is cancelled.
3. *slip and proceed* - leave a mooring or jetty by *slipping the ropes*, then head for sea and the next task.
4. *slips* (FAA) - are *slip *watches* which run from 2000 to 0800 the next day. The *first, *middle and *morning watches all *slip into each other* in this shore routine, which equates to being on nights in the *civvy sense.
5. *slip* - a shore facility where a ship can be *slipped*, by being pulled up a *slipway* on a cradle for examination and repair of hull, propulsion or steering gear.

SLJO   Frequently-heard acronym of complaint, or sympathy, for *Shitty Little Jobs Officer*.

slop chit   A list of responsibilities. Should someone or something be *on your slop chit* then he / she / it is down to you in all respects. The term originated from the clothing list (*chit*) which recorded Jack's issues from the *slops chest.

slop out   Wash a place through, with *slops of water* from a bucket. This term is still very much in use within HM Prisons, even in modern jails where each cell is equipped with *heads, rather than just a bucket.

slope   A trio here:
1. Leave a place furtively, by *sloping off*.
2. Pass a problem on by *sloping shoulders*; the phrase is generally used with a brushing motion of the hand. See also *Coke-bottle shoulders* as an anatomical feature of those unable to accept or carry any form of responsibility.
3. American import for *sloping eyes*, describing a person with an Oriental *fizzog; may also be heard as *slopehead*.

slops Uniform clothing available for purchase or exchange from the Cash Clothing Store (*slop room*). Derives from the old english *sloppe*, meaning breeches, and referring to the former sailors' baggy (petticoat) trousers. *Slops* were originally issued from the *slop chest*, and the purser was entitled to 1 shilling in the pound (5%) commission. See *KUA also.

sloshy A naval chef.

slot (FAA) *Stovie procedure for rejoining an airfield or carrier circuit to land.

slug (RM) A sleeping bag, especially a *green slug.

slush Originally, this was a term for the fat skimmed off by the cook from his cauldrons of boiled meat. This was compacted, and sold to the *purser for making candles. The monies made from this process constituted the very first *slush fund*, a term now in widespread use ashore.

small ships Nowadays, Mine Countermeasures Vessels, Fishery Protection Ships and other Patrol Craft, rather than frigates and destroyers:'*I've been a small ships man for most of my time in the *Andrew..*' It is interesting to note that at the end of WW2, the term would refer to any ship smaller than a cruiser. In WW1 the average destroyer was about 500 tons; by the end of WW2 it was 2 - 3,000 tons. The post war County Class Guided Missile destroyers displaced some 5,500 tons, but they were only called destroyers to get them through the Parliamentary naval estimates. Similarly, our present *carriers (which see) were described as *Through-deck Cruisers*!

smalley Little, as in *smalley eats* for cocktail-type snacks, *Smalley Pigs* for Petty Officers, and (esp. RM) *smalley girls* for under-age jail-bait. *Smalley boys* are Sea Cadets; to *go for a smalley portion* is similar to having *legover, a *quick coat of paint - or a *dash across the prairie.

smalls Underwear, as in *crash out your smalls.

Smartie Tube (RM) Long, filthy tunnel on the *Endurance course at *Lympstone, made of concrete piping and containing mud, stones and running water. This obstacle has to be negotiated on your back, in semi-darkness, with the rifle barrel kept dry at all times - or else you go through again.

Smashex A pair of applications:
1. An exercise which simulates a submarine accident, with all

the relevant responses being taken.

2. (RM) Decriptive term for a really good party, presumably where everyone gets *smashed*.

smeggers Semolina pudding.

smellies (FAA) Nickname for maintainers; **green-and-smellies* are flying overalls.

Smoke Nickname for London: *'I'm off up to the Big Smoke for *extenders..'*

smoked (FAA) Crash into the ground, leaving only a *smoking hole* to mark your passing: *'Then I fell behind on cockpit workload, got a bit distracted, and almost smoked myself and my wingman..'*

Smudge / Smudger Nicknames traditionally associated with the surname of Smith: *'Yessir, that's right - Smudger Smith, sir - and that's Smiff spelt with two f's..'*

SNAFU WW2 acronym for *Situation Normal - All (Fouled!) Up.* Some would say that this is the normal situation pertaining to most military endeavours, but see also **self-adjusting cock-up* and **FUBAR.*

snag (FAA) Process of rendering an aircraft temporarily unserviceable by reporting a defect, and logging this fact in the MoD Form 700.

snake and pygmy pie A steak and kidney pudding.

snake pit Another quintet:
1. Any untidy messdeck.
2. The **scruffs bar of the **Wardroom at **Dartmouth.
3. (SM) Forward lower section of a **diesel drainpipe's engine room.

4. Temporary ladies'*heads set up in a ship during a function.

5. An amusement arcade in Union Street, Plymouth. A favourite place for men looking for women looking for men during the war.

snake's honeymoon / wedding   An unholy tangle of lines and ropes on the *deck.

snap dragon   A male homosexual.

snap one off   Two rather different applications:
1. Defaecate; see also *crimp off a length.
2. (RM) Render a hand salute.

snap roll (SM)   High speed turn in a dived submarine which creates a large angle of heel as the boat goes into the turn.

snapper   See *brownhatter - again!

snaps   The older name for a member of the naval photographic branch; the term is too easily confused with *snapper and *snap dragon these days, so *phots is the preferred usage now.

snarlers   Yet another term for sausages.

snarley   A mess of some kind, although RM usage also has this as a the *green grolly hanging like candlewax from a *snot gobbler's nose. A *snarleypig* is any particularly unpleasant individual - of either sex, whereas a *snarley* *crocadillapig* is a really fierce animal - of any size.

sneaky (SM)   A covert patrol carried out under semi-operational and highly classified conditions. The word can also be employed in RM usage as an adjective, as in *sneaky beaky* for someone who is employed on intelligence-gathering duties; see also *secret squirrel in this respect.

snifter   Smell something: *'Have a snifter of this..'* which led on to a practical application with regard to the *tot: *'Have a quick snifter of my *wet..'* See also *framework of hospitality.

SNLR   Acronym meaning *Services No Longer Required*: *'This geezer reckons 'e served during the Falklands punch-up, but I've 'ad a little *buzz that 'e went outside SNLR the year before..'* See *discharge also.

Snobs   Older nickname for an amateur ship's cobbler, now replaced on larger ships by a Chinese *Tap-tap; this is a shortened form of the term *snobber*.

snookered on red   Discovering that one's wife or girlfriend is at the wrong time of her menstrual cycle.

snorker   Sausage.

snort (SM)   The process of running a diesel *boat's engines while at periscope depth in order to charge batteries; the air is drawn down through a *snort mast*.

snot box   The nose: *'He gets right up my snot box, he does..'*

snot gobbler   Interesting term of abuse, derived from the description of a young child whose nostrils are festooned with *green grollies or candlesticks.

snotty   Older word for a Midshipman; these young men used to have three buttons sewn onto their jacket cuffs, supposedly to stop them wiping their noses on the sleeves. Their uniforms were also designed without pockets so that there would be no temptation to stand around idling, but there was also nowhere to stow a handkerchief. Many officers still carry handkerchieves up one sleeve of the uniform jacket; those who are Communicators traditionally sport silk - which is also allowed to show! *Snotty* also has the adjectival meaning of someone short-tempered and rather conceited, and note also the descriptive term *Snotties' Nurse* - an experienced officer formerly charged with the welfare and training of midshipmen, in the days when they went to sea in their early teenage years.

snotty heap (esp. RM)   Anyone who trips and falls over usually does so in a *snotty heap*; can also be used to describe the manner of collapsing after a really good *run ashore.

snowball   As in tombola. A prize that multiplies with each game until a criteria is met and it is won.

Snowy   Nickname for anyone with the surname Winters or Winterbottom; also for anyone with particularly fair hair, or even - (and esp. RM) as an abbreviation of *Snowball* - for a black *oppo.

snurger   (Pronounced with a soft 'g') Another name for a *toggle-oggler.

snurgle (RM)   Infiltrate: *'The last thing that the Argies expected us to do was snurgle round and attack from the flank..'*

Soapy   Traditional nickname for anyone called Watson.

HMS EXCELLENT

Guns

SOBS (FAA)   The Senior Observer of a squadron: '*SOBS 706 is off to the West Indies as the *guardship's *Jimmy - the *jammy git!*'

social hand grenade (RM)   An individual whose general lack of the social graces makes him really bad news at a party.

sock-footed (SM)   Moving very, very quietly in *silent routine.

SOD's opera   Ship's concert arranged, performed and appreciated by Jack, usually on *Channel night. Some old scores are settled painlessly, and tradition dictates that *Father should sit in the front row of the audience, take some *stick, and then perform himself after due encouragement from the audience:
> '*Sing, you bastard, sing - or show us your *ring -
> We don't want to see your ring, so SING!*'

The word **SODS** is supposed to stand for *Sailor's Own Drama Society*, or *Ship's Drama and Operatic Society*. Take your pick!

sod's law   Variation of Murphy's Law. The original Murphy's Law stated that if any aircraft component could be installed backwards or upside down, then at some time it would be. Now used in a more general sense that if anything can go wrong it will - and at the most inconvenient time. Could be defined thus: *A piece of bread and butter will always fall butter-side down, except when attempting to prove this law.*

soft   A quartet of uses:
1. *soft option* - an easy way out of a problem, but which may not be the best.
2. *soft number* - a really cushy job.
3. *soft tack* - bread; see also *hard tack for ship's biscuit.
4. *softwood wedge* - suppository.

(The) Soldier   The junior of two Royal Marines officers, if two are carried a part of a warship's *Detachment.

soldier's farewell   To obtain good riddance of something worthless. It has also been pointed out to tha author (by a friendly *pongo) that a sailor's farewell was *Goodbye*, but a soldier's one was 7/6 a week (the old maintenance allowance!)

Someone's on our side!   Remark made when things have been going badly, and then the luck begins to run the other way; rather like saying: '*Well, at least the Good Lord is with us!*'

son of a gun   Rough *hand, but a good chap nonetheless. Debauchery on the gundecks in older times was a common feature of life in harbour after a long stint at sea. With women on board in this way, there were even babies born 'tween decks; a male child, born on the gundeck and father often unknown, became the *son of a gun*. Collectively, they all became *sons of the sea*, as in this classic description of Jack:

> *Begotten in the *galley and born under a gun,*
> *Every hair a rope yarn, every tooth a *marline spike*
> *Every finger a fish-hook -*
> *And their blood right good Stockholm tar..*

Although frequently used to mean a good fellow, this is really an old naval expression casting aspersions on a man's parentage. He would be christened *Tom Bowline* or *Bill Backstay* or some such name. Tom Bowline was a famous character who died of wounds in 1790 and was buried at Haslar; he went ashore once in seventeen years.

sonar   Acronym for *Sound Navigation and Ranging* - the name that came from across the *Pond for what the RN initially called *asdic, and which is now the accepted name for underwater sonar detection.

soojie moojie   Mixture used for washing paint work. Has the meaning of *strongers* in the Merchant Navy.

SOP   Acronym of *Standard Operating Procedures* hence:'*The only way to tackle this problem is according to SOPs..*'

sort that bastard out!   Traditional exclamation made as you give up trying to solve a complex muddle or problem, and pass it on to your *oppo instead; also heard when a punch is landed on an adversary.

sound off   Play a bugle call, make a *pipe on the Tannoy - or express an opinion, loudly.

soup jockey   Nickname for a *Wardroom steward.

space cadet   Young Officer who thinks he or she is Captain of the Universe.

spacehopper   A short, fat, adolescent *smalley girl:'*Any talent down the disco, Bill?*' '*Nah, mate - just *gangs of spacehoppers..*'

spadger   Ornithological term; one of the four types of feathered bird recognized by Jack; see also *shitehawks, *arse-up ducks and *oozelum birds.

spanner   Another of Jack's useful catch-all words, of almost lim-

S - 414

itless application, used to describe any implement other than one used to tighten or loosen a nut and bolt! Hence *bottle/can spanner* (opener), *scran spanners* (cutlery), *fang spanner* (toothbrush), **baby spanner*, and so on almost *ad infinitum*. A *spanner wanker* is the rude nickname for a *Mechanician. *Spanner face* is a term of endearment for a pretty woman - because she tightens your nuts.

spare   A trio of usages:
1. Losing patience, as in: '*It's driving me completely spare..*'
2. An unattached female: '*There's a nice bit of spare over there..*'
3. *spare crew* - those SM personnel held at base to provide replacements for *boat crew members who fall ill.

Sparks / Sparkers   Radio operator, the modern version of the old Telegraphist and his *sparking* wireless set.

sparrowfart   Dawn, or at first light; *oh-crack-sparrowfart* is very early indeed, ie. when the sparrow first wakes and breaks wind, long before first light.

spasm chasm   Another of Jack's nicknames for the vagina; find the others yourself!

spazz (RM)   Derisory term for any Marine or recruit who is temporarily sick or injured.

SPDC   Acronym for what was formerly the *Spare Parts Distribution Centre*, one of *pusser's huge stores complexes, carefully sited as far as possible from a Dockyard. Most of these have now closed; they were also generally and rather wryly known by Jack as the *Society for Prevention of the Distribution of Components*.

spear in (FAA)   Crash in an aircraft, usually with terminal results, but can also describe the process of hitting the *pit when extremely tired.

Special Duties list   The older term (pre-2000) for officers select-ed for elevation to *Wardroom status from the *lower deck, and therefore limited in their ultimate promotion prospects unless they manage to transfer *GL; see also *SD List and specific com-ments there. Note that the term *Special Sea Dutymen* (or *Specials*) has a completely different usage in respect of responsibilities undertaken when entering or leaving harbour.

Speechless One (FAA)   Callsign used by Air Traffic Control for an aircraft which has suffered partial or complete radio failure; the term can also be used for an officer who is unusually taciturn and quiet.

speed march (RM)   Technique of double-marching on the flat and downhill, but quick-marching uphill, which forms the basis of the *nine-miler *Commando test - nine miles in ninety minutes as part of a formed squad wearing boots, *fighting order and carrying a weapon. Not easy!

spewing his ring / toenails   Vomiting excessively, especially when suffering from *nautical nausea.

Spick   General nickname for a dark Latino type, but especially a native of Argentina: *'Spicks? Well, as far as I can tell from the history books, they're basically Italians who speak Spanish rather badly, behave like the French - and also wish they were English!'*

Spike / spike   Another useful trio:
1. *marline spike* - pointed tool on sailor's knife, for ropework.
2. Nickname for the surname Hughes or Milligan.
3. Foil a plan by *spiking it*, as in the older ploy of *spiking* (an enemy's) **guns**.

spilled blood   *Father's amendments to a draft *C.206, usually made in *red ink, and usually in disagreement - either to some high opinion expressed, or to the general overmarking.

spin a yarn   Elaborate story to cover up some misdemeanour, or reminiscences that have been fabricated or exaggerated.

spine-shattering (RM)   Qualifying adjective indicating extremely pleasurable sexual congress, and the subsequent dramatic relief of what might be termed *pelvic tension*; can also be used to describe similar sensations when *coiling down a really good one. Also an extremely good foreign port visit or run ashore.

spit and polish   The key ingredients for success when making your uniform boots and brasswork bright, shiny and clean.

spits brown   An old slang expression describing a sailor who chewed his tobacco.

Spithead   An area of sea between the Isle of Wight and the entrance to *Pompey harbour which has given its name both to the *Spithead pheasant* - a kipper, and a *Spithead nightingale* - the whistling sound made by a *Bosun's call.

spitkid   Bucket, *barrico or old brass shellcase, used as a *gashbin on a messdeck; originally used for spitting into, especially when chewing a plug of tobacco - spitting on board other than into a *spitkid* was an offence punishable by flogging. Now most commonly seen as a large, round aluminium ashtray-cum-*gashbin. In a training ship these appeared on deck at *stand easy and disappeared when the *hands *turned to; you could never forget the order:*'Clean aht and stow away spitkids..'*

spitting distance   Ships that are very close, as when *RAZing, are said to be within *spitting distance* of each other.

spitting feathers   Enthusiastic, or rather anxious to get a particular job:*'What do you mean 'was I keen to go'? I was ruddy spitting feathers to get selected..'*

splashed (FAA)   Shot down (even used over land):*'The Seawolf missile system managed to splash three of the four Argentine Skyhawks as they ran in to attack us..'*

splash-target (FAA)   Floating wooden framework towed behind a warship, but at a safe distance; diving aircraft can then fire rockets or cannon shells at the device. See also *bite.

Splice the mainbrace!   Order to carry out the traditional naval celebration involving the issue of an additional *tot of rum to all onboard (including officers on this occasion); possibly derives

S - 417

from the complexity and urgency required in *splicing* (repairing) a broken *mainbrace* (in order to restore a sailing ship's speed and manoeuvrability), which deserved a reward. Some cynics would point out that this emergency rarely, if ever, took place! Nowadays reserved for major occasions (eg. a Royal Anniversary) and, since *Black Day, using any commercial spirit, or beer, although most people prefer the traditional rum. If the Lord High Admiral ordains *Splicers*, then the Exchequer pays. Anyone else requesting this evolution (like General Montgomery, visiting the Mediterranean Fleet during WW2) will subsequently receive a rather large bill.

splice Join something to something else, hence also a euphemism for mariage:*'When you gettin' spliced?'*

split pin Jack's nickname for a *sleaze who has little trouble in parting her legs.

split yarn *'Are we ready for the Admiral?' 'Yes sir, everything's on a split yarn..'* Comes from the practice of lashing rigging, sails etc. with a weak piece of string, so that a good sharp heave would part this lashing and set the sail practically instantly. Therefore something *on a split yarn* is ready for instant use or action.

split-arsed matelot Crude, anatomically-based soubriquet for a female member of the RN; collectively, sometimes known more simply as *splits*. A warship that has undergone a conversion to allow her to accommodate female ratings and officers is said to have been *fitted for split*. Completely divergent from this rather sexist usage, someone who *cracks up psychologically may also be said to have *split right down the middle*. Wrens - if good looking, would be referred to as Jenny, if not, or referred to as a group, they were always *splitarse mechanics* as in:*'I don't know what Blockhouse is coming to, it's full of splitarse mechanics..'*

split-arsed turn (FAA) Tight turn that begins with a half-roll and ends with the second half of a loop in order to reverse course quickly. The term *split-arsed* can also be used for any reckless aerial or terrestrial manoeuvre.

Splot (FAA) The Senior Pilot of a squadron:*'I hear that Nick's off to be Splot of 849..'*

spo (SM) Rhymes with snow; early *TLA for *stoker petty officer*.

spoil the ship for a ha'porth of tar   Older phrase that has come ashore to mean that anything that is worth doing should be done properly and completely, not skimped with regard to the finishing touches just to save a small amount of money, because both efficiency *and* appearance will be affected.

spoil your whole day (FAA / RM)   Lovely understatement, probably of American origin:'*And above all, please don't walk into the tail rotor while it's turning, because that will spoil your whole day - as well as mine with all the paperwork..*'

spondoolicks   19th century Jackspeak word for money:'*Can't go on a *run-ashore tonight - no spondoolicks..*'

spoof   Another trio:
1. Trick or device designed to get a really good *bite; some really classic examples include asking for volunteers' names for the famous *Malta dog shoot, *splash-target cox'n, or a Haggis hunt. Alternatively, a new hand might be sent around the ship on an errand seeking a *fuse* for a *deadlight, some *red and green lamp oil*, the *key* of the starboard *Watch, or five metres of *Fallopian tube*! He might also be asked to get a *sky hook* in order to lift something up with.
2. Deliberate ploy to distract and mislead the enemy.
3. (FAA) Guessing game played to establish who buys the wine at dinner. See also *horse

sports pages   The romantic or sexy bits of a letter written to Jack by his *pash.

spotted dog   Any *duff with currants or raisins (may therefore also be known as *Dalmatian pudding* or *Dalmatian duff*).

spout   As in *toggle.

spring a leak   Pass water, or urinate.

springer (RM)   Physical Training Instructor. Also the nickname for RN officers of the PT&R specialisation: '*The Fleet Springer is based in *Pompey..*'

spring-loaded chicken   Rabbit.

springs   Ropes restricting the *surging or fore-and-aft movement of a warship when she is *secured to a quay or jetty; these may need *easing as the ship rises and falls with the tide.

sprog   General description of any novice, either to the Navy or to some branch of the Senior Service, eg. a *sprog pilot*. Said to be

Handcarted

derived from the word for a baby gannet, but may also be a portmanteau word for *frogspawn*, or perhaps even a confusion and fusion between *sprocket* and *cog*.

Spud   Nickname for the surname Murphy, but note also *spud barber* for anyone on potato peeling duties.

spur-lash   Wonderful excuse for pushing young *middies and *subbies overboard: *'Ever seen a spur-lash, young sirs? No? Well, come and have a look over here then..'*

SQ   Specialist Qualification - words (usually abbreviated to initials) after a person's *rate to indicate his or her branch or specialisation.   For instance, Petty Officer MEM = PO Marine Engineering Mechanic.   Nowadays, advancement and promotion is dependent on SQ proficiency as well as leadership / management skills, but this was not always the case, notably in the old *seaman branch (see *Instructor).   In the Royal Marines, a man will spend part of his career employed in an *SQ billet*, but at other times will fill any *GD job.   Some examples are: DL (Drill Instructor) - *not* Drill Leader!; PW (Platoon Weapons Instructor); ML (Mountain Leader) and PT (Physical Training Instructor).

squad (RM)   A *recruit squad* normally comprised about 30 young men, each squad being consecutively numbered. Unless through injury, sickness or some other reason, when one could be *back-squadded*, you completed your basic training as a member of that squad.   Like an officer's date of commission, *squad numbers* could be used to settle seniority disputes, as (for instance) which one of two *three-badge marines got the corner bed or *cushy number.   A similar distinction was the old divisional prefix to a man's number, which could have a bearing on one's unofficial standing in the hierarchy, with Chatham Marines considering themselves superior to either Portsmouth or Plymouth men.

squadmate   A person who joined up and went through his basic recruit training with you.   Like the YO's *batch members, a *squadmate* is a relationship that exists for life.

square   A word used in a number of phrases:
1. *square meal* - decent *scran; in earlier times, sailor's plates (platters) were square (so that they did not roll around) and were made of wood.
2. *square number* - nice, easy, undemanding job.

3. *square rig* - sailor's uniform (below Petty Officer) with jumper and trousers which used to be creased horizontally, from side to side, plus a blue jean material collar. This was in contrast to the *fore-and-aft rig of Petty Officers and above, where trousers were creased from front to back. In the old days, seamen petty officers also wore square rig.

4. *square yards* (with someone) - a reconciliation process after a disagreement.

5. *squared away* - everything stowed and *secured in a *seamanlike fashion.

6. *squared off* - tidied up neatly.

7. *squared up* - this was the phrase emanating from men o'war sailing ships, which contrived to attack from an *abeam position. This has come ashore to describe the position which a person adopts in order to confront another with the intention of fighting.

8. *square pusher*   Someone who is courting a lady, who is his *squarey*. This latter term is less used nowadays, but was very popular in the 50s and 60s for a girlfriend of a semi-permanent nature.

Squat, Jack!   Dismissive phrase used to describe official indifference to a sailor's problems: *'An' even if you did ask *Pusser, nine out of ten times the answer would be Squat, Jack! - so what's the point of askin' in the first place, eh?'*   See also *face aft and salute.

squawk (FAA)   The semi-automatic process of sending out a numerically coded identification signal to assist the *Air Tragickers when aircraft enter busy airspace.

squawk box   *Bulkhead-mounted speaker of a ship's *Tannoy public address system, or any inter-office intercom.

squeegee   A tool for removing water from the deck. Consists of a broomhandle with a length of shaped rubber attached to one end, and used to clear large areas of surface water. *Squeegee lips* refer to prominent or large lips.

squeeze box   Accordion.

squeeze up   See *catch the boat up and *blob up(2).

squirt (FAA)   Older term for a carrier catapult which *squirted* the aircraft off the front end.

squitters   Diarrhoea and frequent, loose bowel motions. See also *black drizzle, *scatters, *pebbledash and *trots.

stab   Attempt something, as in: *'Go on - have a stab at it..'*

stab out (FAA)   Most Naval helicopters have some form of gyroscopic stabilization system which can be switched off: *'By this time he was well *ratted, lurching, totally stab out..'*

stabbing arse   Euphemism for homosexual activity.

stack (FAA)   Cancellation of the flying programme for some reason, followed by a mass movement to the *Wardroom bar; also an older name for what are now called *funnel uptakes*.

stacks (RM)   Abbreviation for *stacks of effort*, hence: *'Come on lads, last time of asking, give it stacks..'*

stacks rating   Someone who is consistently successful with the opposite sex, and who is *getting yards as opposed to *plums.

staff officer   An Officer who has trained at a Staff College (usually) and who works in an Admiral's or (RM) Major-General's Headquarters. They are members of a general breed which can be either be helpful or unhelpful: *'If you ask that staff officer for the time, he'll just tell you, in enormous detail, how his bloody watch works..'*

Staffy (FAA)   The *staff officer* of a Squadron, responsible for correspondence, duty rosters, etc. - roughly equivalent to a *CorrO in a ship.

stag (esp. RM)   Guard duty, or a period of intensive study for an examination: *'He's away stagging for his *killick's..'* This word was in recorded use during the 18th century for the process of observing, watching or detecting.

stagger juice   Any strong spirit, but especially rum.

stamps   Of no importance, without power or influence: *'*Reggies are stamps when you're home on leave..'* (Not strictly true!)

stanchion   Fixed *deck structure; see also *barrack stanchion.

stand by   A disparate trio:
1. Naval order to get ready to do something.
2. Request for someone to wait: *'Stand by just a tick, please..'*
3. To be appointed to a warship or submarine that is still in her builder's hands, and has yet to be accepted into Her Majesty's Service: *'I stood by CORNWALL while she was building at Yarrow's..'*

stand down   Return to a more relaxed state of alertness after *Action stations, (RM) *standing to or:*'We were at the *dip, ready to assist, but an hour later the Rescue Co-ordination Centre stood us down..'*

stand easy   Another trio:
1. The most relaxed stance when on parade.
2. A specific period of relaxation built into the normal work routine: *'I'm going to the *canteen at stand easy..'* Interestingly, the Army equivalent is a *NAAFI break.
3. The *big stand easy* or the *permanent stand easy* are both euphemisms for death.
Note that in larger ships and establishments, the bugle call which preceded the *pipe for *Stand Easy!* had a tune to which a one line lyric was chanted on the lower deck:*'If you want to have a shit, fall out..'*

stand fast   Substitute for *except* in conversation, or as in the following typical emergency *pipe: *'For exercise, for exercise, stand fast the *Sickbay and medics - FIRE! FIRE! FIRE! - FIRE in the hangar - Attack party and Damage Control teams *close up to the canteen *flat - this is for exercise..'* In the days of the *tot, the *pipe Up Spirits! was made at midday, invariably followed by some wag saying:*'Stand fast the Holy Ghost!'*

Another lovely example of this usage is the pipe made in Malta Harbour when the remains of HMS VOLAGE were towed in after she had been mined in the Corfu Channel incident: *'The ship now entering harbour is HMS VOLAGE, stand fast her bows..'*

stand over   Formal decision for a Captain or Executive Officer, while hearing a disciplinary case at *Defaulters, to close the proceedings and re-open them later - after a specified delay.

stand to   Command to assume the highest degree of preparedness when at *Action Stations, especially after taking self-preservation measures during an attack (see *brace, brace, brace!) or to specific *quarters just before operating a weapon system. In the Royal Marines, *stand to* describes the emergency process of manning defensive positions rapidly when under attack, or the instinctive and routine business of doing so when enemy attack is expected at the traditional times of first and last light. RN use was when at Ready Stations and attack was imminent: *'Stand to - aircraft starboard..'* Of course, A/A gunfire was mainly visual in those early days.

Standard!   Sentry's warning shout on sighting the approaching Royal Standard on a car or motor launch.

standing about (men) (RM)   A collective order given by the senior rank of a working party engaged in a variety of tasks (gash collection, sweeping etc) on the arrival of an officer:*'Men standing about - 'shun..'*

standing charge (SM)   Charging batteries (running diesels) when tied up alongside, as opposed to the running charge usually done at sea.

standing into danger   Maintaining a course that will take the ship into hazardous conditions. To say to someone:*'Listen, you're standing into danger..'* implies that if he carries on doing what he is doing, he will get into trouble fairly soon.

standing orders   The Captain or *HoD's written orders and instructions for what is expected during a normal working day. Note also that any regularly performed *evolution may become a *standing routine*, while a *standing watch* is a period of duty undertaken at the same time each day, rather than in the rotation of a normal *watch system.

star jumps (esp. RM)   In an excitable state; see also *wall of death, *low hover, and *Mexican hat dance.

star system   Method of denoting seniority within *Flag rank; this runs from one star (Commodore) up to five stars for an Admiral of the Fleet.

starboard   The right-hand side of a ship; derives from *steer-board*, ie. the side of the ship that the *steering board* (rudder) was usually fitted in older times. The opposite side was larboard (now *port). Traditionally, and for obvious reasons, *starboard* has always been superior to port.

starbolins   Older term for members of the starboard *watch.

starters (RM)   Any lubricant or easing fluid, but especially one designed for personal use on the skin, such as *Vaseline*; see also *stoppers in this latter context for the vital components of Royal's *run-ashore kit.

State of the Nation   Traditional nickname for the overall message given by *Father at *clear lower deck when he attempts to explain some new *MoD directive, or even the most recent Defence White Paper.

station card   Small coloured card with Jack's name, messdeck, *watch and normal place of duty (*station*) written on it; the colours are *green* (starboard *watch), *red* (port *watch) or *blue* (temporarily employed as a *dayman and therefore not in the harbour *watchbill). In this latter context, see also *blue card man. This card is left on board with the *QM when going ashore, and is also rather wryly known as the *licence to breathe*. Whilst this system is still technically in force, it has generally been superseded by a more self-disciplined approach, whereby Jack and Jenny indicate their presence or absence using a peg board.

stats sheet (FAA)   Daily record of all flying undertaken in a squadron; *stats sheets* are collated and analysed each week.

steady   Adjective describing someone who is a reliable *hand; also a *conning order *steady as she goes* (now seldom used) meaning to stop the turn and *steady the ship* on the compass course shown.

steam   A verb meaning to hurry on or work hard: *'We'e going to have to steam in order to get this finished by *Colours..'*

steam easy   Derogatory nickname applied to a matelot given to boasting about his sea-time.

steamer   Jocular nickname for a warship.

steamie   Mechanical engineer of any rank or rate who specialises in the fast-disappearing methods of steam propulsion.

steaming   Moving fast.

steaming bag   Small extra kitbag.

steaming bats   Shoes with steel toe caps and non-slip direct-moulded soles. Tugg has a lovely cartoon at page X - 512.

steam queen   Another diesel submariners' name for his nuclear colleagues.

steam-shy   A *steamic who has become reluctant to enter the engine-room and its associated machinery spaces.

steel-beach barbie   Barbecue held on the ship's flightdeck.

steely (FAA)   Tough and resolute: *'Two *SHARs against four F-15s! That's a bit steely, isn't it?'*

steer   Take up a heading; the term is not necessarily confined to ships, but is also used for Naval aircraft and, in a more general sense: *'Could you give me a steer on this one please - how do I play it?'* A *bum steer* refers to bad information, rather than the activities associated with *botty bandits.

stern tube   Arse.

Sticks   Nickname for a Royal Marine Bugler; traditionally, drums were used to beat out orders, followed by a bugle call. All RM drummers are trained in these skills, which can be heard and seen to excellent effect in the *Sunset ceremony or *Beat Retreat.

stick   An unusual pair:
1. Punishment of any kind: *'He didn't half give their bowling some stick..'*
2. A group of passengers formed up to board an aircraft, such as a *stick* of parachutists; the term is derived from a *stick of bombs*. See also *chalk in this sense.

stickler   Someone who insists on the exact letter of any regulation being obeyed; see also *by the book.

sticks out like _____   Both Jack and Royal have a number of favourite descriptive comparisons for items such as nipples that are especially prominent:
- *a racing dog's bollocks.*
- *a blind carpenter's thumbs.*
- *the stops on a Hammond organ.*
- *brass check-fire gong buttons.*
- *chapel hat pegs.*

sticky / Stickies   *Sticky greens* are drinks with a base of *creme de menthe*; also the drink that a female would try and entice you to buy in a Far Eastern bar; *tea and sticky buns*, or just *tea and stickies* are both descriptions of any friendly domestic get-together. To Royal, the *Stickies* are members of the Official IRA (as opposed to the Provisionals / Provvies or Provos).

Stiggins (FAA)   Spotty, immature and rather ill-mannered jet pilot from John Winton's novel *HMS LEVIATHAN*. A caricature of the Fleet Air Arm needless to say, but a revealing one: *'Our new Commander seems to think that all Sub-Lieutenants with wings on their sleeves are called Stiggins..'*

Still!   The *pipe made on a *Bosun's call for *Silence and stand still!* at *Colours or other cermonial such as saluting a passing ship - one long steady note of 4 to 6 seconds. The bugle equiv-alent is the *Alert. Also an order much beloved of the *GI, and uttered, or blown on a gunner's whistle, to prevent chaos and destruction. Everybody would freeze on hearing the shout. Then the GI would spell out what was wrong, and unfreeze those present with a *Carry on!*

still on patrol   Those HM Submarines which have not returned, have never been found, are which are presumed lost.

Stills   Nickname applied to *Bennies soon after a local order came out in the Falklands banning the use of the latter term, because - as the logic ran - whatever else you called them, they were **still** *Bennies. However, note the locals' superb riposte concerning *Whens.

S - 428

Stimulator (FAA)   *Sea King and *SHAR cockpit simulators with excellent visual and motion systems that can actually convince a pilot he is coping with a real emergency and get his *adrenalin flowing.

stitch up   Any procedure, trick or *spoof which sets an *oppo up for embarrassment or trouble. Derived from the old trick of *stitching up* the legs of a pair of trousers; getting a good *bite has much the same intent:'*They promised me a gorgeous blonde, which is what I got, but nobody said anything about her husband! I was well and truly stitched up..'* Or:'*Who put me down fer duty on New Year's Eve? It's a bleedin' stitch-up, that's what it is!'*

stocious   Angry, unreasonable, drunk, or all three at the same time.

stoker's friend   Old sailor's slang name for the Ace of Spades in a pack of cards.

Stokes   Nickname for any stoker; *Stokie boy* is the SM equivalent. These were used by the seaman's branch when addressing a member of the *blackhand gang or engine room branch. This, of course, was modified if a stoker was suspected of being a   frequent user of the *five fingered widow*. In that case, he was called *Strokes* instead.

Ston   The cargo of FORT and RESOURCE Class RFAs is looked after by Civil Service warehouse men and managers of the RNSTS. The head of this department is the Supply and Transport Officer (Naval) or STO(N), who is known as *The Ston*. This is carried on further so that all of the RNSTS contingent are known collectively as the *stonnery*, and individually as *stons* or *stonners*. In some locations like the Falklands, the *Ston* is afforded the privilege of wearing a RN Lieutenant Commander's uniform with light green *distinction cloth. During the Gulf crisis, STO(N) (Middle East) became known by all and sundry as *Stone Me.*

stone frigate   Any Naval base or shore establishment with a ship's name.

stoned   Despite the *civvy connotation with drugs, Jack still uses this word in relation to drunkenness.

stonicky   A short thick stick or canvas-covered rope weilded by petty officer instructors in boy-training shore establishments during the navy's brutal days; used for belting boys up the back-side to hurry them along in a *last one out* situation. Boys quickly learned to move fast and avoid being caught - very painful it was too.

stonker   Erection; see also *lob and *lazy lob.

stonking (RM)   Heavy artillery or mortar barrage: *'3 PARA suffered seriously from Argentinian 155's in an all-day stonking of Mount Longdon after they had taken this objective..'*

stoofed in   An aircraft crash into the sea or ground, but may also be used in the non-aviation sense: *'He tried to *trap that gorgeous *Wren-O who works as the Admiral's PA - but stoofed in completely..'*

stooge around   Cruise or fly about in an area while observing.

stoppage   Punishment characterised by the withdrawal of some privilege, as in stoppage of leave etc.   May also be used in a social sense: *'Didn't enjoy the weekend much - the Missus had me on stoppage..'* Stoppage of wine bill is a specific punishment that denies any alcoholic drinks to an officer; while the jamming of an automatic weapon (RM) leads to the performance of *stoppage drills*.

stopped his clock   Another euphemism for death; see also the big *stand-easy.

stopper   Seamanship term for securing a rope or hawser, and very strong.   Hence, to *put a stopper* on something is both powerful and permanent.

stoppers and starters (pre-1918)   Cheese and a laxative.

stoppers (RM)   Local anaesthetic jelly used to delay onset of the *vinegar strokes; see also *starters.

stopping   Anything used to seal a leak, or else to secure a furled sail.

Stores   Items designed to be left on the shelf because, according to *pusser's logic, if they were meant to be given out, then they would have been called *Issues*.   Chief Stores Accountant: *'Now look here, lad. I am a store keeper, not a store giver..'*

stovie (FAA)   Member of the fast jet community, so-called because of the *stove-pipe* appearance of their jet engine exhausts - and the flaming afterburners of the *Toom.

stove in   Seamanship term, but now adapted for other situations.   This is to break in the top of a barrel ie. to open it, but the ship's sides can also be *stoved in*, like a car body panel, as the result of a collision.

stow   Put an article away in a secure and safe manner; *Stow it!* or *Stow your tits!* are both ways of saying:*'Shut up and be quiet!'*

straddle   The process in naval gunnery of getting near misses on both sides of a target, ie. the salvo fired is *bang on target, and perhaps one of the shells might also hit.

straight rush   Older term for a piece of meat (usually not much more than bone and gristle) which was *rushed straight* to the *galley for cooking.   A slightly more imaginative variant, *schooner on the rocks, involved placing the meat on peeled potatoes and possibly surrounded by vegetables.

straight up? / straight up!   *'Is that true?'* / *'Honest, that's exactly what happened!'*

strapadicktomy   Jack's imaginative description of Lesbian activity.

strap-on job   Another rude and disrespectful name for a *split-pin.

strapped   Very short of some commodity, eg. *strapped for cash.*

streak of piss   A long, thin and weedy-looking person.

stretcher   A piece of wood about an inch square, 18-20 inches long, notched at each end. Placed between the corner nettles at the head end of a slung hammock, this *stretched* the *clews apart, and allowed more freedom for the occupant's head.

strike   The process of lowering anything that has been elevated or hoisted, hence:
> *strike your colours* - lower your flag in surrender.
> *strike down* - lower cargo or equipment into a hold
> > using a crane or lifting tackle.
> *strike down* (FAA) - Term used in aircraft carriers to
> > describe the removal of aircraft (at the end of
> > *Flying Stations) from the flight deck, via the
> > main or side lifts, into the hangar below.

Note also the term *dawn strike!*

striker   Usual name for an assistant, perhaps a title inherited from the sailing-ship days of Second Mates who used to *strike out* hard - and often. Could also have been from the days of the ship's blacksmith and the blacksmith's mate, his *striker*, who did all the hard work with a sledgehammer. Note also the *dolphin striker*, a chainstay between the bowsprit and fore foot of the bow itself.

striking sixteen bells   Midnight, 31 December / 1 January is marked by the *striking of 16 bells* - eight for the old year and eight for the new. The youngest officer on board has the privilege of doing this. It used to be a custom to play practical jokes on this officer, such as smearing the bell-rope with marmalade - or even connecting it up to an electricity supply so that the lad got a mild shock when he grasped the rope.

Stringbag (FAA)   Affectionate nickname for the WW2 Swordfish naval torpedo carrier aircraft that slowed the German battleship BISMARCK and also badly damaged the Italian battle fleet at *Taranto.

stripe basis   Method of *divvying up the cost of a *Wardroom function so that a *Subby with one stripe pays a single share, whereas a *Sergeant (Commander)·pays for three.

stripey   Cheeky but also respectful nickname for someone with three good conduct badges, especially a *three-badge AB. Such a person is a rarity these days, but in the past he was usually a totally reliable man who remained devoid of ambition. He also usually had a soft number, and deserved it, but also could be relied upon in any emergency to do *any* task requiring seamanship skills, and perform both quickly and efficiently.

Stroll on!   *'Well I never!'* An expression of surprised disbelief.

strongers   A detergent mixture of soap and soda for washing paintwork and decks, often to the *Buffer's secret recipe.

strop   Any made-up rope used for lifting purposes - or a *looped strap* used in helicopter winching, but note also the word *stroppy* in a general context as an abbreviation of *obstreporous* - someone who is in an argumentative mood and spoiling for a fight. See *Jack Strop as well in this latter context.

stroppy   In the artificer's training establishments, a *strop* was a piece of the driving belt used on lathes, drilling machines etc. If a junior apprentice was cheeky to, or offended a senior apprentice, he was given a few strokes across his backside with a *strop*. So, to *be stroppy* originally meant to be *sufficiently insolent as to merit being stropped*.

struck down   A pair:
1. (*for action*) Anything that can be tied down or thrown over the side before battle, is *struck down* to avoid its conversion into flying and potentially lethal splinters.

Mismuster

2. (FAA) The opposite of *ranging is the process of moving aircraft from the flightdeck down into the hangar as in *strike down.

struck from charge (FAA) An aircraft that has been written off, either because it has crashed, become too badly damaged or become obsolete, is formally *struck from charge* before its subsequent disposal.

stuck in *Get stuck in!* is a traditional exhortation to do better, whereas to get *stuck across* someone has connotations of sexual activity and a *legover!

study for staff college (RM) Fall asleep.

stuff of greatness Sardonic but traditional remark directed at poor quality *Wardroom food.

stumper See *wolverine for definition; *coyote and *wildebeeste are alternatives.

Sub / sub An amusing quintet:
1. A *Sub-Lieutenant RN* (may also be described as a *Subby*). See Tugg's beautiful imagination at work on page X- 514.
2. Stand in, or substitute for an *oppo in a *watch bill: '*Do me a sub this afternoon will you, Shiner?*'
3. A loan of money: '*Anyone got a fiver to sub me?*' See also *rub in this context.
4. (rarely) A submarine.
5. *sub-calibre* Jossman A witty label sometimes applied to a RPO or Leading Regulator.

sublime to the gor-blime From one extreme to the other.

submarine equation (SM) The number of times surfaced must always equal the number of times dived.

submarine rash (SM) Piles - all long serving submariners had them.

submarine service motto This, strictly speaking, is *We come unseen* but is usually translated *We come at dawn, we come unseen, we go at dusk, we go unclean..*'

submarine tactics (SM) This was always said to be *sneak up behind her, slip in a crippler - and then move in for the kill*. This applied, of course, whether hunting women or *skimmers.

submariner's shower / dust bath (SM) Rapid once-over with a tin of *foo-foo powder before going ashore; a *submariner's dhobey* refers to a similar procedure, but with a bottle of deodorant instead. The self-cleaning schedule was top half Monday, bottom half Wednesday, and Friday night all over lightly with an oily rag.

submariner's frock (SM)   A white sea jersey, which got longer with every wash, finishing up below the knees, and worn with leather sea boots.

submiss (SM)   This is not an exercise, but means that a *boat is overdue by more than an hour in getting off her surfacing signal, and preparations are put in hand for *subsmash.

subsmash (SM)   This is signalled after *submiss, and says that a boat is in a possible *smash*, and may be damaged or disabled.

substantive   Confirmed in a rank or appointment, usually after a period in the *Acting rank.

suck back   An *Uckers ploy according to *Wafu rules which drags an opponent's counter backwards just before it can reach home; if this is achieved *around the corner* it becomes a *bendy suck-back*. The process of changing your mind about something or reversing a decision can be announced with *Suck back ten!'

suck back or blow through   This term comes from *razzing at sea. The tanker passes the fuel line to the ship, and when transfer is completed, the tanker tells you how he is going to clear the transfer line before disconnection. Both these terms are also used by stokers as an exclamation: 'F(lipping) suck back!' or 'I haven't had a good blow through since the old King died..'

suck back ten   Added on to the exclamation *Suck back!* if there is need to enhance the sense of surprise. Originates from the evolution desribed at the previous entry. If there was a problem clearing the oil line, the tanker was asked increase pump suction to 10 inches of vacuum.

suck, squeeze, bang, blow   A description of the combustion cycle of induction, compression, ignition, exhaust. Makes a good party piece with four performers - when well rehearsed.

sucker's gap (FAA)   Temporary improvement in poor airfield weather conditions; those aircrew eager to *commit aviation can then find themselves unable to return when the weather *clamps soon afterwards.

sucking on the hind tit   At the bottom of the promotion ladder, or the last in a line.

sucking the monkey   Wonderful *dodge pulled in the West Indies by Jack in older times, when he would fill coconuts ashore with rum and then bring them back on board, thus leading to bouts of unexplained drunkenness that must have had the *crushers going *spare.

suds   Beer.

summarine (SM)   What a submariner calls his boat.

sun dodger   Submariner!

sun over the yardarm   Traditional observation made at midday on the Equator; it has now become a more general cue for the first alcoholic drink of the day.

Sunset, sir!   Shouted when someone dropped something with a clatter.

sunshine pill (SM)   Depth charge

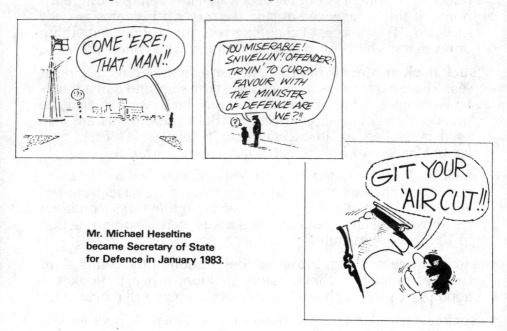

Mr. Michael Heseltine became Secretary of State for Defence in January 1983.

Supplementary List   Officers entered on limited duration Commissions, only some of which are pensionable (unlike the *General List) but whose specialist skills are in particular demand; *SL aviators* of the Fleet Air Arm form the biggest group. Note also the traditional descriptions of *SL shag* and *GL smoothie*.

S - 436

surge 2 distinct meanings:
1. Synonymous with *scend, which see, and used in order not to confuse with (2).
2. The act of easing the pull on a hawser, which has been brought to and is being hove in around a capstan, so that although the capstan is still rotating, the hawser is not actually being brought in. More commonly used for the act of *paying out quickly a hawser that has been turned up around a bollard or capstan, so that the weight does not come on it.

survivor's tot Similar to an *arduous duty tot. A large measure of rum which can officially be made available for issue to the rescued survivors of a *ditching at sea or a shipwreck.

SUSFU *Situation Unchanged, Still Fouled Up.*

SUSO American import directed at those who are not trying hard enough - *Shape Up or Ship Out*; see also *FIFO for Royal's version of these sentiments.

suzzies (a word usually uttered with a low growl) Stocking suspenders.

swab out / boojie out Clean with a mop and bucket.

'swain Shortened form of the abbreviation for *boatswain (*bo'-sun*) or *coxswain (*cox'n*); the *'swain* element means *husband*, as explained in *ship husbandry.

SWALK Typical of a number of inscriptions placed on the envelopes of Jack's letters to wives/girlfriends during the war, but persisting long thereafter. Examples: SWALK - Sealed With A Loving Kiss and BURMA - Be Undressed Ready My Angel. Note also *NORWICH.

swallow the anchor Retire from a career at sea, implying that one has no further use for the implement one has for so long trusted.

swallow the dictionary To come out with a really big word!

swamp / Swampy Nocturnal enuresis, ie. bedwetting, which can also occur in older men who have been drinking heavily and who *swamp their *pits*. The nickname *Swampy* often sticks unfairly in these cases, but it is also traditional for anyone with the surname Marsh.

swanning about Wandering around in a generally aimless way, usually while awaiting orders or instructions.

swapping spit   Graphically accurate term for kissing; the American version is *sucking face*.

sweat money   Jack's description of and additional allowance paid to men working in particularly unpleasant conditions - for example, the machinery spaces of a ship in the tropics. This pittance was only payable to ratings.

sweating drops of bluebell   *Bluebell* was the brass polish that Jack used, and if he was doing a job which caused excessive perspiration from the brow, which then dropped on the polished article and got mixed in - then so be it.

sweating neaters   Very anxious state; a Captain who is *sweating on his Flag* is involved in, and highly concerned about, possible promotion to Rear Admiral.

sweeps   Any cleaner, but especially the RM *block sweeps*; can also be the *mine-sweeping cables* towed by mine warfare vessels.

swept-up   Two applications:
1. De-luxe:'*I've got the swept-up version of that estate car..*'
2. Knowledgeable:'*You'll need to be pretty swept-up on fuel control systems when the *Trappers arrive next week..*'

swig   Short pull on a rope or a drink:'*C'mon, Barney - let's have a swig of yer *goffer..*'

swimmer   Old Navy term for a sailor who was once a prisoner, but chose a life at sea rather than in gaol; nowadays the *swimmer of the watch* is a life-saver dressed to enter the water if required.

swindle sheet   Any expense claim.

swing   A quintet:
1. *swing it* - arrange or achieve something.
2. '*I'll see you swing for it..*' - refers to execution by hanging, and implies that the person being spoken to will be seriously punished for a perceived misdemeanour.
3. *swing the lead* - malinger, or pretend to work.
4. *swing around the buoy* - have nothing much to do.
5. *swing the lamp* - tell stories, usually highly coloured.

switched-on   Alert; RM usage also has *switched on to custard* for someone who is particularly dozy. Jack may be described, in an opposite sense, and when in *Pompey, as being *switched to Brickwoods* (ale) but *switched-off* is the commoner term. See also *thumb in bum, mind in neutral; a *switch-op* is a female tele-phone switchboard operator.

switched to transmit   Someone who is always talking, and who never listens.

swopsies   Something that has been acquired in an exchange.

swords and medals   Formal occasion for an officer eg. for a ceremonial parade, but also used in another, almost disciplinary sense: *'I stood my ground with the Admiral's staff, and it almost became a swords and medals job until someone high up, maybe even the *Flag Officer himself, realised that I might be right after all..'*

syphon the python   Yet another way to *pump ship.

TANGO

441 - 476

T   For *Temperance*, denoting a man who elected *not* to draw a
*tot though entitled to do so, and drew 3d (three old pence) a
day in lieu. This letter appeared against his name in various
ledgers.

tab nabs   Small eats, normally found at cocktail parties; in the
RFA many of the Supply gurus are nicknamed *Tab Nab*.

(the) **Table**   Generic name for the *Captain's or Executive
Officer's *Requestmen and *Defaulter's parade. Under ever-
more complex legislation governing the investigation of
offences, the Officer of the Day (OOD) seldom if ever *holds a*

table nowadays, and alleged offences are usually investigated by
the *Reggies (as Service policemen). Note that the United
States Navy equivalent is a Mast.

table ending   Copulating on the very end of a table, something
that has featured in *Patrol reports!

table money   Entertainment allowance made to Flag and Commanding Officers to ensure that the process of providing the traditional and official hospitality of the Royal Navy does not leave them too far out of pocket.

tablets of stone   Something immovable in terms of policy or doctrine can be said, like the Ten Commandments, to have been *set in tablets of stone.*

tack in a pint of water   A really handy sailing ship; nowadays reserved for sailing dinghies that are particularly responsive to the helm.

tack-line   This was used by the *bunting tossers to separate parts of a signal in a flag *hoist. The first part of the *hoist would be followed by a *tack-line*, and then the next part of the message. The *tack-line* was a length of signal halyard, fitted with Inglefield clips top and bottom to take the lower end of the first *hoist and the upper end of the next. One of the most apt descriptions of a very tall, thin person was *head, tack-line, boots!*

tackle   In the RN this noun refers to an outfit of pulley-blocks and rope, and it is pronounced *tay-kle.*

tactical   Taking precautions not to be detected, ie. maintaining radio silence, getting blacked-out and moving as quietly as possible:*'Sssh! We've gone tactical!'* Can also be pronounced *tattical.*

Taff   General nickname for those with the surname Evans, Williams, but also of course for any Welshman.

TAG (FAA)   *Telegraphist Air Gunner,* and the salt of the wartime Fleet Air Arm; in the *Stringbag the *TAG* was responsible for managing *WT communication and air defence - with a single machine gun. The TAGs are the forerunners of today's Aircrewman branch and have a thriving Association, with regular get-togethers. They are still upset that they were left behind, because of the operational requirement to be replaced by an extra petrol tank, for the attack on *Taranto.

tailor-made   A factory-manufactured *tickler as opposed to the roll-your-own product.

take a turn   Procedure for securing a line around a bollard, and hence also *taking a turn* (walking) around the upper deck.

take charge (esp. RM)   Expression used in a personal, rather than in a leadership sense: *'Breathe in properly, you *big girl's* *blouse! Come on, take charge of yourself!'* Also said of ships' fittings and furniture which break away from their fastenings in bad weather and are thrown about by the motion of the ship.

take the con   Assume directional control of a warship or submarine. This is may be a USN import, but it is now widely used in the sense of having *conduct* of the ship.

taken aback   An expression that has come ashore for shock, surprise or the mental effect of something completely unexpected. A square-rigged sailing ship was said to be *taken aback* when a sudden shift in the wind direction flattened the sails (*flat aback*) and caused the ship to come to a virtual standstill. This could also be a deliberate manoeuvre (such as in a close-quarters battle in order to frustrate the enemy's tactics) but it was also highly dangerous and could damage spars and rigging.

taken off / on charge   A valuable, attractive or important stores item is *taken on charge* when issued, ie. the event is recorded in a Permanent Loan Record book and the item must be then be accounted for at regular intervals. The more dramatic form of *struck off charge* may be used to describe a FAA aircraft that has crashed, or has otherwise been put up for disposal, eg. by by sale.

taking in dhobeying   Jack's beautifully expressed reference to the quantity of material pulled up into the cleft between a lady's buttocks, a feature sometimes displayed by bikini-clad girls on the beach.

taking your time by the dockyard clock   A rather nice reference to the length of time which it used to take for HM warships to re-appear from the Dockyard after entering for refit: *'Taking your time by the Dockyard clock - January, February, MARCH!'*

talent   Quality *clacker in a pub, disco - or at page Z - 521!

talk into the big white telephone   Euphemism for the procedure of vomiting into a lavatory bowl, usually whilst promising never *ever* to get drunk again.

talking baggage / Nav bag (FAA)   Rather disparaging Pilot nicknames for their Observers.

talking trees   Jack's description of Special Forces. When they are embarked and taking passage in an HM Ship, their accommodation is often described as the *Enchanted Forest*.

Homeward Bounders

tally   An interesting term derived from the *tally-stick* which was used in the old days for checking cargo. They were soft wooden batons on which the checkers could cut notches. Also:
1. *cap tally*.   Jack's blue cap ribbon bearing the ship's name blocked out in gold lettering. An exception to this is the SM world where the cap tally simply states HM SUBMARINES. Note also the expression *different ships - different cap tallies*. In wartime, cap tallies had only the letters HMS on them.
2. A nameplate or label mounted on or near a piece of equipment in order to indicate its proper purpose.
3. A *pusser's tally* is any *nom-de-plume* used by Jack when staying ashore in a place like *Aggie Weston's. Favourites included J (for Jack) *Burberry and (SM) *Roger Ballast-Pump.
4. *death tally* is an older term for an identity disk. In a terrible economy measure prior to the Falklands War, these were made from compressed cardboard. Where fire and incineration was involved as the cause of death, this awful expedient made the task of identification very difficult.

tame Crab (FAA)   A Royal Air Force officer serving in a Naval aviation billet on an exchange basis; they are usually excellent men who enter into the spirit of things by developing a shaving rash that can only be resolved by growing a *full set.

tampax towers   A *WRNS accommodation block; originally used to describe the new facility built in Eastney Barracks.

tampion   A pair:
1. Ornamental plug for the barrel of a gun, a name that has been modified and commercially adapted elsewhere as an article of feminine hygiene.
2. (SM) Large cotton item used to stop up the lower voice pipe from the conning tower, in order to prevent ingress of very cold water into the submarine - and onto the surfacing planesman. You always got the odd *tosspot who left the upper voice pipe open when diving.

Tank Another pair:
1. (SM)   Nickname for the Submarine Escape Training Tower at HMS DOLPHIN, a prominent feature on the Gosport skyline near Portsmouth. All those who aspire to *Dolphins must make a free ascent from the bottom (at a starting depth of 120 feet) wearing escape gear. The instructors are splendidly fit men capable of free-diving (just like dolphins!) in the opposite direction, which they all do once a year for an underwater photograph.

They are also known as *water babies*. Further, the smaller 30 foot tank was also known as *The Pot*.   2
Inevitably, a nickname linked with the surname Sherman.

tanked up   Drunk or inebriated: *'Johnno was getting a bit too tanked-up, so we *scrubbed round the other nightclub and dragged him back to the ship..'*

Tanky   Name given to a junior rating with a particular responsibility. Hence *Freshwater Tanky* - responsible for the condition and maintenance of all the drinking water storage tanks and filters, as well as the daily sounding of their contents. In the era of the *Tot he also had another equally crucial role as part of the team that *mustered outside the Spirit Room when *Up Spirits! was *piped. In small ships he might also be in charge of the cold store, and required to do a bit of butchery as well. Previously, the Navigating Officer in big ships also had his own *Tanky*, a *Middy who was responsible for correcting charts and publications, but this person is now a rating, and usually called a *yeoman*. In the SM world, *Tanky* was a junior rating who assisted the *Cox'n with arduous tasks such as issuing provisions, paperwork and football pools.

Tannoy   A internal main broadcasting system in a ship or shore establishment; the name is applied indiscriminately, even if that system is not actually made by Messrs. Tannoy plc. See also *Tartan tannoy.

Tap-tap   Nickname for the ship's Chinese cobbler, if carried; *Snobs was the nickname for an amateur cobbler in a previous era.

taped   Abbreviation of *tape-measured*, in the sense that someone who *has a job taped* has it measured in all respects and can now complete the task with both speed and certainty.

tapes   White tape on a sailor's (blue) collar. The three rows of white tape on sailors' collars were introduced in 1857, solely as an ornamentation. No reference to Lord Nelson's victories was intended. Originally, the rows of white tape on the collars of RNVR seamen were waved, hence the name *Wavy Navy*.

tapped   Two different applications:
1. To be *tapped for a fiver* means that some *oppo has borrowed £5 from you.
2. To be *tapped up* implies that some *brownhatter has made an approach or physical advance to you.

Taranto (FAA)   The Fleet Air Arm's epic night attack on the Italian naval base at Taranto; twenty *Stringbags from the carrier HMS ILLUSTRIOUS equipped with long-range tanks, and dropping bombs, flares and eleven torpedoes (fitted with newly-designed Duplex magnetic firing pistols that allowed the *tin fish to pass beneath torpedo nets before exploding under the steel hulls) took out the anchored Italian battle fleet as an effective force, despite their many defensive precautions. Only two of the Swordfish aircraft were lost; one crew survived to imprisonment. The actual *Men of Taranto*, and their justly-celebrated feat are remembered on or near the anniversary of November 11th 1940 wherever FAA and former Royal Naval aviators gather around the world. The message behind Churchill's summary: *'By this single stroke the balance of naval power in the Mediterranean was decisively altered..'* was one also well-heeded by the Imperial Japanese Navy. Lt Cdr Minoru Genda was an assistant Naval attache in London. This very able Naval pilot went home, drew up the plans and built a torpedo-dropping range in one of Japan's inland seas. Nearly thirteen months after Taranto, they staged something of a repeat performance - at Pearl Harbor, Hawaii, on the morning of Sunday December 7th 1941.

tarbreeks   Jack's older name for a sailor whose speech was laden with *Avasts* and *Belays*.

target (SM)   According to submarine lore there are only two kinds of vessels that go to sea - other submarines, and *targets!*

tarmac tiff   Parade ground instructor; see also *tick tock tiff.

tarpaulin   Originally *tarpawling*, this was old sailcloth dressed with tar and cut up by Jack to make waterproof clothing for wet or heavy weather. Later on the name described, as it still does today, a heavy waterproof material used to cover hatches and deck cargo. A *tarpaulin captain* was a 17th/18th century officer who had risen to his command position on merit and experience rather than by influence at Court - like a *Gentleman Captain; a *tarpaulin muster* was the precursor of the modern day *kitty, because it refers to Jack's pooling of mutual resources (emptying of pockets) prior to a *run-ashore.

tartan tannoy (esp. RM)   Nickname for a particularly noisy Scotsman.

Tarzan course (RM)   Agility and co-ordination test conducted against the clock as part of the *Commando course at *Lympstone; not for the faint-hearted or those frightened of heights.

'tash (RM)   A *moustache*, the growing of which is strictly Royal's privilege - except on those ocasions when Jack decides to have a *'tash growing* competition, for charity, while at sea.

tatticks   *Tactics:*'Doan' listen ter humm - 'e couldny fight hus way oot a wet pepper bag, boot the boogger's allus talkin' tatticks..'*

taut ship   An efficient, smart and well-disciplined ship in which there is very little slack:*'He ran a taut ship down South and it really showed in the results..'* A *taut hand* is a general expression used to describe someone possessed of these same qualities.

TCBO   Acronym for *Tout Circulair Bon Oeuf* - someone who is regarded as an all-round good egg!

tea and stickies   Formal afternoon tea in the sense that cake, sandwiches or *sticky buns are served, hence its current usage to describe any generous non-alcoholic hospitality, even if it actually involves coffee and biscuits!

tea boat   Originally a pot of tea, now the kitty, or a money pool collected for provision of tea *makings.

Teacher (SM)   Nickname for the Officer in charge of the *Perisher course who lives cheek-by-jowl with his students, as they put the *Perisher boat through the increasingly complex *evolutions that he demands of them. All the while, *Teacher* is watching, correcting, encouraging, worrying - and then, if necessary, sacking.

tear off a strip   Naval slang expression for the giving of a reprimand. Possibly derived from the sound made by tearing a strip of calico or canvas.

teased-out   Well-worn, rather like a frayed rope's end:*'What's up with Chiefy? He's been looking rather tired and teased-out recently..'*

Technical Ted   Older term for anyone who excelled in the theory of electronics or wireless telegraphy.

Technicolour yawn   An episode of vomiting; see *Dockyard omelette for a complete list of alternatives.

teeny-weeny airways (FAA)   *Junglie nickname for the light helicopters of what used to be the 3rd Commando Brigade Air Squadron, based alongside them at *Yeovilton, and also of the Army Air Corps.

tell-tale   A repeater instrument (eg. the compass in the Captain's *cabin).

Tell that to the Marines!   When flying fish were being described to general disbelief at King William IV's Court, it was a Captain of Marines who confirmed the traveller's tale. The Royal response was that, henceforth, when the truth of a story needed verifying, his Marines would do this job.

telling you, not asking you   Emphasis of an order.

telling-bone   Telephone; see *bone for an interesting assortment.

Ten A's   *10 A's* was a punishment dished out in the late fifties. It consisted of marching round the barrack square, or if you were at sea, extra work. It follows then that an arduous task could be described as Ten A's: *'He told me to clean that tank out on my own, and that's really 10 A's, that bastard..'*

tender A *small ship, not carrying a Supply Officer, and which is therefore not self-accounting; her pay, cash and stores accounts are held and maintained by a Headquarters ship, or nowadays an establishment. Small Naval establishments can also be *tenders to* larger ones nearby.

ten pint pretty A lady with whom you would had to have consumed at least 10 pints before she started to look attractive. See *gronks as well.

tent peg (FAA) Euphemism for crashing fatally on land; *smoked, *spear in and *stoof are alternatives.

TEWT (RM) *Tactical Exercise Without Troops*, covering any section, troop or other ground movements rehearsed and discussed, without actually having people on the ground. Can also be indoors on a scale-modelled sand table.

texture never varies, only the depth The material referred to is manure, and the phrase describes someone who is always in trouble.

Thames barges Very large shoes or steaming *bats. Another expression in this context: *'Those aren't shoes, sunshine - they're the boxes that they came in..'*

that clears me This was said to indicate that you had finished or that you were no longer either capable, or wishing to continue. After a big meal you would say: *'Well, that clears me..'* If you were knocked out of a game, or really *dicked in *Uckers, you might say: *'Well, that clears me, as Nelson said when the musket ball hit him..'*

That is all! Traditional phrase used to end any *pipe that begins with the words *D'ye hear there?*

the grace of God The Admiralty chart. An old Merchant Navy saying was *'We navigate by the grace of God and the Admiralty chart'*. This was adapted and came home!

thickers Condensed milk; see additional reference under *B's, but also a measure of stiffness in paint or soup.

thicket (SM) The derisory collective noun that submariners use for any group of *skimmer officers.

thief's cat A special *cat'o'nine tails in which the ropes were knotted along their length to inflict extra damage; a thief might also be punished by *cobbing or the *gauntlet for less serious crimes.

thing (RM)   Lovely label for a useless individual: *'What's my opinion of him? Well sir, that man - that man is a thing..'*

thinks bubble (FAA)   Cartoon device carried over into real life: *'Approach told me to report when I was passing south *abeam the airfield. When I reminded them that we were twenty miles to the north, you could almost see a big thinks bubble forming in the distance, over the Control Tower..'*

thin out   Originally a *bootneck phrase. To *thin out* was to leave, as in: *'OK lads, that's it now, time to thin out..'*

third nostril   Amusing simile: *'It will be about as much use to you as a ruddy third nostril..'* See also *ashtray and *chocolate.

third pronger (FAA)   Pilot who goes to *Lynx and a Ship's Flight after gaining his *Wings, thereby leaving the two other training pipelines that flow towards the *Pinger or *Junglie worlds.

thirst after righteousness   Paraphrase of the Biblical expression, used in this context to describe the first *wet taken in the *Wardroom after Church service on Sunday!

thirty miler (RM)   Final *Commando pass out test for the *green beret; a thirty mile group *yomp aross Dartmoor, in fighting order, while carrying weapons, safety stores and a radio. The time allowed is eight hours for recruits, seven-and-a-half hours for *YOs.

thousand miler   A piece of *kit that has seen much service during its time, or an item of clothing that gets *dhobeyed at these intervals.

thousand yard stare   The haunted look of battle veterans who have yet to complete the process of emotional decompression following combat, and who are at risk of developing Post Traumatic Stress Disorder (PTSD) unless helped.

threaders (esp. RM)   Run ragged, or about to blow one's top in a very big way: *'On the bus, off the bus - and then on the bloody bus again - the boys were getting really threaders by now..'* A contraction of the word *threadbare*.

three badge   In possession of three Good Conduct Badges, which are displayed as three chevrons (not to be confused with those of an Army / RM Sergeant) and worn on the sleeve of Jack's uniform suit up to, and including, the rank of Petty Officer.

Hurt Certificate

An *AB who is a *three-badger* is often a stalwart of great experience and character who has not sought promotion during his career - see *stripey. But note also the expression *three badges gold - too bloody old!*

three in one   The Montague whaler (seaboat) could be propelled by oars, sails and an engine.

three golden rules   Advice given to young RN and RM personnel at the start of their careers. You will do well in your career as long as (a) you never get separated from your kit, (b) you don't rely on the Royal Air Force - especially at a weekend, and (c) you don't march on Moscow!

three lies   You will probably hear these at least once during your time in the *Andrew:
1. *This appointment will be good for your career..*
2. *The *FOST staff are here to help you..*
3. *We will have air superiority by the time you get there..*

three sheets to the wind   Older description of a sail that is almost out of control because its sheets - or control ropes - are flapping in the wind. Now used to describe someone who is drunk; see *legless for a complete listing of the regular terms.

three-Yankee   A higher *Damage Control condition of watertightness, usually adopted when entering and leaving harbour, or when operating in very close proximity to other ships (eg *RAS-ing). When Jack describes a fellow rating as being *in three-Yankee* he is implying that the chap is a bit *piso, and reluctant to damage the contents of his pockets by paying for a round of drinks.

throats and legs   Female attendees (regular) at ships' *CTPs; the modern equivalent of the old *fishing fleet.

throbbing   Socially active and exciting: *'Fort Lauderdale in June? The place was absolutely throbbing..'*

throw off   Deflection in gunnery practice which must be incorporated into any calculations, in order to avoid actually hitting and thus destroying the (expensive) target.

throw the book at ____   When referring to *QRRN the expression implies that someone has committed a number of misdemeanours, or a single offence so serious that a number of charges can be *framed against him: *'Of course that was the last straw, so *Father threw the book at him..'*

throwing   Adjective used to mock someone being pompous about wine: '*What would you like to drink after dinner? I've got a rather nice little throwing brandy..*'

thrunge   Event, enhanced to *megathrunge* if a socially impor-tant, but highly entertaining event.

thruster   Ambitious and determined officer: '*Mike's being a typ-ical *In Zone thruster at the moment. Hope he gets *selected and back to normal soon..*'

thumb up bum, mind in neutral   Apt description of someone who is daydreaming while on a task, and therefore not paying the necessary attention; may be abbreviated as **TUBMIN*. See also **switched-off*.

thundie   Abbreviation for *thunderflash*; an enlarged firework banger used for simulating the explosion of a hand-grenade, or for emergency signalling underwater as when recalling divers to the surface. **Bopper* is an alternative.

Thursday War   See **Weekly War*.

tick in the box   Some routine stage in a ship or officer's progress: '*I went and did that course, but it was only to get a tick in the box..*'

tick tocking   Marching badly on a parade ground, swinging the right arm with the right leg in a very awkward-looking motion; a *tick tock tiff*, like a **tarmac tiff*, is a Naval drill instructor.

ticker   Known to any matelot who has done time in a Military Corrective Training Establishment (the Army equivalent to DQs), as the device used to light a fag when more legal means of ignition were unavailable. A twisted spill of paper - the insu-lation - was doubled on itself, while holding a curved sliver of lead carved from the end of a toothpaste tube. Between the horns of the metal you positioned the scrapings of fluff from almost any article of clothing. The method was to remove a light bulb, carefully insert the *ticker* in its place, with the horns touch-ing the two electrical contacts, and switch on. The resultant short circuit caused an explosion which ignited the fluff. Bingo - a ball of flaming material from which to light the only curren-cy available. Of course, it blew the fuse - but who worried about smoking in the dark when the official ration was but three fags a day!

ticket   Four applications here:

1. Certificate of Qualification: *'I got my watchkeeping ticket in BRILLIANT..'* In theory, you couldn't get your ticket until you had kept watch on your own, and you couldn't keep watch on your own without a ticket. Thank God for sensible captains!

2. Expression of approval: *'That's just the ticket!'*

3. (FAA) Instrument Flying qualification.

4. To *work ones's ticket* - to behave in such a way as to ensure early *discharge. Nowadays, with everyone able to give 18 months notice to leave the Service, it is no longer necessary, but the expression is still used.

ticklers   Shredded or cut tobacco - also known as *pusser's leaf - issued to the old Navy in half-pound tins at duty free prices. The scale of issue was one pound per person per month, as cigarette or pipe tobacco. When you went foreign, the issue was doubled. Cigarettes which were self-rolled from this source also became known as *ticklers*. The actual origin of the term is most interesting, because around 1904 jam preserves became *issue, and one of the main suppliers were Messrs. *Ticklers*! A new class of rating joining for only twelve year's service was also created at about this time; these men much preferred the shredded baccy to the tough *periques of pipe tobacco smoked (or chewed) by the old salts, and they were themselves immediately and rather disdainfully labelled as *Ticklers*. The actual creation of these traditional plugs is discussed at the entry for *prick. The shredded tobacco could also be made up into *tailor-mades, by a contractor with a cigarette-making machine mounted on the back of his truck which came round the larger shore establishments. These cigarettes would incorporate the ship's crest in the paper, obviously the antecedents of *blue liners! Note also the term *Jack-me-tickler* - a sailor who knows all the answers.

tiddly   A famous naval expression, but of surprisingly recent origin; it appears merely to be a whimsical corruption of *tidily* (*tid - i -ly*) and dates only from the 1920s. It still means tidy, or of neat appearance, and in some contexts has overtones of *bullshit:

1. A *tiddly suit* is Jack's Number One uniform suit, often tailor-made rather than issued from *Slops, and always kept clean and neatly pressed in a *messdeck locker or hanging space; a *tiddly bow* is a perfectly and flamboyantly tied bow on a cap *tally worn, if Jack can get away with it, above the forehead rather than the left ear.

2. *tiddly work* - any elaborate and decorative piece of decorative work, designed to impress.
3. Details, often of a ceremonial or procedural nature: *'The *Master-at-Arms will precede you on *Rounds to do the tiddly bits..'*

tiddy oggy   Traditional nickname for a Cornish pasty, and an older name for a sailor born and bred in Devonport.

tide over   Another old sailing term that has come ashore to a wider meaning.   Ships beating down the English Channel against the prevailing winds could not also make headway against a *flood tide*; instead they would drop the *pick until the tide began to ebb, thus *tiding over* the temporary difficulty.

tied up   A boat is *tied up* to a jetty, whereas a woman is *tied up* if she is married - or into bondage!

Tiff / Tiffy   Nickname for an Artificer. *Tiffy's toenails* was the nickname for Parmesan cheese.

tight   Abbreviation for *watertight*, with no leaks - but also for someone in the condition of *having had drink taken*.

Tiger / tiger: A quartet here:
1. Nickname for a big strong lad.
2. Occasional nickname for a steward: *'I was the *Captain's tiger in ARROW..'*
3. tigernuts are prolapsed haemorrhoids - also *bumplums.
4. Corned beef used to be called *tinned tiger*!

tiller   Rudder post extension for steering a sea boat. Detached for *tiller soup* when a *cox'n belabours the crew. Also seen in sexually profligate individual as: *'He uses his prick as a tiller..'*

tiller flat   The most inspected part of any Mine Counter Measures Vessel, especially during parties when many a female guest has been invited to *tour the tiller flat*.

tilly   Shortened version of the old (Bedford) *Utilicon* van, now a word used in its own right for almost any kind of light transport.

Timber   Nickname associated with the surname Woods.

timbershifting   Cheating; derived originally from secretly moving the matchsticks used to score with on a cribbage board. The word is now employed in *Uckers as well. See also *fifteen-two that bastard!

timberwolf An ugly lady or *gronk; the *timberwolf* is supposed to eat through its own leg if caught in a snare or trap. Should Jack or Royal *trap a *timberwolf*, he would rather do the same thing than wake her up by removing his arm from around her the following morning! *Coyote, *stumper, *wolverine and *wildebeeste are variations on this rather cruel theme, but then see *booze and *ten pints pretty as well.

time to sling your hammock The Naval way of describing the period - usually 24 hours - given to many officers and ratings in which to find their way about a new ship or on taking up a new appointment.

tin burberry Your car.

tin fish (SM) A torpedo; see also *kippered.

tin man Older expression for someone trying to dominate any conversation or discussion without having the necessary knowledge or experience, and therefore in danger of being knocked down like the *tin* and *man*-sized targets on a rifle range: *'Don't you come / go the tin man with me, my friend!'*

tin trousers A Captain's Mess Dress uniform trousers embellished with *lightning conductors.

tingel Strictly speaking, a wooden or metal patch on a crack or hole in a small craft, but also used to describe other emergency repairs: *'Better get a tingel on those overalls before I see you again..'*

titfer Hat; Cockney rhyming slang.

tit / tits Not surprisingly, more than half-a-dozen entries under this heading:

1. Tomatoes in tomato sauce - see *-ITS.
2. Expression of annoyance:'*He gets right on my tits..*'
3. '*It's about as much use as tits on a bull..*'
4. A *tit hammock* is a 44 inch D-cup brassiere.
5. (SM) To *push the tit* was for the Officer of the Watch to sound the klaxon, using the conning tower bellpush, just before diving.
6. A *tit* is another name in *Uckers for a *blob, with extensions such as *mixy-tit* or to *tit up*.
7. '*I couldn't give a fish's tit..*' '*I don't care at all..*'
8. *tits up* (esp. FAA)   Lying on its back, ie. broken or useless: '*We were due to *launch at *oh seven dubs, but the aircraft went tits up as we taxyed out..*'

Tizzysnatcher   Two explanations:
1. Very old nickname for the Paymaster (now part of the *white empire); a *tizzy* was Cockney slang for a sixpence. The Navy paid men up to the nearest sixpence below their wages, the odd coppers being carried over on the ledger until next payment. Many sailors maintained that the Paymaster had snatched the odd *tizzies* from them.
2. Also a name for the *Schoolie, rather than the Pusser, dating from the days (very long ago) when a *tizzy* (sixpence) per day was deducted from a midshipman's pay as a tuition fee for the instructor.

TLA   A *Three Letter Abbreviation* - like this one!

toast   The **Loyal Toast** is the privilege accorded to the Royal Navy of remaining seated whilst drinking the Sovereign's health, and is of long standing, but obscure origin. There are three popular beliefs about this (a) that King Charles II when on board the ROYAL CHARLES bumped his head on rising to reply to the toast; (b) that King George IV when Regent, dining on board one of HM Ships said as the officers rose to drink the King's health,'*Gentlemen pray be seated, your loyalty is beyond suspicion*' and (c) that King William IV while Duke of Clarence (Lord High Admiral) bumped his head as he stood up at dinner in one of HM Ships. In many wooden ships it was almost impossible to stand upright between decks except between the deckbeams. Furthermore, in ships having a pronounced *tumblehome* i.e. steeply sloping sides, anyone seated close to the ship's side would find it difficult to stand at all.

Toasts of the week (*sotto voce* additions in brackets):
    Monday : Our ships at sea

Tuesday :   Our men
Wednesday :   Ourselves (*since no-one else will think of us*)
Thursday :   A bloody war or a sickly season (*and a quick promotion*)
Friday :   A willing foe - and sea room
Saturday :   Sweethearts and wives (*may they never meet!*)
Sunday :   Absent friends

toddy   Rum (or whisky) with hot water and lemon.

toe rag (esp. RM)   Frequent term of abuse:'*Just look at him working on the *Boss - the snivelling toe rag..*'

toe rot   Athlete's foot, or any other fungal infection of the skin - often used with the qualification *chinky.

toe the line   Older Naval term that has now come ashore. When the ship's company was *mustered for *victualling or pay, each sailor stepped forward to a line marked on the deck, and then gave his name and place of duty in the ship. This line was placed sufficiently far away from the Paymaster's table so that Jack could not sweep the whole lot into his cap as he leaned forward to scoop up his pay. This procedure has developed in shore parlance into an expression which indicates an acknowledgement of authority and a willingness to obey the rules.

toffologist   Anyone on the lower deck who spoke with a public school, Oxbridge or other cut-glass accent was labelled as a *toffologist*. The term was particularly prevalent during the days of *HOs and National Service. Contrast this with a *bad speaking bastard..

toggle (and two)   The male genital apparatus: '*Well - wozzit a baby boy then?' 'Fink so - at least it 'ad a toggle an' two..*' A *toggle pin* can be found opposite a *becket on a duffle coat. Note also: '*His toggle was that big it looked like an elephant's trunk. We used to throw buns to it in the showers..*'

toggle-oggling   Gazing at someone else's *parts, eg. in a stand-up urinal: '*Shiny shoes you've got!*'   Or: '*New shoes?*' *Snurging is another name for this activity.

tombola   Shipboard version of bingo or lotto: '*You've got skin like the lee side of a winning tombola ticket..*' Sometimes heard as *tombollocks*.

tonsil varnish (older)   Really strong tea.

took the wind out of his sails   A *windward vessel steals the wind from another to leeward; this can be seen in the covering tactics that are supposed to make the America's Cup races exciting. The expression is now used ashore for someone who is rather *taken aback and splutteringly speechless.

tool screecher (esp. RM)   Female schoolteacher.

Toom (FAA)   The McDonnell Douglas F-4K *Phantom*, powered by Rolls-Royce Spey turbofan engines, and the last conventional jet fighter operated by *Stovies in the fighter/ground attack role from the previous *Ark. These aircraft, like the *Bucc, all passed onwards into Royal Air Force service, before being finally *struck from charge.

toot   A trio of interest:
1. An opinion given in a discussion:*'Once we'd all had a toot, the Admiral then said what he wanted done, and when..'*
2. Depending on the context it is used in, a *quick toot* can also mean a short weeping episode.
3. To have a *toot on* describes a state of annoyance and anger.

toothie / toothwright   Dentist; see also *gnasher basher, *fang farrier, *molar mangler and *Top Gum. A *Wisdom Tooth* is the Senior Dental Surgeon.

Tommy Pipes Very old Navy nickname for the *bosun's mate.

top bollocks Jack's alternative name for the female breasts.

top heavy in the fore peak A very busty party.

top cover (FAA) The presence of friendly fighters overhead during a mission, now adapted to describe having someone more senior than you present on some escapade: '*The Commodore came ashore with us for a pub *run, so with top cover like that there were no problems..*'

Top Gum The head of the Royal Navy Dental Branch.

top shelf run A visit to a pub, like the *Perisher Course's visitation to the Victoria Hotel Rothesay, when the only liquor taken comes from the bottles on the *top shelf* behind the bar.

toppers Full up, or topped up: '*The *gash bin was toppers, so these idiots simply *ditched the stuff behind a nearby tent..*'

topsides Two usages:
1. On top of something: '*When I shared a cabin with Jim, his bunk was topsides..*' Note also *cheesy hammy eggy topsides.
2. On deck: '*What's happening topsides?*'

Torbay steaks (SM) Faggots (the food); following the incidents involving a homosexual *Jimmy in HMS TORBAY, a submarine *Wardroom steward will now refer to faggots as: '*Torbay steaks on the menu this evening..*'

tore him up for arse paper A serious rebuke; in mixed company this becomes *tore him up for rice paper*.

torpedo dish (SM) Galley tray.

Torpoint Cornish town situated on the Hamoaze river, just opposite Devonport and its Naval Dockyard. In older times it was where warships and other vessels could be ballasted and careened for the tarring and caulking of their hulls, and was known then as *Tar Point*. See also the entries for *pay and *Devil. It was also the scene of a thriving rope-making industry, hence the expression of someone bandy-legged as having legs like a *Torpoint rope-maker*. Nowadays it is the thriving run-ashore for the *nozzers of HMS *RALEIGH who are often to be found in the *Royal Navy School of Dancing, or the many other adjacent hostelries.

Torps The Officer who was to *Torp*edoes and Mines what

*Guns was to the arts of Gunnery and (parade) Drill. He was also, when electricity was introduced into ships, responsible for its distribution; this, of course, was direct current (DC) or straight amps initially. All ships had either 100v or 240v DC. **Torps** was never allowed to get his hands on the *wiggly amps*. He only ever looked after straight ones. There are those who could say he didn't/couldn't understand wiggly amps. Equipment that needed *wiggly amps or alternating current (AC), eg. radio and subsequently radar, was the responsibility of the operators (Telegraphists and Radar Plotters). After WWII, the electrical (L) branch was created, which subsequently became the Weapons Electrical (WL) branch, then the Weapons & Electrical Engineering (WEE) branch, and finally the Weapons Engineering (WE) branch. See also *engineering.

toss (FAA)   Method of attacking a distant target from low-level, using a *SHAR equipped with freefall or laser-guided precision weapons, pulling up into a half-loop as it releases the ordnance; also known as a *loft attack* because the bombs are projected *a-loft* before they descend. Note also the more general use of: '*I couldn't give a toss about that..*' by someone who can't care less.

tosser / tosspot   Fairly serious and derogatory terms of abuse for an individual. They have also been heard as a nickname for the son of a Mr and Mrs Kerr, parents who were daft enough to give their boy the Christian name Wayne!

TOT (FAA)   Acronym for *Time On Task*, ie the time that you propose to turn up for some rendezvous or meeting.

tot   A half-gill measure of *pusser's previously issued (prior to the *Black Day) to entitled individuals at the *tot time* of around 11.30 am - an eagerly awaited event in a warship's day. There were some benefits - ship's Welfare Committee business meetings could usually be held at 11.25 and completed by tot time! Some Navies with links to the RN (such as the Royal New Zealand Navy) still retain the tot custom. Note also the conversational put-down by an older sailor to a young 'un: '*I've had more ripples in my tot than you've steamed over..*' If a Senior Rates mess meeting was held *after* tot time it could easily degenerate into *tot time frolics*.

Tot Fund   An Admiralty Fund established for the welfare of RN sailors out of monies saved on rum purchases when the Tot was withdrawn in 1970; see *Black day and the entry on *rum. Currently some £1.5 million of non-public funds are distributed annually in this way.

Tote displays Standard nickname in a warship's Operations Room for the small television screens adjoining the main display units, from which information similar to the *Tote* betting prices of horse-racing can be extracted and stored using a light pen. In the pre-TV and computer era, *Tote Boards* were used. These resembled the chalk boards used by bookies at race tracks, and the information was written on them in chinagraph pencil. A big wartime carrier like IMPLACABLE had 129 aircraft embarked, and the Air Direction Room was run by the FDO and two Assistant Direction Officers. It was quite exciting keeping tabs on all the aircraft up when using manual plotting, especially if the other carriers in the Pacific Fleet had their squadrons airborne too.

touch and go An expression commonly used to mean uncertainty. It is of maritime origin and refers to a ship touching the sea bottom and then slipping off. Also used by the FAA in the pre-*SHAR era for a roller landing with the tailhook up.

tough titty! *'Hard luck, mate!'*

towed array roll New term, and a play on words describing the uncomfortable movement in a seaway of frigates employed in the towed array role!

tower (SM) Double hatch access route to the fin (called a sail across the *Pond) from inside a submarine - derived from the older term of *conning tower.

townie Shipmate or *oppo coming from the same area as you.

towpath copy An unofficial or *silent copy of an important document or letter; subtle response to the 1987 *Court Martial of a certain well-decorated Naval Officer. Certain important and suppressed truths emerged when the contents of his private MOD briefing notes became public knowledge after they had been mislaid on a towpath near the Thames. Really a modern version of the older *drop copy.

toybox The engine room.

TQ (RM) *Technical Qualification* (RM). Once a man is trained in one of these he is transferred from the General Duties to the Technical Branch, and will be employed in his *TQ* for the rest of his career. Divided into tradesmen and non-tradesmen sub-branches, eg. VM (Vehicle Mechanic), K (Cook), SA (Stores Accountant and C (Clerk).

(the) Trade (SM)   The Submarine Service's nickname for itself.

trade (FAA)   Direction Officer's term to fighters on *CAP for enemy aircraft targets: *'Hello Silver Leader - we have trade for you at ninety miles to the north - four hostiles on the *deck at six hundred knots - inbound..'*

Trafalgar   A crucial battle in Britain's destiny which, although finally thwarting Napoleon's plans for a cross-Channel invasion by the total defeat of the combined French and Spanish fleets under Villeneuve, also cost the life of Lord *Nelson, the country's premier maritime warrior.   The battle, and his peerless example, are still celebrated on the anniversary of his death, in RN *Wardrooms at sea and ashore all over the world; see also the *Immortal Memory.   October 21st is also a *Corps memorable date, because of the Royal Marines' splendid contributions on that day, off Cape Trafalgar, in 1805.

train smash   *Car smash with sausages.

trained monkey (FAA)   *Observers fighting back (at last) with a nickname for their Pilots; see also *monkey on a stick.

Trainer   Second-in-command to the gun *Layer on a cannon or in a gun turret not under a Turret Captain, and directly responsible for the weapon's azimuth setting.   The name lived on with the *Field Gun Team *Trainers* who were not called this, as is generally supposed, because they were responsible for the physical condition of their *Field Gunners. These days however, it would not really be possible to call their superiors *Layers!

training wheels (FAA)   Disparaging nickname for the retractable wingtip-mounted wheels of the *SHAR.

transmit   When a rating got the social disease it used to be said that he had had his *safe to transmit boards* removed.   These were boards positioned physically over the radio transmitter and radar switches that prevented any transmissions while a man was aloft.

transom   Bottom: *'How's your transom, my handsom'?'*

trap   Half-a-dozen applications here:
1. Acquire a female friend on a *run ashore: *'Lauderdale was fantastic - most of us trapped every time we went ashore..'*
2. A large serving dish eg. a *mess trap*.
3. (FAA) Check flight with the RN Flying Standards Unit - who are therefore known as *The Trappers*!

Jack Dusty

4. (FAA also)   Deck landing with the tail-hook catching an arrester wire; the (steam) catapault-assisted take-off is called a *boost.
5. Jack's (older) name for the Bermuda Fleet Canteen.
6. Alternative name for a toilet or *heads.

tree stop (RM)   The process, while out of control on *pusser's planks, of decelerating suddenly and painfully; see also *yeti.

trench foot   Non-freezing cold injury of the foot, a circulation disorder caused by prolonged exposure to cold and damp conditions outdoors; common amongst the poorly-shod British ground forces towards the end of the land battles for the Falklands in 1982.

trice up   Fix something up with strings or rope.

trick   Period on duty at the wheel; this is generally shorter than a full *Watch because of the intense and steady concentration needed. Any period of watch - not just helmsman duty.

trick cyclist   Another term for a head shrinker or *sky artist.

trickle drafting   System whereby the ship's company of a warship is always being turned over in small increments, so that her fighting efficiency is never really at a constant peak. However, both administrative convenience and financial considerations outweigh this former aspect.

trim (SM)   A submarine's state of neutral buoyancy and also balance; to *trim down* in harbour implies adjustment by allowing water into the main ballast tanks, whereas to *catch a trim* is to get it just right. Note also the older applicatopn of *trimming someone's lamps* - by giving him a black eye. See also *racing trim.

trim the dish   When several people were sitting on one side of a launch, the boat would heel over to that side. The coxswain might shout: '*Come on lads, trim the dish..*' to even up the load.

trip the anchor   *Evolution carried out before lifting the anchor, designed to free its flukes from the sea-bed. Sometimes not done intentionally - it happens when a ship swings, the cable catches a fluke and then lifts the anchor out. When *weighing anchor, the anchor is *broken out*. The state of the anchor, when working cable, used to be signalled to the bridge by a flag. Cable up and down was flag U; *anchor aweigh* was port or starboard, depending which anchor, and *anchor clear* was the affirmative. *Foul anchor* was the negative - and an awful lot of bad language. Occasionally, impatient captains or pilots would shout down: *'Mr Bloggs, what is the delay?'* The classic reply to this was: *'There is no delay sir, it always takes as long as this..'* This was considered a little insubordinate by some captains. In such an instance, the cable officer would usually hold his hand up high and say nothing. This was equally infuriating to the bridge, but could not be called insubordinate!

tripewriter   A *Scribes who cannot spell.

triple-hatted   A senior officer who has three distinctly separate areas of responsibility to attend to.

trog (RM)   Term of abuse derived from *troglodyte* - a brainless caveman type whose knuckles brush the ground as he walks. In some quarters the word is also an appropriate abbreviation for a *trained rating of *Ganges*!

trolley   To have sexual intercourse.

trolleys   Underpants; see also *keks and *smalls.

troop (RM)   Older name for a trained soldier with Good Conduct badges: *'He's a good troop..'* Now used more in the sense of the Army's word *platoon* to describe a sub-formation of a rifle company. The *Troop Bible* is a crucial and constantly-modified notebook or Filofax carried by the *Troop Sergeant* which contains every single personal military detail anyone could think of: *'If it's not in the Troop Bible then it's just a *gash *buzz..'*

trooped (RM)   Royal's equivalent of being put in the *rattle.

troops   An important pair:
1. Collective term for Jack: *'A *run-ashore in Sydney will certainly be highly popular with the troops..'*
2. (RM) *Out Troops!* - the order to leave a landing craft.

tropical routine   The modified working day in tropical climates whereby non-watchkeepers were called at 0600; they worked throughout the remaining relatively cool two hours of the morning, all the forenoon, and *secured for the day at 1300.

trot   Five different applications:
1. *on the trot* - absent from place of duty, having deserted.
2. *trots* - diarrhoea; see *squitters for some alternatives.
3. A line of mooring buoys or ships at anchor, hence this quote about London buses: *'..and then six came along on the trot..'*

4. (SM) A group of submarines tied up alongside. The *trot sentries* look after the security and safety of a *boat in harbour, and may be an *Upper Deck trot* (casing sentry) or the *Downstairs Trot* ('tween decks). A *trot fob* referred to the daily shuffle of submarines alongside a depot ship.
5. The *trot boat* could also refer to the working vessel which took Jack ashore when his ship was anchored off.

trouser trout / snake   The penis.

truck   The circular wooden cap to a mast or *jackstaff, containing a set of sheaves. Another adaptation of the word comes from the solid wooden wheels of a gun carriage which were its

truck wheels. This has now come ashore - to the M25 orbital motorway in particular.

Truckie
1. Wartime nickname for a *WRNS *truck driver*.
2. Nickname for any member of the Royal Corps of Transport, now subsumed into the Royal Logistic Corps.
3. Label applied to the type of flying carried out by the C-130 *Hercules* transport crews of the RAF.

true colours   Another phrase with a Naval origin; *false colours* were permitted during an approach to another ship, but the *true* (nationality) *colours* had to be broken out once battle was joined and fire exchanged.

True dit!   Qualification for a statement or story which sounds completely implausible but which is actually true (at least in the mind of the teller!).

Trunk a monk!   *'Well I never!'*

trunking   Another pair:
1.   **Fan / cable trunking** - air-conditioning / electrical cable ducts passing throughout a ship.
2.   Sexual intercourse - see also *trolley.

Trunky   Nickname for a Chief Electrician (or *'Lecky) responsible for the condition of wires in *cable trunking*. Can also be a nickname for someone with a big nose.

tub   Two usgaes again:
1.   An unwieldy, or poorly handling vessel.
2.   Decorated and polished wooden barrel from which the *tot was issued by *Tanky - *neaters for the *Chuffs and *Puffs, *grog for the *messdecks. See *rum also.

tube (FAA)   *Pinger nickname for a submarine.

TUBMIN   See entry under *thumb.

Tug / Tugg   Nickname for the surname Wilson, after an Admiral Wilson who repeatedly ordered a battleship to carry out the *evolution of entering harbour, before finally offering her Captain, in exasperation, to **tug** (tow) his *pusser's wagon in for him. Also, of course, the Fleet Air Arm's celebrated and most favourite cartoonist!

tumbled   Found out.

tune for maximum smoke   A highly unorthodox method of finding out where an earth was in a long cable run, especially in the older days when all wiring was of the lead-cased variety. Somewhere in those miles of *electric string was a fault that, with lots of clipping and unclipping, could take weeks to find. This dangerous technique involved swapping the fuse that kept blowing for a six-inch long, countersunk head, brass screw. Then, where the smoke came from - there was your earth!

Tunney Cup (RM)   Association Football challenge cup analagous to the *Argyll Bowl of rugby football. Officially, it is the United States *Marine Corps Trophy and yet another celebration of the close links between the two Corps; in practice it is named after Captain Gene Tunney USMC, the much-admired former World Heavyweight boxing champion who actually presented this piece of silver to the Royal Marines in 1928.

Tupperware fleet   The new generation of glassfibre-reinforced and plastic-hulled Mine Countermeasures Vessels.

turdburglar   Wonderful term of general abuse and disparagement, but in some quarters also specific for a *brownhatter.

turd tank   Occasional nickname for the rectum.

turk   See *trolley and *trunk, both euphemisms for the act of copulation. *Turk Town* is Gosport, a small Hampshire town on the western side of Portsmouth Harbour, and home to many naval establishments.

Turk's head   Ornamental and decorative ropework.

turn a blind eye   Witness some misdemeanour yet ignore it, derived from Lord *Nelson's conduct at the Battle of Copenhagen where he chose not to see a signal ordering him to break off the action at a critical moment; he then went on to destroy the Danish fleet.

turn and turn about   A spell of continuous duty under a two-watch system.

turn in   The process of preparing for sleep; note that it can also be used in an active sense, such as putting an incapacitated colleague to bed:'*At that stage, the boys turned him in to sleep things off.*.'

turn in the barrel (SM)   This stemmed from the old joke about legionnaires in an isolated desert fort. Watches in the older submarines were only two hours long; the theory being that you could only be alert for this period of time. A *boat was most vulnerable when it was *snorting, for very obvious reasons. The whole boat crew's lives at that moment depended on the engine room *tiffs, because apart from the ease at which you could write off the main engines, it was pretty disastrous to crash dive with the snort mast still open. It was a 14 inch pipe, almost as wide as a *barrel*. Snorting watches were kept, with a tiff on each engine. If playing war games, the *old man would try and snort at every opportunity to keep the box (*batteries*) up. Sometimes, these attemps would be of a very short duration, and sometimes you would not even get going. This could be a fairly exhausting routine, especially with the amount of concentration required. If it was your *turn in the barrel*, then you were the one who was *shaken to start snorting, and the one who had the longest to go before you went off watch.

turn of leave out of watch   A method whereby Jack can go *ashore when he is in the duty *watch, provided he has a *sub; also used to describe someone who is seeking sexual gratification other than in the marital bed. *Getting a bit, *out of station* has a similar meaning.

turn out   Can mean the opposite of *turn in, as in: '*The duty *watch then turned out to meet this threat..*' but it is more often used to describe general appearance, or the standard of uniform and accessories. For Royal, this will always be *immaculate!

turn to   Start work.

turn turtle   A ship that goes right over and lies overturned and hull-up, looking just like a turtle.

turning trousers (FAA)   Anti-G device worn by fighter pilots over the lower half of their flying suits. Expanding rubber bladders prevent blood draining into the legs and abdomen during high-G manoeuvres, thereby helping to prolong consciousness. See also *speed jeans.

twat hat (esp. RM) Soft tweed hat with an all-round rim.

tweaking Fine tuning of a ship's operational performance.

'tweendecks The accepted abbreviation of *between decks*, and properly refers to any area inside the ship, although usually just to accommodation and other communal spaces. In big ships a junior seaman officer is usually designated **Mate of the 'Tweendecks*.

twelve (year engagement) *'Roll on my bloody twelve, that's all I can say..'*

twenty-four about Auxiliary watchkeeper's round of watches were 24 *about*, ie. afternoon, first and morning, then 24 hours off, followed by dogs, middle and forenoon, then 24 off again, and so on.

Twirler! (FAA) R/T call transmitted when a 2 inch unguided rocket was fired and some of the folding fins did not deploy, thus making the device fly on a totally unpredictable trajectory.

twist a burn Roll a cigarette.

twitched An interesting duo:
1. (FAA) A state of nervous exhaustion or combat fatigue, often characterised by a tic or *twitch* of the facial muscles, especially around the eyes.
2. Frightened:*'He's a bit twitched about seeing the Admiral at noon, although he doesn't yet realise it's for a *BZ..'*

twitter Brainless chatter:*'Come on you lot - stop bloody twittering - and get on with it!'*

two-and-a-half (rings) The rank **lace* of a Lieutenant Commander, namely two gold rings, with a half (**scraper) ring in between; the author's late son put this nicely into perspective when he proudly announced in 1978 that his newly promoted Dad was now a *two-and-a-bit*!

two and one The dilution ordered by Admiral Vernon when **grog* was first issued; see also **two water*. This weakened strength persisted until the **Black Day* was visited upon the Fleet.

two and two An administrative punishment based on becoming Second Class for both leave and pay.

two and two make five? Drawing the wrong conclusion to something: *'So because of that happening, you think that we're off to the West Indies, and that two and two make five?'*

two badger   Eight years unblemished service, as evidenced by two *GCBs worn on the left uniform sleeve.

Two blocks!   Means: *'I've had enough - I'm fed up'*. Derived (as with *chokker) from two blocks in a *tackle coming together when they have been pulled up as far as they can go. No further movement is possible. *Two blocks!* was also a recognised order to stop hauling, and has survived from the era of sailing ships.

two-oh-six   See also *flimsy; Form *S.206 was the report format for RN and RM officers. Now computerised, it has become the C.206, although Royal tends to refer to a *two-nought-six*. A more complete collection has been assembled by the author in a companion volume entitled *IN CONFIDENCE*, details of which are inside the back cover of this book. As a taster, however, some of the classic comments are repeated here:
His men would follow him anywhere, but only out of curiosity..
I would not breed from this Officer..
This Officer is really not so much of a has-been, but more of a
        definitely won't-be..
When she opens her mouth, it seems that this is only to change
        whichever foot was previously in there..
He has carried out each and every one of his duties to his entire
        satisfaction..
He would be out of his depth in a car park puddle..
Technically sound, but socially impossible..
This young lady has delusions of adequacy..
Since my last report he has reached rock bottom, and has now
        started to dig..
He has the wisdom of youth, and the energy of old age..

two shakes of a (duck's) tail   In no time at all, or very quickly.

two - six, heave!   Two completely different explanations for something that may even be directly related:
1. Exhortation to the gun numbers in a sailing warship responsible for pulling the cannon back into position after reloading; the word heave is pronounced *hevvy*. Often used, without the suffix, for a task ashore where some form of co-ordinated physical effort is involved: *'Everyone got a hand on it? Right - two six..'*
2. (FAA)   An alternative to the above, and a parallel explanation, is that this was an order given to push an aircraft into a new position, tail first. To do this, two men lifted the tail while six others pushed against the wings, three on either side. This goes right back to the First World War.

Loblolly Boy

two thirds A double measure of spirits.

Two's up! A way of reserving your position after somebody: *'Two's up on that magazine, Bill!'* Or:*'I went two's up on that Magic Mountain ride after Ginge - wish I hadn't now..'*

two watches *Watches of equal length, eg. four hours on, four hours off, around the clock - a very tiring routine. The expression *eyes in two watches* refers to the eyes being in different *watches and hence, whether due to alcohol or tiredness, not focusing very well.

two water Another version of *two and one - *neaters that has been diluted by this amount in the original version of *grog.

twofers Two drinks for the price of one, eg. at a Happy Hour in the *Wardroom.

Type Since WWII, most classes of warship of up to destroyer size have been allocated a Type number; notable exceptions were the Daring Class (super destroyers) and the County Class of Guided Missile Destroyers (actually of cruiser size). The *Types* (in roughly chronological order) have been:

Type 15/16 (late 40s) - conversions of a variety of wartime destroyers and frigates to Anti-Submarine (AS) frigates.

Type 14 (early 50s) - small A/S steam frigates.

Type 12 (50s) - AS steam frigates.

Type 41 (50s) Anti-Aircraft diesel frigates.

Type 61 (50s) - Aircraft Direction diesel frigates.

Type 81 (late 50s/early 60s) - very popular Tribal Class of general purpose (GP) steam & gas turbine frigates.

Modified Type 12 (60s) - The Leander Class of GP steam frigates, subsequently extensively remodernised into separate specialist roles.

Type 82 (late 60s) - HMS BRISTOL, only one built of a class designed to provide AA protection for the new class of aircraft *carrier (CVA-01), plans for which were scrapped in the mid-60s.

Type 21 (70s) - hugely popular GP gas turbine frigates.

Type 42 (70s) - Anti-Air Warfare gas turbine destroyers.

Type 22 (late 70s/80s) - primarily Anti-Submarine, gas turbine frigates, fitted with the Seawolf air defence missile system.

Type 23 (late 80s/90s) - GP gas turbine frigates.

Type 45 Newly announced class (2000) of area air defence ship, the first in class to be HMS DARING.

Tyro (FAA) Prefix to aircraft's radio call sign used by a student doing his first few solos, so that other pilots in the circuit can watch out for him and, if necessary, take avoiding action.

UNIFORM

477 - 484

UA Under Age; see *G, T and UA.

Uckers The old family game of ludo, modified by Jack to include strategy and tactics, and played at all levels throughout the Royal Navy from minesweepers to the *Yacht (when she was still in service). The piling up of counters creates *blobs which, depending on their size, require varying challenges to overcome. A *mixy blob loses those challenge rights. *Wafu rules are not played in *General Service, but include such subtleties as *suck backs and *siff on his donk. See also *double six, *Out piece and hack!, *Look for the rules!, *Up table!, *Up tit!, and *eight piece dicking. There are so many varieties, it would probably be nigh impossible to compile a comprehensive set of Fleet rules. Many messdecks and crew rooms have a permanent Uckers board incorporated into the furniture, somewhere, ready for use. In the old HMS CUMBERLAND there was a large Uckers board let into B gun deck for championship games - with spectators!

Ugh man (FAA) The grunt of effort *Ugh!* was associated with a big, strong individual lifting a heavy weight; it often involved *stovie *bombheads of a past era who all seemed to be well-built *muscle bosuns.

ugly Some choice and wholly chauvinistic figures of speech used by both Jack and Royal when describing a certain lack of feminine beauty. In these days of strict equality of course, they could easily be adapted the other way:

She wasn't just ugly, she was (flipp)ing ugly!
Her mouth looked like a torn pocket..
*Her *moosh deserved its own *Hurt Certificate..*
Those teeth! They looked like a row of condemned houses..
She looked a bit like a bulldog chewing a wasp..
Helen of Troy's face launched a thousand ships - this one

would have caused the boys to *scuttle the fleet..
*Every time she stood up, I thought someone had switched
    the lights out..*
*She told me she worked for an airline - if it's true, then I bet
    she bump-starts them Jumbo jets..*
She was as ugly as a robber's dog..
*'Er teeth stuck out so far it looked like 'er nose was playin'
    a piano..*
*Honest, her face was / enough to stop a clock / like a bag of
    spanners / like a choked weedtrap..*

Although not really a measure of beauty as such, Jack has a nice statement regarding those impossibly skinny fashion models who are supposed to represent normal people when displaying the latest fashion designs: *'She's that thin she could tread water in a sight gauge..'*

ugly rush (FAA)   Any unorthodox, or dangerous approach to a landing by an aircraft.

ullage   Worthless residue in a beer barrel, can also be used to describe the overall quality of a group, as well as the residue left in the *tub after the tot had been issued. *Grog becomes **ullage** after about 45 minutes. This was supposed to be ditched under the eye of the Officer Of the Day. There is a lovely *dit called *'Arpin'* in which the Chief *Buffer Archangel says to Both Watches of the Angels:*'Right you lot, Guard and Celestial Choir is required today. We shall be welcoming on board a *three badge *killick *dusty wot never sold Jack short on 'is tot, and always ditched the ullage..'*

ulu (FAA and RM)   The Malay word for jungle, sometimes written incorrectly as *ooloo*; the term is now employed conversationally to describe any remote location that might be occupied by *Junglies or *Booties - even in Arctic Norway!

unbutton   De-code or de-cypher a signal.

uncork   Older term for decoding a signal.

under way   Strictly speaking, no longer secured; a ship that *slips and proceeds is getting *under way* as she starts to move, and *making way* when well established in forward motion.

underwater butler (SM)   Officers' steward or Tiffy's messman.

underwonder-gun   A device, fitted in boats, which can fire a variety of pyrotechnics to the surface when dived, i.e. smoke canisters, a multitude of coloured grenades, message buoys and the legendary bubble decoy of WW2, Portland and Firth of Clyde fame.

undetected crime   In Jack's eyes, fifteen years of this is what the *Blue Peter or *pea-do is awarded for.

unhook   Older term for *proffing.

Unknown Warrior   Used, without any disrespect intended, to describe a total *sack rat:*'He spends more time in his bunk than the Unknown Warrior..'*

unlatched   Term used for someone on detached and loan duty away from his normal appointment.

unrig   In the old days of compulsory attendance at Sunday church services on the quarterdeck of cruisers and capital ships, forms were carried from the messdecks and chairs from the wardroom for the congregation. After the blessing and the disappearance of the Captain's cap as he descended the after hatch, there would be a cheerful bosun's *pipe to accompany the loud order: '*Second part of the starboard watch, unrig church; boys down prayer books..'*

unscheduled sunrise (FAA)   The effect of detonating a nuclear weapon; see also *bucket of sunshine and *CND.

up all hammocks   It is ironic that in the morning when hammocks were taken down, the pipe was *Up all hammocks!* In the evening when hammocks had to be up on their hooks or bars, the pipe was *Down all hammocks!* This order originates from the days when hammock nettings (stowages) were situated on the upper deck, along the bulwarks between the quarter deck and the forecastle. Therefore hammocks had to be taken *up* on deck to be stowed and brought *down* to be rigged for sleep.

up Channel night   See *Channel night.

up funnel, down screw   The order given when steam was auxiliary to sail, with screw and funnel retracted when sailing. Sometimes used nowadays to indicate a major change of mode.

up homers   Any family hospitality shown to Jack when he is away from his own home. Tugg shows this perfectly at B - 74.

up my nose   Frequently heard expression indicating a sense of irritation or annoyance with someone: '*Usually he's a really good *hand, but his whole attitude to this particular problem gets right up my nose..'*   See also *tits.

Up or down, but not sideways!   Standard cry to a person blocking access by being stationary on an accommodation ladder.

Up spirits!   *Pipe made in the era of the *Tot to initiate the daily collection and issue of *pusser's from the Spirit Room. Throughout the ship, countless lips would be muttering the classic rejoinder: '*Stand fast the Holy Ghost..'*

up sticks (RM)   *Turn to, strike camp and get *yomping; see also *pull pole.

up the creek   In physical difficulties, or in some other hopeless situation. The author has often wondered if there is any connection with the dismal prospects facing a sick *matelot* being transferred by water, in the old days, from his ship in the Solent or Plymouth Sound, *up Haslar Creek* or *up Stonehouse Creek* respectively.

up the line   Up country somewhere from *Guzz or *Pompey,

U - 480

but generally at home. Also, a description of someone who is a bit dozey, whose mind is *up the line* and elsewhere.

up there A phrase used, with the jerk of a thumb, to describe the location and whereabouts of those *Whitehall warriors, who are not necessarily all in Whitehall these days!

Up table! A desperate ploy in *Uckers, used to end the game by lifting the table and causing the counters to slide off. As in *Look for the rules! both the fist size and degree of inebriation of your opponents should both be very carefully considered before employing this tactic.

Up tit! Exhortation to move a counter forward on the *Uckers board after dice have been thrown.

up to speed (on something) Briefed and fully aware of the facts or details of a case: *'Are you up to speed on the latest developments concerning the replacement amphibious ships?'*

up top On deck or *topsides

uphill gardener One of many alternatives for *brownhatter.

UPO Yet another *TLA, this version standing for *Unit Personnel Office*, a one-stop personnel administration centre in ships and establishments.

Upper Yardie Properly *Upper Yardman* - a rating under 21 who has been selected for, and has volunteered for, training and commissioning as an Officer. Formerly, only the brightest seamen were selected to *man the upper yards*; the hazards involved required people who could think and react very quickly. *Special Duties Officers have now been renamed *Senior Upper Yardmen* and their training arrangements altered at *Dartmouth.

upper deck Collective term to describe all external areas of a ship; generally synonymous with *weather decks, but which see for subtle differences. Note that the opposite of *upper deck* is not *lower deck, but *below decks or *'tweendecks, and in addition, the term *upper deck* does not properly refer to officers (see *quarterdeck). An *upper deck ape* is a stoker's nickname for a seaman, or *sandscratcher.

upper scupper Rhyming slang for the above; the term is often used by the *lower deck to mock some piece of deliberately officer-like behaviour: *'I say, old chap - that was just a bit upper scupper, don't you think?'*

upside-down head   A bald man with a beard; see also *VFR.

upstairs (SM)   The surface of the sea.

uptake   Correct name for a warship's funnel. The funnel is that part of the *uptakes* which is physically above the weather decks. The uptakes were the gathering-together of the flues from the different boilers,* 'tween decks, before reaching the funnels. In the older carriers, there were as many as sixteen boilers, and the exhaust gases were gathered in the uptakes before ascending about 100 feet to the top of the island. Close examination shows the exhaust system (boilers and gas turbines) to be a trunk within a trunk. Both skins below decks are uptakes, but above the weather deck the outer becomes the *funnel* but the inner skin is still the uptake. The system was designed to keep the funnel cool but even so, in a destroyer at full power, the paint would char.

u/s (esp. FAA)   Abbreviation for *unserviceable* - an expression that is rather difficult for American exchange officers to come to terms with!

uselessness   Note the terms *ashtray on a motorbike, *chocolate fireguard and *third nostril, but in a more general sense of describing a totally useless person these gems may occasionally also be heard:
  He couldn't pull the skin off a rice pudding..
  He couldn't spot a new sixpence on a chimney-sweep's bum..
  He couldn't fight his way out of a wet paper bag..

Malta Dog

VICTOR

485 - 488

Van Heusen   Famous clothing manufacturer which used to advertise a *semi-stiff collar* as a feature of its shirts; quickly adopted by Jack to describe a *lazy lob, or incomplete erection.

Vasco   Classic nickname for the Navigating Officer (but see also *pilot), from *Vasco da Gama*, the 16th century Portuguese explorer.

'vast!   See *avast. An order to stop: *''vast heaving!'*

veer Two different meanings:
1. A clockwise shift in wind direction; see also *back.
2. Ease out a rope or hawser, under control, around a capstan or winch.

Velcro back   Someone who is stuck to his *pit; a similar expression to *canvas back.

Velcro rating   A man who has been promoted to, and then demoted from the same rank on several occasions in his career: *'He's been made up to *killick and then busted down that many times, his badges must be backed with Velcro..'*

verbal   Encouragement or vocal support: *'Don't just stand there and watch your team, lads - give it some verbal!'*

vertrep   Portmanteau word for *vertical replenishment*, now widely used to describe the procedure for any stores ashore or at sea that are delivered by helicopter.

Very good!   Acknowledgement by the Officer of the Watch of an action completed by the *Quartermaster or helmsman. A steering order of say, 257 degrees, is acknowledged by an exact repetition of the order, followed by: *'Course 257, sir'*, and the response by the OOW of *'Very good!'* Note that in the RN this is never from a junior to a senior, but Royal Marines, as ever, are different!

very seldom up top   Bald as a coot; may also be termed an *upside-down head.

vetting   Screening process for an appointment; all Naval personnel are supposed to be *Normally Vetted* to a certain degree, a process involving a search through records held by the Home Office. Some, in sensitive appointments, are also *Positively Vetted* or *PV'd*, where colleagues and referrees are actually interviewed.

VFR on top, IFR below (FAA)   The *TLAs stand for *Visual* and *Instrument Flying Rules*, and the whole phrase refers to a bald, bearded man. See also *upside-down head.

VG   *Very Good*   The highest character (or *conduct*) assessment on Jack's, Jenny's or Royal's *Service Certificate; continuous *VG Conduct* is a prerequisite for the award of Good Conduct *Badges (4 years for each) and for the *pea doo (15 years).

vicky verky   Jack's traditional mis-pronounciation of the Latin phrase *vice versa*.

victualled   A quartet of different meanings:
1. On the ship's *Victualling Book*, ie. living on board.
2. *well victualled* - first class food and drink.
3. '*Is our Caterer competent ? I tell you, the fellow couldn't victual two woodpeckers into Sherwood Forest..*'
4. Note the special RM application of *vittled up.

Viet Taff   Jack's name for extremist Welsh Separatist movement.

vin d'honneur   Formal invitation by the *Wardroom, for an officer who is leaving the ship, to attend for lunchtime drinks as their guest. Used to be a PPC, *pour prendre conge*.

vinegar strokes   The phase immediately prior to orgasm, or as Jack would put it: '*Almost there!*' This is also the very last opportunity to get out at *Fratton.

vino collapso   Any rough, strong local wine.

virginity screen   Canvas *dodger rigged under a ladder or *companionway to stop Jack looking up the skirts of lady visitors to the ship. This is the polite version of a much cruder phrase.

virgins on the verge   Jack's nickname for a group of officers who seem collectively unable to make their minds up.

visiting firemen   VIPs scheduled to visit a ship and for whom special reception and hosting arrangements are required.

visual (FAA)   Single word used in radio traffic to indicate that something is in sight:*'Roger, visual the tower..'* Or, as an amusing up-market version of *See you, Jimmy!* (usually spoken in a slurred voice, with a strong *Jockanese accent) how about: *'I have you visual, James!'*

vittled up (RM)   Special application of the word *victualled to describe the impact of machine-gun bullets or cannon fire, as in strafing:*'We were in HMS PLYMOUTH on June 8th when she was vittled up good and proper by a gaggle of Argentinian Air Force Mirages..'* Some of those cannon shell marks can still be seen on the old war horse, now alongside as memorial and floating museum in Liverpool.

VMT   Abbreviated signal group for *Very Many Thanks*.

vodka & windolene   Jack's wry description of an imaginary *wet which gives you much the same headache the morning after as any other mixture, but at least with this one you can see clearly.

volret   (Premature) *voluntary retirement*; composite word which can also be used as a verb: *'I'm volretting next year..'* See also *PVR.

Plushers

WHISKY

489 - 510

wacky baccy   Cannabis.

wafter   WW2 term for a convoy escort vessel which *wafted* the ships in a convoy from place to place. The word achieved public recognition in a television advertisement for an aperitif: '*Were you truly wafted here from Paradise?' 'Nah, mate - Luton Airport!'*

wafu   *General service nickname for a member of the Fleet Air Arm, or anything to do with the FAA; the acronym is supposed to stand for *wet and (flipping) useless*. In fact, it is derived from the *Pusser's stores category of *WAFU* which used to refer to the sleeveless, anti-static and sheepskin-lined leather jerkins for issue only to *Weapon And Fuel Users* like *chockheads, *bombheads and Air mechanics, especially when they had to work up on the cold, windswept and spark-dangerous spaces of an aircraft carrier's flight deck. Some authorities spell the word as *wafoo* and state, rather jealously, that this is because the embarked squadrons in a carrier have the operating philosophy of *we always fly off - offshore!*

wah-wah (RM)   Royal's generic name for a cavalry officer - based on the noise that a group of them make in conversation; see also *rupert and *seagulls.

wailing wall   Formerly, the wall surrounding the *Wrens' quarters in a shore establishment, and the scene of much *swapping of spit in the very late evening. The girls had to be in by midnight.

waister   Older term used by Jack for an incompetent novice, incapable of doing anything really useful on a ship such as climbing the mast and getting out on the *yards. Instead, all he could do usefully was swab the deck in the *ship's waist* and pull on ropes when told to. This word, now often but incorrectly

Pongo

spelt WASTER, comes from the fact that only the best hands in a sailing ship were employed aloft in the rigging; the others were employed in the waist of the ship. Thus the name *waister* came to be an implied reproach on a man's efficiency or experience. Even as late as 1900 the word still appeared in the quarter bills of HM Ships - referring to stewards, bandsmen and artificers whose action stations were in the waist of the ship, armed with sharp-edged or pointed weapons, and ready either to repel boarders or to cross over onto an enemy ship.

wait one   An injunction to hold on for a minute, usually on the telephone. The *one* can easily become up to a quarter of an hour, depending on the conscientiousness and/or sense of humour of the person making the call.

Wakey, wakey!   Traditional early morning *bosun's call, heard in the Royal Navy long before Billy Cotton made the phrase his trademark, and classically followed by: *'Rise and shine, You've had yours - now I'll have mine!'* See also *rise.

Walcheren (RM)   *Corps memorable date of 1944 now commemorated every November 1st; this difficult amphibious assault cleared the entrance to the Scheldt river and was crucial to Allied operations in the Low Countries.

Wall of Death (esp. RM)   The excitable state of a Senior NCO or officer when he is responsible for something that's either about to go wrong - or has just done so. See also *star jumps and *high hover.

wall-safe   At sea, the equivalent of a *File 13. The request to *put something in the wall-safe* is much the same as saying: *'Chuck it through the *scuttle!'*

wallop   Either:
1. A resounding blow. Or:
2. Beer: *'Pint of wallop please..'*

Wanchai burberry   A *burberry is a quality raincoat, synonymous with the famous London rainwear makers; the *Wanchai* version is a Chinese oiled paper umbrella available in *Honkers.

wandering lead   A useful extension to take electric light into some dark corner, but may also be used to describe a rather gormless electrician who lacks direction or purpose.

wangle   Obtain something by craft, trickery or deception: *"Owja wangle that then?"*

wank you very crutch *'Thank you very much!'*

war canoe   Affectionate nickname for a warship.

Wardroom   Strictly speaking it is the *compartment where officers eat, and derives from the term *Wardrobe Room*. By extension and usage it has come to be both a collective term for all officers of a warship or establishment, as well as the generic term for the officers' accommodation area. In a large ship or shore establishment, the term *Wardroom* properly applies to the dining area only; the relaxation area (usually with a bar) is the Ante Room. Uniquely, in the Royal Navy, the *President of the Wardroom Mess* is invariably the *Executive Officer; the *captain is offered honorary membership, but (except in the smallest ships) messes separately and only enters the Wardroom by invitation. The Royal Marines conform to this convention at sea, but in establishments, the Officers' Mess is run on military rather than naval lines.

Wardroom Two (FAA)   Alternate Wardroom in former aircraft carriers for aircrew relaxing or eating while still in their flying clothing. The term is also used to describe any particularly favoured local pub near an air station.

Warfare Branch   At the time of writing, the latest evolution of the former Operations branch, which itself replaced the old Seaman branch in the early '70s. This embraces, at junior rating level, the concept of the operator maintainer (ie. those who *use* it, also *fix* it).

warmers into the butts (RM)   A few rounds fired deliberately down a range, without really being aimed, purely in order to heat up the rifle's barrel prior to some competitive shooting. Now used to describe a few drinks taken prior to a social event, ie. the RM equivalent of getting up *flying speed.

warming the bell   The process of heating the bowl (*bell*) of an hour-glass to (theoretically) make the neck expand slightly - so that the sand falls through slightly faster, thus ending the *watch prematurely. An older but exactly similar expression is to *flog the glass*. Now in general use to describe any early arrival, for instance at a party, or the process of preparing the way for the introduction of some new idea or concept. Often used in addition to describe a baby born less than nine months after a marriage ceremony - because its parents had *warmed the bell* a bit.

warn in / warn out   The process of making a Movement Occurrence Report in a special *Wardroom book, so that proper allowances can be paid (or deductions made!) by *CENTURION.

Warrant Officer   The highest rate/rank a rating/NCO can aspire to without becoming a officer. The Navy (but not the RM) has had an on/off relationship with this rank. In the mid-20th century the rank was abolished and the commissioned branch introduced; hence Commissioned Gunner, etc., for the non-technical branches, and Commissioned Branch Officer for the technical side. These officers wore a thin (half) ring on their sleeves. In 1956, this was abolished and the *SD (Special Duties) List was introduced; this (a) enabled ratings below Chief Petty Officer to transfer and (b) provided promotion prospects up to Commander rank. For the next 15 years the Navy managed without Warrant Officers, but in 1971 the *Fleet Chief rate was introduced, which was a Warrant Officer in all but name. The new name was popular with everyone except the Fleet Chiefs - who perceived themselves to be at a disadvantage compared with the other Services, and so in 1986 the name reverted to Warrant Officer. The RM and the other services have two classes, WO1 and WO2; the RN has only one which equates to a WO1. The Warrant Officer abbreviation has produced a small crop of dark-blue *funnies such as the WO(OPS) of Operations, and the WO(CK) Chef. The latter was particularly amusing in the days of locally-entered Chinese personnel in Hong Kong.

warry   Abbreviation for *warlike* or to do with a *war story*:'Wow - you look really warry in that gear..' Or:'You tellin' warries again - or just *swinging the lamp?'

warshot   An explosive-filled torpedo or missile, as opposed to a dummy or practice round. Someone who is *firing warshots* is not taking any contraceptive precautions when *giving the ferret a run; after a successful *bricking these warshots, rather like a submarine simulating the discharge of a torpedo, become *watershots.

Wart   Historic nickname for a Midshipman or *Snotty, because each one is generally held to be an unwelcome and persistent excrescence on the face of Nature.

wash-out   Cancel something; also a description of someone or something totally useless. This term originated before the days of signal pads, when messages were taken down on a slate.

After the signal had been noted, the message was rubbed or washed off the slate, since it was no longer of any significance.

wash-up   Post-exercise analysis and discussion; note that a *hot wash-up* is just such a meeting held immediately after *Endex, and not something to do with dirty dishes.

washers   Newer name for *klebbies - foreign coins of little real value that might just as well be drilled through and then used as **washers**.

waste of rations   Someone not worth having on board; also heard occasionally as: *'He's a complete waste of space..'*

watershot (esp. SM)   Release of water from a dived submarine's torpedo tube, thereby simulating a firing of this weapon during exercises. See detail on *warshot for another more general application. In effect, this is firing the torpedo tube without a torpedo. Nuclear *boats don't give their position away by discharging compressed air! For the Polaris missile system, this water discharge was known as a *sabot*. If the latter was done alongside at Faslane, the *goofers on the jetty got very wet indeed!

watch   Two distinct, but related meanings, and a number of applications:
1. The naval day is divided into *watches*, which are spells of duty undertaken by Jack in order to *watch* (out) *and ward* (off danger) therby ensuring the ship's safety. These *watches* are, in chronological order:

Middle Watch:	0001-0400
Morning Watch:	0400-0800
Forenoon Watch:	0800-1200
Afternoon Watch:	1200-1600
First Dog Watch:	1600-1800
Last Dog Watch:	1800-2000
First Watch:	2000-2359

Note that the *dog watches are split into two, to avoid people keeping the same watch every day.
2. A ship is also organised into two watches, *Port* (red) and *Starboard* (green), and everyone on board is allocated to one watch or the other. Each watch is sub-divided into 2 parts (1st and 2nd), which thus provides the normal 1 in 4 *watchkeeping* system.
3. Note also the following additional applications:

(a) *watch and watch* (about)   Duty in alternate watches of four hours on and four off throughout a twenty four-hour period, which can itself continue in war for an indefinite period of time. When *closed up in this state while at war, the ship's company is said to be in *Defence Watches.

(b) *watch on stop on*   Jack's rueful description of any continuous duty undertaken without relief.

(c) *watch & station bill*   A schedule of the whole ship's company, setting out in vertical columns where a man works, his station in the event of abandoning ship, his cleaning duties and any *special sea duties he may have when entering or leaving harbour. The *watch & station bill* is derived from the Scheme of Complement, which itself is derived from the Quarter Bill - both these latter documents being generated by the relevant MoD departments.

(d) *anchor watch*   A special watch kept when anchored in rough weather or a strong tideway in order to detect any signs of the anchor's dragging.

(e) *watch keeper*   Formal description of someone standing a watch ,or as Jack would put it, a sailor who works irregular hours on a very regular basis!

(f) *watching*   A buoy, float or paravane is said to be *watching* when just visible, i.e. in position and doing its job.

(g) *watch doggy*   Older term for a warship on convoy escort duties.

(h) *watch my lips!*   Encouragement to pay close attention, derived from the RM fire-control order: '*Watch my tracer!*' Now also used by politicians on telling pariculary horrid *porkies.

(i) *watchcoat*   A thick woollen outer garment, like a *lammy or duffel coat, to keep those *on watch* nice and warm.

water-hen   Jack's affectionate and admiring description of Jenny when she is employed in boatwork or seamanship duties.

waterlogged / waterwedged   Unable to consume any more alcohol, even if not yet totally *handcarted.

Wave   The US Navy's equivalent of a *Jenny Wren.

Wavy Navy   A RNVR (Royal Naval Volunteer Reserve) Officer's rank was denoted by a narrow and wavy gold *lace braid, but this is now used only by Sea Cadet Force Officers. The RN Reserve Officers of today have the same braid as their regular counterparts, but with a gold letter *R* sewn inside the curl.

way   To *get under way* is the naval expression for getting moving. In this sense, *way* means progress, rather than direction, although her rudder (which controls the direction of this progress!) will not be effective until a certain minimum speed is reached, and the ship is said to have enough *way on*. Another important point is that the ship is technically *under way* when her anchor is free of the sea bed. However, this word should not be confused with *weighing the anchor, which is the physical operation of hoisting the anchor from the sea bed to the hawse pipe.

ways of the navy   The often unwritten traditions and customs of the Senior Service which one learns by experience - sometimes painful.

wazzing (FAA)   Low flying without any purpose, or any unauthorized aerobatics; note that in RM usage a *feat of wazz* can describe something brilliant.

we come unclean   The motto beneath the device on a Submarine Old Comrades Association member's blazer badge is *We come unseen*. Due to the deplorable state that most *old soaks lived in on board those older *boats, the phrase *We come unclean* was seen as having a more truthful ring about it!

weaken   *'It's a great life if you don't weaken..'* An often-heard phrase with the underlying sentiment: *'I'm very seriously pissed off with all this..'*

wearing a *flag   A warship that has become a *flagship as opposed to a *private ship, because she has a *Flag officer embarked. Note that ships *wear* this flag; entitled senior officers *fly their flag*.

weasel out Excuse oneself from some duty or task: *'How on earth did you weasel out from under that one?'*

weather eye Watch any situation carefully for change or deterioration. The term is not strictly meteorological.

weather gauge In the days of fighting sail the fleet that held the weather gauge had the advantage, and Nelson was very good at obtaining this. Generally, it meant manoeuvering to ensure that the wind was behind you when you began the battle. Being *up sun* and higher up for fighter aircraft conveyed similar advantage in the pre-missile era.

weather guesser The Met(eorological) Officer - who may be WRNS; see also *Professor Fog.

webbing check The process of establishing, by a Braille technique, whether or not a lady is sporting *suzzies.

wedding garland An evergreen garland is hoisted to the masthead when an officer or rating of the ship's company gets married. This was originally the signal indicating that women were welcome on board - in the days when Jack was *pressed and likely to go on the *trot if allowed ashore.

wedding tackle The male genitals, also known as *marriage tackle*.

wedge A sandwich (older term).

wedge technician (FAA) Newish label for a *chockhead.

weed a pack Remove any non-current or superfluous papers from a file docket.

weejie A word similar to *bazzy, in that to *get a weejie on* implies that the person involved is both angry and upset.

weekend admiral An amateur yachtsman who visits a warship and then dispenses advice on nautical matters; *weekend sailors* are members of the RN Reserve but this time the name is far from derogatory.

weekly war Major air, surface and sub-surface exercise that takes place in the waters around Plymouth. Traditionally, but not necessarily, this occurs on a *Thursday, and is for ships undergoing *sea training or pre-deployment work-up; it usually also incorporates *FOST's final inspection.

Gizzet

weighed-off   The different meanings of this phrase depend on the context that it is used in:
1. *'He had the whole thing completely weighed-off..'* implies that at least someone knew what was happening and how to cope with the problem.
2. *'*Father's just weighed Johnno off for seven days *chokey..'* means that some bad lad is about to spend a week in cells, and the term implies usage of the Scales of Justice.

weight   Refers to the *weight of responsibility*. Thus:*'Who's got the weight this evening?'* means:*'Who is the Duty Officer?'*

well deck   Upper deck, midships.

welly   A super trio:
1. Hit something.
2. Try harder (esp. RM) as in the expression:*'Give it some welly!'*
3. *wellies from the Queen* are condoms held by the *QM at the *brow during foreign port visits and available (free) to Jack on his way ashore.

wendy   Excitable and upset in a rather womanish way:*'*Jimmy the One's got a wendy on about smoking in the canteen *flat..'* Or: *'Their *Splot's nothing but a great big wendy..'* Note the specialist application of *Wendy House* for a Flag Planning Room. In a big ship, wearing a *flag, this is the compartment where the Admiral's staff conduct their operational business.

Wessex / Wezzy (FAA)   What used to be the Fleet Air Arm's main workhorse helicopter, initially in the anti-submarine, but latterly in Commando and SAR roles. Very sadly, the aircraft retired from RN service in 1988:*'I reckon the only suitable replacement for a Wezzy 5 is another one, whatever the Staff say..'*

wet   Many applications!
1. *wet a stripe* - celebratory drink on promotion, similar to *wetting the baby's head* at its birth in rehearsal for the christening!
2. *wet as a mess deck scrubber* - totally useless.
3. *wet behind the ears* - a complete novice.
4. *Wetdream* (FAA) - Jetstream training aircraft.
5. *Wet List* - officers selected and in line for a seagoing command appointment.
6. *wet Navy* - either the RN, RAN or RNZN, because alcohol in various forms may be consumed on board, under strict control.
7. *wet nurse* - officer or senior rate in charge of first-timers in a sea training ship.

8. *wet of tea / coffee* - a mug of either fluid, as in:'*I don't care what it is - just as long as it's hot and wet..*' Or:'*Tea's wet!*'

9. *wet ship* - a really hard-drinking outfit; also a ship which, by some quirk in her design, regularly *ships it green.

10. *wet your whistle* - have an alcoholic drink.

11. *pre-wetting* - an installed system in a ship which generates a continuous film of water all over the upperworks, to wash off and therefore minimise contamination by chemical agents or radioactive fallout.

12. *wet weather routine* - the alternative arrangements for an *evolution that is noramallt conducted outdoors.

whack   Unit of quantity, based on punishment of older times, but now used for any share: '*Come on - you've had your fair whack..*'   Note also the nickname *Whacker* associated with the surname Payne.

whaler   Double-ended wooden boat designed on whaleboat lines; these were powered by oars (three on one side, two on the other) or sail (*Montagu whaler*) in the first instance, but later on small engines were fitted (*three-in-one whaler*). It was the standard *sea boat in the RN, but since the mid '80s it has been replaced by the *RIB, and whalers are no longer carried in HM ships.

Whaley   Whale Island ; see *Guns.

whanged into   Collided with something; see also *graunch.

wheaties   All-purpose nickname for any form of breakfast cereal.

wheel   A fairly important person such as a Head of Department (**big wheel**); see also *mudguard! '*Blessed be they who go round and round in circles, for they shall be called wheels..*'

wheel spanner   A tool for opening and shutting valve wheels. No Engineering officer, *outside Wrecker or *tiff, or stoker would be properly dressed without one.

wheeze   An idea, usually something with an underlying humorous intent.

whens   Falkland Islanders' nickname for British servicemen impolite enough to call them *bennies or *stills. This is based on the newcomers' tendency to precede most discussions with the phrase:'*When I was in..*'

which wax? (RM)   Traditional Arctic battle cry, referring to the many compounds available to smooth (or retard) the progress of a pair of *pusser's planks through snow.

which way it's screwed on   Someone who is possessed of *common dog, as opposed to pure intelligence, is described as knowing *which way it's screwed on*; see also *pickle jar and *jam-pot lid in this context.

whip   Single rope *rendered to a block for hoisting and lowering something. The Parliamentary meaning of *whip* and *three-line whip* for the importance attached to a Vote or debate, as well as the actual office held by those responsible for enforcing this interest, is derived from hunting. To get a mechanical advantage with ropes and blocks, you require one fixed block, and one moving block, joined by ropes. This at once becomes a *tackle or a *purchase. If each block merely has one sheave, it is a *single purchase*; two sheaves, a *two-fold purchase*, and three, which was the largest normally used in a ship, a *three-fold purchase*. In fact, a three-fold purchase was normally a *deck tackle* and used, for example, for weighing anchor by hand, if the capstan broke down.

whipper-in (FAA)   A formation leader's assistant who flies above the *Balbo while it assembles, and then calls with advice (and names!) on tidy and correct positioning. Again, this has a hunting derivation.

whipping   Yarn lashed neatly around a rope's end to prevent it *fagging and becoming frayed.

whistle up   Call someone forward, or create something quickly. The act of *whistling* has always been banned at sea, for superstitious reasons, and also because of possible confusion with the *boatswain's *pipes - except for the ship's cook while he was stoning prunes, who was required to whistle and thus show that he wasn't actually eating them!   To *whistle for a wind* was a superstition that, in order to get a breeze going when becalmed, all one had to do was whistle loudly and stick a knife into the mainmast.

whistling handbag (FAA)   Portable filter/blower unit carried by aircrew wearing chemical warfare protection equipment.

White Empire   The Supply and Secretariat Department, based on their old *distinction cloth, still used in the Merchant Navy; note also *white Mafia.

white around the gills   Seasick; see also *nautical nausea.

white barge   A *QHM's barge.

white front   Jack's term for the square-necked, short-sleeved white shirt worn as part of *square rig.   The correct *slops description is - or was - a *flannel.

white gloves   A Captain's *Table at which there are no *Defaulters; this expression commemorates the rare event at County Assizes when the visiting Judge had no cases to try and was presented with a pair of white gloves instead.

white-knuckle (FAA)   Frightening:'*Constant-attitude *autorotation? Complete white-knuckle job from start to finish..'

white Mafia   Collective nickname for the Supply and Secretariat Branch; see *distinction cloth for explanation.   May also be heard as *White Empire, or white striper.

white man's magic   Something clever and easy to do, usually because of modern technology.

white rat   Older name for an informer on the messdecks.

white silk   Unofficial collar tape and bow traditionally worn by Jack when he gets *spliced to whichever *pash is destined to become his *CINC-NAG-HOME.

white telephone   Toilet bowl; the confusion is often induced by excess alcohol, but may be secondary to *nautical nausea.

Whitehall warrior   An officer who is appointed to the *MoD in London for staff duties, and therefore slightly divorced from the practical realities of life at the *sharp end.

whizzer (FAA / SM)   A helicopter's rotor blades, or a ship's or submarine's propellers.

WIA   *TLA for the term *Wounded In Action*. In a battle, those particpants who are injured by blast, bullet or fragment may be overwhelmed and become KIAs in the statistics - *Killed In Action*. The WIAs, by contrast, should pass down a casualty treatment and evacuation chain. If they don't, they are likely to become *DOWs - Died of Wounds*. The Surgeon General only has one primary purpose - to ensure that WIAs do not become DOWs, but this simple mission statement often seems to be forgotten in a plethora of Defeence Cost Studies and Implementation Teams! For the land battles of the 1982 South

Atlantic Conflict, the KIA figure was 78, and the WIA/DOW ratio 580:4.

widger (FAA)   Either a perspex protractor used on maps and navigation charts, or a word used as a substitute for *doobrey, *doofer, *skrinser or *johnson - in other words, practically anything. Can also be a *widget*.

widow's hop   See *grab-a-granny night, and the RN *School of Dancing.

wife and kids (FAA)   Phrase used to describe caution induced by family responsibilities: *'I've calculated the fuel required, and added three hundred pounds extra for the wife and kids..'*

wife's best friend   The *toggle or *bedroom boatrope: *'I'm going to shake hands with the wife's best friend..'* is a less than polite announcement that you intend to *pump ship or *syphon the python. Also heard as *wife's wedding present*.

wigging   Any severe reprimand.

wiggle   Escape:*'Just try and wiggle out of that one!'*

wiggly amps   Electrical current of the alternating kind.

Wiggy   Traditional nickname for the surname Bennett.

Wilco (FAA)   *'Will comply..'* ie. the response to a message or order that indicates it is understood and will be carried out.

wildebeeste   Alternative to *stumper and *coyote when describing those in attendance at a *grab-a-granny night; see also *wolverine for a more complete definition.

willy waving   Posturing, usually rather ineffectually and part of a *pissing contest.

win   Similar meaning to *proff or *acquire.

wind and water   The part of a sailing ship or yacht's hull which is above the waterline in harbour or to windward, but below when heeling while on a tack. Much the worst place in which to be hit and perforated by a cannonball.

wind up   Teasing someone in an attempt to get a *bite:*'You're really winding me up now, aren't you?'* Note also the extended version of *winding* (someone) *up a treat*, meaning that the response generated has been a really *senior one.

wind yer neck in!   *'Shut up!'*

windfall   Many English and (in the days of the colonies there) American landowners were not allowed to trade in timber, as this commodity was reserved exclusively for the construction and fitting-out of warships. Such restrictions did not apply to trees blown over by the wind - which became gifts described, quite literally, as *windfalls*.

windscoops   A curved metal shape inserted into a *scuttle which projects outside the hull and *scoops in* fresh air. Near the waterline, these had to be used with caution because of the risk of scooping in a *goffer (wave). Can also be used as a descriptive label for large ears.

windward   Getting to *windward* of someone, as in all sailing, implies gaining an advantage of some kind. See also *weather gauge.

Windy / windy   A quartet:
1. Traditional nickname for the surname Gale.
2. Frightened:*'Fran got a bit windy about it all, so he cancelled..'*
3. *windy hammer* - pneumatic drill/hammer or rivet gun driven by compressed air.
4. *windy burbs* - upper deck working jacket.

winger   A term applied to a sailor who helps voluntarily in another department; the rating who helps a *sin bosun to rig the chapel for a service is the *chaplain's winger*. The word originated from WW1 when all Active Service personnel were encouraged to take a Hostilities Only rating *under their wings*, but the term is also used now for a regular *run-ashore *oppo. It used not to be complimentary term, but this aspect has changed now. Sometimes heard as *wingsybash*.

wingnuts Traditional nickname for someone with large or bat ears; note also the label *assy when the condition is only one-sided. See also *windscoops!

Wings (FAA) Two related usages:
1. General nickname for a Commander (Air), the senior officer who is in overall charge of all flying, deck or runway operations in a carrier or naval air station.
2. Pilot, Observer, or Aircrewman's Flying Badge, worn on the left uniform sleeve and presented at a Wings Parade following basic flying training. In older times, if a pilot was grounded, he was said to have *folded his wings*, not by ceasing to wear them, but by having his flying pay withdrawn. Note also that some naval personnel are parachute-trained, and also wear these wings on their sleeves as a result.

winker Marginally more polite version for the common term of abuse which implies *self*-abuse!

wiped out Drunk, or severely *frapped at sport.

wired (FAA) Two aviation-related applications:
1. Simulated attack by fighter aircraft:'*The Sea Harriers wired the airfield very effectively from two directions..*'
2. Description of a *Balbo:'*The whole formation wired up nicely - and stayed that way for a change..*'

wiring diagram An organizational chart.

WMP Standard affirmative response to an invitation or *RPC. The *TLA stands for *With Much Pleasure*; a badly-organized ship might also add *PSB - Please Send Boat*!

wobbleheads (FAA) Another *stovie term of derision for *chopper puke helicopter aircrew.

wobbly Adjective applied to anything containing alcohol, such as *wobbly coffee* or *wobbly pie*. When used in the sense of *throwing a wobbly*, it implies a severe sense of humour failure.

wobbly-o A Warrant Officer.

wokka-wokka A helicopter, especially one of American manufacture (like the tandem rotor Chinook in RAF service) which has this characteristic blade-slapping sound; see also *paraffin pigeon for some alternatives.

Rosy Dawn

wolverine The *wolverine* is an animal of great determination in that it will gnaw through its own leg to escape if the limb is caught in a steel trap. Jack now uses this label, along with *stumper, *coyote, *timberwolf and *wildebeeste, to describe a *gronk who he has *trapped for a spot of *all-nighters, but then would rather gnaw through his own arm than actually wake her up the following morning.

Wombat (RM) Obsolete 105mm recoiless anti-tank weapon with an open rear venturi, and which produced an enormous noise and back-blast when fired - hence the expression: *'She *bangs like a *belt-fed Wombat..'

wood butcher Carpenter; see also *chippy.

wooden topsails Oars.

Woodbury rash (RM) An infectious skin condition apparently unique to *Lympstone, actually proven to be caused by a persistent streptococcus bacterium on the gymnasium ropes, but generally held by *Royal to be caused by the prickly gorse bushes of Woodbury Common.

wooden ships and iron men The old sailing warship cry, to which the reply was: *'Now it's iron ships and wooden bastards..'*

woof run Going *ashore specifically to eat large quantities of food in some facility where quantity matters more than quality.

woofter Homosexual (rhyming derivative of *poofter*).

woofted / woofting Portmanteau words used at *Dartmouth, and derived from the *TLA *WFT* (*Withdrawn From Training*).

woolly pully Blue or green (RM) woollen jersey pullover with reinforced elbow and shoulder patches in the same colour. Widely adopted now in the RN as a standard working *rig. Interestingly, Lord Nelson wrote to their Lordships of the Admiralty in November 1804 about his seamen's Guernsey jackets.

woolworth carrier WW2 escort aircraft carriers converted from merchant ships, relatively cheaply.

word salad Any statement, whether written or spoken, which fails to make sense when closely examined.

work one's ticket Exploit the appropriate regulations quite deliberately in order to get *outside.

work-up Traditional and wryly-affectionate name for the period of intensive sea and harbour training (and now officially called *Operational Sea Training*) undergone by newly-built or refitted warships when all systems are thoroughly tested, then *evolutions run through repeatedly until the ship is at maximum efficiency and assessed capable of operational deployment. After the closure of the legendary WW2 work-up base at Tobermory, this was, until 1996, conducted at *Portland under the auspices of the Flag Officer Sea Training (FOST), with ever-increasing attendance by ships from allied navies. Since *Portland's closure, FOST has been based in Devonport, but the legendary high standards and rigorous routines remain unchanged. After all, as one previous FOST put it, war is a come-as-you-are party. It is FOST's aim to make sure ships and their companies are, as it were, fully dressed for that occasion. *Work-up* is also used to describe any gradual process of moving from slow to top speed, or (FAA) a squadron working up to operational standards before deploying to sea.

world fell out of my bottom *'I have just had a very satisfactory bowel evacuation..'* See also the splendid American import*five turd crap.

worming **Worming a rope** consists of filling in the spaces between the strands with lengths of spunyarn or small stuff along the lay of the rope. A rope, or part of a rope is *wormed, *parcelled and served* to protect it from chafe, to make it less liable to chafe other ropes, and with a wire rope, to protect the hands of the men handling it.

worms A rather disparate trio:
1. Older nickname for sailors employed on gardening duties ashore, also known as a *worm gunner*.
2. *worms in red lead* - tinned spaghetti in tommato sauce.
3. Turned into a *can of worms* - everything went disastrously wrong.

worse things happen at sea *'Can things get any worse than they are at this moment?'*

Wot sir - me sir? *'No sir, not me sir - not me never sir!'*

WRA *Wardroom attendant. Often a retired Royal Marine, but nowadays more likely to be a contracted *civvy.

wrap Give up, also applied in this sense in the phrase *wrap your hand* (or *tits*) *in*. Also seen as *rap, although this word has other meanings, mainly to do with pop music.

wrecker A pair of very different applications:

1. (SM) The *ERA who is reponsible for everything mechanical, air and hydraulic *outside* the *donk shop. The label is probably a pun of contraction, but since it is particularly used in the submarine world, there is the wrecking of surrendered German U-boats in both world wars to consider. Because of their vast knowledge of systems, the *wreckers went down these captured vessels and opened them up ready for scuttling or neutralising for trials, or by usage in mine and torpedo testing. See also *outside wrecker.

2. The FOST staff who wander round a warship while on duty, letting off smoke canisters and *thundies to rot everyone up - except themselves!

Wren Although the Women's Royal Naval Service, or *WRNS*, has been fully absorbed into the RN and has ceased to exist as a separate organisation, *Wren* is still a word used by all but the most politically-correct to describe a female member of the Navy. Formerly, *WRN* (pronounced *wren*) was the most junior rate (rank) in the WRNS. Collectively they are known as *Wrens*, although a group of more than two or three may be specifically described as a *wriggle of Wrens*. A *Wrenlin* is an older term for a *Fleet Air Arm* Wren for whom nothing ever seems to go right (compounded from the two words Wren and *gremlin*). The *Wrennery* is where the girls live. Before they became sea-going, any shore job or appointment that had been given to the WRNS in order to free male sailors for sea duty was described as having been *wrennified* or *wrennerized*. Note also the frequent description of female officers as *Wren-Os*, and that splendid creature the *Maren*, who works with the Royal Marines.

wriggle stuff Management bullshit, associated with an unwillingness or inability to speak (or write) the truth.

wrinkle A *nice little wrinkle* is a short cut, or some hint or tip that makes a task easier to carry out.

write The expression: *'May I write for you?'* is explained at the entry concerned with the *no treating rule.

write-off Useless, when used to describe a person, generally when they have become incapable through drink; *written-off* is the process whereby non-consumable stores held *on charge have been destroyed for some accidental reason and must be removed from the accounting books. Note also the specific application of *writing your name astern* - the inablity to steer a steady and straight course.

Writer   Rating employed on clerical duties: '*Scribes? He's been working his trousers to the bone..'* See also *cross-dressing.

WT   Abbreviation for the **Wireless Telegraphy** of Morse code, rather than the radio-telephony and RT using voice.   Sadly, Morse is no longer taught in the *Andrew.

X-RAY

511 - 512

X-chaser   Anyone with a reputation for being brainy. Derived from **x** as the unknown in algebraic equations. An officer joining his first ship might be asked where he had come in the passing out list from *Dartmouth. If he had done pretty well, he might then be told: *'You must now get down to some practical work - we don't need any x-chasers on board here..'* The term was particularly used for *dagger gunnery officers, who were one level above the normal gunnery officers, and could also do calculus in order to plot their ballistic probabilities - and a fat lot of good it did them!

X-factor   A pseudo-additional component of Jack's pay which is supposed to compensate him for the uncertainties and exigencies of Service life.

Xmas tree (FAA)   A well-robbed *Hangar Annie that people with *robbing chits keep taking presents from. also described at *Christmas tree.

Steaming Bats

YANKEE

513 - 518

Y-bone steak   One of Jack's favourite dishes, especially when going down for lunch - it could be described a choice cut from below the female waistline.

Yacht   Formerly, the *Royal Yacht*, HMY BRITANNIA, which *paid off in 1997; when Jack referred to a *Yachtie* or a *Yachtsman* he was not talking about the off-shore racing fraternity, but about a member of BRITANNIA's ship's company. The Yacht provided a floating trade facility for *Great Britain Inc.* as well as secure accommodation for the Royal Family on visits abroad to countries with a maritime border. The ability to reciprocate hospitality in an impressive and uniquely British style was also particularly important. Sadly, there are no plans for a replacement Yacht.

yaffle   Eat voraciously; note these additional applications:
yaffle fish - a barracuda or shark.
yaffling irons - knife and fork.
yaffle gear - mouth and teeth.

yam seng   Drinking toast that has persisted since Royal and Jack's China Station and Singapore days, now used in a direct sense to mean draining a glass in one continuous swig: *'So, seein' as it was 'is birthday, the bleeder went and yam senged it..'*

yammering   Complaining.

yardarm   Outer portion of the horizontally-positioned spar attached to a mast. Signal flags and - in the days of capital punishment at sea - condemned men were hung from this structure. Note also the term *clear (your / his) yardarm*. When the sun goes *over the yardarm*, it is time for a G&T or a *HN.

yarn (to) / **spin a yarn**   Naval expression meaning to tell a tale.

Subby

The expression originates from the days when rope was made and remade on board ship; men repairing the rope-yarns could do this and chat at the same time.

yarpie   South African.

yellow   Another interesting colour with several important Naval applications:
1. *Yellow List* - old Admiralty list of those officers for whom no further employment is planned. See also (6).
2. *yellow Jack* - a quarantine flag, not a sailor with hepatitis!
3. *yellow peas and Bonsai trees* - sweetcorn and broccoli.
4. *yellow peril* - smoked haddock.
5. *Yellow Peril* - Pernod with water or lemonade.
6. *yellow admiral* - Used to describe an officer using a flag rank who was only given it on retirement, as at one time all *Post Captains were.

Yeoman of Signals   Descriptive and historic rank of a senior *bunting tosser.

Yeovilton   Headquarters base of the Fleet Air Arm , and spiritual home of all *Junglies as well as, until 2002, the *Sea Harrier. Immediately adjoining this busy Naval Air Command Fighter Station is the excellent Fleet Air Arm Museum. From the steps up to the entrance one can appreciate the massive bulk of the *Bucc, then view the *Toom, Concorde and some fascinating exhibits on both current and historical themes. Then, if the weather is reasonable, your picnic in the Museum car park should be enjoyed to a backdrop of the sound of Falkland Islanders' freedom - the Rolls-Royce *Pegasus jet engine of the *SHAR.

Yes and no!   The question: *'Are Royal Marines Officers any good at taking quick decisions?'* Answer (after a very long pause): *'Well - yes and no!'* See also *positive perhaps and *definite maybe.

yeti (RM)   Royal's description of falling over while ski-ing; if the resulting *yeti-hole* is big enough (as a direct consequence of carrying a *chacon for instance) then it can be described as an *elk's nest: *'You should have seen us on that hill! Carl mega-yettied into a ditch and broke his skis, while I did a *tree-stop that shook all the snow off its branches and buried me completely..'*

yinyang   In Chinese philosophy, *Yin* is the passive female principle, and *Yang* is the active male element of the universe. By extension, they is used to describe female and male sexuality.

Thus a hybrid mixture of the two has come to mean a confused or *don't know* situation, which has in turn become a portmanteau word describing a river (the *Yangtze* of AMETHYST fame?) as in: *'We're completely up the yinyang now on manpower..'*

yockered   Spat, a slang word of *Scouser origin that is based on the sound made at the back of one's throat when clearing it, or when expressing disgust at something revolting- *yuck!*

yodel in a bucket   Vomit copiously; see also *pavement pizza, *dockyard omelette, *technicolour yawn and *white telephone.

yomp   A word that has always had, as its principal meaning, the rapid consumption of food. The process of *yomping your meal* in big mouthfuls then became adapted to Royal's *yomping* across the ground with huge strides. It was this latter sense which caught the British public's imagination during the Falklands campaign, rather than the Paras' equivalent activity of *tabbing*, and the former has now become part of the vernacular.

yonks   A long time

You have the ship!   Formal expression of handover from an Officer of the Watch to his *relief. In the FAA, modified to *You have control!* when changing pilots, but in either case the transfer is confirmed by the response: *'I have the ship / I have control..'*

you-can't-bend-it   Optional extension of the *all-singing, all-dancing, **you-can't-bend-it** label applied to some new piece of *kit.

Young Officer / YO   Until recently, and uniquely, these terms applied to Royal Marines new-entry officers. Royal's future leaders are trained alongside other recruits at *Lympstone, although their training is twice as long, and they must achieve all the *Commando tests to a slightly higher standard. They are known as the *Young Sirs* by their NCO trainers, and collectively as The *Batch. This latter phrase is always used when describing a colleague: *'He was in my *Batch..'* and not: *'We went through training in the same year..'* In 1991, the Royal Navy decided to abandon the much-ridiculed term Officers Under Training (OUTs) for RN new-entry officers, and to adopt the term *Young Officer* as well.

young butcher   Junior Surgeon / deputy PMO, or Little *Doc.

You're a scholar and a gentleman, sir!   *'Thank you very much..'*

yuloh   Single sculling oar for propelling a Chinese sampan, a technique also seen with the Maltese *dhaigsa*.

ZULU

519 - 521

Z man   Someone paid a bounty, on demobilization or service expiry at the end of the war, to go on a special reserve list for recall if necessary. Many *Z men* were caught up on this scheme at the time of the Suez emergency.

zap lead (FAA)   Grounding wire carried by helicopter winchmen, designed to conduct static electricity earthwards by a route other than the crewman's body.

zebedee   A *zebedee* is a tired old bastard, from Jack's favourite children's TV programme *Magic Roundabout*. Good old *Zebedee* was always saying: *'Time for bed..'*, a sentiment much endorsed by Jack, in both a social and physical context!

zed shed   The main lecture theatre at *Dartmouth has heavily damped acoustics, and is known locally as the *zed shed*. Hence the definition of a lecture given there as *someone talking in everyone else's sleep*.

zeds   General purpose word for sleep; the word is used in a number of expressions such as *racking up the zeds, piling up the zeds, zeds *merchant (F - 182) or:'I'm off to crack out a few zeds..'

Zeebrugge   A specific *Corps memorable date for this harbour on the Belgian coast, long before the ferry tragedy that shocked the world in 1987. This St. George's Day attack on 23 April 1918, against what was then a German naval base, was designed to block the harbour entrance and destroy the outer Mole. In this aspect the operation was only partly successful, but tremendous gallantry under withering enemy fire was shown by personnel of the 4th Battalion RM. There were heavy RN and RM casualties; two of the eight Victoria Crosses awarded went to Royal Marines.

zero (FAA)   Newish nickname for an *Observer based on his (or her now!) **O** qualification in the *Navy List, and according to some *stick monkey opinion, also indicative of overall value!

zero crack zero *ringbolt   *Really* early in the morning.

zip lip (esp. FAA)   Radio silence: *'From then on in - it's zip lip..'*

zit   A facial spot; see also *pluke. Allegedly, this name is derived from the sound made when the item is squeezed, and its contents hit the mirror; note also *zit bar* as Jack's description of a large piece of *nutty.

zizz   Alternative to *zeds when describing sleep. A *zizz *duff* is a particularly stodgy and coma-inducing pudding.

zonk   As for *zeds and *zizz.

zoomboots (FAA)   Jack's nickname for those Royal Marine pilots who were trained by the Fleet Air Arm. There were at least three such *zoomboots* among the 56 FAA pilots present at the 1940 Battle of Britain, a fact which most *Crabs are ignorant of, and usually also quick to deny. Their names were Lieutenants Marsh, Wright and Hay. At the time of writing, there is another Royal Marines officer, besides the former *Sea Hawk* pilot, Major Terence Murphy, going through the *stovie training pipeline to become a *SHAR driver. A *Sea Jet *stovie *zoomboot*! Yes!! All the author can say, as a former *bootie MO and *wafu *Avquack is: *'Time to *cheer ship..'*

zoomies   Another rotary-wing aircrew nickname for *stovies.

Zulu   Three usages in the final entry of this handbook:
1. *Zulu Time* is Greenwich Mean Time.
2. *zulu warrior* - A ritual, male stripping routine performed when most of the participants are fairly well *handcarted.
3. Battle cry of Z *Company* 45 *Commando RM, when they did the necessary business on the twin peaks of Two Sisters, during the night of 11/12 June 1982, in the Falkland Islands.

Talent

Notes

All additions and suggestions to:

Dr Rick Jolly OBE
c/o Palamanando Publications
PO Box 42
Torpoint
Cornwall PL11 2YR

(Mark envelope PLEASE FORWARD
TO 'JACKSPEAK' AUTHOR)

Notes

Notes

Notes

Notes

FORTHCOMING TITLES
(Planned for 2001, also by Rick Jolly)

Publication in late Spring 2001 - <u>Non fiction</u>

FOR FRIEND & FOE   (illustrated in colour and B&W)

Originally published by Century and Corgi as the
RED AND GREEN LIFE MACHINE, this book tells the
triumphant story of an abandoned building at Ajax Bay,
Falkland Islands, during the 1982 War. The author was the
field hospital's commander. Quite incredibly, despite dust,
dirt, poor lighting and the unwelcome presence of two
unexploded bombs in the converted mutton packing plant,
every wounded British soldier who reached Ajax Bay alive
also went out alive - despite their horrific injuries. For these
services the author was appointed OBE.

But Rick Jolly was also Staff Medical Adviser to the 'Man of
the Match' - his Brigade Commander, Julian Thompson.
He now reveals how their close and trusting relationship,
which continues to this day, survived constant meddling
and interference which might otherwise have wrecked Ajax
Bay's brilliant track record. He also explains the background
to the demanding physical training, and the realistic
professional preparations of his red and green-bereted
medical teams. In addition, he tells of the unique
circumstances whereby Argentina's Government, 17 years
after the events of 1982, formally acknowledged the care
given to their wounded.

*The author is one of the very few people in military history
who has been decorated by both sides in the same conflict.*

Late 2001 - <u>Fiction</u>

FOR QUEEN AND PRESIDENT

May 1982:   Thousands of miles from Britain, and just prior to the landings which precede the main battles of the Falklands war, a heavily-laden Sea King helicopter crashes into the freezing waters of the South Atlantic.
Only a few of the passengers and crew survive.
One is a Royal Marines officer seconded to the SAS...

Decmber 1982:   A scientist working at the Murmansk Submarine Research Institute in Russia makes an accidental but spectacular discovery in the field of high-energy laser physics. Personal tragedy also invades her life and, in desperation, she makes plans to escape to the West...

January 1983:   A US Navy senior medical corpsman, on exchange posting to the British Royal Marines to learn about their field medical techniques in the Falklands War, is sent off to Norway for Arctic Warfare training...

Late March 1983:   The President of the United States of America announces his *Strategic Defense Initiative*, quickly renamed *'Star Wars'*. Based on the development of a newly discovered scientific breakthrough, he proposes the creation of a high-technology defensive umbrella to protect the citizens of America from surprise missile attack...

Set in London, Washington, Moscow, Murmansk and Arctic Norway, **FOR QUEEN AND PRESIDENT** *is an exciting and completely authentic tale of Anglo-American co-operation, at a human level, to bring a vital secret out safely to the Free World.*

HOW TO ORDER

You can order any or all of these titles very easily, and get them direct from Palamanando Publications.

Either use a photocopy of the order form overleaf, or just make sure all the necessary details are put on your own notepaper or letter.

Follow the instructions carefully, and then send your order in by post*, by fax** or by e-mail***.

FOR CAMPAIGN SERVICE   (Red&Green Books)   £7.95

Belfast 1972. The Provisional IRA's gunmen and bombers have been given an important but deadly task. Can anyone stop them?
Take a look at **www.redandgreen.com** for more detail and some extracts.

JACKSPEAK   (Palamanando Press)   £9.95

The second edition of a hilarious reference guide to the vivid and colourful slang and usage of the Royal Navy and Royal Marines. Cross-referenced, and includes the terms and words unique to the Fleet Air Arm and Submarine Service as well! Perfectly illustrated by the famous *Navy News* cartoonist, **TUGG**.
Visit **www.jackspeak.com** for more detail and samples.

IN CONFIDENCE   (FoSAMA - Friends of SAMA82)   £9.95

Nearly 600 side-splitting comments taken from periodic confidential reports completed for British officers, servicemen and servicewomen - from the Royal Navy, Army, Royal Marines and Royal Air Force. Completely politically incorrect! Inspect **www.fosama.com** for more detail and a few examples of each personalty trait covered!
(*Publisher's Note: All profits from this book go to maintenance and upkeep of the unique SAMA82 Garden of Remembrance dedicated to those who fell in the Falklands War, which can be visited at www.sama82.org.uk*)

FOR FRIEND AND FOE   (Red&Green Books)
FOR QUEEN AND PRESIDENT   (Red&Green Books)

Both these titles will be published in 2001.
See previous pages for details, and also check the **www.redandgreen.com** website for breaking news.

Don't forget to add £1.00 per book for postage and packing, although if you order THREE books or more, p&p is *FREE*!

ORDER FORM
(Transcribe or photocopy this)

Please make sure that **all** the information requested is given. Your personal details will **not** be released to any third party. Follow the instructions, check your method of payment, and then send your order in by post*, by fax** or by e-mail***.

By post* to: **Orders** Section,
Palamanando Publishing,
PO Box 42, Torpoint, Cornwall
PL11 2YR

*Make your cheque payable to Palamanando Publications, and ensure that you have signed it! Please also write your own abbreviated address and full post code on the back.

By fax** to: (UK 44)   **(0)1503 230 421**

**Complete your credit card details clearly, in block letter, and don't forget these items in a letter!

By Email*** to: **orders@palamanando.com**

***The website at **www.palamanando.com** will <u>not</u> be 'Ecommerce' enabled until December 2000, but you can also download a faxable order form from there.

Name:...

Address:...

Town ....County / State..........................

Post / Zip Code ....

Credit Card Orders   Please tick the appropriate box:-

Visa ☐   Delta ☐   Mastercard ☐   American Express ☐   Switch ☐

Delivery Address (if different) ....

Cardholder's Name ....

Card Number ☐☐☐☐ ☐☐☐☐ ☐☐☐☐ ☐☐☐☐ ☐☐☐

Card Start Date ☐☐☐☐   Card Expiry Date ☐☐☐☐

Cardholder's Signature:

Don't forget the (subsidised!) UK postage and packing charge!!